INTRODUCING LITERARY THEORIES

INTRODUCING
LITERARY THEORIES

A Guide and Glossary

Julian Wolfreys

EDINBURGH UNIVERSITY PRESS

© the contributors, 2001

Edinburgh University Press Ltd
22 George Square, Edinburgh

Typeset in Sabon and Gill
by Hewer Text Ltd, Edinburgh, and
printed and bound in Great Britain by
MPG Books Ltd, Bodmin

A CIP Record for this book is
available from the British Library

ISBN 0 7486 1483 4 (paperback)

CONTENTS

CONTENTS

ALTERNATIVE CONTENTS

PREFACE AND ACKNOWLEDGEMENTS

Introducing Literary Theories: A Guide and Glossary has developed in part from a previous publication, *Literary Theories: A Reader and Guide* (1999). For the most part, the essays in the current volume, including the introduction, are revisions, in some cases involving extensive reworking, of the introductions to each area of theoretical discourse which were commissioned for the earlier book. Broadly defined, these areas of discussion are structuralism, feminism, marxism, reader-response theory, deconstruction, poststructuralism, new historicism, postcolonialism, gay studies and queer theory, and cultural studies. The essay on postmodernism is new, and the essays on Bakhtinian criticism and cultural materialism are also new additions.

Each of the essays in *Introducing Literary Theories* speaks to the complexities of specific analytic discourses, examining the interpretative strategies, the epistemological assumptions and the tensions by which such reading praxes are informed. To this end, rather than seeking simply to provide a general overview, the majority of essays in the present volume, in tracing the contours of its subject, takes as exemplary two or three essays, looking in some detail at features of those essays (which are to be found reproduced in *Literary Theories: A Reader and Guide*).

At the same time, each essay turns its attention, and directs its readers towards, the consideration of literary texts, films on a couple of occasions, or, broadly put, matters of cultural representation. Each essay concludes with a brief sketch of a reading of a particular text or two so as to provide the reader with an example in miniature of the different ways in which the specifics of analytical or theoretically inflected practice can serve to illuminate what is already at work in the literary, the textual. At the same time, each of the sketches seeks to open for its readers further pathways of critical engagement, rather than providing definitive accounts of a text. The reader is directed towards these sketches of possible readings as an alternative pathway through the present volume.

Following the 'notes towards readings', each of the essayists has provided a series of questions for further consideration. In each case the questions are directed towards both the theoretical or epistemological issues which the essays raise in relation to matters of analysis, and towards specific problems presented in the act of reading developed from specific analytical premises. Also at the end of each essay there is an annotated bibliography and a bibliography of further reading, intended to orient the reader towards further independent study of the subject or area.

In addition to the essays, there is also a glossary of keywords often found in what is broadly defined as literary, critical or 'high' theory. While the glossary incorporates terms used in the various essays of this volume, it also provides the student with a number of other definitions of terms beyond the immediate scope of *Introducing Literary Theories* but which are commonly encountered elsewhere in the study of the theory and practice of criticism.

I would like to thank the contributors to this volume for their participation and their willingness. At Edinburgh University Press, I would like to thank Jackie Jones for suggesting revisiting the earlier volume in order to reinvent it in the present fashion, and also for her continued unflagging support and encouragement for this and other projects. Finally, and most importantly, there are those students who have taken classes in what we are pleased to call 'literary theory' who, whether they know it or not, have been instrumental to the shaping of all the chapters in this volume.

Gainesville, Florida
September 2000

ABBREVIATIONS OF WORKS CITED

IM   Alfred, Lord Tennyson, *In Memoriam A.H.H.*, in *Tennyson: A Selected Edition*, ed. Christopher Ricks (Berkeley, CA, 1989)

LT   Julian Wolfreys (ed.), *Literary Theories: A Reader and Guide* (Edinburgh, 1999)

M   George Eliot, *Middlemarch*, ed. and intro. Rosemary Ashton (Harmondsworth, 1994)

MD   Virginia Woolf, *Mrs Dalloway*, ed. Stella McNichol, intro. Elaine Showalter (Harmondsworth, 1992)

PAYM   James Joyce, *A Portrait of the Artist as a Young Man: Text, Criticism, and Notes*, ed. Chester G. Anderson (New York, 1968)

PL   John Milton, *Paradise Lost*, ed. and intro. Christopher Ricks (Harmondsworth, 1989)

S-P L   Alan Hollinghurst, *The Swimming-Pool Library* (New York, 1989)

T   William Shakespeare, *The Tempest*, in *The Complete Works*, eds Stanley Wells and Gary Taylor (Oxford, 1988)

INTRODUCTION

Julian Wolfreys

THE QUESTION OF 'LITERARY THEORY'

What is 'literary theory'? How has it developed? What does it do? Why is it necessary, and/or what is it good for? What are the arguments for it and why the resistance to it? Is it, in fact, an 'it' at all, a single definable entity or phenomenon? All of these questions sound as if they belong in an exam, none of them are easy to answer, certainly not in so short a space as a foreword or introduction. But I want to begin by outlining very broadly a few responses.

In their challenging, groundbreaking *An Introduction to Literature, Criticism and Theory: Key Critical Concepts*, Andrew Bennett and Nicholas Royle offer the following comment: 'Literary theory is an unavoidable part of studying literature and criticism. But theory – especially when it takes the form of "isms" – can often be intimidating or else, frankly, boring' (1995, ix). Without risking a definition of 'literary theory', Bennett and Royle manage succinctly to identify their subject's conventional location and reception. While the authors scrupulously avoid all immediate determination of the phrase in question as an interesting rhetorical strategy resistant to a somewhat normative institutional practice, nonetheless they provide an insight into that which we are calling 'literary theory' as possibly understood to exist and having a recognized and recognizable situation and role which belongs and is subordinate to the function, organization and place of the university.

Therefore, while Bennett and Royle are correct in their identification of the intimidating and boring aspects of this badly named thing, it has to be said that, from their comment, we can risk the strong reading that 'literary theory' has assumed its identity specifically in the context of higher education. ('Why' is, however, another question, and another matter, which has far less – if anything – to do with the academics who teach it as a subject defined by a curriculum than with the organization and the politics of the institution.) This is especially the case when the teaching of 'theory' has resolved itself into the dissemination and explication of 'isms' (see the commentary on 'poststructuralism' in the essay on deconstruction). Of course, as Martin McQuillan has argued, 'high theory as a form of knowledge like any other exists to be encountered, learned and taught' (1999, 384). A corollary of this is that '[p]edagogical practice implies selection' (McQuillan, 1999, 384), and in this process of selection there is, equally, an act of the accommodation of those aspects of theoretical discourse which are most easily assimilated. Part of this assimilation is naming and, with that, the imposition of an identity and the concomitant erasure of differences. The application of those names which share the suffix 'ism' are thus involved in assembling a family portrait. The various praxes of critical analysis become subsumed within the pragmatics of a 'general likeness' theory of knowledge and use-value necessary for the practical day-to-day operation of places of higher education – and this is especially the case in England today where there is, more and more, an emphasis on 'learning outcomes' and 'transferable skills' – while, simultaneously, constructing an aura around the various discourses of so-called 'literary theory' by which these discourses are maintained at a certain distance, familiarized and yet never quite at home.

Literary theory is, then, and in as broad and neutral a definition as possible, the name given to a range of disparate critical practices and approaches which are used by members of the humanities in the exploration of literary texts, films and aspects of contemporary and past cultures. Literary theory is also the name given to the teaching of such practices and approaches in the university, particularly in English departments. Literary theory is an umbrella term which gathers together conveniently and for the purpose of identification or definition various texts concerned with the study of literature and culture by, amongst others, feminists, marxists, and those who teach literature but are interested in certain branches of linguistics, psychoanalysis or philosophy.

Historically, literary theory, as a convenience term or label, defines work influenced by the practices, discourses (language and its power relations within specific disciplines) and texts of feminism, marxism, psychoanalysis, linguistics, semiotics (the study of signs) and continental philosophy of the last 40 years, including all the various disciplines, fields and, again, discourses, ideas and approaches gathered together under the label 'structuralism' or 'poststructuralism'. This last term is a particular example of a now widespread 'ism' generated during the late 1960s in the Anglo-American academic world for the purpose of identifying a quite often radically heterogeneous range of analytical practices of critics, philosophers, historians and psychoanalysts from France which were first being encountered in universities in Great Britain and the United States. Literary theory, owned as belonging to both literary criticism and literary studies, has come into being as a subject on the curriculum during the same period. It may well be the case, as some critics claim, that literary theory has been around as long as there has been literature, even if it has been termed 'poetics' for example. However, aside from the fact that such remarks are not really helpful, it remains the case that the advent of courses concerning themselves with 'theory' first occurs in the 1970s. Literary Theory has been therefore the name given to a number of different, differing, occasionallly overlapping or related ways of reading and interpreting, and is defined thus for economical purposes, first within the university, and subsequently beyond the university, in publishers' catalogues, in reviews, journals and news media.

Before moving on to the next question, 'How has it developed?', I would like to point to what is, for me, a problem with the term 'literary theory'. As everything in the previous paragraph should suggest, the nature of so-called literary theory is complex and multiple. There is more than one aspect or identity for/to literary theory. Hence the plural used in the title of this volume: Literary Theories. 'Literary Theory' is problematic for me because it names a singular object or point of focus. However implicitly, 'literary theory' names a single focal point, rather than something composed, constructed or comprised of many aspects or multiple, often quite different identities. If we name several identities or objects as one, not only do we not respect the separateness or singularity of each of those subjects or identities, we also move in some measure towards erasing our comprehension of the difference between those objects and identities, making them in the process invisible.

Indeed some would say that the act of providing a single name or single identity is done precisely to make things simple for ourselves, or for whoever does the naming. If we can reduce, say, feminist literary criticism, marxist literary criticism, psychoanalytic approaches to literature, to 'literary theory', we have a catch-all term which puts everything together effortlessly. The act of naming implies a great power for whoever controls the act, whoever has the ability. At the same time, the act of naming does a degree of violence to the different objects. In making the different identities all the same, we make them manageable, we contain them, we don't respect their differences, we make life a little bit easier for ourselves.

This may seem to be making too much of this question of a single identity, but the harm implicit in such an act cannot be underestimated. The importance of the point can be seen if we think for a moment, not of literary study but of attitudes towards cultures, or, even more simply, if we name everyone who comes from some place other than where we are from, foreigners. In doing so, we immediately engage in a way of thinking about the world which is reliant on an ability to define, and separate, an 'us' from a 'them'. And as the example of 'literary theory' demonstrates, the act of separation is also an act of containment. All those feminists, all those marxists, all those . . . well it's all just literary theory, isn't it?

This leads me to the second question, though with a qualification, given that I wish to resist thinking about 'literary theory' in the singular. How has it developed? Let's begin straight away by saying that 'literary theory' is not an 'it', and precisely for the kinds of reasons I've already suggested or at least implied. If we accept the argument that literary theory is composed of many strands, the question of how 'it' developed can be re-cast as 'how have theories developed?' Various theoretical approaches to literature have evolved and developed in part because in the twentieth century the study of literature had itself developed from a limited range of perspectives, beliefs, and ideological or philosophical assumptions which had not been questioned from other places and the proponents of which largely did not examine their own assumptions or grounds of articulation. This meant, in brief, that certain questions could not be asked about literature or even that only certain works were deemed worthy of study in the first place. Indeed, when I speak of 'theoretical approaches' or otherwise use the potentially vacuous term 'theory', I wish merely to signal an analytical engagement with the process of reading from a number of different positions which respond to that which, in the names of criticism and reading, has been overlooked, elided, suppressed or silenced, consciously or otherwise.

Theoretical approaches developed, employing the language of other disciplines from outside the field of literary studies as a means of redressing the balance, of finding ways of asking previously unarticulated questions, of responding patiently and attentively to those strange and strangely troubling moments in textual form and matter, and as a means of bringing back into focus texts which have been neglected. At the same time, theoretically informed approaches to the study of literature and culture provided various vantage points from which different 'voices' could be heard, different identities other than those implicitly understood (Christian, humanist, western, male European) in the conventional institutional approaches to literary study. Not all these voices agreed with each other, although out of the disagreement and debate came yet other inflections, further positions and identities, yet more ways of addressing what it is we call 'literature', as Ruth Robbins suggests in her essay, where she makes the point that there are various feminist discourses and philosophies, and that feminisms themselves cannot, today as we enter the twenty-first century, be reduced to a single feminism.

All questions of what has been termed 'literary theory' come down therefore, as Martin McQuillan suggests, to questions of reading, even if the concerns of various readings are neither the same, nor reducible to an agreed understanding. Not just reading in the narrow sense of picking up a novel and gleaning the story from it; rather 'reading' suggests a manner of interpreting our world and the texts which comprise that world. No one single manner of reading will do, so heterogenous is the world, so diverse are its peoples and cultures, so different are the texts, whether literary, cultural or symbolic by which we tell ourselves and others about ourselves, and by which others speak to us about their differences from us, whether from the present, from some other culture, or from the past, from whatever we may think of as our own culture. Reading thus becomes a heavily encrypted, if not haunted, word. Apparently singular, yet 'containing multitudes' as it were, 'reading' names an act which cannot be reduced to a formula, and therefore rendered in some abstract fashion as a 'theory'. Every reading will, of necessity, be different from every other, and this not least because every act of 'good reading' – to use J. Hillis Miller's oft-deployed phrase – is always a response to the singularity of the text being read. At the same time, no reading ever comes to an end, and if there is something shared, if there is a resemblance between the various discourses of so-called literary theory, it is this: a recognition of the responsibility which reading entails when understood as a figure of incompletion or, perhaps, an open system.

If reading then cannot be reduced to a theory but is understood in McQuillan's and my own use as a complex renaming of what goes by the names 'theory', 'high theory' or 'literary theory', then 'theory' must perforce be comprehended differently, as both different from itself and in itself. 'Theory', as Tom Cohen has remarked, 'never quite meant "theory" to begin with, but a different sort of praxis; one that, for the moment, we may call anti-mimetic, epistemo-political' (1998, 7). To unpack this a little: whatever has gone by the name 'literary theory' or is identified as such has concerned itself not with a view of literature as an undistorted representation of the 'world-as-it-is'. 'What nice, faithful, true descriptions of the English countryside Austen and Hardy provide us with' reads according to a notion of mimetic-aesthetic fidelity which occludes both the knowledge – the epistemological bases and assumptions – by which we recognize both the apparently prevailing 'truth' of descriptions by Hardy or Austen (or Lawrence, or Forster, or . . .) and its political dimensions (the recognition of and identification with a landscape as *English*, that is to say, marked in some mystified manner by the traits of a supposedly shared national identity). Whatever the differences of so-called 'theory', the practitioners of these different, differing analytical praxes share, however roughly, this 'epistemo-political' concern with the power of what reading effects, and what words can do in all their materiality. What is called 'Literary Theory' has no pretense to being a theory of anything. Indeed, in being grounded in analytical acts, the questions of reading with which we are here concerned seek either implicitly or explicitly to exceed, escape or otherwise resist the generalizing and totalizing contours, the very idea, of a theory.

So-called theoretical approaches to literary study have developed and established themselves in part in the academic world, though not without often bitter struggles which still persist, as a means of comprehending, acknowledging and respecting heterogeneity and difference, rather than seeking to reduce the difference to one identity which is either a version of ourselves, a version of the same, or otherwise as an other which cannot be incorporated into a single identity. This is what 'theoretical approaches' to literary and cultural studies can do, what they are 'good for' to put it both baldly and pragmatically; it is also why they are necessary: as the beginning steps in a process of revising how one sees, how one reads. Such approaches are also necessary because they provide the means, as already remarked, for alternative voices, even dissenting voices, instead of being spoken for by some single authoritative voice, to challenge the power of those who had previously assumed the right to speak for all, whether in the form of a single, dominant political party or politician, or through the voice of a critic such as F. R. Leavis, who presumed to tell us that there was a 'great tradition' in English literature and what exactly did or did not belong to that tradition. The analytic approaches considered in this volume contest not only the composition of the tradition but also the right of any one voice or group of aligned voices to argue for a single tradition, while, at the same time, share a 'primary focus', from their various locations, 'on what is powerful, complex and strange about literary works' (Bennett and Royle, 1995, ix).

One of the reasons why the various analytical practices with which we are concerned have proved challenging and provoking and have caused on some occasions hostile resistance is their insistence on addressing epistemological or ideological dimensions of the text in the act of reading. At the same time, such approaches to literature have led to both the broadening of the literary canon, the texts we study, and to the raising of questions, concerning, for example, race, gender, national identity, which previously had not been asked – which could not be asked because of the implicit ideological and philosophical assumptions behind the study of so-called great literature. Forty years ago it would hardly have been understood as appropriate to raise the issue of either Shakespeare's or Dickens's depiction of Jews or women. Today, Caliban can no longer be considered merely as a somewhat fantastic figure, the offspring of a witch; instead, his role and *The Tempest* in general are explored in relation to questions of race, of miscegenation, and the cultural history of England's colonial expansion.

Another aspect of theoretical discourse which encounters objection is its difficulty. The obviously political question aside, there is, as Michael Payne points out (1991, vii) the sense, especially expressed by those who are 'anti-theory' that it is, well, hard to read, drawing as it does on the specialised languages of other disciplines. As I discuss below, such a reaction has more to do with the challenge felt to the identity of literary studies as a 'single community' on the part of members of that community, than it has to do with theoretical discourse itself. Theoretical discourse often is difficult, not simply because of the ways in which theories of literature are expressed but also because of the questions differing approaches to the literary text demand we ask, often of ourselves and our understanding of what we think of as literature, as 'good' or 'great' literature, and how we come to think of the literary in such a manner in the first place.

In the next part of this introduction, and in order to introduce the study of literary theories in the broader context of literary study in the univer, I turn to particular debates, using the work of Terry Eagleton as an example. Beginning with an epigraph, I draw on Eagleton's agricultural or rural metaphor as a means of introducing the debates around so-called 'literary theory'. Looking at how Eagleton has returned over the years from his position as a marxist to question the need for theoretical approaches, I move from this and from Eagleton's own arguments to a consideration of the significance of theory and its sometimes fraught relation to the more conservative elements in the institution of literary study.

Following Eagleton's metaphors as a means of addressing the movement of 'theory', I develop the idea of critical analysis as something which crosses over the border of literary studies from other places. In doing so, I suggest that the various identities of theories, in being perceived as 'foreign' to some 'native' identity of literary studies, have had to undergo some form of naturalization process, some reinvention of their identities in order to allow them into the field of literary studies. Yet, this being the case, it is now necessary to recognize what has happened and to find ways of reading, looking again at literary theories so as to return to the theoretical a sense of the radical difference of theories in order to question the very process of institutionalization which Terry Eagleton had been concerned with, back in 1976.

FROM THE COUNTRY TO THE CITY

> . . . yet one more stimulating academic 'approach', one more well-tilled field for students to tramp . . .
>
> Terry Eagleton

The epigraph – that sneaking rhetorical device which insinuates itself onto the page between the title and the body of the text, and yet which has the hubris to assume the role of summarizing, encapsulating, the argument of the entire essay or book in a nutshell – is taken, as you'll see, from Terry Eagleton, in 1976. Eagleton is bemoaning the possible, perhaps even inevitable, institutionalization and canonization of marxist politics in the form of a literary approach to texts. Politics diluted to a method. In Eagleton's view, the translation from the realm of politics to that of literary studies signalled some form of entry into academia, which was also a form of domestication for marxism. To enter the 'United States of Criticism', if not of 'theory', meant that the discourse or practice in question had been suitably vetted, vetoed if and where necessary, and granted the requisite visa for entry into the land of literary studies. Therefore, Gary Day was inaccurate when he stated that '[t]heory imposes worlds . . . it generates conformity' (Day, 1998. 25). If anything, we can see from Eagleton's response that it is perhaps the world imposed by the academy on ideas which runs the risk of both instituting and generating conformity.

Eagleton's organic metaphor of the field and students tramping across the marxist farmland is instructive, not least for the fact that such a figure is readable, despite Eagleton's ostensibly oppositional political discourse, as being rooted, so to speak, in the epistemological soil of a discourse which is markedly English. It ties the practice of marxism, once located within the study of literature and English departments, to an agrarian way of life, perhaps even one that is feudal. marxism, once the wild and glorious countryside of ideological practice, has been transformed into manageable soil. Interesting also is the pessimistic manner in which the critic invokes hoards of ramblers pursuing their path unthinkingly across arable and fertile land. It does not seem to occur to Eagleton in his vision of the study of literary criticism and theory that there might be a form of crop rotation at work here, where a Jethro Tull-like figure (the agricultural theorist, not the band) sets out the theory of circulating the seeds of marxism, feminism and so on, in order to produce a varied crop and to maintain the fertility of the soil at the same time, through the process of rotation. Be that as it may, the field has been entered. The topographical image serves a useful starting point here. It speaks of the land, suggesting an act of trespass. The boundary line broken, the well-ordered soil is churned up, the field will need to be reworked.

This was in fact to be the case with Eagleton himself. For, only seven years after his concerned and somewhat cynical caveat, there occurred the publication of a book which served, to a great extent, to change the outlook on literary study for a generation of students in Great Britain, *Literary Theory: An Introduction*. As is well known, Eagleton was the author of this book.[1] Instead of standing by like some alarmed woodsman watching in disbelief as packs of day-trippers disported themselves in so cavalier a fashion across his land, here is the same author helping in the reconstruction of the landscape. The landscape has changed, however, and we will find ourselves no longer, like Tess, rooting for the dirt-covered crops of critical thinking, but being brought face to face with an imposing architectural structure.

Beginning with the assertion that, if there is something called literary theory then there must equally be something called literature, about which theory can circulate, about which it can make its theoretical statements (1983, 1), Eagleton traces the question of what is to be considered 'literature'. He concludes his introduction by stating, correctly, that what we term 'literature' relies for its identity on a complex and interrelated series of value-judgements relating to 'deeper structures of belief', the 'roots' of which are 'as apparently as unshake-able as the Empire State Building' (1983, 16). I'm not sure whether buildings have roots (I know they have foundations), but at least Eagleton's comment has the virtue of resisting obfuscation and occlusion concerning the 'materiality of language' (Cohen, 1998, 7), unlike Gary Day's remark that 'literature is the place where language can breathe and expand . . . literature visualizes' (1998, 25). However, if literature, or rather its ideological, cultural and institutional maintenance, is now akin to the structure which supports an undeniably urban architecture, the implication is that 'theory' is there in order to comprehend the structure, the structures of the text and the 'deeper structures' out of which the structure of literature grows or is constructed. What is the purpose of a theoretical approach to the structure beyond merely seeing how the structure functions? Eagleton concludes his book, in a discussion of political criticism, by asking a similar question: 'What is the *point* of literary theory?' (1983, 194). The brief answer is that literature is not value free, nor is it merely a question of aesthetic evaluation, as though aesthetic questions were themselves somehow outside the realm of the political or economic. As Eagleton puts it, 'the history of modern literary theory is part of the political and ideological history of our epoch . . . literary theory [is] . . . indissociably bound up with political beliefs and ideological values. Indeed literary theory is less an object of intellectual enquiry in its own right than a particular perspective in which to view the history of our times' (1983, 194–5).

Continuing, Eagleton points out that 'Departments of literature in higher education, then, are part of the ideological apparatus of the modern capitalist state' (1983, 200). The purpose of the various methods of criticism and theory is to work to expose the ideological apparatus, to show its workings and structures, and to question an immovable notion of 'literature', to understand 'literature' not as being distinct from other cultural forms or having some immutable and universal value, but as itself being the product of broader discursive and ideological practices. The feminist theorist, Eagleton argues by example, 'is not studying representations of gender simply because she believes that this will further her political ends. She also believes that gender and sexuality are central themes in literature and other sorts of discourse, and that any critical account which suppresses them is seriously defective' (1983, 209). Thus the purpose of the theoretical analysis of literature is not solely for the purpose of looking at literature in another way, taking one more 'approach'. 'Literature' and its conventional study are wholly conventional constructs of the societies in which we live and the systems of belief which maintain the operation of those societies. The theorized – and for Eagleton, politicized – study of the literary is not an end in itself, but, rather, a means of making oneself capable of seeing beyond literature, to see how literature functions and is made to function in silent and invisible ways.

THE SIGNIFICANCE OF THEORY

I don't want to spend too much more time with Terry Eagleton (not because the debate is done; this is, however, an introduction, and we need to move on), but because of his central significance to 'literary theory', it is necessary and instructive to take the measure of literary theory through brief consideration of Eagleton's move from worried sceptic in 1976 to advocate of the theoretical in 1983, which is a wholly understandable move for the politicized critic. In a sense, this also helps to explain, in retrospect, Eagleton's adoption of various critical-political positions throughout his writing career; from marxist to Althusserian marxist, to postcolonial marxist.[2] Eagleton's breathless and trenchant political commentaries on the literary and its institutionalized positions have demonstrated the political necessity not only of adopting theoretical positions but also of shaping one's political response in different ways strategically as a means of resisting becoming solidified into a single position, which itself is then accommodated by the 'ideological state apparatus'. Eagleton's shift is part of an attempt to prevent the fall of theory into the hands of those who he sees serving the institutional and ideological needs of dominant discourses and structures. Theory in the 'wrong hands', say that of the 'dominant political order' (Eagleton, 1990, 37), becomes merely one more tool, one more weapon, involved in acts, to paraphrase Eagleton, of intensive colonization (1990, 36, 37). Who gets colonized? We do, says Eagleton, as subjects disciplined and contained within various social modes of production, in which modes of production literature serves as an apparatus for colonization of the subject (1990, 37). What this means is that, in being told that literature has a restricted range of timeless humanist values, which it is your purpose to comprehend through a literary education, you are being asked to accept these values as a form of truth. Thus, as a reader, you are 'colonized' through being asked to accept such values as your own. 'Theory', if divorced from often political contexts, can be transformed – if it has not been altogether rejected – into a merely formal method of proving the same or similar values as those produced by conventional criticism. On the one hand, the result may be, as Bennett and Royle suggest above, intimidation and boredom. On the other hand, the will-to-formalism has been generated within and as a symptom of an increasingly commodified higher education system, where taming so-called 'theory' has gone hand in hand with the production of courses which put, as it has been charmingly and accurately described, 'bums on seats' (McQuillan et al., 1999, xi). This is not an either/or situation; intimidation, boredom and success, statistically speaking, can all quite happily accommodate one another in the same space.

However, if it is the case that 'Theory's claims of radicalism are greatly exaggerated, then by the same token the radical effects of Theory are greatly undervalued' (McQuillan et al., 1999, xi). Retaining the radicality of the theoretical is, for Eagleton, a means of comprehending the cultural, historical and material aspects of literary texts, while also providing forms of resistance to 'colonization', ideologically speaking. The image of colonization is an important one, for it suggests the use of force to take over what is assumed to be a sovereign state. It speaks to the image in my title of border crossings. Theory, for Eagleton, and, indeed for me, provides a means not only of understanding how borders get crossed, how locations become colonized and made to speak almost unconsciously in a voice we never realized we had (see Martin McQuillan in this volume on the novels of Jane Austen); the significance of 'theory', for Eagleton in 1990, is that it helps maintain 'radical ideas' in the face of the attempted erasure of those very same radical ideas in both Britain and the USA (1990, 38).

ARRIVALS

Those analytical and reading practices called 'theory' have always been understood, in various guises and manifestations, to have arrived from elsewhere. Most immediately, theory, in the forms of 'poststructuralism', 'psychoanalytic literary criticism', 'deconstruction', is usually identified, in introductions, encyclopedias, guides and so on, as the result of the import of French theoretical discourses prevalent in the 1960s, which subsequently became translated into English and into departments of English. There were also some German incursions, in the form of one version of reader-response theory, the influence of members of the Frankfurt School and other hermeneuticists, but the simple narrative of theory is that its origins were markedly Francophone, if not specifically Parisian. Like so many tourists on a trip to Britain and the USA, theoretical discourses arrived, dressed themselves up in Anglo-American guise and had the nerve to stay, long after the visa expired. What occurred is, as they say, history, but English and criticism have never been the same since, and the change in the national identities of literary study has lasted now for more than thirty years. This is, of course, one possible, somewhat familiar narrative of the arrival of a range of analytical approaches. As such, it has no greater claim to truth than any other narrative we might care to tell. Whether or not it is 'theory's founding myth', as Gary Day has somewhat archly overstressed it (Day, 2000), I'm not in a position to say. However, what is undeniable is that, on both sides of the Atlantic, a sea change began to take place in English studies. However, this provisionally identified initiating instance of intellectual transition and, more specifically, the forms of resistance and struggle over the sites of criticism which have subsequently taken, and continue to take, place (see Bennington, 1999, 103–22; Cohen, 1998, 1–7; Easthope, 1988; Kamuf, 1997) belongs to a much broader historical narrative of tension between Anglo-American and continental epistemo-political discourses and institutions concerning matters of modernity and nation of which the struggle for criticism is merely symptomatic (see Ackroyd, 1993; Easthope, 1999; Mathy, 2000).

Two commentators on the import of theory and the subsequent changes in literary studies are Michael Payne and K. M. Newton, who provide us with historical-cultural accounts of continental analytical discourse, in the US and the British Isles respectively. First, Michael Payne:

> Fundamental and far-reaching changes in literary studies, often compared to paradigmatic shifts in the sciences, have been taking place in the last thirty years. These changes have included enlarging the literary canon not only to include novels, poems and plays by writers whose race, gender or nationality had marginalized their work but also to include texts by philosophers, psychoanalysts, historians, anthropologists, social and religious thinkers, who previously were studied by critics merely as 'background' . . . Many practising writers and teachers of literature, however, see recent developments in literary theory as dangerous and anti-humanistic. (Payne, 1991, vi–vii)

Now, K. M. Newton:

> . . . theory or critical principles that have some theoretical base underlie *any* form of reading, even the most naïve, of a literary text . . . The reason that there is so much controversy and debate in literary studies . . . is that critics and readers feel they belong to a single community, even though they may have made quite different choices as to how they read literary

texts . . . [However,] literary criticism . . . is like a parliament . . . in which two parties dominated . . . What has happened to the 'parliament' recently is that this two-party dominance has been threatened because numerous small parties have entered the parliament, depriving any single party of an overall majority . . . Literary criticism is thus revealed as a struggle for power among parties . . . The debate also has significance for society in general in that it raises questions that have implications beyond the purely literary sphere. (Newton, 1997, xv, xviii, xix)

Between Terry Eagleton, Michael Payne and K. M. Newton, you might get the sense that what is called literary theory is something to be feared; indeed many do fear it, often without knowing exactly what it is, other than it does derive from numerous disciplines outside literary studies, such as feminism, marxism, psychoanalysis and philosophy, and, worst of all, *continental* philosophy, not the good old, home-grown varieties of the analytical tradition in Britain or pragmatism in the USA.

Another fear, already mentioned, both within and outside universities, is that 'theory' is difficult, as Michael Payne suggests in pointing to the worries of the detractors (see Payne, 1991, vii). What could represent more of an affront than language about literature, about material which is supposedly part of a cultural heritage – that which puts the *English* in *English Literature* and also in *English Departments* – yet which is hard to understand? Canonical Literature should be taught either historically, from Beowulf to, well, Virginia Woolf and cultural studies should be abandoned; or literature should be taught because of its timeless, formal and aesthetic qualities which transcend cultural and political issues; what we need is a sense of *value*. You can find letters of objection similar in content or tone in, for example, *The New York Review of Books*, the *Times Literary Supplement*, the *Times Higher Education Supplement*, *The Chronicle of Higher Education*, even in non-specialist newspapers, such as *The Guardian* or the *Los Angeles Times*. What is the reason for this? Largely it's a question of media misrepresentation, because, to assume an Eagletonian tone for a moment, the newspapers and other forms of media are all part of the dominant order, they all serve in the colonization of the subject, of which Eagleton speaks.

Literary theory as the English translation of continental analytic praxes is, then, something to be afraid of, like so many illegal immigrants, like the 'contamination' of the English language with *modish* foreign words or, as far as some Britons are concerned, with the importation of 'Americanisms'. The fear of such discourse on the part of many, whether inside or outside the university, is precisely a fear of the foreign, the alien, the intruder, that which gets across the national boundaries, that which crosses the borders and comes to live in the homeland of English Literature, eventually taking it over, and changing its terrain forever. To borrow K. M. Newton's analogy, even the consensus politics of English Literature is no longer a safe discourse between ruling parties, assaulted as it is by those who no longer speak the same language. Literary Theory, so called, speaks in tongues, a

Babelian hoard not even waiting at the checkpoints to have its passports stamped. Perhaps the most far-reaching challenge which the reading practices in their many forms gesture is the inadequacy of the representation of the literary on the part of traditional and institutional beliefs as the 'best' that can be known and taught, to paraphrase Matthew Arnold. And the extent to which 'theory' has already crossed the border, infiltrated the mother country of English Literature, is marked by, on the one hand, the native distrust of whatever 'theory' may be (mis)taken to be, and, on the other, the way in which the institution of higher education, as a representative of Eagleton's dominant social order, has sought to quiet the difference of analysis down, to domesticate it, to reify it in English departments.

One way in which 'theory' has been given its rabies shots, put into quarantine, and then, having been taught to sit up and pay attention, let into its new homeland, is through the establishment of courses on literary theory. This is an effective form of containment, because it marks 'theory' off from, say, Shakespeare or the Victorian novel as merely one more subject to study. In this form it has become that which Eagleton in 1976 feared it would: a series of approaches (if this is week six it must be feminism). Even with the best will in the world on the part of those of us who teach on Literary Theory courses, the danger of such an approach is double: on the one hand, we isolate 'theory' from its engagement with literature, because if the course is about 'theory', then to a certain extent, we have to trust in the student's – that's to say your – willingness to go away and address literary texts from theoretical perspectives. With so much to study, this doesn't always happen. Theory, that which is associated, in the words of Tom Cohen, 'with a philosophically inflected amalgam of programs interfacing linguistic concerns with the redefinition of "history" (or, for that matter, human agency, meaning, impositions of power, and so on)' (Cohen, 1998, 5), merely ends up an adjunct of literary studies, an optional course for those who wish to take it. What could be better for those who fear 'theory' than this version of events. Theory in this guise is not going to represent a threat to anyone or anything if it's put in its place. (This is assuming of course that what is a named theory is a threat; it may or may not be radical or political, but it is only a threat if you fear being asked to think differently from the usual tired complacent habits of thought and belief which can come to constitute an identity for you, without your awareness.)

On the other hand, the other form of 'theory's' institutionalization is its absorption into the mainstream. Take the following statement: 'These days most academics are, to some extent, theorized.' These are the words of an ex-colleague, or as close to what he said as I can remember (though I believe it's fairly accurate). I'm not going to suggest that there is any overt agenda behind the utterance of this statement, in fact I believe it was uttered, as far as was possible for him, in absolute good faith. Yet, it can be read in a number of ways which suggests something of the institutional fortunes of 'theory'. While 'theory' may be contained through being given its own place in the curriculum as yet one more course, it can also be consumed, rendered relatively ineffectual and reduced to a series of formalist tools. To simplify greatly: the study of the function of metaphors and rhetorical figures has been replaced, as a result of, for example, the influence of Foucault and the Anglicization of his radical foreign identity, with the study of images of the body, or of incarceration, acts of policing, and so forth. Feminism, to take another example, is merely the examination of the depiction of women, of female characters and women writers. One can read the formalist, 'common-sense' domestication of 'theory' everywhere (not least in the name, the very idea, of 'theory') in literary studies, where 'domestication' means simply the replacement of old figures of analysis with newer ones, while maintaining the same principles behind the act of reading. If we are all, to greater or lesser extents, theorised, then the debates and battles, spoken of by Newton, Payne and Eagleton, are won. Aren't they? Theory, in this formula, has done well and no longer needs to keep going on about political issues or to insist on being political. One can't keep waging a war with the foreign, so one has to find ways of accommodating it, always supposing of course that this accommodation occurs according to one's own identity and values. If we are all more or less theorised, then 'theory' no longer has to be an issue, its erasure begun as surely as that of radical thought gestured towards by Eagleton.

BORDER CROSSINGS

As if to anticipate the institutionalization and domestication of 'Literary Theory', critical theories have, repeatedly, energetically and ceaselessly, formed and reformed themselves, forging allegiances with, and involving themselves in, critical debate with other theoretical discourses, models, paradigms. There is no single literary theory, if there ever was, even though the anti-theorists make the mistake of assuming a single identity for theory. The application of the title 'Literary Theory' is merely one form of domestication. The title operates to silence and erase differences, to hide contention, to ignore the complications, the heterogeneity, the protean energies, not only of disparate theories, but also within any supposedly single theory, such as, for example 'feminism'. As Ruth Robbins' title, 'Will the Real Feminist Theory Please Stand Up?' suggests, it is impossible to tell which is the 'real' theory, if only because, as she goes on to argue, there is no single true feminist theory. And this perhaps is feminism's, or any theory's, 'threat', that being hybrid, heterogeneous and protean, 'it' is not an 'it'; the theoretical discourse, by virtue of its own nature, resists all efforts at identification. This can be seen in any number of the essays in this collection. Martin McQuillan states that there is no such thing as reader-response theory, precisely because what is called reader-response theory draws upon so many other theoretical discourses, and all theoretical discourses are, in a sense, responses of the reader. Postmodernism cannot be represented because the discourses called 'postmodernism' are, themselves, so diverse and differentiated, while at the same time, the discourse on postmodernism is a post-modernist discourse inasmuch as it seeks to stress or represent the unrepresentable. K. M. Newton's article on Roland Barthes and structuralism similarly stresses that Barthes was a critic who never stood still, and could not therefore be pinned down as a structuralist critic (even supposing some simple identity called 'structuralism' existed, which, as Newton shows in differentiating Barthes from other structuralist critics, it did not).

Thus there are border crossings from one analytical practice to another, and within so-called theoretical positions. Indeed, the mobility of – in and among, across – analytical configurations points to an active resistance to, erasure of, anything so simply, so reductively defined as literary theory or, even, particular 'theories' (supposing they can be defined as such) as discrete discursive, epistemological phenomena or self-identical intellectual structures not already riven by internal fractures, contradictions, paradoxes, aporia, silences and omissions, or otherwise hermeneutically closed off. To return to the image of countries and states, theories exist in a state of productive tension, rather than in some utopian location of pluralist consensus, as is imagined by those, such as my previously mentioned acquaintance, for whom theory represents a club, determined to exclude those who don't know the language. It is not the case that there is the land of non-theory, and that of theory, where, like the Lilliputians and Brobdingnagians, wars are waged over which end one's egg should be opened (a case might be made for the comparison to be made in terms of Yahoos and Houyhnhnms, although this is not the place to do so), even though anti-theorists such as Gary Day in England or, in the US, Alan Sokal and David Lehman – who typifies Anglo-American parochial distrust in remarking that the 'American lit-crit profession [is] slowly but steadily shed[ding] its tweedy image in favor of foppish French fashion' (Lehman, 1991, 48) – might wish it were that simple (as their anti-theoretical narratives seem to suggest they do). Rather, theories cross each others' borders constantly; there are borders, limits, the demarcation of lines, to be certain. But these get redrawn constantly, as you will see from the essays in this collection. For example, the effects and legacies of various structuralisms mark theoretical readings of textual forms in a number of places. Theories not only cross the borders of an assumed identity in order to demonstrate the unspoken assumptions which serve to articulate that identity in the first place, they also, to reiterate the point, cross and recross each other's borders, remapping their own boundaries as they go. It is perhaps this very sense of excess, and of the constant outgrowing of a self which so troubles those who need the definition 'Literary Theory', if only so as to keep 'it' in 'its' place, in their minds at least. 'Literary Theory' is itself a form of border erected so as to keep 'theory' contained. It names an act also of border patrol, of policing, keeping the foreign, the other, the potentially dangerous under surveillance. The border patrol operates in a number of ways, for it seeks to erect a boundary within its own territory, rather than ultimately expelling the theoretical. To take the example of 'deconstruction', a very singular example unquestionably, and yet an example which serves to exemplify the treatment accorded all such singular examples, whether we name these feminism, marxism, postcolonial or gay theories, the institutionalized response is summed up by Peggy Kamuf: 'Concerning the institution that is the university put in question by the PC debate, the term "deconstruction" is most often presumed to refer to a theory, a method, a school, perhaps even a doctrine, in any case, some identifiable or localizable 'thing' that can be positioned – posed and opposed – within that institution, but also that can be excluded from this defined enclosure' (1997, 141).

CLOSE ENCOUNTERS OF THE TEXTUAL KIND

As Peggy Kamuf continues, what is more interesting than the reasons for establishing boundaries – the reasons present themselves more or less obviously or immediately, as the reasons *for* identification and location – is the revelation of a certain 'unfigurable space . . . the space for different kinds of effects' (1997, 141). It is precisely the opening of a space, unfigurable by any border, – which does not have installed already within it as a condition of its structure the possibility of its own erasure – which gives rise to such animosity in the face of the perceived threat of theory or theories. Indeed, the use of the plural *theories* is intended to signal that the opening of the space is already underway. If the work of Jacques Derrida in a certain way, in a translated form, is remarked in queer theory or postcolonial studies for example, this is less a comment on the signal importance of Derrida's work to a number of areas and disciplines, discourses and practices in the twentieth century, than it is an exemplary sign of the opening of channels of virtual communication which pass easily across all imagined borders and boundaries. The virtualization of theoretical movements reinscribes the space of the theoretical with a certain haunted quality, an uncanny effect as one of the possible effects described by Kamuf, in the unfigurable space of theories. Another effect, if it can be described this way, is to counter the formalization of critical thinking in the institution of literary criticism. For what has emerged have been new forms of political thinking, which, in adapting radical discourse and crossing the borders of literary study, have reinvented textual encounters, as the examples of postcolonial theory, queer theory and gay and lesbian studies, and cultural studies show. Critical practices such as these address not only questions of what we read, but also how we reread what we've already been told how to read. This is not to say that other theoretical discourses have not been political, have not stressed the necessity for rereading in ways which seek to emancipate the differences of the text. Rather, it is to suggest that literary theories have responded to the immediate danger of institutional enclosure through redrawing the political lines of analysis, of textual encounter. The textual encounter has become one, once more, of proximity, the close encounter of the title above. If theoretical discourse is markedly political, it has also, by virtue of its production of different effects, come close to the text, to read with energy and urgency textual structures. With this in mind, each of the essays here speak to the question of the interactions between philosophically inflected discourse, language and a re-thinking of the historical or historial, along with matters of agency and power, the constitution of the subject and so on, in order to work with, and thereby move beyond, institutional definitions of the theoretical and its identified subsets, moving also towards the idea of reading in excess of the notions of 'a feminism', 'a marxism' and so forth. In doing this *Introducing Literary Theories* endeavours to make available to its readers the possibility of coming to terms with the openness and energy made possible by the difference of the critical act, and to begin a process of crossing various epistemological, political and critical borders themselves.

NOTES

1. Although, subsequently, other studies introducing 'theory' in general have appeared (Andrew Bennett's and Nicholas Royle's already referred to, or Peter Barry's marvellous *Beginning Literary Theory* are just two of the most successful), Eagleton's study, whatever its shortcomings, remains significant in its engagement and the moment of its appearance, in the British Isles at least.
2. This sentence sketches Eagleton's engagement with different theoretical discourses, none of which he has simply accepted. Rather he has sought to mediate the insights of various theories from a marxist orientation. Louis Althusser was a French marxist whose own work engaged with structuralism and aspects of psychoanalysis.

WORKS CITED

Ackroyd, Peter. *Notes for A New Culture*, rev. edn. London, 1993.

Bennett, Andrew, and Nicholas Royle. *An Introduction to Literature, Criticism and Theory: Key Critical Concepts*. Hemel Hempstead, 1995.

Bennington, Geoffrey. 'Inter', in Martin McQuillan et al., eds. *Post-Theory: New Directions in Criticism*. Edinburgh, 1999.

Cohen, Tom. *Ideology and Inscription: 'Cultural Studies' after Benjamin, de Man, and Bakhtin*. Cambridge, 1998.

Day, Gary. 'Slapstick Meanings', *Times Higher Education Supplement*, 19 June 1998.

Day, Gary. 'A New Take on Old Questions', *Times Higher Education Supplement*, 2 May 2000.

Eagleton, Terry. *Literary Theory: An Introduction*. Oxford, 1983.

Eagleton, Terry. *The Significance of Theory*. Oxford, 1990.

Easthope, Antony. *British Post-structuralism since 1968*. London, 1988.

Easthope, Antony. *Englishness and National Culture*. London, 1999.

Kamuf, Peggy. *The Division of Literature or the University in Deconstruction*. Chicago, 1997.

McQuillan, Martin. 'Review', *Textual Practice*, 13: 2, Summer 1999.

McQuillan, Martin, et al. 'The Joy of Theory', in Martin McQuillan et al. (eds), *Post-Theory: New Directions in Criticism*. Edinburgh, 1999.

Mathy, Jean-Phillipe. *French Resistance: The French-American Culture Wars*. Minneapolis, MN, 2000.

Newton, K. M. *Twentieth-Century Literary Theory: A Reader*. Basingstoke, 1997.

Payne, Michael. *Reading Theory: An Introduction to Lacan, Derrida, and Kristeva*. Oxford, 1991.

CHAPTER

1

MIKHAIL BAKHTIN AND BAKHTINIAN CRITICISM

R. Brandon Kershner

Mikhail Bakhtin has been hailed by Tzvetan Todorov as 'the most important Soviet thinker in the human sciences and the greatest theoretician of literature in the twentieth century' (Todorov, 1984, ix), and has had a serious impact on the thinking of literary critics as diverse and distinguished as Roman Jakobson, Wayne Booth, David Lodge and Julia Kristeva. By any standards he is a stunningly original thinker, whose work has implications for philology, semiotics, philosophy (especially ethics and aesthetics), psychology and cultural anthropology as well as for literary history and criticism. Yet, virtually his entire life passed in obscurity, not only from the viewpoint of the West but within the Soviet Union as well. The son of a bank manager, Bakhtin was born in Orel, south of Moscow, and studied classics at Petersburg University (1913–17). On moving to Nevel, Bakhtin dominated a group of intellectuals, the first 'Bakhtin circle', including philosophers, linguists, literary scholars and a musicologist. In Vitebsk, the group was joined by Pavel M. Medvedev, a critic who had some official standing with the government.

Throughout the mid-1920s Bakhtin was quite productive, working on a number of essays and monographs in aesthetics and moral philosophy (some of which have been translated under the title *Art and Answerability*) as well as an early version of his book on Dostoevsky; the surviving notebooks show him moving away from the neo-Kantianism of Ernst Cassirer and Hermann Cohen which had been an important influence. In 1929 *Problems of Dostoevsky's Creative Works* was published to some acclaim, but meanwhile Bakhtin was arrested, apparently for his questionable religious affiliations. His sentence was commuted to 'internal exile' in Kazakhstan, and by the mid-1930s Bakhtin was able to find employment in obscure academic posts. In the late 1930s, fearing a purge of the faculty, Bakhtin moved to Savelovo. He did some reviewing and finished a book on the novel of education whose publication was stopped by the war. Only fragments of it survive. Meanwhile several of his circle, including Medvedev, were executed or died in camps. By 1940 he had prepared a doctoral dissertation for the Gorky Institute on 'Rabelais in the History of Realism' but the war postponed his defence. When he was finally allowed to defend the thesis, in 1952, for political reasons it was awarded only a candidate's degree.

During the late 1950s his old formalist antagonist Shklovsky mentioned the Dostoevsky work respectfully, as did Jakobson, and by 1960 several young Russian scholars, believing him dead, were making efforts to republish that book. Bakhtin was persuaded to revise the book and the final years of his life were marked by increasing recognition. Both the surviving formalists and the Tartu semioticians (on the left) celebrated him, as did a young group of Russian Orthodox scholars (on the right). Bakhtin's ability to appeal simultaneously to thinkers of widely divergent positions has continued to characterize his work during its reception in Europe and the Americas. Meanwhile, during his last years he worked on the Rabelais manuscript (which was published in 1965), his notebooks and a host of earlier manuscripts he wished to revise. In 1973 the semiotician Vyacheslav Ivanov claimed that Medvedev's book *The Formal Method in Literary Scholarship*, a critique of formalism published in 1928, was actually written by Bakhtin, as were *Freudianism; A Critical Sketch* (1927) and *Marxism and the Philosophy of Language* (1929), both signed by Voloshinov, and several essays published under Voloshinov's name. Bakhtin did not con-clusively either affirm or deny these assertions, and by 1975 he was dead. His final words were 'I go to thee'.

Bakhtin has been claimed by formalists and their successors the structuralists as one of their own, and he shares with both of them the conviction that language must be the fundamental key to analyzing and evaluating art and experience. Poststructuralists, beginning with Julia Kristeva (1980), often claim him as a precursor because his attack on the notion of a unified speaking subject as the guarantor of *logos* and his vision of language as inevitably a patchwork of citations anticipates poststructuralist positions. The self, for Bakhtin, is always provisory and in dynamic interchange, while the text can never be said to 'belong' to any fixed source. Marxists have claimed him because of his conviction that language is always already ideological and his championing of the dispossessed and admiration for 'the people'. And after all, whatever we consider the source of the disputed texts, with their explicitly marxist orienta-tion, they were certainly the product of his circle. Yet anti-marxists often see him as a fundamentally religious thinker, pointing out the parallels between his work and that of Martin Buber, with its highlighting of the 'I – Thou' relation. Further, his emphasis on resistance to authority, and the disruption and mockery of what he terms 'official culture', certainly make him an unusual marxist. He is a hero to a neo-Aristotelian like Wayne Booth because he proposes analytic categories for thinking about narration, like a formalist, but also clearly sees literary issues as ethical.

The question of the disputed texts exacerbates some of these problems, since the Voloshinov and Medvedev works are much closer to conventionally marxist thought than are the works published under Bakhtin's name. At this point, though, it is probably the consensus of scholars that while the disputed texts may indeed incorporate many of Bakhtin's ideas, they are not directly his work. But although Bakhtin is not a conventional marxist, neither are most of the western marxists such as Althusser, Adorno or Benjamin. His approach and values are certainly more 'sociological' and anti-idealist than was the work of most Anglo-American literary critics up until the last twenty years. But he is unlike both marxists and many contemporary theorists in his opposition to 'theoretism', the explanation of human phenomena by invoking a set of abstract rules, norms or analytic categories. He is not himself a wholly systematic thinker, and the state of being 'unfinished' or 'unfinalizable' is in fact one of his highest values and is basic to his definition of humanity.

Bakhtin's idea of the self is radically dependent upon others; the self, for him, is an act of grace, the gift of the other. Human consciousness is formed only in a process of perpetual negotiation with other selves by way of their 'languages'. Selfhood is supremely social, and a person who grew up without ever having been exposed to speech would not be fully human for Bakhtin: a passage in *Marxism and the Philosophy of Language* asserts that 'Consciousness becomes consciousness only once it has been filled with ideological (semiotic) content, consequently, only in the process of social interaction' (Voloshinov, 1986, 11). For Bakhtin, in a sense, intersubjectivity precedes subjectivity. Paradoxically, while consciousness is where Bakhtin locates selfhood, consciousness for him is fundamentally linguistic, and thus in his terms an extraterritorial part of the organism. For most who share in the Western philosophical tradition with its Cartesian emphasis, the idea that consciousness, where we most immediately locate our sense of being, is not really 'us' or even 'ours' is difficult to assimilate. As he remarks, language 'lies on the border between oneself and the other' (Bakhtin, 1981, 293). In his early writings on self and other Bakhtin points out that all people benefit from the 'surplus of vision' that others enjoy in looking at him or her and incorporate that vision into their vision of themselves even while opposing or partially assenting to it. So by definition, one's finalizing vision of another is never adequate; people, like successful characters in novels, 'do not coincide with themselves'. Bakhtin has little interest in the unconscious, and ascribes to consciousness most of the conflicts, contradictions and complexities that Freudians see in the interaction of conscious and unconscious minds.

Bakhtin makes a division between the natural sciences and the human sciences: in the former, objective *knowledge* is the goal, whereas in the human sciences, the goal is a dialogical *understanding*. Understanding is always determined by the concrete sociolinguistic horizon of the speaker and listener, and in literary studies in particular, understanding is always historical and personal. Language, the semiotic system that most interests Bakhtin, is not an abstraction for him, nor is it a closed system. In structuralist terms, we might say that he is always concerned with *parole*, the individual instance of speech – rather than *langue*, the system that orders speech. From Bakhtin's perspective, formal study of language systems is useless, and the early formalists were essentially wrong-headed – because it ignores the way in which speech is always rooted in a particular material situation that contributes a significant part of its meaning. We might say that every example of actual speech is a 'social enthymeme', relying on unstated premises. The 'sentence' is objective and can be reiterated, but the 'utterance' is unique and unrepeatable. Where the sentence has signification, the utterance has a 'theme', which is nonreiterative and concrete; the utterance also includes values, so that it can be beautiful, sincere, false or courageous.

Further, language is always, in Bakhtin's terms, ideological: that is, each utterance carries with it the aura of a particular idea-system (which may be more or less explicitly political) out of which it was spoken. The most significant aspect of an utterance for Bakhtin is what he terms its addressivity, its quality of being in some respect spoken *toward* someone. Bakhtin calls for a 'metalinguistics' or a 'translinguistics' which would investigate not merely the forms of language but the kinds of material situations in which speech occurs, because each speech act involves not only a theme but at least two interlocutors plus an invisible 'third', a 'superaddressee' providing an imagined absolutely just response, God, human conscience, 'the people', science, etc. (Bakhtin, 1986, 126). Bakhtin uses the term 'heteroglossia' to refer to the fact that speech, insofar as it is always embodied in a particular situation, is always multiple, always a mixture of languages which themselves can be further reduced. Everyone participates in numerous 'languages of heteroglossia', each of them claiming privilege. Obviously one of the problems of such a system is to establish any sort of final typology, but Bakhtin was happy to generalize about language types in a strictly provisory way. Toward the end of his life he was wrestling with the problem of what he termed 'speech genres', 'whole utterances belonging to particular generic types' (Bakhtin, 1986, 89).

The key to understanding language for Bakhtin is that

> our speech, that is, all our utterances (including creative works) is filled with others' words, varying degrees of otherness or varying degrees of 'our own-ness', varying degrees of awareness and detachment. These words of others carry with them their own expression, their own evaluative tone, which we assimilate, re-work, and re-accentuate. (Bakhtin, 1986, 89)

Thus language is always *double-voiced*, embodying both the language of the speaker (itself an amalgam of that speaker's important interlocutors, such as parents, lovers, intellectual influences and so forth) and any immediate or anticipated addressee, towards whom the speaker may linguistically assume a great variety of postures. Bakhtin has a particular interest in – and sensitivity to

– *intonation*, which is located on the boundary of the verbal and the nonverbal, and which must always be intuited in a written work. He sometimes finds a particular passage in a novel to be surrounded by invisible 'intonational quotation marks', signifiying that the phrase is another's language. To a remarkable degree, Bakhtin's theories of self–other relations, of language and consciousness, of ethics and of literature interpenetrate and support one another, so that Gary Saul Morson and Caryl Emerson have offered the term 'prosaics' to suggest both the way Bakhtin's thought is always rooted in the ordinary, the everyday and the immediate and the way his literary system elevates the prose genres over the poetic ones (Morson and Emerson, 1990). To a great extent, the 'actor' or 'performer' of Bakhtin's philosophical and ethical writings is the same as the 'author' of his later specifically literary ones, and both groups of writings celebrate the confrontation with alterity, the radical otherness the confrontation with which produces selfhood.

Bakhtin's approach is radically revisionary, and his agenda can often be seen as a defence of genres that have conventionally been seen as lesser. His championing of the novel should be seen as a reaction to the classical view in which poetry is the 'highest' literary form and prose fiction as a lesser one. He is also a champion of the popular – we could say of literary 'impurity' – and so stresses the way novels feed upon popular, 'subliterary' genres, as well as the way a writer like Rabelais includes profanity, obscenity and a host of rhetoric rooted in popular speech rather than in formal literary models.

For literary criticism, Bakhtin's most important essays are probably 'Epic and Novel', 'From the Prehistory of Novelistic Discourse' and 'Discourse in the Novel', all collected in *The Dialogic Imagination*. In an unsystematic but highly suggestive way he lays out a theory of literature that inverts most of the classical assumptions about the hierarchies of writing and what constitutes formal excellence. First, he opposes the novel and its earliest Hellenic forms, such as the dialogue, the symposium or Menippean satire, to epic and lyric poetry (and, less convincingly, to drama as well), arguing that the prose forms are superior in that they are *dialogic* – founded upon and constituted by dialogue – whereas poetry always tends toward the *monologic*, the state of a single, authoritative voice. In his book on Dostoevsky, Bakhtin argues that that novelist most fully realized the potential of the form. Dostoevsky's aesthetic process is best described as *polyphonic*, referring to the interplay between the author's own language and the fully realized languages of his protagonists. While in one sense no real speech or writing can be truly monologic, Bakhtin uses the term to refer to patriarchal, authoritarian, consciously ideological speech that reifies and totalizes. The authorial speech of Tolstoy seems this way to Bakhtin, as opposed to the polyphonic speech of Dostoevsky, in which we can easily find dialogized heteroglossia, a living dialogue of worldviews. In the genuine novel, Bakhtin claims, 'the "depicting" authorial language now lies on the same plane as the "depicted" language of the hero, and may enter into dialogic relations and hybrid combinations with it' (1981, 27–8). Indeed, it can be said that in the fully realized novel the 'author participates in the novel (he is omnipresent in it) *with almost no direct language of his own*. The language of the novel is a system of languages that mutually and ideologically interanimate each other' (1981, 47).

Bakhtin's conception of the novel attacks the assumptions inherent in the very Anglo-European names for the genre. Where much Western criticism has followed Ian Watt's model for 'the rise of the Novel' in the eighteenth century as a response to and to some degree a product of the rising middle class, Bakhtin in contrast stresses the novel's roots in Hellenic fiction; there is nothing new about it, he implies, because human narratives, whether in realistic or fantastic forms, are among the most ancient of literary expressions. His extensive and idiosyncratic classical training enables him to find predecessors for the novel form among the least studied Greek narratives. Similarly, he demonstrates that the other major European terms for the genre, which are variations of the term for romance, are equally misnomers because in his system the romance is a more monological branch of prose fiction, one leading to an inferior variant of the modern novel. We might also note that there is a class aspect to his argument, in that through these arguments he refuses to accept the novel's purported links to either the aristocracy or the middle class, implying that it is nearer to a popular or even 'folk' expression.

Bakhtin is at his most formalist in categorizing dialogical relations in the modern novel, although he does so very differently in different works. He talks of the enormous number of ways in which language is stratified, by genres and subgenres of literature (lyric, oratorical, penny-dreadful), by social professions (lawyers, businessmen, politicians), by social differentiations among groups, by artistic circles, journals and even particular artistic works, all 'capable of stratifying language, in proportion to their social significance' (1981, 290). But his main interest is reserved for different ways in which the language of the author may interact with other languages in the novel. For example, he explores what he terms 'character zones' in novels, areas of the text in which the authorial language changes to reflect the consciousness of a character even when that character is merely mentioned by the author and no direct attempt is being made to represent his or her thoughts. Much later and independently, the critic Hugh Kenner described this as the 'Uncle Charles effect', in reference to a passage in James Joyce's *Portrait of the Artist as a Young Man* where Stephen Dedalus's Uncle Charles 'repairs' to the outhouse, where he finds the air 'salubrious', a passage that Wyndham Lewis, missing the point, attacked as inflated late-Victorian prose. A character zone is a clear example of hetero-glossia; another is the way the novel form uses incorporated genres, short stories, songs, poems, newspaper stories, scholarly or religious genres, for example, as well as the familiar confession, letter, diary and so forth. This is another strength of the novel for Bakhtin, and shows how it is not simply another genre of literature but a 'super-genre', capable of assimilating all the others.

In *Problems of Dostoevsky's Poetics* Bakhtin gives his most elaborate schema for classifying novelistic discourse (1984, 199). His first category is direct, unmediated discourse directed exclusively toward its referential object, essentially the monologism of the author (and thus something not found in a true novel). The second category is objectified discourse, in other words a character's speech. Bakhtin notes that this can be more or less 'typed', and insofar as it is *not* typed, the relationship between author's and character's speech approaches dialogue. Double-voiced discourse, or discourse with an orientation toward someone else's discourse, is the third category, and the one that Bakhtin finds crucial. There are several subtypes of double-voiced discourse, the first of which he terms 'unidirectional' and 'convergent'. Examples of this type include stylization, the narration of an independent narrator, the unobjectified discourse of a character who is in part an authorial spokesperson and first-person narration. One might note that the author is fundamentally sympathetic to all these voice-types. The reverse is the case with 'vari-directional double-voiced discourse' (where the voices are 'divergent'), including parody, the discourse of a character being parodied and 'any transmission of someone else's words with a shift in accent'. The last sort of double-voiced discourse is the reflected discourse of another in which the other discourse exerts influence from without, including the 'hidden internal polemic' (where another's language is being contested without ever being explicitly identified), the discourse 'with a sideward glance' toward someone else's discourse (which is never directly addressed but is indirectly highly influential in producing the speaker's language), or a rejoinder of a dialogue (either explicit or hidden). Elsewhere Bakhtin deploys very different paradigms, but his main areas of interest remain.

A second characteristic of the novel which is not derivable from his concept of dialogism is the form's participation in a sense of life Bakhtin labels *carnival*, from the medieval ritual celebration. It is a simplification but perhaps helpful to say that if dialogism is the novel's proper form, carnival underlies its optimal content; the true novel is *carnivalized*. Carnival is probably Bakhtin's most influential formulation, and unsurprisingly it is also the most easily susceptible to abuse. As he develops the notion, principally in *Rabelais and His World* and *Problems of Dostoevsky's Poetics*, carnival embodies a kind of folk wisdom that celebrates the body and opposes all forms of authority. It is 'a pageant without footlights and without a division into performers and spectators' (Bakhtin, 1984, 122). Bakhtin derives his utopian notion of carnival from various medieval celebrations in which a sort of 'licensed misrule' was practised, usually through mockery directed toward the church and the town's established hierarchy. Often the mighty were ridiculed and a fool was crowned and uncrowned and there was general indulgence in 'base' pleasures of the body. Bakhtin emphasizes the free and familiar contact among people in carnival without regard to hierarchies, in 'carnival misalliances', as well as the free indulgence in blasphemy and profanation. For Bakhtin carnival expresses the 'joyful relativity' of all structure and order, and through its celebration of the 'bodily lower stratum' affirms a perpetual organic process of birth and death, nourishment and decay that is wholly transindividual. Although Bakhtin interprets carnival as almost entirely oppositional, it should be noted that many historians view this officially tolerated ritual as a mere 'safety valve' whose effect is to reaffirm the dominant power.

Most kinds of symbolic expression associated with carnival Bakhtin finds in 'carnivalized' literature, including the all-important carnival laughter, the ritual exchange of insults, parody, creative blasphemy, crowning and decrowning, the highlighting of base bodily functions, including sex, ingestion, defecation and urination, drunkenness, flatulence and a host of material appetites. Carnival levels all pretence, and in literary formulation tends toward a 'grotesque realism' that Bakhtin celebrates as the natural form of 'unofficial culture'. Rabelais's works are for Bakhtin the best examples of the tendency of the novel toward carnivalization, though he finds many traces of carnival in Dostoevsky as well. Indeed, Bakhtin traces two separate stylistic lines of development for the novel. One of them originates in the relatively monological language of the 'Sophistic novels' and runs through the medieval novels of gallantry, the Baroque novel and the fictions of Voltaire; the other is rooted in the dialogues and in Menippean satire, the works of Apuleis and Petronius, and runs through the uncategorizable works of writers like Rabelais, Sterne and Dostoevsky. The Second Line, as Bakhtin calls it (1981, 371–88), shows the novel's fundamentally dialogized relationship to heteroglossia, while the First Line tends towards objectification and monologism. And as it happens, where the First Line usually strikes a serious tone and involves itself in idealizations, the Second Line is more or less carnivalized from the beginning. Bakhtin's implication is that the traditional genealogy of the novel culminating in the social realism of Stendhal, Austen, Trollope, Balzac, Thackeray and James is actually a diversion from the more anarchic and fertile line running through Rabelais, Cervantes, the picaresque novelists, Goethe, Hugo, Dickens, Sterne and perhaps, in the twentieth century, writers like Joyce, John Barth and Thomas Pynchon.

A final term of Bakhtin's that has found some currency in contemporary literary criticism is the *chronotope*, a coinage that literally means 'time-space' and that Bakhtin uses to refer to the characteristic qualities of these parameters within any given fictional genre. Unusually, Bakhtin gives primacy to neither, and is particularly interested in their interaction. He understands the chronotope as 'a formally constitutive category of literature', and asserts, 'In the literary artistic chronotope, spatial and temporal indicators are fused into one carefully thought-out, concrete whole. Time, as it were, thickens, takes on flesh, becomes artistically visible; likewise, space becomes charged and responsive to the movements of time, plot, and history' (1981, 84). Bakhtin takes the term from Einsteinian physics, referring both to the interconnectedness of time and space and to the variety of time-space concepts implied by relativity theory. Chronotopes do not exist only in literary genres, where they help constitute the genre, but in human experience as well. In different contexts we experience time and space differently. Indeed, chronotopes are historical, as the ground for human activity, and may rise and fall, interacting with one another in a way Bakhtin describes as dialogical.

But although Bakhtin suggests that the chronotope has applications much wider than the literary, his discussion focuses on chronotopes of literary precursors of the modern novel. His treatment of the chronotope of the Greek 'adventure novel of the ordeal' (200–600 AD) and of the 'adventure novel of everyday life', Apuleius's *Golden Ass* and Petronius's *Satyricon*, somewhat resembles European phenomenological criticism of the 1960s in its attempt to give the inner sense of a literary universe, in which time, space, causality, selfhood and other fundamental categories of experience can be deployed in a variety of ways (1981, 86–129). Bakhtin may well have developed the idea of the chronotope because he is determined to trace the origins of the amorphous form of the novel through its ancient precursors, including locations (such as Menippean satire) where few critics had looked for pre-novelistic traces. But because Bakhtin's idea of the destiny of the novel is something very different from social realism, the chronotope helps him to re-map the literary past in radical ways.

Over the past fifteen years or so a large number of books have appeared using Bakhtin's thought as a point of entry to a variety of writings, and in the process exploring or contesting aspects of his ideas and method. David Lodge's *After Bakhtin* is a collection of essays dealing directly or indirectly with Bakhtin, emphasizing his relationship to structuralist criticism and arguing the question whether Lawrence or the Eliot of *Middlemarch*, for example, are monological or dialogical authorial voices. Peter Stallybrass and Allon White's *The Politics and Poetics of Transgression*, on the other hand, deals mostly with Bakhtin's notion of carnival, extending Bakhtin's idea of the 'grotesque body' to the 'body of the city'. Their analysis is also influenced by Foucault and other poststructuralist thinkers, and has special application to nineteenth-century culture and texts. Bakhtin has also been useful to feminist critics, even though his idea of carnival has been seriously challenged by women who point out that it is primarily female figures who are abused and exploited in carnival's madness. Nevertheless, Patricia Yaeger in *Honey-Mad Women* suggests that women writers have characteristically incorporated men's texts into their own and revelled in the polyvocality of the novel. For her, both carnival and dialogism contribute to an emancipatory strategy of playful writing for women. Terry Castle's *Masquerade and Civilization: The Carnivalesque in Eighteenth-Century Culture and Fiction* is another attempt to incorporate carnival into a sophisticated reading of British culture. Readers interested in further ideas on Bakhtin and feminism might look to Dale Bauer and Susan McKinsky's collection of essays *Feminism, Bakhtin and the Dialogic*.

Despite Bakhtin's assertion that the romantic lyric is mainly monological (in Pushkin, for example), Don H. Bialostosky argues in *Wordsworth, Dialogics, and the Practice of Criticism* that the poet's work is in fact dialogical. In *The*

Politics of Voice: Liberalism and Social Criticism from Franklin to Kingston
Malini Schueller traces ideological conflicts in American autobiographies
through their dialogical relationships with competing or contributing voices.
Less immediately interested in ideology, Calvin Bedient in *He Do the Police in
Different Voices: 'The Waste Land' and Its Protagonist* uses Bakhtin's methods
toward a sensitive exploration of the voices of that poem, combining Bakhtin
with Kristeva's work on abjection and Angus Fletcher's on allegory. Another
twentieth-century application of Bakhtin is R. B. Kershner's *Joyce, Bakhtin and
Popular Literature*, which concentrates mainly on dialogical relations in Joyce's
early works, through the play *Exiles*. The following discussion is based on
sections of that book.

NOTES TOWARDS A READING OF *A PORTRAIT OF THE ARTIST AS A YOUNG MAN*

Dialogism offers a fruitful way of approaching Joyce's *Portrait*, despite the fact
that its narrative differs from those Bakhtin normally considers. In *Portrait* there
is no single 'authorial voice' and the relationship between the author-narrator
and the protagonist, Stephen Dedalus, is notoriously difficult to specify. Not
only does the apparent authorial 'distance' change from virtual identification to
ironic detachment in different passages, but the narrative style as a whole
changes as Stephen develops. The majority of the text is an intense example of
the indirect free style, at times verging on stream-of-consciousness narration.

The author-protagonist aspect of dialogism is difficult to trace in *Portrait*, but
the book is particularly rich in other aspects. Stephen is constantly exposed to
other languages in the course of the book, of which the most dominant is the
conflict between the language of the church – Bakhtin's original model for a
monological language – and the language of romantic nationalism. This is most
vividly embodied in the 'Christmas dinner' scene, where Dante proclaims that
Stephen will remember 'the language he heard against God and religion and
priests in his own home', while Mr Casey cries, 'Let him remember the language
with which the priests and the priests' pawns broke Parnell's heart' (*PAYM*, 33–
4). It is important that as an English-speaking Irishman, Stephen feels that there
is no language in which he is 'at home'. English, the language of the dean of
studies, he feels to be alien: 'His language, so familiar and so foreign, will always
be for me an acquired speech. I have not made or accepted its words' (*PAYM*,
189). One irony we might note is that insofar as Stephen stands in for the young
Joyce here, he more than any other modern author later becomes responsible for
shaping that language.

As Stephen develops, we see him mulling upon the universe of 'given' words
and phrases he hears around him, which are surrounded by invisible 'intonational quotation marks'; through these he forms what Bakhtin calls 'vertical'
relationships between the outer world and his own psyche, even as he forms
'horizontal' relationships with the language of other individuals. These processes can be see most clearly in the repeated passages of chapter one, where he

broods on, for example, Wells shouldering him into the square ditch (*PAYM*, 10, 14) or Eileen's long white hands (*PAYM*, 36, 42). Such examples of incremental repetition show us a mind whose mode of conscious preception is in a radical sense *narrative*. Stephen not only thinks, but also perceives in phrases and sentences. His consciousness, we might say, is 'narratized'. This effect is so prominent in this novel because, after all, we are dealing with an artist as a young man.

Throughout the book Stephen studies accents, vocabularies, intonations and delivery much like an actor unsure which of an infinity of possible parts he will be called upon to play. He repeats to himself schoolboy or adult phrases like 'he would be captain of the third line all the fellows said' (*PAYM*, 8) or 'his father had told him whatever he did never to peach on a fellow' (*PAYM*, 9). He imitates for his friends the 'mincing nasal tone of the provincial' Father Conmee (*PAYM*, 72) or the patricians giving orders 'in highpitched provincial voices which pierced through their skintight accents' (*PAYM*, 238) or the 'genteel accent, low and moist, marred by errors' of the old captain in the 'National Library' (*PAYM*, 228). For all of his 'objectifying' analysis of the social and literary languages surrounding him, all of his attempts to eschew 'the language of the marketplace', Stephen eventually must become aware that his own language is a hybrid, that he is 'spoken through' even in his private thoughts, in a sort of mental ventriloquy. Even his formal education has been based upon the inculcation of key passages from a variety of sources, and his accomplishment has been evaluated with an eye to his ready and graceful application of passages and tags from textbooks advertised as *Synopsis of the Philosophy of X or Y*.

A different aspect of dialogism in the novel is represented by Stephen's encounter with texts in the world around him. Some of this can be seen in his adaptation of classical texts in his thought, such as his development of an aesthetic of what he terms 'applied Aquinas' or of ideas from Shelley, Pater and others. This territory, of course, has been thoroughly covered by conventional Joyce criticism through the history of ideas approach. But a relatively unexplored area to which Bakhtin points is Stephen's encounter with popular literature, such as his attendance at Bulwer Lytton's drama *The Lady of Lyons* or his schoolboy reading of *Peter Parley's Tales of Greece and Rome*. Each of these contributes to his sense of selfhood and to the romantic project which culminates in the desire to 'create the uncreated conscience of [his] race' (*PAYM*, 253). Perhaps the most important such text is Dumas's *Count of Monte Cristo*, a narrative that contributes substantially to his psychological set toward feelings of ultimate alienation, potentially unlimited power and romantic abnegation through the betrayal of a young woman. Without taking into account his modelling himself on Edmond Dantes it is difficult to understand the degree to which he imagines himself betrayed by E. C. or the way in which, even before meeting her, his most romantic vision of himself is of saying to his own Mercedes, 'Madam, I never eat Muscatel grapes' (*PAYM*, 63). When Dantes explains himself to one of his betrayers as a man with allegiance to no sovereign but who speaks all languages and can move among the citizens of all countries easily, we have the first intimation of Joyce the cosmopolite, empowered by his very deracination.

A final area to which we might look for dialogical relationships is intertextuality. Again, conventional criticism has explored the relationship of *Portrait* to a host of literary examples of the *Bildungsroman* or *Kunstlerroman*, but little attention has been paid to popular examples, including the most obvious ones. Thomas Hughes's *Tom Brown's School Days* (1857), for example, set the pattern for school stories throughout the British Isles and to a degree in America as well. Despite their obvious differences in temperament and experience, Stephen and Tom go through a large number of parallel experiences, down to the interrogation about their names and origins by schoolfellows. Reading the Rugby novel makes it clear how much of British schoolboy ideology persists in Clongowes school, and to what extent that ideology is embodied in language. Indeed, the last part of the first chapter of *Portrait*, where Stephen appeals to the rector because of his mistreatment by one of the priests and is then celebrated by his fellows, follows the pattern of schoolboy stories in all but the details of style. A more surprising intertext for *Portrait* is Tom Greer's very popular Irish adventure novel, *A Modern Daedalus* (1885), which tells the story of a young Irish boy who is scorned by his father and brothers because of his intellectual and artistic interests while they are dedicated to revolutionary action. The boy manages to invent wings and at the end of the story returns to Ireland at the head of a revolutionary air force, winning his country's independence and the acclaim of his family. The book, for all its silliness, captures the tone of Stephen's aspirations after heroism as well as his sense of alienation, and even his devotion to Parnell. Bakhtin enables us to see how *Portrait* stands in dialogue with a host of texts of many genres and social levels, just as Stephen is formed by many of the very languages with which he battles.

QUESTIONS FOR FURTHER CONSIDERATION

1. Explore the feminist critique of Bakhtin, concentrating on carnival. Is it significant that Bakhtin nowhere recognizes a 'woman's voice'?
2. In some ways, Bakhtin's belief in the liberatory potential of carnival is opposed by some of Foucault's followers, with their emphasis on the ability of regulatory discourse to assimilate opposing voices. Is there a way of mediating between these different paradigms?
3. Despite Bakhtin's lack of interest in the unconscious, several critics have attempted to combine his insights with those of Freud and his followers. How might this be done?
4. The reading of *Portrait* sketched above concentrates on the voices forming Stephen's consciousness. Can an 'original' voice be detected in Stephen as well?

5. Despite the closeness of authorial and protagonist's voices, how might we distinguish Joyce's voice in the book?
6. What might be the main characteristics of 'school ideology' as it is exemplified in Clongowes?

ANNOTATED BIBLIOGRAPHY

Bakhtin, Mikhail. *Rabelais and His World* (1965), trans. Hélène Iswolsky. Cambridge, MA, 1968.
Bakhtin here gives his most fully developed discussion of carnival.
Bakhtin, Mikhail. *The Dialogic Imagination: Four Essays by M. M. Bakhtin*, ed. Michael Holquist, trans. Caryl Emerson and Michael Holquist. Austin, TX, 1981.
Contains 'Epic and Novel', 'From the Prehistory of Novelistic Discourse', 'Forms of Time and the Chronotope in the Novel' and 'Discourse in the Novel', all fundamental essays for Bakhtin's thought.
Bakhtin, Mikhail. *Problems of Dostoevsky's Poetics* (1963), ed. and trans. Caryl Emerson. Minneapolis, MN, 1984.
Includes a thorough discussion of internal dialogism in the novel, with examples from Dostoevsky.
Bakhtin, Mikhail. *Speech Genres and Other Late Essays* (1986), eds Caryl Emerson and Michael Holquist, trans. Vern W. McGee. Austin, TX, 1986.
Includes the title essay as well as essays on the *Bildungsroman*, essays on 'The Problem of the Text in Linguistics, Philology, and the Human Sciences' and 'Toward a Methodology in the Human Sciences', as well as suggestive notes made shortly before his death.
Bakhtin, Mikhail. *Art and Answerability: Early Philosophical Essays by M. M. Bakhtin*, eds Michael Holquist and Vadim Liapunov, trans. Vadim Liapunov. Austin, TX, 1990.
Somewhat neo-Kantian work of the early Bakhtin, showing the ethical dimension of his literary thought.

SUPPLEMENTARY BIBLIOGRAPHY

Bakhtin, M. M., and P. N. Medvedev *The Formal Method in Literary Scholarship: A Critical Introduction to Sociological Poetics* (pub. under Medvedev, Moscow, 1928), trans. Albert J. Wehrle. Cambridge, MA, 1985.
Bauer, Dale, and Susan McKinsky, eds. *Feminism, Bakhtin, and the Dialogic*. Albany, NY, 1991.
Bedient, Calvin. *He Do the Police in Different Voices: 'The Waste Land' and Its Protagonist*. Chicago, 1986.
Bialostosky, Don H. *Wordsworth, Dialogics, and the Practice of Criticism*. Cambridge, 1992.
Booker, M. Keith. *Joyce, Bakhtin, and the Literary Tradition: Towards a Comparative Cultural Poetics*. Ann Arbor, MI: 1995.
Castle, Terry. *Masquerade and Civilization: The Carnivalesque in Eighteenth-Century Culture and Fiction*. Stanford, CA, 1986.
Clark, Katerina, and Michael Holquist. *Mikhail Bakhtin*. Cambridge, MA, 1984.
Coates, Ruth. *Christianity in Bakhtin: God and the Exiled Author*. New York, 1998.
Emerson, Caryl. *The First Hundred Years of Mikhail Bakhtin*. Princeton, NJ, 1997.
Emerson, Caryl, ed. *Critical Essays on M. M. Bakhtin*. New York, 1997.
Hirschkop, Ken, and David Shepherd, (eds). *Bakhtin and Cultural Theory*. Manchester, 1989.
Holquist, Michael. *Dialogism: Bakhtin and His World*. London, 1990.
Kershner, R. B. *Joyce, Bakhtin, and Popular Literature: Chronicles of Disorder*. Chapel

Hill, NC, 1989.

Kristeva, Julia. 'Word, Dialogue, and Novel', *Desire in Language: A Semiotic Approach to Literature and Art*, trans. Leon S. Roudiez. New York, 1980.

Lodge, David. *After Bakhtin: Essays on Fiction and Criticism*. New York, 1990.

Morris, Pam, ed. *The Bakhtin Reader: Selected Writings of Bakhtin, Medvedev, Volosinov*. London, 1994.

Morson, Gary Saul, ed. 1986. *Bakhtin: Essays and Dialogues on His Work*. Chicago, 1986.

Morson, Gary Saul and Emerson, Caryl (eds). *Rethinking Bakhtin: Extensions and Challenges*. Evanston, IL, 1989.

Morson, Gary Saul and Emerson, Caryl. *Mikhail Bakhtin: Creation of a Prosaics*. Stanford, CA, 1990.

Schueller, Malini Johar. *The Politics of Voice: Liberalism and Social Criticism from Franklin to Kingston*. Albany, NY, 1992.

Sebeok, Thomas A., ed. *Carnival!* (1984). New York, 1984.

Todorov, Tzvetan. *Mikhail Bakhtin: The Dialogical Principle* (1981), trans. Wlad Godzich. Minneapolis, MN, 1984.

Voloshinov, V. N. *Marxism and the Philosophy of Language* (1929), trans. Ladislav Matejka and I. R. Titunik. Cambridge, MA, 1986.

Voloshinov, V. N. *Freudianism: A Critical Sketch* (1927), eds I. R. Titunik and Neil R. Bruss, trans. I. R. Titunik. Bloomington, IN, 1987.

Yaeger, Patricia. *Honey-Mad Women: Emancipatory Strategies in Women's Writing*. New York, 1988.

2

ROLAND BARTHES AND STRUCTURALIST CRITICISM

K. M. Newton

A common description of structuralism is that it is a method of analysing cultural phenomena founded on Saussurian linguistics. This description is borne out if one reads such structuralist critics as Roman Jakobson, in his later critical writings, Tzvetan Todorov, A. J. Greimas, Gérard Genette. These critics were concerned to apply structuralist methodology – in Jakobson's case to the analysis of poetic language and in the case of Todorov, Greimas and Genette to the study of narrative – without explicitly engaging in philosophical or ideological conflict with non-structuralist forms of analysis. Roland Barthes, the most famous of structuralists, was also capable of such neutral forms of structuralist analysis, notably in one long essay entitled 'The Structural Analysis of Narratives'. However, Barthes was essentially a critical controversialist. For him, structuralism was primarily important as a weapon that could be used to attack two of the dominant forces in western ideology – science and its counterpart in the social sciences, positivism – both of which had their basis in empiricism.

One might see Barthes as fighting an old battle here. The French tradition of thought had been predominantly based on rationalism, a form of thinking that posited that knowledge of reality is possible without reference to sensory experience, Descartes being the major French philosopher in this tradition. Opposed to this rationalist tradition was empiricism, the theory that all knowledge is derived from sense experience and that no knowledge is innate or a priori. The latter tradition had been dominated by Anglo-Saxon thinkers such as Locke and Hume, and this tradition was much more in tune with science than the rationalist tradition. Since the rise of science in the seventeenth and eighteenth centuries, therefore, empiricism can be seen as the major influence on western thinking. In the conflict between rationalism in the philosophical sense and empiricism, the latter could be said to have prevailed.

Yet it could be argued that the rationalist tradition encouraged critique much more forcibly than the empiricist tradition. In the empiricist tradition the world was seen as an independent structure which it was the task of the human mind to try to understand. The mind's relation to the world could then be seen as essentially passive, thus encouraging conservative attitudes. Marx, one recalls, blamed philosophers for only interpreting the world instead of endeavouring to change it. The attraction of structuralism for a radical like Barthes was that it had the potential to reassert rationalist critique and undermine empiricist passivity, for central to structuralist thinking is that the mind's relation to the world is active and not passive.

Before Saussure, linguistics had tended to be studied on a positivistic basis grounded in empirical investigation. Language was treated in historical terms, with the emphasis being on how language had developed and changed over time. Saussure shifted the emphasis from this diachronic aspect of language to the synchronic aspect. His predominant concern was with how language as a system of signs functioned at a particular point in time rather than with language as a historical product. For Saussure, language has two fundamental aspects: *langue* or the underlying system that governs language use, and *parole*, how language is employed for communicative purposes through the use of words and sentences. Saussure's overriding interest was in *langue*. One can see that this is a return to a more rationalistic approach in the philosophical sense, since *langue* is not empirically present as the object of investigation but is a mental construct. *Langue* governs *parole* but it can only be reconstructed from *parole*, that is from empirically existing linguistic data, but such data are essentially secondary. Noam Chomsky's linguistic theory departs from Saussure's in important respects but for Chomsky also it is the linguistic system that allows individual users to generate sentences which may never have been uttered before yet which can be understood by others, and significantly the title of one of Chomsky's books is *Cartesian Linguistics*, indicating his identification with a rationalist tradition of thought.

An implication of Saussurian linguistics is that language structures the world since language as a system of signs mediates between the human mind and external reality. For Saussure words are arbitrary signs and, more important, meaning is relational: it is produced by the differences between linguistic signs and not by words having discrete independent meanings. In the relation between mind and world, therefore, one cannot forget about language: it refracts the mind's relation to the world. In an essay first published in 1967, 'From Science to Literature', Barthes attacks science for viewing language as 'an instrument' and as 'transparent' and 'neutral' so that it is 'subjugated to scientific matters (operations, hypotheses, results) which are said to exist outside it and to precede it' (*LT*, 25). Literature, in contrast, is made up only of language – 'language is the *being* of literature, its very world' (25) – and this allows it to question reality and not merely accept it passively: 'Ethically, it is solely by its passage through language that literature pursues the disturbance of the essential concepts of our culture, "reality" chief among them' (25). The rise of science had seemingly consigned the study of rhetoric to the dustbin of history but Barthes claims that the discrediting of rhetoric – 'grandiose effort of an entire culture to analyze and classify the forms of speech, to render the world of language intelligible' – was ideological and that it is structuralism's 'glamorous ancestor' (26).

However, Barthes goes on to argue in this essay that structuralism has itself been infected by the scientific aspiration towards objectivity, and in contrast argues that its 'logical extension can only be to join literature, no longer as "object" of analysis but as activity of writing' (27). This involves recognizing the role of the subject in any analysis of the object. This will allow structuralism more effectively to contest the view of positivistic science that 'a neutral state of language exists, from which would branch off, like so many gaps and orna-ments, a certain number of specialized languages, such as the literary language or the poetic language' (28). Science has no claim to be 'a superior code; writing seeks to be a total code, including its own forces of destruction' (28). Barthes makes clear the social and ideological implications of this when he writes: 'It follows that only writing alone can break the theological image imposed by science' (28).

This literary writing is called by Barthes *écriture*. Writing which seeks to be transparent and is thus complicit with the prevailing dominant ideology with its basis in positivistic science is, in contrast, *écrivance*. For Barthes the objection to the realist novel is that it has its basis in *écrivance* rather than *écriture*, and throughout his writing Barthes is hostile to realist fiction because it is seen as reinforcing a conservative ideology that essentially accepts the world as given. However, there would seem to be an obvious distinction between formulaic realist novels that have no claim to literary merit or interest and novels by writers such as Balzac or Stendhal who are categorised as realists by literary historians. It is perhaps the need to distinguish between different types of realism that leads Barthes to produce *S/Z*, his study of Balzac's novella, *Sarrasine*, which is perhaps his most influential critical text.

In the introductory sections of *S/Z*, Barthes introduces a distinction that qualifies his earlier distinction between *écriture* and *écrivance*, namely that between *scriptible* and *lisible*, usually translated as 'writerly' and 'readerly' respectively. *S/Z* can be seen as a transitional work in which Barthes is moving beyond structuralism into poststructuralism, with the emphasis being on textual rather than structural analysis. It is generally agreed that poststructuralist thinking emerged most powerfully in 1966 with Jacques Derrida's paper 'Structure, Sign and Play in the Discourse of the Human Sciences', first delivered at a conference at Johns Hopkins University, a conference Barthes had attended. Derrida followed this up with the publication of three major texts in 1967, notably *Of Grammatology*. In the opening section of *S/Z* Barthes distances himself from the earlier structuralist project:

> Precisely what the first analysts of narrative were attempting: to see all the world's stories . . . within a single structure [is] a task as exhausting (ninety-nine percent perspiration, as the saying goes) as it is ultimately undesirable, for the text thereby loses its difference. *LT*, 30)

Barthes then goes on to discuss this 'difference' and the word has a distinctly Derridean ring. He shifts the focus from narrative in the general sense, which was the main preoccupation of structuralist narratology, to the individual text: 'the single text is valid for all texts of literature, not in the sense that it represents them . . . but in that literature itself is never anything but a single text: the one text is not an (inductive) access to a Model, but entrance into a network with a thousand entrances' (35).

However, Barthes maintains his hostility to realism. The 'writerly' is from the beginning elevated above the 'readerly' text: 'Why is the writerly our value? Because the goal of literary work (of literature as work) is to make the reader no longer a consumer, but a producer of the text' (31). The 'writerly' text 'is a perpetual present, upon which no *consequent* language . . . can be super-imposed'; it is '*ourselves writing*, before the infinite play of the world . . . is traversed, intersected, stopped, plasticized by some singular system . . . which reduces the plurality of entrances, the opening of networks, the infinity of languages' (31). This is very like Derrida's second form of interpretation in his 'Structure, Sign and Play' essay which 'affirms freeplay and tries to pass beyond man and humanism' (Macksey, 1972, 265), yet it could be argued that both owe something to Barthes's concept of 'writing degree zero' in his first important book of that name, published in 1953. In contrast 'readerly' texts 'are products (and not productions), they make up the enormous mass of our literature' (31). Whereas the 'writerly' text is 'a galaxy of signifiers' and 'the codes it mobilizes extend as far *as the eye can reach*' (32), the readerly text is open to interpretation and governed by a restricted number of codes. However, Barthes accepts that certain 'readerly' texts have a limited plurality, texts by such writers as Balzac and other literary realists. The basis of that limited plurality is 'connotation'. The aim of his study of Balzac's *Sarrasine* is to reveal the 'difference' at work within the text, that difference being created by the space between 'denotation' and 'connotation' in a text. Connotation, for Barthes, is 'a correlation im-manent in the text . . . one may say that it is an association made by the text-as-subject within its own system . . . connotations are meanings which are neither in the dictionary nor in the grammar of the language in which the text is written' (33).

Conventionally connotation is contrasted with denotation in language, that is meaning in a literal sense, the meaning that can be found in a dictionary. But Barthes claims that denotation has no intrinsic priority over connotation: 'denotation is not the first meaning, but pretends to be so; under this illusion, it is ultimately no more than the *last* of the connotations (the one which seems both to establish and close the reading) (34). This suggests that denotation or literal meaning is more of an ideological than a linguistic product. Certain meanings have a greater power than others for ideological reasons and these meanings are termed denotative or literal.

In demonstrating that a text is a plurality of connotations, with denotation being displaced from the centre of meaning and having no separate existence from connotation, one can see Barthes's structuralism moving towards Derridean deconstruction. Not only is the text dismantled by being shown to be a plurality of coded connotations, but in the process, the reader as a centred 'I' figure is also dismantled: 'This "I" which approaches the text is already a plurality of other texts, of codes which are infinite or, more precisely, lost (whose origin is lost)'. Subjectivity is a construction since it is only a 'deceptive plenitude . . . merely the wake of all the codes which constitute me' (34). However, Barthes's claim that the 'readerly' text is the product of five codes of reading which organize its intelligibility is something of a return to a more structuralist form of narratology: the *proairetic* code controls the reader's construction of plot; the *hermeneutic* code presents the reader with a question or a problem or an enigma which gives the plot its momentum; the *semic* code is concerned with characteristics, such as psychological traits; the *symbolic* code is concerned with the organization of symbolic meanings; the *referential* code consists of references in the text to cultural phenomena. However, there is an element of playfulness in Barthes's presentation of these codes, which distances his approach from orthodox structuralism. He does not argue in detail for them or make any scientific claim for them in the manner of other structuralist critics who believe that literary criticism should aspire to a kind of scientific objectivity.

Yet to discuss literary texts in terms of codes is clearly an implicit attack on the kind of criticism that sees literature as being above ideology and having transcendental powers. A code, such as morse code or the barcodes one finds on items in supermarkets, triggers meaning mechanically and automatically and for Barthes writing as *écrivance* does the same. Literary texts such as the novels of Balzac and other realists may be more complex in that a multiplicity of codes are at work but essentially a similar mechanical generation of meaning operates, with the codes triggering certain effects in the reader's mind. And more is at stake here than just reading. Such texts are responsible for constructing the reader's view of reality, but Barthes's critical aim is to demystify the realist literary text and its claim to offer a true representation of reality. For Barthes what is being represented is only a 'reality effect', the title of another of his essays: in *S/Z* the aim is to show in detail, by dividing a text into numbered *lexias* or units of meaning and discussing each of them in turn, how this reality effect is produced by an interplay of codes.

One might compare Barthes's five codes to Kant's categories of mind which order our understanding of the world. For Kant any reality beyond the forms of our consciousness and categories of mind, such as quality and causation, is unknowable but without such categories our relation to the world would just be a chaos of sensations. But whereas Kant believes that his categories are intrinsic to the mind, Barthes suggests that codes of reading are socially constructed; therefore one is not necessarily condemned to accept such codes. It is possible for the 'readerly' to be replaced by the 'writerly'. Since the 'writerly' text does not operate in terms of a limited number of codes, it has the potential to allow the reader to escape from a reality determined in advance by codes rooted in ideology and potentially to create a new reality.

Clearly there was an implicit revolutionary aspect in a political sense to Barthes's structuralist criticism and this made his work very influential with certain British critics. Stephen Heath was one of the first critics to write a study of Barthes and in a later book on the *nouveau roman*, which Barthes had supported for its implicit attack on conventional realism, Heath argues that the realist novel is readable because it 'is relayed by a series of codes and conventions, by the text of the already known and written: that work is readable, therefore, which is cast within their horizon, which repeats them in their naturalized transparence' (Heath, 1972, 21), and whereas Barthes selects Balzac as his exemplary realist, Heath selects George Eliot: 'Thus George Eliot, for example, can offer her novels naturally as an attempt to "give a faithful account of men and things as they have mirrored themselves in my mind". This is the same kind of "innocence" that was encountered in Balzac's description of the *Comédie Humaine* as "visual dictation"' (Heath, 1972, 20).

These ideas were further developed by Colin MacCabe in a study of James Joyce. Joyce for MacCabe represents writing aspiring towards the 'writerly' while the 'readerly' text is again represented by George Eliot. MacCabe uses a phrase which was to become very influential in the work of British critics who were influenced by Barthes. Discussing narration and the use of inverted commas to separate characters' speech from the discourse of the narrator, MacCabe argues that this creates a hierarchy of discourses with the narration functioning as a metalanguage which 'refuses to acknowledge its own status as writing' and 'functions simply as a window on reality. This relationship between discourses can be taken as the defining feature of *the classic realist text*' (MacCabe, 1978, 15).

Other British critics interpreted Barthes's critical ideas in relation to realism in more directly political terms. In a discussion of *S/Z* in their book *Language and Materialism*, Rosalind Coward and John Ellis write that 'realism stresses the product and not the production. It represses production in the same way that the mechanism of the market, of general exchangeability, represses production in capitalist society' (Coward and Ellis, 1977, 46). The idea of 'the classic realist text' was particularly fundamental to Catherine Belsey's influential book, *Critical Practice*, first published in 1980. She states that 'Classic realism . . . is what Barthes in *S/Z* defines as the readable (*lisible*), the dominant literary form of the nineteenth-century, no longer "pertinent" in the twentieth' (Belsey, 1980, 73), and she sees it as no accident that 'classic realism' is the dominant form during the period of industrial capitalism. But though Belsey draws on Barthes to declare that the 'readable text is merchandize to be consumed' (Belsey, 1980, 105), again linking 'classic realism' with capitalism, she recognises that *S/Z* is a very different kind of critical text from her own *Critical Practice*. Rather it is 'itself a polyphonic critical text' and 'impossible to summarize adequately, to reduce to systematic accessibility'; it is 'at once frustrating and exhilarating . . . it would almost certainly not be possible (or useful) to attempt a wholesale imitation of its critical method(s)' (Belsey, 1980, 105–6).

This brings out a distinction between Barthes and his British followers. Although ideas are important to Barthes, he seems more aware than critics like Belsey of a potential contradiction in attacking the 'readerly' text or 'classic realism' but at the same time using a form of critical discourse that is itself 'readerly'. For Barthes, 'writerly' language in itself is political: by refusing to conform to 'readerly' conventions that assume that language should be transparent in its meaning and paraphraseable one is undermining the 'readerly' not just at the level of ideas but at the deeper level of form.

Although Barthes's structuralist writings were massively influential on British critics, they were less well received by American criticism. When Barthes gave a paper entitled 'To Write: An Intransitive Verb?' at the Johns Hopkins conference on structuralism in 1966, there was a question and answer session following the paper. Paul de Man, who was later to become the major figure in American deconstruction, was scathing in his criticism both of Barthes's type of structuralist analysis and of his conception of literary history. He attacks Barthes in particular for promoting 'an optimistic historical myth', one that 'represents historical progress and extremely optimistic possibilities for the history of thought'. Barthes's stylistic analyses do not, de Man claims, 'show any progress over those of the Formalists, Russian or American, who used empirical methods, through neither the vocabulary nor the conceptual frame you use'. As regards literary history 'you say things that are false within a typically French myth'. Whereas Barthes places writing since Mallarmé, particularly the *nouveau roman*, in opposition to Romantic writing as regards the treatment of the ego, de Man asserts that Barthes is simply wrong:

> In the romantic autobiography, or, well before that, in the seventeenth-century story, this same complication of the ego (*moi*) is found, not only unconsciously, but explicitly and thematically treated, in a much more complex way than in the contemporary novel. I don't want to continue this development; it is simply to indicate that you distort history *because* you need a historical myth of progress to justify a method which is not yet able to justify itself by results. (Macksey, 1972, 150)

Barthes's reply was interesting. Although he was conventionally thought of as being a demythologizer because of his book *Mythologies*, he states that

> I never succeed in defining literary history independently of what time has added to it. In other words, I always give it a mythical dimension. For me,

> Romanticism includes everything that has been said about Romanticism. Consequently, the historical past acts as a sort of psychoanalysis. For me the historical past is a sort of gluey matter for which I feel an inauthentic shame and from which I try to detach myself by living my present as a sort of combat or violence against this mythical time immediately behind me. When I see something that might have happened fifty years ago, for me it already has a mythical dimension. (Macksey, 1972, 150–1)

This suggests that Barthes's anti-empiricism goes all the way down, as it were. He is not concerned about the 'empirical facts' of history; these are always in any case distorted by the 'mythical dimension'. Again the driving force of his writing is to create change and if this requires what de Man sees as 'a historical myth of progress', then so be it. De Man, in contrast, believes that one should try to separate fact and myth and is sceptical about the possibility of progress, both in life and literature.

De Man's main objection to Barthes is that his myth of progress leads to a distortion of literary history, with modernist writing being elevated above the literature of earlier periods. Barthes's criticism also operates with oppositions between *écriture* and *écrivance* and 'writerly' and 'readerly' and this makes him vulnerable to a Derridean criticism that deconstructs such oppositions. De Man in his later career was the leading theorist among the so called Yale deconstructionists and one of his ex-students, Barbara Johnson, subjected Barthes's *S/Z* to a deconstructive analysis which sets out to show that Barthes's attempt to confine Balzac's *Sarrasine* to the category of the 'readerly' becomes entangled in contradictions.

The plot of *Sarrasine* centres on the passion of the sculptor Sarrasine for an opera singer, La Zambinella, but he is ignorant of the fact that *castrati* – castrated men – sang the soprana parts on the Italian operatic stage, and he eventually discovers that La Zambinella, whom he had considered to possess a perfect female body, had been born a man. Johnson uses this collapse of oppositions within the story to undermine Barthes's opposition between the 'writerly' and the 'readerly' text. Barthes's distinction is made up of a difference *between*, but like the difference between male and female in the text of *Sarrasine*, this collapses into a difference *within*, since Johnson argues that the qualities Barthes associated with the 'writerly' are evident in the very text he has used to exemplify the 'readerly': 'Like the readerly text, Sarrasine's deluded image of La Zambinella is a glorification of perfect unity and wholeness . . . But like the writerly text, Zambinella is actually fragmented, unnatural and sexually undecidable' (Johnson, 1980, 8). Instead of the text thematizing the 'writerly-readerly' opposition, the text itself shows an awareness of the fact that such oppositions cannot be sustained since Sarrasine, 'In thinking that he knows where difference is located – between the sexes – he is blind to a difference that cannot be situated between, but only within' (Johnson, 1980, 10). It is the text itself which 'demystifies the logocentric blindness' of Sarrasine's conception of

La Zambinella so that Balzac's text has already deconstructed the most basic of oppositions: that between male and female: 'Balzac has already in a sense done Barthes's work for him. The readerly text is itself nothing other than a deconstruction of the readerly text.' The text 'does not simply reverse the hierarchy between readerly and writerly by substituting the truth of castration for the delusion of wholeness; it deconstructs the very possibility of naming the difference' (Johnson, 1980, 11–12).

De Manian deconstruction thus attempts to outflank Barthes, the anti-positivist, by demonstrating that in operating with oppositions that are open to deconstruction, he is complicit with positivist thinking which is also dominated by similar value-laden oppositions. However, Johnson perhaps does not give sufficient credit to the playful nature of a text such as S/Z. As mentioned earlier, Barthes makes no scientific claims for his codes and he would not be surprised, I think, by the fact that the 'writerly-readerly' opposition could not be made hard and fast. Though differences may collapse into each other when subjected to deconstructive scrutiny this does not mean that one can operate without them, even if one has to qualify certain terms by placing them 'under erasure', that is, writing them but also crossing them out. De Man as an extreme sceptic shared none of Barthes's political goals so that the kind of criticism he favoured was free to take deconstruction to its extremity, concluding notoriously that 'reading is impossible'. Barthes, in contrast, wants reading to make a difference even if that involves making use of myth and oppositions which may be vulnerable to the rigours of deconstructive logic.

Though in S/Z Barthes seemed to be leaving structuralism behind in favour of what came to be called poststructuralism, his later work indicates that it would be an oversimplification to draw such a conclusion. Again it is difficult to pin him down. In his essay, 'The Struggle with the Angel', first published in 1971, which focuses on a particular text – part of the thirty-second chapter of Genesis – one sees a partial return to the more objective approach to structural analysis associated with the earlier Barthes of 'Introduction to the Structural Analysis of Narratives'. Barthes points out in a footnote that the discussion of Sarrasine in S/Z 'belongs more to textual than to structural analysis' (Barthes, 1977, 137) but in contrast his treatment of the Genesis passage is predominantly structural: 'the piece under discussion lends itself to an extremely and almost canonical structural analysis' (Barthes, 1977, 126). But he goes on to say that the methodology of S/Z has not been wholly discarded:

> I shall allow myself every so often (and perhaps continuously on the quiet) to direct my investigation towards an analysis with which I am more at home, textual analysis . . . Such an analysis endeavours to 'see' each particular text in its difference – which does not mean in its ineffable individuality, for this difference is 'woven' in familiar codes; it conceives the text as taken up in an *open* network which is the very infinity of language, itself structured without closure; it tries to say no longer *from*

where the text comes (historical criticism), nor even *how* it is made (structural analysis), but how it is unmade, how it explodes, disseminates – by what coded paths it *goes off*. (Barthes, 1977, 126–7)

The end of that passage conjures up Derridean deconstruction. This essay, therefore, is an ambitious effort to bring together the various phases of Barthes's critical career: his connections with the kind of structuralist analysis associated with such figures as Greimas; the textual analysis he developed in *S/Z*; and the more Derridean influenced approach of his last phase.

Roland Barthes was a critic who never stood still. As with such modernist artists as Picasso one has to talk of his work as falling into different phases. He can never be securely pinned down though the term 'structuralist' perhaps has greater force than any other that could be applied to him. But his structuralism interacted with his commitment to modernism, his concern with the politics of writing and reading, his refusal to accept the artist-critic division, his awareness of the work of poststructuralists such as Derrida. All of Barthes's critical phases continue to be influential and this makes him one of the major critics of the latter half of the twentieth century.

NOTES TOWARDS A READING OF *MIDDLEMARCH*

As discussed above, Roland Barthes's British followers identified George Eliot's fiction with the kind of classic realism which Barthes associated with the 'readerly', and certainly in a novel such as *Middlemarch* the narration would seem to function as a metalanguage superior to any other form of discourse contained in the novel. A Barthes-based approach to the text, operating along similar lines to his critique of Balzac's *Sarrasine*, would expose how this narration is constructed so as to exert power over the reader by representing itself as embodying truth or wisdom or an unchallengeable view of reality. But as Barthes's exposure of Balzac was vulnerable to a counterattack, so *Middlemarch* can likewise be defended against Barthes-influenced critiques. This can be seen if one looks at the following passage from the opening of Chapter 27 of *Middlemarch* in which the narrator addresses the reader:

> An eminent philosopher among my friends, who can dignify even your ugly furniture by lifting it into the serene light of science, has shown me this pregnant little fact. Your pier-glass of extensive surface of polished steel made to be rubbed by a housemaid, will be minutely and multitudinously scratched in all directions; but place now against it a lighted candle as a centre of illumination, and lo! The scratches will seem to arrange themselves in a fine series of concentric circles round that little sun. It is demonstrable that the scratches are going everywhere impartially, and it is only your candle which produces the flattering illusion of a concentric arrangement, its light falling with an exclusive optical selection. These things are a parable. The scratches are events, and the candle is the egoism of any person now absent – of Miss Vincy, for example. (*M*, 264)

This passage is typical of many in the novel in which the narrator addresses the reader in direct terms and expresses a particular perspective or viewpoint with no disagreement or objection being apparently envisaged. In discussions of narration in nineteenth-century fiction, the narrator is often identified as a God-like presence. The narrator in the passage appears to assume that the reader will accept the account of the pier-glass as an incontrovertible fact, based on science, which the reader has no alternative but to accept. Language is thus used merely to reflect or mirror a world of fact, thus identifying it with *écrivance* in Barthes's terms.

Yet it may be significant that Eliot uses a mirror as an exemplification of how appearances do not necessarily reflect reality. It seems likely that there is an allusion to the common use in the eighteenth century of the mirror as an analogy for the mind's relation to reality, one which was challenged during the Romantic period when that analogy was called into question and the mind was compared rather to a lamp. Though a mirror may appear to reflect the world without distortion even the very object which produces that reflection cannot be trusted. From a scientific point of view – presumably arrived at by examining them under ordinary daylight conditions – the scratches on the pier-glass go in every direction but if a particular source of light is applied they appear to be concentric. The narration identifies the scientific view with truth but scientific truth can only be a particular perspective on the world, one which is produced through its own procedures and rules of operation. Truth in science, unlike truth in a metaphysical or religious sense, cannot aspire to an absolute status. The passage goes on to construct the phenomenon of the scratches on the pier-glass into a parable, with the human ego forming concentric arrangements out of events which like the scratches have no intrinsic organization.

Clearly this parable does not apply only to egocentric characters in the novel such as Rosamond Vincy but also even to the narrator since every human being is born into egoism. The narrator has earlier informed us, in Chapter 21, that 'We are all of us born into moral stupidity, taking the world as an udder to feed our supreme selves' (*M*, 210), and though one can 'emerge from that stupidity', it is clear that egoism can never be eradicated but at best only sublimated; in Chapter 18 the narrator refers to 'inevitably self-interested desires' (*M*, 177). Therefore what appears to be a categorical statement by the narrator under-mines itself by the relativistic implications of the statement itself. The apparent God-like command that the narrator exerts over the narrative so that we identify its account with incontrovertible fact and truth is exposed as a construction by a particular mind which will inevitably have its interests and prejudices.

Has a Barthes-like analysis of nineteenth-century narrative again been under-mined by being anticipated by or contained within the text as a literary construct? One can argue that it has but on the other hand a Barthes-influenced structuralist critic could respond that though the narration of *Middlemarch* may acknowledge relativism at the level of statement, this insight is not incorporated into the novel at the level of form. Though the narrator by implication accepts that narration as metalanguage is only one possible perspective on reality the reader is still denied any other perspective. Indeed, it might be argued that this apparent acknowledgement of relativism is a mere rhetorical device to disarm the reader into accepting passively the metalanguage of the narration. In contrast, later modernist fiction recognizes that relativism, or more precisely perspectivism, is irreconcilable with the kind of dominating metalanguage that one finds in a novel such as *Middlemarch*. This leads novelists like Joyce and Virginia Woolf to incorporate relativism or perspectivism into fiction at a formal level through fragmenting narration and developing techniques such as a radical use of free indirect speech and stream of consciousness which undermine the need for 'omniscient' narration.

QUESTIONS FOR FURTHER CONSIDERATION

1. In what ways can structuralism make available or otherwise enable a critique of the ideologies which inform conventional reading habits?
2. Consider the role of the five codes of reading and how these operate in different cultural forms, such as an advertising poster, a commercial or a narrative film.
3. How do narratives produce the illusion of a central, coherent subject who we take to be the narrator?
4. To what extent does the narrator of *Middlemarch* rely on connotation in the Barthesian sense in order to position the reader? Consider some of the rhetorical and structural features by which the narrator does this.
5. Consider the various functions of the narrator in *Middlemarch* in the light of Barthes's distinction between *écriture* and *écrivance*. While Barthes claims that realist writing aims at a certain transparency with regard to its language, thereby showing itself to be complicit in prevailing dominant ideologies, to what extent is it possible to consider the narrator's occasional appeals to the reader as breaking the narrative frame and thereby calling into question the ideological assumptions which rest upon the implicit empiricism and mimeticism inherent in realist narrative?
6. Consider the role which various binary oppositions throughout *Middlemarch* (e.g. science/belief, past/present, tradition/innovation) play in either supporting or subverting the novel's social hierarchies and institutions, and the dominant ideologies embedded or expressed through these. To what extent is Eliot's figure of the web as a figure for society a structural model?

ANNOTATED BIBLIOGRAPHY

Barthes, Roland. *Writing Degree Zero*, trans. Annette Lavers and Colin Smith. London, 1967.

Barthes's first book published in 1953 and one which formulates some of the pre-occupations that recur throughout his writings. It establishes him as a writer and critic whose fundamental sympathies are with the modernist movement in art. Barthes focuses on classical French writing (*écriture classique*), a way of writing that was so powerful that it was not seen as a particular literary style but merely as a reflection of reality, natural and innocent. He particularly attacks the appropriation of this style by the bourgeoisie in the nineteenth century when it became encoded with bourgeois values and he supports twentieth-century writing which resists it by apparently being devoid of style.

Barthes, Roland. *Mythologies*, trans. Annette Lavers. London, 1972.

Barthes's most popular book and one which showed that structuralism was not an opaque methodology that was relevant only to such fields as social anthropology and literary criticism but could be applied to virtually every cultural area, both low and high. The book also showed how structuralist criticism could operate as political critique. The discussion of myth as a second-order semiotic system is particularly important.

Barthes, Roland. *Criticism and Truth*, trans. Katrine Pilcher Keuneman. London, 1987.

Barthes's response to an attack on him by a traditional French academic critic, Raymond Picard. Picard scathingly criticized Barthes's book *Sur Racine*, which made use of psychoanalysis and marxism, and accused it of intellectual irresponsibility when compared with objective, historically-based academic criticism. Barthes argues against Picard that traditional academic criticism is not ideologically innocent, that literature has an inherent plurality and cannot be pinned down to a restricted set of meanings.

Culler, Jonathan. *Structuralist Poetics: Structuralism, Linguistics and the Study of Literature*. London, 1975.

Still probably the best general study of structuralism. Particularly useful on the relationship between structuralism and linguistic theory. Full discussions of Jakobson, Barthes, Greimas, Todorov, Genette and other significant critics and theorists. Culler's belief that one can construct 'a poetics which stands to literature as linguistics stands to language' is more controversial.

Macksey, Richard (with Eugenio Donato), ed. *The Structuralist Controversy: The Languages of Criticism and the Sciences of Man*. Baltimore, MD, 1972.

The proceedings of a conference in 1966 at which most noted structuralists spoke, including Barthes, Todorov and Lacan. Also contains Derrida's essay, 'Structure, Sign, and Play in the Discourse of the Human Sciences', a major critique of structuralism and arguably the beginning of poststructuralism. An interesting feature of the volume is that it reproduces the discussions that followed the delivery of papers. Thus Barthes's paper, 'To Write: An Intransitive Verb?', is followed by contributions from Todorov, de Man and Derrida, among others.

SUPPLEMENTARY BIBLIOGRAPHY

Barthes, Roland. *Elements of Semiology*, trans. Annette Lavers and Colin Smith. London, 1967.

————. *Critical Essays*, trans. Richard Howard. Evanston, IL, 1972.

————. *The Pleasure of the Text*, trans. Richard Miller. London, 1976.

————. *The Rustle of Language*, trans. Richard Howard. Berkeley, CA, 1989.

————. *Image, Music, Text*, trans. Stephen Heath. London, 1977.

————. *The Grain of the Voice: Interviews, 1962–1980*. Berkeley, CA, 1991.

Belsey, Catherine. *Critical Practice*. London, 1980.

Coward, Rosalind, and John Ellis. *Language and Materialism: Developments in Semiology and the Theory of the Subject*. London, 1977.

Culler, Jonathan. *Saussure*. London, 1976.

————. *Barthes*. London, 1983.

Ehrmann, Jacques, ed. *Structuralism*. New York, 1970.

Gadet, Françoise. *Saussure and Contemporary Culture*, trans. Gregory Elliott. London, 1989.

Genette, Gérard. *Narrative Discourse: An Essay on Method*, trans. Jane Lewin. Ithaca, NY, 1980.

Harland, Richard. *Superstructuralism: The Philosophy of Structuralism and Post-Structuralism*. London, 1987.

Hawkes, Terence. *Structuralism and Criticism*. London, 1977.

Heath, Stephen. *The Nouveau Roman: A Study in the Practice of Writing*. London, 1972.

Jackson, Leonard. *The Poverty of Structuralism: Literature and Structuralist Theory*. London, 1991.

Jameson, Fredric. *The Prison House of Language: A Critical Account of Structuralism and Russian Formalism*. Princeton, NJ, 1972.

Johnson, Barbara. *The Critical Difference: Essays in the Contemporary Rhetoric of Reading*. Baltimore, MD, 1980.

Lavers, Annette. *Roland Barthes: Structuralism and After*. London, 1982.

Lévi-Strauss, Claude. *Structural Anthropology*, trans. Claire Jacobson and Brooke Grundfest Schoepf. New York, 1963.

Lodge, David. *Working with Structuralism: Essays and Reviews on Nineteenth- and Twentieth-Century Literature*. London, 1981.

MacCabe, Colin. *James Joyce and the Revolution of the Word*. London, 1978.

Miller, Joan. *French Structuralism: A Multidisciplinary Bibliography*. New York, 1981.

Moriarty, Michael. *Roland Barthes*. Cambridge, 1991.

Riffaterre, Michael. *Essais de stylistique structurale*. Paris, 1971.

Robey, David, ed. *Structuralism: An Introduction*. Oxford, 1973.

Saussure, Ferdinand de. *Course in General Linguistics*, trans. Roy Harris. London, 1983.

Scholes, Robert. *Structuralism in Literature: An Introduction*. New Haven, CT, 1974.

Sebeok, Thomas A., ed. *Style in Language*. Cambridge, MA, 1960.

Sontag, Susan, ed. *A Barthes Reader*. London, 1982.

Sturrock, John, ed. *Structuralism and Since: From Lévi-Strauss to Derrida*. Oxford, 1979.

Thody, Philip. *Roland Barthes: A Conservative Estimate*. London, 1977.

Todorov, Tzvetan. *The Fantastic: A Structural Approach to a Literary Genre*, trans. Richard Howard. Ithaca, NY, 1975.

————. *The Poetics of Prose*, trans. Richard Howard. Ithaca, NY, 1977.

————. *Introduction to Poetics*, trans. Richard Howard. Brighton, 1981.

Wiseman, Mary B. *The Ecstasies of Roland Barthes*. London, 1989.

CHAPTER 3

WILL THE REAL FEMINIST
THEORY PLEASE STAND UP?

Ruth Robbins

Did I mention a girl? Oh, she is out of it – completely. They – the women I mean – are out of it – should be out of it. We must help them to stay in that beautiful world of their own, lest ours gets worse. (Joseph Conrad, *Heart of Darkness*, 1900)

'I have always been in favour of a little theory: we must have Thought; else we shall be landed back in the dark ages . . .' (Mr Brooke in George Eliot's *Middlemarch*, 1870–1)

The answer to the question posed by the title is, of course, no. Feminist literary theory is not a unified theory with a single corpus of work that has to be read and mastered before you can begin: there is no feminist Marx or Freud whose work defines feminism as theory and method. This fact is both a strength and sometimes a frustration of feminism. It is also part of its politics since one of the things that feminism resists is what might be called the 'authorized' version, the ready-made responses to texts and life that are habitual and unthinking. Feminist theories are necessarily adaptable to different contexts because they make very few assumptions about the nature of the enterprise; nor does feminism presume an absolutist common political purpose. This means that anyone can do 'it', and can do 'it' to any text – but what 'it' is is not proscribed. Feminist literary theories are perhaps best understood as an ongoing series of interventions in reading practices, interventions that pursue a politics of reading, and that also presume that reading practices can make some difference to our experiences of the world.

In broad terms, I would identify as feminist any literary theory and practice which bases itself on the following three propositions.

1. THE WORD AND THE WORLD ARE RELATED

Feminist literary theories presume some relationship between words and the world – between texts and the reality from which they arise and in which they are subsequently read. The relationship is never transparent, but that does not mean that it is not there. Feminist theories assume that Literature is not some transcendent space in which the contingencies of everyday life are somehow elided or absent. Literature, in literate cultures, is *part* of reality. It *reflects the real* (though the mirror may be distorting or defective); *it creates the real* (through getting us to believe in its fictional worlds and/or by suggesting that we might behave in particular ways); and *it offers alternatives to the real* (through critiques of reality as we live it, or through imagining alternative modes of being in fantasies, utopias, dystopias, science fictions and so on). Texts, feminist theories argue, are always produced out of a specific reality, and they bear the marks of their time, place and mode of production. They are always to be understood as relating to historic and geographic specificity, both in terms of the moment when they are first produced, and at the moments when they are reproduced by our readings of them. These principles align feminist literary theory to both marxist and historicist/materialist approaches.

[To this extent, the fifty years between the publication of George Eliot's *Middlemarch* and Virginia Woolf's *Mrs Dalloway* have to be taken into account when comparing their very different versions of female subjectivity. One might presume that historical development means progress, especially in terms of the liberation of women. Reading in the twenty-first century, one might be surprised to notice, for example, how consistently we think of the twentieth-century heroine, Clarissa as '*Mrs* Dalloway' – named for her husband – and of Dorothea as Dorothea Brooke – named for *herself*, though she ought more properly to be named Mrs Casaubon. Why does the historically later character, a woman who can vote and have a public life in her own right, should she choose, think of herself as lost in her husband's identity? 'She had the oddest sense of being herself invisible; unseen; unknown . . . this being Mrs Dalloway; not even Clarissa any more; this being Mrs Richard Dalloway' (*MD*, 11). The answers are local and individual – Mrs Dalloway is happily married by her own lights, but is almost an anachronistic being in 1923, ageing and old-fashioned, content to accept the limitations of wifedom, whereas Dorothea is clearly inappropriately married and is swiftly widowed. But even as a wife, Dorothea is separate from her husband, a source of sorrow to him, and of discomfort to her, as when he asks her to promise to continue his work after his death and she cannot promise immediately: 'you would use your own judgement,' he says to her: 'I ask you to obey mine; you refuse' (*M*, 519). The point is that Dorothea is in quest of a kind of life of *action*, a life of active doing, which resists the expectations of the world into which she is born. We first meet her drawing up plans for new cottages intended to make a material difference to the lives of others (texts that will eventually have their effects on the real world); her marriage is unsatisfactory to her among other reasons because it leaves her with ample liberty for 'being' but with no scope for doing:

> There was the stifling oppression of that gentlewoman's world, where everything was done for her and none asked for her aid . . . 'What shall I *do*?' 'Whatever you please, my dear': that had been her brief history since she had left off learning morning lessons and practising silly rhythms on the hated piano. Marriage, which was to bring guidance into *worthy and imperative occupation*, had not yet freed her from the gentlewoman's oppressive liberty. (*M*, 274, my italics)

Eliot's narrator gently pokes fun at Dorothea's little pang of disappointment that there was 'nothing for her to *do* in Lowick' (*M*, 78, my italics) since the parishioners are relatively well off. What we see in Dorothea is a resistance to simply 'being' and a desire to act.

But the reasons for the different naming and the different sense of self the two heroines each inhabits are also historical and, as it were, global. Comparatively speaking, *Middlemarch* is set in an age of innocence, distanced from its own narrative perspective (written from the late 1860s to the early 1870s but set in the late 1820s to early 1830s). It does not exactly chart a golden age, but there is nostalgia – albeit tinged with irony. *Mrs Dalloway* is absolutely set in the present. There is no perspective and distance, and the year 1923 is necessarily haunted by the very recent global events of the years 1914–19 (the war years, and their aftermath, the great influenza epidemic which claimed more victims than the war itself – a global phenomenon, yet one which has individually, locally, affected Mrs Dalloway's heart (*MD*, 4). Dorothea's individuality and her yearnings for an individual life come from the time in which she has her being. By the same token, Mrs Dalloway's acceptance of the duties and obligations of marriage, her will to maintain social forms, even her decision to give a party, are an indirect response to the horrors of recent history. Mrs Dalloway lives the same kind of life as Dorothea does – ministered to by servants, choosing her own occupations, free to do whatever she pleases. But Mrs Dalloway is satisfied with 'oppressive liberty', indeed does not experience it *as* oppressive. By Dorothea's lights, Clarissa's world is trivial: a whirl of socializing and pretty clothes (Mrs Dalloway dresses well and hates the insult of Miss Kilman's deliberately ugly clothing; but Mrs Casaubon has 'that kind of beauty that seems to be thrown into relief by poor dress' (*M*, 7)). But it is, nonetheless, a political response to history. In another novel, *To the Lighthouse*, Woolf suggested that this world of surfaces and the small lies of social interaction have their own purpose and function in maintaining civilization. Mrs Ramsay, that other matriarch named by her husband's name (without in her case even a passing reference to a forename or a maiden name), knows that her own function is to smooth other people's lives – to tell the necessary small lies. When her husband pursues truth too forcibly, she perceives it as violation:

> To pursue truth with such astonishing lack of consideration for other people's feelings, to rend the thin veils of civilisation so wantonly, so brutally, was to her so horrible an outrage of human decency . . . There was nothing to be said. (Woolf, 1992, 37)

Civilization is here a woman wearing thin veils – a figure that is fragile and easily assaulted – and civilization was certainly assaulted by 'the horror, the horror', as Conrad might have put it, of the First World War.

In other words, one woman maintains a status quo that has been exposed as only too fragile, while the other, at a different point in history, kicks against the social expectations of femininity in her own time and place, against a social edifice that appears massive and potent.]

2. WORDS AND THE WORLD ARE POLITICALLY RELATED

The second proposition is that the relationships between texts and worlds are necessarily political – political in the broad sense of having to do with power. Texts and our readings of them can be coercive, representing and encoding 'proper' behaviour and 'proper' structures of belief and feeling. Texts and readings can also be subversive, attacking dominant modes of understanding, offering alternative ways of living and thinking. If texts are related to the world, texts (and the ways we read them) can *change* the world. At the heart of feminist literary theory, therefore, is a will to political agency – reading in a particular way, writing about what one has read with this in mind, these things can make a difference. Again, the potential links with marxist approaches to literature are clear.

[Not, of course, that the politics of a text is always easy to see, nor, indeed, acceptable when it *is* seen. I can love novels like *Mrs Dalloway* or *Middlemarch* and yet still find myself deeply uncomfortable with the political positions they appear to endorse. This may be politics in the 'party' sense – Sir James Chettam is a land-owning Tory and is presented as decent if rather dim; Mr Brooke as a wrong-headed independent radical, with no real political convictions at all; Richard Dalloway is a Tory MP, and toes the party line. But it may also be a politics of representation. After all, the stories of Dorothea Brooke and Clarissa Dalloway concentrate almost all their sympathetic attention on the lives of very privileged women. Dorothea might be upset by her 'oppressive liberty', but I'd be prepared to bet that hers is the kind of oppression that lots of working-class women of her own period would have relished. She is 'free' because other women wash her clothes, clean her house, provide her food; she is also free because she has inherited money, which is presumably the result of the labour of others. The politics of representation that disguises these facts, that reduces Dorothea's lady's maid Tantripp to a comic minor figure, or Mrs Dalloway's servant Lucy into a pure – and rather unlikely – conduit of affection for her mistress, and which makes the middle-class consciousness of the 'heroines' the sympathetic fulcrum of the texts, is exclusionary and even hurtful. Feminist theories have to read the exclusions as well as the inclusions, have to bring to the surface connections that the texts might seek (consciously or not) to repress. We cannot just accept representation as reality, and in reading what is not represented, or what is under-represented, as well as what is represented plainly for either disapproval or agreement, we can see anew elements of disclosure and disguise in our own world.]

3. FEMINIST THEORIES FOCUS ON WOMEN IN RELATION TO THE POLITICS OF WORDS AND THE POLITICS OF THE WORLD

The third proposition is perhaps the most important. What all feminist theories share is a focus on women. That bald statement conceals a multitude of possibilities because the collective noun 'women' disguises, as I suggest above, the many differences between individual women, the differences in individual women within the space of a single life, and the differences between women from different groups: Eve has many faces. The focus on women, however, constitutes feminism's main impetus. Marxism argues that human subjects are formed by economic conditions of competition and oppression; psychoanalysis argues that human subjects are formed by psychic conditions of repressed trauma. Feminist theories argue that women are also formed by other structures that build on economic subjection and psychic repression, and that these structures have tended to operate as structures of oppression because of the social and psychic inequalities of gender. Among those structures, feminist theories identify social deprivations specific to women (poor access to education and well-paid work); physiological oppressions based on the female body (the facts that bearing and rearing children is largely 'women's work', that women are physically weaker than men and can be subjected to violence and rape); cultural oppression (in which women are devalued into cultural objects rather than being valued – and being able to value themselves – as cultural subjects); and psychological oppression (where women are denied masculine status, and often come to believe in their own inferiority because they lack masculine bodies and minds). The name given to this complex of oppressive structures is patriarchy – literally the rule of the father – and feminist theorists identify patriarchy at work in the home, the state, the church or other religious systems, the law, education, the workplace, in culture at large, and even in women themselves since women often internalize the values they are fed by powerful external institutions. Both marxism and psychoanalysis speak also of these structures: but feminism concentrates on their effects on women, arguing that any structure of oppression rebounds more strongly on women than on men. That is not to say that in white western societies, a black working man is less oppressed than a white middle-class woman; but it does tend to suggest that a black working woman is more likely to be oppressed than her black male counterpart. Feminist thinking seeks to uncover – and thence to challenge and change – these structural inequalities. A feminist practice of literary theory might be one of the tools by which discovery and transformation can come about. Reading, thinking, criticizing, writing are all forms of action that can underpin oppression: they might also be made to serve the undoing of oppression. Feminism is aligned therefore with the theories that account for many different kinds of inequalities – with psychoanalysis and marxism, with black theories, postcolonial theories, and with lesbian and gay (or queer) theories.

[Not all of these ideas can be brought to bear on readings of *Middlemarch* or *Mrs Dalloway*. There are no black characters in either text – a marker of historical and geographical specificity rather than deliberately racist exclusion; and there is only just the faintest glimmering of a postcolonialist sensibility in Peter Walsh's wasted career as an imperial civil servant in India. Indeed, because the focus is on privileged women there is little sense of a world in which child-rearing or paid work impinge on our consciousness except at the home of the Garths in *Middlemarch*. Dorothea, it is true, feels herself woefully under-educated, but that is an individual quirk, unique to her character, which the novel satirizes, rather than a structural failing in the education system in general. Rosamund Vincy's education is mercilessly criticized:

> She was admitted to be the flower of Mrs Lemon's school, the chief school in the country, where the teaching included all that was demanded of an accomplished female – even to extras, such as the getting in and out of a carriage. Mrs Lemon herself had always held up Miss Vincy as an example: no pupil, she said, exceeded that young lady for mental acquisition and propriety of speech, while her musical execution was quite exceptional. (*M*, 123)

In other words it has consisted almost entirely of learning the deportment of femininity. Rosamund has acquired knowledge but has no idea what to do with it; has learned to speak well, but has nothing to say; and can play complicated music efficiently – but, so what? Although Miss Vincy ends up being well served by her education – she pursues her own ends entirely single-mindedly and ends up quite content with her life – it nearly destroys her husband, for she is incapable of sympathy with his intellectual pursuits. Incidentally, though, Dorothea's inadequate education has not made her similarly obtuse – she can sympathize both with the deeply unprepossessing Casaubon to the point of marrying him, and with the more attractive but still flawed Lydgate to the point of loaning him a very large sum of money. So, Eliot's text tends to argue that the fault is individual rather than structural. Only in comparing Rosamund's education with Fred's can the systematic faults be seen, and they are not to be understood as gender-inflected. Fred, too, has an inadequate education, despite the fact that he has been to the University. His schooling is intended to fit him for the career of clergyman, but he has no temperamental aptitude for this vocation. He needs an education that will prepare him for practical life, and receives that only later when Caleb Garth undertakes to teach him estate management (and handwriting – which his expensive sojourn at college has done nothing to improve). Neither Vincy sibling has been taught what they will later need. Fred is nonetheless a pleasant enough character – a bit irresponsible but fundamentally decent deep down. His education has made no difference to that. Rosamund has been taught to catch a man, her accomplishments listed above being precisely the things that attract Lydgate: 'She is grace itself; she is perfectly lovely and accomplished. That is what a woman ought to be: she ought to produce the effect of exquisite music,' he says to himself (*M*, 94). But she knows nothing about the practicalities of her future career – how to continue to love the man once she has caught him. But then, Eliot seems to suggest, that cannot be taught in Mrs Lemon's school or elsewhere: that is a matter of individual personality. Rosamund lacks what it takes and the result is horrible.

My point is that Eliot's emphasis remains very forcibly on the individual character. While it's clear that Mrs Lemon's methods of training do not meet with her narrator's approval, it is just as clear that Rosamund must nonetheless take responsibility for her own failings. *Middlemarch* establishes itself very firmly and explicitly as a novel about society and the interconnections between individual in a communal group through its repeated metaphor of the web. Frankly, though, the novel is much more concerned with the choices, the moral responsibilities, duties and obligations that each person must take on for him/ herself. The connections and structures, the lines of cause and effect, are largely incidental. How, for example, did Dorothea get to be so soulful as she is when we first meet her? Her character has no external causes; her education has scarcely impinged upon her; what she is, Eliot implies, comes from inside her, not from external circumstance or from connections with other people. Only, as I may have mentioned before, to imply this is to disguise the conditions that allow Dorothea to be soulful – those others who maintain the practical world for her so that she is free to dream her dreams, draw her plans, learn Hebrew and Greek, and so on. In other words, *Middlemarch* is very selective in its emphases on structures, and very selective indeed in the kinds of individual it admires, tolerates and castigates.

In a most unacademic moment (these are characters, not real people, but then the novel asks me to make this kind of identification, and for once I shall oblige) I imagine a meeting that does not take place in *Middlemarch*: Rosamund Lydgate née Vincy stands for a moment next to Celia Chettam née Brooke. In the novel as we have it, Celia is silly and childish, but she is largely approved; Rosamund is silly and childish, but we know she is wrong. I wonder if Rosamund is wrong because she is discontented, if she is wrong because she is not married to a wealthy landowner who indulges her every whim, if she is wrong because of circumstances rather than character. If, finally, she is wrong because she disappoints her husband's (admittedly unrealistic) expectations, and Celia is 'all right' because she does not. These two women are both objects within culture, figures to be looked at and admired, but finally figures with underdeveloped subjectivities. Celia, to be sure, is mocked; but Rosamund is castigated. The novel, in other words, focuses on individuals rather than on the processes that produced them and separates self from circumstances. There are other stories that could be told.]

Finally, feminism is always an idealist position, but it remains always in touch with knowledge that real (by definition) is not ideal, that it should change, and, indeed, that it could change, if we could think through a way to enacting the necessary revolutions. That means sometimes rethinking out old responses, whether to *Middlemarch* (is Dorothea really the heroine and why?) or to more urgent problems in reality.

One of the dangers of writing a 'history' of feminist theory is that history necessarily operates as a narrative of exclusion – defined by what it leaves out. The temptation is to write a history that begins at a specific point, 1968, say, when Mary Ellmann published *Thinking About Women*, or 1949 when Simone de Beauvoir published *The Second Sex*, and to argue that subsequent developments in feminist theories constitute a story of progress from naive, simplistic beginnings to our current state of sophisticated knowingness. That kind of narrative of progress, however, risks systematizing what is really a series of ongoing interventions, and implies that the older insights can be left behind without a backward glance. It implies, too, that we all *must* be doing what others are doing right now. For me, however, feminist theory is not prescriptive. It doesn't tell us what to do, say, think, read. Rather it offers possibilities of approach – things you *could* do, say, think, read. The only prescriptions are: feminist theories must never forget to be politicized in the joys of reading differently, and they must offer some commitment to reality, to real women's lives.

Feminist literary theory began by looking at the images of women in literary texts. The texts were largely male-authored, and the women in them were generally stereotypically represented as either ideal (virginal, beautiful, passive, dependent, nurturing) or monstrous (whorish, sexually voracious, independent, ugly and dangerous). Two sets of conclusions were drawn from these images. First, male writers wrote unrealistically (badly) about women; second, male writers themselves produced and reproduced these images to enforce their own ideals of femininity on women. There were honorable exceptions but they were few and far between.

This approach has seemed simplistic to many commentators. It assumes a transparent connection between image and reality and between the writer's sex and his (or sometimes her) attitudes. Moreover, it ignores the 'literariness', the textuality of the text. It is also of limited use to an overtly feminist politics since it notices a textual oppression (women are represented by stereotypes) but does nothing to change the oppression, to offer an alternative to the stereotypes of which it disapproves. But before it is dismissed too easily, two important points should be made. In the first place, what underpins this approach is a revolutionary assumption – that the reader of the text is a woman, not a man. It mounts a gentle, not always explicit, but still significant attack on the universalizing tendency of criticism to presume the reader is male. In the second place one might often notice instances where the apparent binary opposition of the stereotypes (what is often described as the angel/whore dichotomy in Victorian literature in particular) collapses to subversive effect. Think again of Dorothea Brooke, perhaps the narrator's ideal, and of Rosamund Vincy, the feminine ideal of Middlemarch society. Dorothea's image is plain and quakerish, Rosamund's pretty and coquettish, and a judgement is made that the former is better than the latter. When Lydgate first thinks of Rosamund, it is as fine music, as the epitome of female charm. We should, however, be warned by the first appearance of her name in the novel, when her praises are sung in comparison to Dorothea's at a dinner held by Mr Brooke. Mr Chichely, one of the guests, says:

> I like a woman who lays herself out a little more to please us [than Miss Brooke does]. There should be a little filigree about a woman – something of the coquette. . . . there should be a little devil in a woman . . . And I like them blond, with a certain gait, and a swan neck. Between ourselves, the mayor's daughter is more to my taste than Miss Brooke. (M, 89)

Or, to put it another way, a woman should be obliging to masculine egos and to their sense of beauty; she should look like an angel, but be a devil underneath, appealing both to aesthetics and to the sensual. Mr Chicheley has no intention, however, of marrying Rosamund and so is safe from the consequences of his preferences. Lydgate believes in the angel he sees, not in the devil lurking under the surface, and will suffer for it. In a moment of great bitterness, he calls Rosamund his basil plant, explaining that 'basil was a plant which flourished wonderfully on a murdered man's brains' (Eliot, 1994, 835). Rosamund inhabits both sides of the stereotype, looking one part and acting quite another. Her appearance is deceptive and those who see only images are misled into misjudgement by a faulty taxonomy. That goes for Lydgate but it also goes more significantly for a whole society that sees Rosamund's prettiness as feminine perfection. Eliot's narrator implies that Middlemarch's judgement is also the real world's judgement, and the novel thereby suggests to us ways of rethinking our interpretations of the real.

The next phase of feminist criticism moved towards the consideration of women as producers of texts as well as consumers of them. The focus shifted towards what Elaine Showalter ([1979] 1986) called 'gynocritics' – towards the woman as writer. This did not mean the end of image criticism; women writers, after all, also write about women. But the shift to the woman writer was significant for several reasons. It is a historicist and materialist approach which considers the practical issue of writing for women – their relationships with education (did they have any?), with publishers (were they paid as men were?), with spaces to write (both publication outlets, and what Virginia Woolf was to term 'a room of one's own'), and with language itself. This was a revolution in the academy. It demanded a rewriting of the canon of literature to include the voices that were excluded by the assumptions that a 'great' text transcended its conditions of production and reception. It demonstrated the structural inequalities between male and female writers, their opportunities to publish and their critical reception; and it suggested that literary value could legitimately be located elsewhere than where the male-dominated tradition had placed it. It also suggested new places to look for literature, and a project of rediscovery was inaugurated to find the women writers who had been hidden from literary history, to republish their works, to edit them in scholarly editions, and to make a female tradition of literature to set beside the so-called 'great' tradition of great men. As Elaine Showalter pointed out, there were women writers who had always shared in the great tradition – and George Eliot and Virginia Woolf are two of them. But in her own book, *A Literature of Their Own*, she argued that 'it is only by considering . . . Millicent Grogan as well as Virginia Woolf . . . that we can begin to record new choices in a new literary history, and to understand why, despite prejudice, despite guilt, despite inhibition, women began to write' (Showalter, 1977, 36). My own readings of Woolf and Eliot in this essay do not consider their less well-known contemporaries: but they could, and the comparisons would be instructive. Placing the sage George Eliot next to the writer of potboilers Mary Elizabeth Braddon demonstrates the extent to which they were both imbricated in the cultural questions of their time, and often shows that their narrative solutions and political blindnesses are remarkably similar despite the differences of genre, audience and subject matter.

There have been criticisms of this phase, too. For one thing, the concentration on the woman as writer, like image criticism, is liable to gloss over textuality. For another, as Toril Moi (1985) put it, female scholarship might be ultimately sterile, leading to an impasse when the feminist scholars ran out of texts to rediscover (though this certainly has not happened yet). There was also the fear that this kind of feminist activity still excluded vast numbers of women – those who never learned to read or write, for example – and risked constructing a very partial history of female subjectivity through texts written largely by and for privileged, mostly white, mostly middle- or upper-class women. Finally, some suggested that gynocritics risked essentialism in its assumption that the only 'authentic' representations of women would come from women themselves, a dangerously naive position which played into the hands of patriarchy by seeing sex (biology) and gender (the cultural attributes of sex) as the same thing.

Writing after these revolutionary changes, it's easy to take them for granted, to assume that there are indeed scholarly editions of Mary Wollstonecraft and popular editions of Elizabeth Barrett Browning, that I can read collections of 'forgotten' women writers and have my readings taken seriously as a legitimate academic enterprise. But we should not forget that it's not that long ago that *major* writers like Barrett Browning and Wollstonecraft were out of print, and that reading them was not quite respectable. And if I don't quite believe in a separatist account of women's writing, gynocritics at least offers lots of opportunity to expand the canon and to rethink literary tradition as a whole. Some of the most significant works of feminist theory have been gynocritical, an approach that is still ongoing. The questions about women reading and women writing have not all been answered, and it is certainly still worth revisiting the pioneering works of Moers (1977), Showalter (1977) and Gilbert and Gubar (1979) because their arguments were certainly not naive, and their insights still have force, despite the often exclusionary aesthetics (no consideration of black women writers, no sustained interest in lesbian women for example) of their subject choices. There is a dialogue that contemporary feminist theorists must continue to have with the past so that we are not condemned merely to repeat feminist literary history because we do not know it.

From the early 1980s another phase of feminist theory is discernible in the English-speaking academy as some of the important texts of French feminism were translated for the first time, in particular the works of Hélène Cixous, Luce Irigaray and Julia Kristeva. These writers have all been influenced by the discourse of Lacanian psychoanalysis, by linguistic theories and by poststructuralist accounts of language and human subjectivity. Irigaray and Kristeva, for example, take very seriously Lacan's idea that rather than the subject speaking language, language in fact speaks the subject (you cannot say 'I' without language, you cannot have a concept of selfhood without words). They concentrate therefore on linguistic formations, and on their psychic effects on speaking subjects, motivated in part by the fact that French is an absolutely gender-inflected language. The subjects they discuss are not always women. But women may well have a different response to a language and culture which defines them as 'lack' and as 'other', and which is the language which shores up the patriarchal law of the father. They seek, then, the gaps and fissures of language into which the displaced feminized (though not always female) subject may insert him/herself. (Septimus Warren Smith, for example, is a man: but in his madness he occupies a feminine position of powerlessness in cultural terms.) Kristeva (1986), for example, coins a new meaning for the word 'semiotic', meaning the disruptions of language, its silences, elisions, ellipses, its rhythms and sounds rather than its semantic functions, and sees the semiotic as the space of femininity. Where gynocritics often insisted on a mimetic relationship between literature and reality, to the extent that it could not properly account for the textuality of avant-garde writing by women, the writings of French feminists have, in different ways, provided tools for thinking about experimental writing, whatever the gender of the writer or character described.

There have also been attacks on what is thought of in Anglophone countries as the French approach, especially in Britain where there is a strong resistance to a feminist theory which appears not to be explicitly aligned to the politics of change. Some disapprove too of the inherent difficulties of the works of these theorists, and of their alignment to Lacan – a patriarchal figure if ever there was one. Nonetheless, it ought to be clear that psychoanalysis – a medical or scientific discourse of a sort – is also a political and politicized discourse. In France this has been more obvious than in Anglophone countries, signalled in the name of one of the most significant Francophone feminist groupings, Psychanalyse et Politique (Psychoanalysis and Politics). The politics of psychology, psychiatry and medicine more generally has been described in more traditional gynocritical models by Elaine Showalter's study of madness, *The Female Malady* (1987) where doctors are sinister, powerful and above all masculine figures, Sir William Bradshaws, pronouncing on sickness and health, in particular in relation to female patients. The Francophone tradition, however, goes beyond a *description* of the political structures of medicine, and attempts to undo its logic by attending to its language. The dissemination of Lacanian psychoanalysis as a positive tool for feminist theories has led to a much greater emphasis on textuality, though perhaps this is sometimes at the expense of materialist, historicist and overtly politicized reading and action.

More recently still, from the late 1980s and early 1990s, feminist theory has started to engage with its own inherent essentialism by revisiting the question of what is a woman? Judith Butler (1990, 1993) and Diana Fuss (1989) have eschewed the common-sense biologist view that we all 'know' what a woman (and what a man) is. They argue instead that sex as much as gender is culturally constructed, and that sexual identity is a kind of masquerade or performance. Thus, the reading of texts is itself a performance that calls into question the authenticity of readers and writers who are always performing multiple identities. Their arguments arise in part from alignment of feminist thinking with queer theories, in which sexuality rather than sex is the basis of the argument. And since sexuality is learned behaviour rather than biologically given, and since sexuality is performative rather than just 'there', the theory leads to the practice of a playful politics of identity that undermines the idea of essence, including the strategic essentialisms of feminist criticism used in order to argue for women's writing. This is not the end point of feminist theory; rather it is another way to think about doing 'it'.

There are so many methods and examples. One might write a critique grounded in both historical research and psychoanalytic theory, as Claire Kahane has done (*LT*, 59–71). One can search for alternative paradigms and genres as does Terry Castle in her reading of Sylvia Townsend Warner and the possibility of a lesbian fiction in *The Apparitional Lesbian* (*LT*, 72–83). And feminist theories can also be playfully political, reconstructing the objective masculinist voice of traditional criticism as Mary Lydon's work exemplifies (*LT*, 73–92). I suggest these three not as a catalogue of the only ways to 'do feminism'. Rather, they represent different exemplary strands which might be characterized as: feminist reading against the grain, lesbian-feminist textual exploration and as the performance of the feminist scholar.

Claire Kahane's essay, 'Medusa's Voice: Male Hysteria in *The Bostonians*', is in some ways the most traditional feminist approach of the three essays I want to consider. Combining historical research, psychoanalytic theory and close textual reading, it takes a male-authored canonical text by a very canonical author, Henry James, and reads it against the very assumptions that made the text canonical. Those assumptions include the idea that the text is a coherent whole that makes sense consistently, that the text contains the voice of reason, and that the voice of reason is male/masculine; also there is the suggestion that the text is somehow 'timeless', transcending its own conditions of production and consumption. In opposition to those assumptions, Kahane argues that *The Bostonians* is rather contradictory and incoherent, hysterical rather than rational, and that it is profoundly implicated in the history of its own era and place (the late nineteenth century in the north-east of the US). She suggests that the text dramatizes the links between apparently oppositional terms, first the realms of the sexual and the political, and then the oppositions of female and male, speech and writing, North and South, fluidity and solidity. (In addressing these binary distinctions, we can witness a feminist critique which puts to work the insights of structuralism for the purpose of ideological demystification, which aspect of structuralism in the context of Roland Barthes's work is discussed in the previous chapter by K. M. Newton.) In each of these oppositions, the privileged or victorious term would usually be the second – and that, indeed, is James's apparent assumption in the novel. But careful reading, Kahane argues, shows that the oppositions are not separate. Instead, they flow into each other with a radically destabilizing effect that unsettles the critical judgment of James's novel that places its value in terms of consistency and coherence. She suggests further that this fluidity of difference within the novel was not in the control of the writer, who thought he was saying one thing, but can be shown to have been saying something quite different in the fissures of his text. As an example of this, Kahane, drawing on Freud, defines hysteria as the fear of femininity. By close reading, she suggests that James's text exposes a hysterical fear of the feminine in its multiple disjunctions between what is explicitly stated and the manner in which it is said.

In a very different way, Terry Castle's essay might also be understood as a piece of traditional feminist criticism, though it 'does' feminist criticism 'differently' in that its focus is on the figure of the lesbian in fiction, and on defining a lesbian mode in fiction. Castle, responding to the invisibility of lesbians in culture, asks what a lesbian fiction might be and whether it exists. This invisibility, she suggests, is not just a simple and obvious example of patriarchy, but has been compounded by the refusals of straight feminists and queer theorists to imagine the lesbian as a significant figure.

It is to address this inequity that Castle turns to Sylvia Townsend Warner's novel, *Summer Will Show*, in her essay 'Sylvia Townsend Warner and the Counterplot of Lesbian Fiction'. Castle's interpretation is at once playful and serious. She uses her example to draw a large conclusion about a definition of lesbian fiction which is structural rather than merely biographical (and therefore implicitly essentialist). She suggests defining characteristics might include the elements of fantasy and stylization which resist 'realism' since this is where male homosociality is valued. She also suggests elements of parody and satire in relation to more canonical texts, taking their situations and rewriting them, for example. In *Summer Will Show* this procedure is exemplified as Warner 'borrows' indirectly from Dickens, Scott, Balzac, Hugo and George Eliot. Such rewriting, Castle argues, is political because it unsettles realism as a version of the real that holds true for everyone. These are methods and ideas of a traditional feminist approach placed in the service of radical lesbian interpretation. Making lesbian women visible to a heterosexual culture that does not want to see them combines aesthetics and politics through the act of criticism.

Mary Lydon's essay, 'Myself and M/Others: Colette, Wilde and Duchamp', offers a radical attack on traditional modes of male-defined academic scholarship, especially in terms of its vivacious style. The essay eschews the usual process of argument, operating instead in a performative mode, enacting its critical position. The essay acts as an exemplary instance of how one might read differently and how such different readings make critical spaces for those usually excluded from the academy.

The title arises from the biological fact that Lydon is a mother; but by thinking through the effects of wordplay in puns and researching the etymologies of words, the essay deals not in an essentialist or biologistic identity (mothers) but in the 'staging of the self', or the figuring of the self as other. Because the mother is, in some sense, the figure of the eternal feminine, both nurturing and monstrous, encompassing oppositions, the essay explores juxtaposed oppositions and developments. Beginning with the *Mona Lisa* and Pater's description of it as both monstrous and perfect, Lydon moves to Marcel Duchamp's 'daring art', which took this iconic figure and drew a moustache and beard on it, rendering it as a parody, as monster, as homage and as a figure of sexual indeterminacy. It is in the light of Mona Lisa's transvestism that Lydon goes on to read Duchamp's own transvestite appearance as Rrose Sélavy, a name which inscribes not single essence, but performance and multiplicity.

The question of the performative aspects of identity, and the strategic uses to which these may be put, is followed through with a turn to Oscar Wilde, with whom the essay begins, who reappears in relation to his mother, who had much to say about the relationships between clothes, meaning and thought, and whose pronouncements seem to imply that language acts as a disguise rather more than it expresses essential selfhood. Similarly, the figure of Colette, who shares her father's name and fulfils his unfulfilled ambition to be a writer, is disguised by the language of her name, dresses herself as it were in a name that is both feminine and masculine, feminine because this is signified by the diminutive *ette*, and masculine because this is the name she receives from her father.

The point of all these substitutions and disguises is to undo two types of identity. First, the essay attacks sexual identity as a given, and insists that sex is a disguise, in which you can dress up at will: identity is therefore a choice. Implicitly, following on from this, the essay also unsettles the coherent, sincere, authentic, reasonable voice of criticism by pointing out through its style that this too is a disguise rather than an essence. Lydon's is an eclectic, performative text, that shows the political importance for feminism of playing roles as well, but which also insists that we know that it is *just* playing, and that we might choose roles quite other from the ones that have already been inscribed. The question is one of choice, of being able to choose, and feminist theories are about the choices you make. Those choices include the kind of critique you want to make but also the kinds of text you choose to discuss: that choice can also be a feminist choice.

NOTES TOWARDS READINGS OF
MIDDLEMARCH AND *MRS DALLOWAY*

... but why always Dorothea? Was her point of view the only possible one . . .? (*M*, 278)

When the narrator of *Middlemarch* asks these questions he (this is a thorough-going impersonation of a masculine voice) presumes really that Dorothea's point of view is a more laudable one than Casaubon's, with whom Dorothea's point of view is about to be compared. He also presumes that Dorothea is more right than most of the other women in the novel, and especially when she is contrasted with Rosamund. It is Dorothea's intellectual problem with marriage ('what shall I do?') that is given more approval than Rosamund's unreflective presumption that the world owes her the life she desires. Dorothea is approved because she learns both sympathy and submission in her relations with her husband; Rosamund, on the other hand, appears to learn nothing at all. Why, though, are the feminine virtues embodied by Dorothea 'better' than the feminine vices embodied by Rosamund? Why can we not think of Rosamund as a feminist heroine while we almost unthinkingly endorse Dorothea as one despite the fact that she achieves almost nothing?

There are obvious and common-sense answers to these questions. If we think of feminism as an emancipatory ideal, as a set of communal aspirations, as intellectual practices and practical interventions in the world, then Rosamund has no place in feminism. The only emancipation she dreams of is her own in relation to economic and social privilege; she has no sense of communal life – sisterhood is not a word that would immediately apply; there is no evidence of intellect and no practical work in the world: not even charity of the Lady-Bountiful-Dorothea-type. Instead, Rosamund is castigated for having a will of her own in opposition to her husband, for failing in sympathy and empathy, for ruining Lydgate in the service of her own far more petty considerations. Her assertion of self is consistently presented as bad, unfeminine, monstrous. What, though, are her alternatives?

It is instructive for all kinds of reasons to read *Middlemarch* and *Mrs Dalloway* side by side. It's very obvious, for example, that the young Clarissa, though less soulful than the young Dorothea, has much in common with her. But the point of comparison I want to concentrate on here is in the presentation of the two doctors' wives in the two novels. Placing Lady Bradshaw alongside Rosamund Lydgate illuminates some of the reasons why what Eliot calls Rosamund's egotism is not an altogether bad thing.

We are supposed to think, of course, that Sir William and Lydgate are very different kinds of doctor. Lydgate is a kind of hero to his narrator, albeit a flawed one. His quest to extend human knowledge is admirable even if his methods (including his inability to oil the social wheels that will help his research) and his scientific paradigms are sometimes misguided. Sir William, on the other hand, is the undisputed villain of *Mrs Dalloway*. If Lydgate struggles financially, Sir William is a self-made man: 'his income was quite twelve thousand a year' (*MD*, 111). And he reads his material success as a vindication of his methods of treatment – 'Sir William not only prospered himself, but made England prosper, secluded her lunatics, forbade childbirth, penalised despair' (*MD*, 109) – despite the fact that he works on an 'exacting science which has to do with what, after all, we know nothing about – the nervous system, the human brain' (*MD*, 108). Lydgate, we are led to believe, wants knowledge for its own sake, and for the good it can do – the material rewards of his profession are not exactly indifferent to him, but they are not his main motivation. Sir William uses his knowledge to enhance his power. He pronounces on health and sanity and coerces his patients into his views, since they cannot cease to be his patients until he is satisfied that they have capitulated.

Compared to Rosamund, Lady Bradshaw is a very minor character indeed in *Mrs Dalloway*, and that in itself might be an indictment of her husband, as well as being indicative of her own failings. She is described in Sir William's terms as the apotheosis of feminine virtue – significantly in parenthesis: '(she embroidered, knitted, spent four nights out of seven at home with her son)' (*M*, 109), as if feminine virtues are so self-abnegating that they are always already under a kind of erasure. The erasure they are under is her husband's will imaged as a cannibalistic, violent, bullying urge towards conversion to his own point of view:

> Conversion, fastidious Goddess, loves blood better than brick, and feasts most subtly on the human will. For example, Lady Bradshaw. Fifteen years ago she had gone under. It was nothing you could put your finger on; there had been no scene, no snap; only the slow sinking, water-logged, of her will into his. Sweet was her smile, swift her submission. (*M*, 110)

She has been both eaten alive and drowned in her husband's ego, though the social conventions are still adhered to in her sweet smile and swift submission. (Dorothea, incidentally, also smiles sweetly, and though she manages to negotiate the terms of her own submission to Casaubon, it would, nonetheless, have been a submission if her husband had not died so conveniently.)

Now Rosamund and Lady Bradshaw are not real people, but hypothetically and indeed rhetorically speaking, which would you rather be? Is it better to be sweetly smiling and crushed or sweetly smiling and powerful? Victim or bitch? (Another binary, of course, with its own categorical failings; but I presume that the Victorian answer is 'victim', and from the 1980s onwards, the answer has been 'bitch', a word that has even come to have its own real, if limited, positive value.)

For me, in many ways Rosamund is the crux of a feminist rereading of *Middlemarch*. She is a character who embodies the stereotypes of femininity against which much feminist thought has rebelled. She is pretty, mindless, egotistical, too interested in appearances, too unrealistic in her assessments of the world and her place in it, and also too grossly materialistic. But by refusing to submit to her husband's will, by refusing even to recognize his claims on her submission, she survives to live the life she wants to live. She lives the doctrine of individualism that was, for mid-Victorian England, supposed to be the sole prerogative of the male subject; she may not know that is what she is doing, but she does demonstrate a different version of female subjectivity. In addition, she undoes the taxonomy of binary stereotypes by being both, as I've suggested, angel and devil. In the process, of course, Lydgate is sacrificed, which is a shame for him personally; but I'm at a loss to understand why it is assumed that the woman reader naturally weeps for the sacrifice of the man to his wife's private whim when it is unimaginable that she should weep for the woman sacrificed to his public ambition. Intentional fallacy notwithstanding, of course, this is not the message that George Eliot wanted me to take from her novel. The language in which she describes Rosamund, and the thoroughgoing structures of comparison made between her and both Dorothea and Mary Garth as exemplary females, militate against the perverse interpretation of her as any kind of heroine, let alone a feminist one. But if we agree that Dorothea is indeed exemplary, we have to think about what we are agreeing to: self-sacrifice as the ultimate feminine ideal. And if we agree with Eliot's narrator and dismiss Rosamund's life as futile, we support a very uncomfortable version of a woman's life as necessarily unimportant compared to that of her husband. Rosamund does not live the 'authorized version', and the complexity of the politics of representation means we must take seriously the resistance she makes. It would be so much easier if she were likeable, or if she sacrificed Lydgate for higher reasons – or even if she didn't have to sacrifice him to live her own dream. But it may just be that she makes the only resistance she can – the only resistance open to a woman in her time, with her education and social status, with her narrow intellect. And we should not be too easily seduced into the habit of seeing only what the narrator wants us to see – that Dorothea is the heroine.

QUESTIONS FOR FURTHER CONSIDERATION

1. Consider the contention that feminist literary theory not only uncovers essentialism in texts, but also participates in essentialism. (In other words, is feminist literary theory necessarily essentialist because of its focus on women? If it is, how can/does it justify its essentialism?)

2. The terms 'woman' and 'women' cover a multitude of difference. How can/should feminist literary theories be attentive to the politics of difference?

3. Where, in your opinion, should the emphasis of feminist literary theory lie: on issues of representation (however broadly conceived); on women writers; on women's history and present (on their material existence today and in the past, on current and historical oppression); on women's psychological repression; on women's use of textual formations? What is the political impact of each of these choices? How might they be usefully combined?

4. Is the feminism of a text intrinsic or extrinsic? That is, does the feminism of a text come from the text itself or from the ways in which we choose to read it? Does it make sense to describe *Middlemarch* (or *Mrs Dalloway*) as a feminist novel? And if it does, where does the feminism reside?

5. My suggestion that Rosamund Vincy is a feminist heroine depends on a liberal humanist version of feminism that privileges individual gains over collective ones. What are the problems with this? What are the alternatives to an individualistic feminist theory?

6. In *Middlemarch*, the centres of reader attention are the middle-class young women and their stories of courtship and marriage. What are the roles of the other women – the older middle-class, more 'minor' female characters such as Mrs Cadwallader, Lady Chettam, Mrs Vincy, Mrs Bulstrode, Mrs Garth? How might attention to these characters alter our view of the novel as a whole? How might it address the problems of essentialism and difference? (And for good measure, how do you imagine that Trantripp – an older woman who is also working class – sees the events? What difference would sustained focus on her point of view of events make to a feminist reading of the novel?)

ANNOTATED BIBLIOGRAPHY

Ellmann, Mary. *Thinking About Women*. New York, 1968.
A founding text of literary feminism, Ellmann's method is an 'images of women' critique, but it works on assumptions that are still current and appropriate in literary theory. Her interest is in 'women as *words* – as the words they pull out of mouths' (xv). She argues that words make realities, and that the judgements of women in literature (as writers or characters) depend on the layers of meaning that go with certain words. She also identifies and analyses nine stereotypes of femininity, demonstrates the inconsistency of thinking through stereotypes, and implies that these literary representations have real effects.

Felski, Rita. *Beyond Feminist Aesthetics: Feminist Literature and Social Change*. London, 1989.
Felski's book draws together Francophone and Anglophone traditions of feminist theory to argue that an adequate feminist account of women's writing requires marxist-materialist explanations combined with psychoanalytic and linguistic models. She concentrates on contemporary 'realist' writing largely by European women in order to

resist too easy a withdrawal from materialist feminism such as French theory appears to threaten. But the book does not resist psychoanalysis, postmodernism or linguistics; rather it seeks a broad, inclusive framework for theory and practice.

Gilbert, Sandra M. and Gubar, Susan. *The Madwoman the Attic: The Woman Writer and the Nineteenth-Century Literary Imagination.* New Haven, CT, 1979.

A classic of early feminist practice, this book considers the material and the psychological position of women writers in the nineteenth century. It argues that anger and madness are the displaced subtexts of women's writing, and that these themes are a direct result of social constraints on women. It discusses the 'canonical' writers of the female literary tradition (Austen, the Brontës, Eliot, Rossetti and Dickinson); but they also place these writers into the larger contexts of the male tradition and the relatively unknown tradition of the so-called 'minor' women writers. For a revision of their ideas, see Armstrong's *Desire and Domestic Fiction.*

Poovey, Mary. *Uneven Developments: The Ideological Work of Gender in Mid-Victorian England.* London, 1989.

A development of the practice of Gilbert and Gubar's book, Poovey provides a rigorous historical analysis of gender relations in mid-Victorian England, and analyses the relationships between legal, statistical and medico-moral discourses and literary writing by both men and women. It includes sophisticated contextual discussions of the life and work of Caroline Norton, *David Coppefield, Jane Eyre* and the figure of Florence Nightingale, examining the matrix of discourses, a hidden history of ideological formations, that reproduced 'uneven' gender relations.

Spelman, Elizabeth V. *Inessential Woman: Problems of Exclusion in Feminist Thought.* London, 1988.

Spelman's book was one of the first to call into question the strategic essentialism of feminism – the view that all women share common experience. In readings of Greek philosophy, the writings of de Beauvoir and Chodorow, and discussions of race and language, she demonstrates that the inclusion of all women in the category of 'Woman' is actually a process of exclusion. While not strictly a book about literature, Spelman's insights have been influential in feminist literary theory undoing a politically naive position about the ahistorical, trans-racial and cross-class vision of women's oppressions.

SUPPLEMENTARY BIBLIOGRAPHY

Armstrong, Nancy. *Desire and Domestic Fiction: A Political History of the Novel.* Oxford, 1987.

Beauvoir, Simone de. *The Second Sex*, trans. H. M. Parshley. Harmondsworth, 1972.

Beer, Gillian. *Reader I Married Him: A study of the Women Characters of Jane Austen, Charlotte Brontë, Elizabeth Gaskell and George Eliot.* London, 1974.

Butler, Judith. *Gender Trouble: Feminism and the Subversion of Identity.* London, 1990.

————. *Bodies that Matter: On the Discursive Limits of 'Sex'.* London, 1993.

Castle, Terry. *The Apparitional Lesbian: Female Sexuality and Modern Culture.* New York, 1993.

Cixous, Hélène. *The Hélène Cixous Reader*, ed. Susan Sellers. New York, 1994.

————. 'The Laugh of the Medusa', in *New French Feminisms: An Anthology*, eds Elaine Marks and Isabelle de Courtrivon. Hemel Hempstead. 1981.

————, and Cathérine Clément. *The Newly Born Woman*, trans. Betsy Wing. Minneapolis, MN, 1986.

Elam, Diane. *Feminism and Deconstruction: Ms en Abyme.* London, 1994.

Faderman, Lillian. *Surpassing the Love of Men: Romantic Friendship and Love between Women from the Renaissance to the Present.* London, 1985.

Felski, Rita. *The Gender of Modernity.* Cambridge, MA, 1995.

Fuss, Diana, *Essentially Speaking: Feminism, Nature and Difference.* New York, 1989.

Gallop, Jane. *The Daughter's Seduction: Feminism and Psychoanalysis*. Ithaca, NY, 1982.

Gilbert, Sandra M., and Susan Gubar. *No Man's Land: The Place of the Woman Writer in the Twentieth Century*, 3 vol: Vol. 1, *The War of the Words*; Vol. 2, *Sexchanges*; Vol. 3, *Letters from the Front*. New Haven, CT 1987–94.

Greene, Gayle, and Coppélia Kahn, eds. *Making a Difference: Feminist Literary Criticism*. London, 1985.

hooks, bel. *Ain't I a Woman? Black Women and Feminism*. London, 1982.

Irigaray, Luce. *This Sex Which is Not One*, trans. Catherine Porter with Carolyn Burke. Ithaca, NY, 1985.

————. *The Speculum of the Other Woman*, trans. Gillian C. Gill. Ithaca, NY, 1985.

————. *The Irigaray Reader*, ed. Margaret Whitford. Cambridge, MA, 1991.

Jacobus, Mary, ed. *Women Writing and Writing About Women*. London, 1979.

Kahane, Claire. *Passions of the Voice: Hysteria, Narrative and the Figure of the Speaking Woman, 1850–1915*. Baltimore, MD, 1995.

Kaplan, Cora. *Seachanges: Culture and Feminism*. London, 1986.

Kristeva, Julia. *The Kristeva Reader*, ed. Toril Moi. Oxford, 1986.

Lydon, Mary. *Skirting the Issue: Essays in Literary Theory*. Madison, WI, 1995.

Marks, Elaine and Isabelle de Courtivron, eds. *New French Feminisms: An Anthology*. Hemel Hempstead, 1981.

Mitchell, Juliet. *Psychoanalysis and Feminism*. Harmondsworth, 1974.

Moers, Ellen. *Literary Women: The Great Writers*. London, 1977.

Moi, Toril. *Sexual/Textual Politics: Feminist Literary Theory*. London, 1985.

————, ed. *French Feminist Thought*. Oxford and New York, 1987.

Munt, Sally, ed. *New Lesbian Criticism: Literary and Cultural Readings*. Hemel Hempstead, 1992.

Robbins, Ruth. *Literary Feminisms*. London, 2000.

Rose, Jacqueline. *Sexuality the Field of Vision*. London, 1986.

Showalter, Elaine. *A Literature of Their Own*. London, 1977.

————, ed. *The New Feminist Criticism: Essays on Women, Literature and Theory*. London, 1986.

————, *The Female Malady: Women, Madness, and English Culture 1830–1980*. New York, 1987.

Ward-Jouve, Nicole. *Female Genesis: Creativity, Self and Gender*. Cambridge, 1998.

Weedon, Chris. *Feminist Practice and Poststructuralist Theory*. Oxford, 1987.

OTHER WORK CITED

Woolf, Virginia. *To the Lighthouse* (1927), ed. Stella McNichol, intr. Hermione Lee. Harmondsworth, 1992.

CHAPTER

4

THE POLITICS OF LITERATURE: MARXIST LITERARY THEORIES

Moyra Haslett

No doubt we shall see Marxist criticism comfortably wedged between Freudian and mythological approaches to literature, as yet one more stimulating academic 'approach', one more well-tilled field for students to tramp.

(Eagleton, 1976, vii)

Marxist literary theories are as much a political as a literary choice. While a marxist literary theory is almost impossible to describe such are the differences in approaches and arguments among marxist literary theorists, marxist literary theory might be defined in terms of common goals and political commitments. The marxist theorist is committed to the interrelationship of word and world, of theory and practice, and to exposing and challenging the inequities of the capitalist system in its various forms. So that, notwithstanding the ways in which marxism has both informed and been informed by other theoretical perspectives, marxism is impoverished as a theory if it is thought of as just one option within many. This conviction has made marxism unpopular and explains, just as much as the fall of state, communism in 1989, why marxism is an identification which increasingly fewer theorists are prepared to make. Marxist theory is so pious, so humourless, so out-of-date, its detractors claim. But marxist literary theories – like feminism and postcolonialism, those theories which also define themselves as both a theoretical and political practice – continue to ask the most challenging questions within the discipline of literary study: what is the relation between literature and society? does literary value exist and if so in what? what is the relation between my study and the lives of others outside of the academy? Few marxist theories today would claim to reveal absolute truths, but they do assert a *situated* argument of what is true or false, for that specific historical moment. For example, marxism argues that all viewpoints are socially determined, but that does not entail that all viewpoints are equal in value. A prisoner is more likely to recognize the oppressive nature of a particular juridical system than a judge. (In classical marxist terms, the working classes will recognize the injustices of capitalism rather than the capitalists.) All marxist theories continue to assert that certain inequities – such as class exploitation and poverty – will always be 'wrong', and marxist literary theories continue to assert that these issues are not unrelated to literature. Marxism is thus both a political movement and a form of intellectual resistance. Most commentators today – marxist and non-marxist – would agree that the end of the twentieth century has been marked in the West as a time of political quietism. Marxist commentators warn that we are in danger of forgetting not just how to act but how to think in resistance to capitalism.

Marxist literary theories inevitably refer us to the writings of Karl Marx, the first major critic of capitalism as a system. Writing out of and within the experience of capitalism in the mid-nineteenth century, Marx's work bears the traces of its own context and tells us something of our own. Undoubtedly, much of Marx's work has dated: the working classes no longer seem likely to be in the vanguard of revolution, at least in the industrial West, and the activism of feminists, anti-racist movements and gay people reminds us that Marx's work contains as many silences and blind spots as we can read in, say, Jane Austen's exclusive focus on the gentry. But capitalism continues to have the same kinds of consequences as it did in the nineteenth century. We still have a wide gulf between the richest and the poorest of our society, many people still find their work unrewarding and repetitive, we are witnessing the growth of the working poor, of an 'underclass', of homelessness, slave labour, and insecure and part-time labour. That Marx's writings bear the imprint of their own time is as unimportant to contemporary marxist theorists as the collapse of the Soviet Union and the economic changes within Chinese society. The theories of western marxism, and especially its cultural theories, have been marked by their divergence from rather than fidelity to communist dogma and the most deterministic readings of Marx, identified with Engels and Lenin. And Marx's works have been retranslated, variously interpreted and critiqued within marxism. The interviews which the editors of *New Left Review* conducted with Raymond Williams in 1979 reveal something of the debates *within* and *between* marxisms. Williams is a tremendously influential and significant figure within marxist literary theory, but his importance is due as much to his arguments with orthodox 'Marxism' as it is to any fidelity to marxist precepts. Thus, long before 'postmarxism' was discussed, or postmodernism repudiated 'grand narratives', many marxist theorists were already repudiating marxist teleologies, or what Williams calls 'formulas'. In an interview titled 'Marxism and Literature' (*LT*, 116–31) Williams rejects the kind of marxism which confidently knows what the next epoch of history has in store, and objects to the implicit celebration in speaking of a 'mastery' of nature. In his quarrel with certain forms of marxism, Williams demonstrated that it was possible to remain marxist and still disagree with received orthodoxies. For this reason I have refused the traditional capital 'M' in my writings on marxist theory, since marxist theories are, on closer inspection, much more diverse than the idea of fidelity to a founding father would suggest.

Despite their diversity, marxist cultural theories, however, do share common characteristics and commitments. First and most fundamental of these is the refusal to separate art from society. Even those aestheticist artworks which attempt or claim to resist context – abstract painting, a Mills & Boon romance, Lewis Carroll's 'nonsense' poem 'Jabberwocky', the aestheticism associated with Walter Pater and Oscar Wilde, improvisatory jazz – are social for they are all created and received in concrete contexts. In all marxist readings, art is interpreted as a material practice, perhaps because it relies upon a 'technology' (the pen, the printing press), is concretely realized in situations which themselves are material (the folkballad sung in a bar or courtly masque performed for royalty) or is bought and sold like other commodities (and is thus subject to such factors as sponsorship, marketing, financing, production and distribution). One marxist reading of ostensibly aestheticist artworks, such as those suggested above, argues that aestheticism is itself an attempt to disguise their very implication in the kinds of commercial concerns which they so disdain. The attempt to escape from commercialism is still a response to that same commercialism. Indeed, marxist writers such as Raymond Williams and Terry Eagleton have argued that art began to perceive and represent itself as 'outside' of society only in the late eighteenth century, the very time in which art was becoming increasingly commodified. At the level of the producer of art – the novelist, folksinger, cartoonist – art is also already social, since the artwork is created by an individual with a class, gender and racial identity, and whose fashioning of the artwork is determined by such factors as education and affluence. In place of the author as expressive genius, whose intrinsic talents means that she transcends her own time and place, we have the author as producer who is inevitably part of her own context. At the level of the word too, art is social, since language is a social convention rather than a merely individual one (as Voloshinov argues contra Saussure). Marxist literary theories thus attempt to situate the artwork within a total context, an ambitious project which will always be an aspiration rather than a necessarily completed task. Raymond Williams's theoretical habit of gesturing towards greater complexity is exemplary here.

Marxist theories are then distinguished from other approaches in the way in which they prioritize the materiality of culture, the way in which it is produced, distributed and received as a concrete and social practice. For marxist theorists the economic mode of society is crucial here because it is the economic system which frequently – though not always – determines how art will be so constructed. The relationship between the economic and the literary is both the central concern of marxism and the subject of its most heated debates. Williams wrote of how the economic determines a 'whole way of life' and that non-economic (in marxist terms superstructural) forces, such as literature, should be related to this rather than to the economic element alone. In practice indeed, no separation between spheres is possible: the 'economic' sphere includes the social relations of people, and the 'literary' is marketed and bought like any other product. The theoretical persistence with which marxist theories situate the artwork within society is also a political resistance to the ways in which capitalism separates the social and the individual, culminates in the division of labour and specializes spheres of human activity. So that when marxist approaches to literature attempt to describe and understand this splitting of aesthetics and society, they also attempt to rectify this splitting, to change it.

Within these parameters, marxist approaches to literature are surprisingly varied, and there is no programmatic way of 'applying' marxist ideas. Of course, marxist critics will continue to discuss such issues as class struggle, commodification, the alienation of labour and so on, but these shared concerns have not entailed that marxist readings are always identical in approach, or even that their conclusions will be the same. Literature might be seen to reflect life under capitalism: for example, in arguing that modernist art portrays and even exacerbates the individual's solipsism and isolation (Lukács) or that art is split between elitist 'high' art and popular 'low' art (cultural studies theorists, such as Bourdieu). Alternatively, however, literature might be seen as opposing the ill-effects of capitalism: specifically artistic traditions may be 'relatively' free of economic determination so that this relative autonomy permits art to critique capitalist relations (Adorno), or that art alone resists appropriation by the market (Bürger on Cubism and avant-garde art); or that new technologies make a collective imagination possible (Benjamin on photography, newspapers and cinema). Marxist approaches to literature are thus attempts both to articulate the relationship between literature and society and to call the separation which this implies into question. Pragmatically, we may have to separate art and society in order to explain their relation, but simultaneously we need to resist this separation by remembering that art is *part of society*. The theoretical complexity involved in this double manoeuvre has often been overlooked, as marxist theorists have been accused of 'reducing' literature to a passive reflection of society, rather than seeing literature as fully implicated within society.

That thought itself is also socially determined, and that this makes the relationship between art and its contexts more complex still, is explored in marxist analyses of ideology. Ideology might be described as the material production of ideas, values and beliefs. This description, however, fails to address the way in which values and beliefs are often conflictual and are overdetermined by power relations. Certain classes and groups of people are able to influence and even manipulate more than others and to disguise the ways in which their values are inherently self-interested. It is in the interest of free-marketeers, for example, that they persuade us that the 'free market' is synonymous with choice. In practice, however, free choice is a myth, since we are limited by what we can afford and what is available. 'Best-selling' lists of books, for example, are commonly accepted as those books which people most want to read. But this implies that people are 'free' to read, or indeed buy, any book they please. The desire for reading, however, is influenced by other factors: suggestive advertising, price, availability, education, peer experience (we read what others read) and, relatedly, class, gender or racial identity. The demand for books is related to what publishers and booksellers make available and how they make it available. Depending on your ideological viewpoint, then, the lists of best-selling books signal popular 'free' choice or mystify the concept of 'choice'. And in an era of global, multinational capitalism, the first ideological stance is the more powerful.

Many of the most significant marxist theories have discussed the ways in which literature permits us to perceive the ideology of its context. When the country-house poems of the seventeenth century (such as Ben Jonson's *Penshurst* and *To Sir Robert Wroth* and Thomas Carew's *To Saxham*) praise the great estates of England, one of their conventions is to describe the way in which nature bestows its plenty upon the lord's dinner table. Nature itself honours the aristocracy. But this conventional poetic hyperbole disguises human labour. It omits the labourers, whose toil in the gardens and fields permits the estate to 'yield' its abundance. That Johnson and Carew were dependent upon the patronage of such lords reveals the way in which their idealised, arcadian representation of the English country house is an accommodation with the feudal relations which sustain their own lives. The dissimulation within the poems helps to legitimate the interests of the English ruling class (see Williams, 1973).

Literary texts, however, do not always reflect ideology in such an obvious manner, nor is ideology always simply a matter of the imposition of a set of erroneous beliefs ('false consciousness'). Definitions of ideology as a form of 'false consciousness' suggest that ideology is always imposed by the ruling classes. These definitions appear to doom the underclasses to subjection, to being dupes in believing that which is against their own interests. But accepting the imposition of beliefs 'from above' may be in the underclasses' *own* interests too: self-deception might make life more tolerable, so that, rather than their beliefs being at odds with their interests, they have conflicting kinds of interests. Gramsci was the first marxist to theorize the ways in which people collude in or consent to prevailing ideological values. Election campaigns are one place we might look for contemporary ideological formations. Here we can see what is appealing, and what is considered as a campaign blunder, and the ways in which they tap important aspects of ideological power relations in complex societies. Neither are these values always negative. In the analogy of best-selling books discussed above, for example, readers who clamour for romantic fiction may not merely have been fooled into buying by, say, Mills & Boon's marketing machine or because it is seen to be a 'feminine' type of reading. They may also *want* to read such books, and their desire to do so may be quite legitimate.

Gramsci's reworking of ideology as a consensual formation was an attempt to explain why Italian workers failed to seize power in the years following the First World War, when it had appeared that all the 'objective' material conditions for a worker's revolution were in place. Marxist analyses of ideology thus became ways of explaining capitalism's continued existence, and of understanding the ways in which we accept its system. Althusser's writings in the 1970s were influenced by the translations of Gramsci's work just becoming available. Althusser's twist on Gramsci's own theories of ideology was to argue that our acceptance of capitalism is achieved at an unconscious level, and that there is a contradiction between the ways in which we think of our position within society and the ways in which we really live it. In Althusser's famous phrase: 'Ideology represents the imaginary relationship of individuals to their real conditions of existence' (1984, 36). This means that our identity is constituted within ideology, so that ideology is not only a matter of performing but also of living in ideology. This theory might appear to be the very opposite of an emancipatory theory: if we live in ideology, how can we ever come to know it, since no 'outside' of ideology is possible? For Althusser knowledge of ideology is possible through theory-as-science and through art. And this latter argument was developed in the 1970s by Macherey and Eagleton. Literature, they argued, could make ideology visible, for in giving ideology a form, literature foregrounds its typical contradictions. A 'symptomatic' reading could thus read the gaps, inconsistencies and limits of a text, as Freud has suggested we might read dreams and slips of the tongue so as to reveal the traces of what they repress. *The Prelude*, for example, partly because of its complex dating (begun in 1798, Wordsworth reworked the text until his death in 1850), exposes inconsistencies in political viewpoint between the young Wordsworth of the 1790s and the later, 'Victorian', Wordsworth. Textual tensions and inconsistencies abound in the descriptions of France and the French Revolution in Books IX and X since the poem is written after disillusionment with revolutionary ideals has set in but attempts to recreate youthful idealism. Wordsworth's epic poem – like all autobiographies – is marked as much by revision as vision, by self-censorship as much as self-expression.

An exemplary instance of a symptomatic reading is to be found in Terry Eagleton's consideration of the critical reception of Thomas Hardy in *Towards a Revolutionary Criticism* (*LT*, 109–15). Eagleton argues that the 'rustic' and 'educated' languages of Thomas Hardy's novels are incommensurable for his critics, who fail to see that this 'inconsistency' reveals the ideological nature of our definitions of 'literature' itself. In Eagleton's consideration, the reception of the novels of Thomas Hardy can tell us much about twentieth-century values, since many of the readings to which Eagleton draws our attention can be seen to illustrate their own concerns rather than that of late Victorian society. And, as we can see from the genealogy of Hardy criticism provided by Eagleton – where

Hardy has successively been read as 'anthropologist of Wessex . . . the melancholic purveyor of late nineteenth-century nihilism'; as a novelist whose work was 'irreparably violated by ideas' and as a novelist available on the one hand for 'formalist, organicist and anti-theoretical assumptions', while on the other hand being recuperable into 'sociological' readings (*LT*, 112–13) – the definition of 'literature' itself is constantly changing.

That section of *Towards a Revolutionary Criticism* from which the consideration of the reception of Hardy comes, demonstrates a distinction between Eagleton's work and that of Pierre Macherey and Renée Balibar. Eagleton resists the latent formalism in Macherey's work, and while Eagleton demonstrates a familiarity with Balibar, his own work is clearly more aligned with established and emergent concerns of British marxism.

Macherey's original work was quickly criticized by other marxists than Eagleton (Bennett, for example) for its latent formalism. In arguing that literature puts ideology into contradiction through literary form, Macherey's theory suggested that all literary texts are subversive. But this is to essentialize a definition of 'Literature', and to forget that such a definition itself might constitute an ideology. In Macherey's early writings, the literary text, instead of being considered in its particularity (in its historical, social, economic, ideological, technological or institutional matrices), becomes a manifestation of the invariant structure which is 'Literature'. In his later work, Macherey revised his writings on literature, influenced by Renée Balibar's study of the use of literature in the French educational system, *Les Français fictifs* (1974). 'Literature' in nineteenth-and twentieth-century France is defined according to how it is constructed within the classroom and there moulded according to the ways in which language itself is taught. In this shift we see something of what would become known as cultural materialism, a British tradition of marxist literary theory which focuses on the changing and contemporary contexts of historical texts. Eagleton's marxism is often of this kind – in his arguments, for example, that a literary text is not inherently conservative or radical, ideological or oppositional, but is so only in relation to its contexts. Because its contexts of reception change, the literary text does not remain the same throughout the history of its reception. No text can be immutably either 'ideological' or 'oppositional' because such judgements will always be determined by other relations which are constantly changing. If the film versions of Jane Austen today portray a conservative, nostalgic image of rural England, it is not so much a matter of the intrinsic conservatism of Austen's work as that the conservative aspects of her own society are still with us. Britain in the 1990s is still a society deeply divided according to class and one in which the countryside alliance of large landowners and landed gentry continues to exercise wide influence.

There is a danger in work of this kind of treating literature as an ideology, as Raymond Williams points out in the interview 'Marxism and Literature'. While literature is certainly not immune to ideology it is also not straightforwardly commensurate with it. Much marxist literary theory of the 1970s and 1980s was written against a received idea of 'Literature' which needed to be resisted – that selective body of canonical texts which were to seen to transcend their own contexts in transmitting eternal literary values. The transformations of university syllabi in the 1980s and 1990s under the challenge of marxist, feminist, postcolonial and queer studies theorists make this a less pressing issue for marxist theorists today, though 'canonical' Literature maintains its dominance and the question of literary 'value' remains contentious. Marxist approaches to the question of literary value have often argued that it would be naive to think that we could eradicate judgement, so that the best we can do is to continue to judge but to reveal as much as possible the way in which that judgement is situated. We should recognize and recontextualize as much as possible our own and others' judgements. In Williams' words, we should try: 'to seek the maximum disclosure of the circumstances of judgement, which would allow someone else to dissociate himself [sic] from it; but then openly and not by a presumptive category' (*LT*, 123). This too may be a limited response to the problem of literary value, but it is also the most attractive and disarming. For marxism – like feminism and postcolonialism – wears its commitment openly, and does not hide behind the pretence of impartiality.

For critics of marxist literary theories, it is this very commitment, however, which makes their readings suspect. A common accusation of marxist approaches to literature is that they are insufficiently attentive to the form of literature. (In the convenient opposition of formalism and marxism, the first pays undue attention to form at the expense of context, the second to context at the expense of form.) One marxist critic who has explicitly addressed this question, and through specific readings of literary texts, is Fredric Jameson in *The Political Unconscious*. Jameson's principle argument in this work is that narrative provides complex resolutions to the more basic contradictions of history. In his readings of Conrad, for example, the literary modes of impressionism and romance are seen as recourses against the rationalization and reification of nineteenth-century capitalist society. Conrad's use of the sense perceptions of impressionism can be understood as both a consequence of this transition and a strategy by which his novels resist it. In the style's foregrounding of the senses, reality is turned into image. This is an embodiment of reification, but it also projects beyond it. So that the literary text in its potential to resolve real contradictions on the level of symbol is both a figure of ideology in Althusser's sense and also an emancipatory ideal. Literature transcends the real, even if only symbolically.

Jameson's discussion of the ways in which narrative is a 'socially symbolic act' also demonstrates how marxist readings need not read literature merely as a reflection of its particular context. It is not a matter of learning something of the historical context and then reading the text off against that as a form of 'background', as the historicist approaches to Shakespeare of, for example, Dover Wilson and Tillyard tended to do. Rather history is read in the *formal* fissures and contradictions within a text. Jane Austen's novels, for example, notoriously do not refer to the French Revolution, Enclosure Acts or Luddite agitations which constitute the history we associate with the Romantic period. Yet her novels do dramatize the tensions between a precapitalist, feudal order in which status hierarchies are strictly maintained and a capitalist order in which social mobility is more possible through 'merit'. These tensions are embodied in the figure of Mr Knightley in *Emma*. He criticizes Emma's attempts to raise Harriet Smith 'out of' her station and his estate of Donwell Abbey represents the fixed, stable, stratified and coherent order associated with this vision of society as inherently hierarchical. Yet Knightley is also a figure of the agrarian capitalist, who spends the little spare money he has frugally and who sensibly reinvests his profits in the farm. He prefers looking over his accounts than dancing and recognizes in his tenant Robert Martin a man who shares his own values, despite their differences in rank. The character of Knightley, then, can symbolically resolve the determinate contradictions which are registered within the novel. He combines the elegance and refinement of the natural aristocrat with the moral, capitalist virtues of industry and thrift. And this symbolic act is possible within Austen's notorious limit of '3 or 4 families in a country village'. what Jameson would call narrative's 'strategy of containment'.

Austen's novels are then thoroughly 'historical', since, like all narratives, their ultimate horizon, their political unconscious is History itself. This makes such questions as whether Austen's novels refer to the French Revolution or the abolition of slavery misplaced. The novels inevitably exist within the context of such events and whether they 'refer to' these events is not the only or even the most significant question of the relationship between narrative and history. Jameson refutes the idea that this historical subtext is 'extrinsic' to the work, something which he, not the text, brings to bear upon it. Instead his 'formal' analysis is defined as 'contextual', a definition we think of as paradoxical only because such theoretical strategies have tended to be situated as oppositional to one another. Formal patterns in the work are read as symbolic enactments of the social within the formal (Jameson, 1983, 77). Jameson's readings are thus attempts to combine heuristic with deductive procedures. His initial approach to the work is an immanent description of its formal and structural properties. It is deductive insofar as its hunt for formal contradictions is motivated by its aim of transcending the purely formalistic, its ultimate intention of relating these contradictions to history as the subtext of the work. And such contradictions will enable a political analysis, in its widest sense.

Jameson's reconciliation of formal with contextual concerns is not the only synthesis within his work, however. The way in which it unites diverse, and often antithetical, theoretical influences is the most controversial synthesis from a marxist perspective. Indeed much of the diversity of marxist approaches alluded to at the beginning of this introduction can be traced through his work. Jameson draws upon such marxist theorists as Althusser and Macherey (structuralist marxists) and Sartre and Lukács (Hegelian marxists), and combines their approaches with those of psychoanalysis, structuralism and poststructuralism. That Hegelian and structuralist marxisms are antithetical does not unduly trouble Jameson. (Hegelian marxisms position history as the dominant form of totalization – Sartre, for example, prioritizes History as the totalization of individual agency in which consciousness is the basis of that totality. Structural marxisms decentre the idea of totality, for example in Althusser's theory of overdetermination and his argument that history is a process without a subject.) In part this unabashed eclecticism is the attraction of Jameson's theory. But it also makes his work problematic from a marxist perspective. Jameson's synthesis of antithetical marxisms and his emphasis upon social *totality* as a standard of judgement for the literary text are both 'Hegelian' manoeuvres. In subsuming all other approaches within marxism, Jameson's theory parallels Hegel's view of history as the unfolding of progressive stages in which new ideas and cultural forms develop by 'sublating' older ones, that is by simultaneously adopting and transcending them, reconciling and preserving them. So too in Jameson's writings, no theory, however 'partial', cannot be usefully assimilated. In Bhaskar's discussion of dialectics, we can see obvious parallels between Hegel and Jameson's approach: 'For Hegel truth is the whole and error lies in one-sidedness, incompleteness and abstraction; it can be recognized by the contradictions it generates and remedied through their incorporation in fuller, richer, more concrete conceptual forms' (in Bottomore et al., 1991, 144). Yet the suspicion remains, as Eagleton has argued, that Jameson is able to assimilate competing theories only because his analysis remains on the level of pure theory, suggesting, to put it in its crudest terms, that we need only see the 'whole' in order to put the world to rights.

This is to end this essay, as it began, with an emphasis upon differences within marxist approaches to literature. In his studies of canonical 'Literature', Eagleton has argued how the institutional matrices make Literature an inherently ideological construct, so that we should be alert to the ways in which we might participate in such formations. Williams argues that literature need not be *inherently* ideological, but that its modern forms have been 'compromised' by increasing specialization. Jameson refuses to condemn literature as ultimately ideological, by tracing the ways in which all ideologies are simultaneously, potentially utopian. That the more structuralist marxisms associated with Eagleton and Hall in Britain have been less popular among American marxist theorists is often read as revealing the absence of a grassroots marxism in America since the McCarthy era. Yet as the essays on new historicism, cultural studies, postmodernism and feminism in this volume suggest, marxism's presence can be traced in the formation and critical practices of other theories. In the 1990s gender, sexuality and race have become the more popular sites for political praxis, and this is reflected in current theories and in the academic study of literature. But the importance and even priority of economic factors such as class, education and literary production for the study and theorizing of literature remains. One of the challenges of future criticism is to combine these determinants and politics – of gender, race, sexuality and class – without seeing them as competing claims.

NOTES TOWARDS A READING OF *MRS DALLOWAY*

In what ways does *Mrs Dalloway* represent the social and economic conditions of capitalism? How does the novel treat the individual subject in relation to society? Does the novel reflect or expose the dominant ideologies of its time? What are the material conditions under which the novel is produced and received? What are the cultural politics of subsequent and contemporary readings of Woolf's fiction? These are some of the questions which marxist readings of *Mrs Dalloway* might ask. Least interesting, and potentially the most reductive, of these readings would be to scrutinize the apparent, 'intended' politics of its author. It was popular in the earlier part of the last century to focus on Virginia Woolf as the aristocratic lady-novelist of Bloomsbury. But too often this reading led to a quick dismissal of her as an elite, 'ivory-tower' writer, ignorant of class struggle and void of any empathy with working-class lives. F. R. Leavis (though not, of course, a marxist critic himself) was guilty of this kind of class determinism when he accused Woolf of a 'sophisticated aestheticism' which masters 'beautiful' writing but which shuts out any experience which is not felt as 'preoccupation with one's consciousness of it' (1942, 295–8). Here Leavis might almost have been speaking for Lukács, whose defence of classic realism against the perceived degeneracy of modernism, would surely have censured the portrayal of Mrs Dalloway as that of the isolated heroine of modernism 'imprisoned' within her own consciousness. More recently (in a Channel 4 programme for British television, 1991), Tom Paulin railed against the limitations of Woolf's views, accusing her of snobbery and conservatism.

Mrs Dalloway – like Woolf's other fiction – is set within the aristocratic and elite circles of Woolf's own cultural background. Mrs Dalloway spends the day delineated by the novel preparing to be the perfect hostess for that evening's party. The wife of a respectable Conservative politician, Clarissa Dalloway's function in life seems to be to bring together family friends to the greater credit of her husband's social standing, but to remain ignorant of, even indifferent to, the political cares of his world:

> He must be off, he said, getting up. But he stood for a moment as if he were about to say something; and she wondered what? Why? There were the roses.
>
> 'Some Committee?' she asked, as he opened the door.
>
> 'Armenians,' he said; or perhaps it was 'Albanians' . . .
>
> He was already half-way to the House of Commons, to his Armenians, his Albanians, having settled her on the sofa, looking at his roses. And people would say, 'Clarissa Dalloway is spoilt.' She cared much more for her roses than for the Armenians. Hunted out of existence, maimed, frozen, the victims of cruelty and injustice (she had heard Richard say so

over and over again) – no, she could feel nothing for the Albanians, or was it the Armenians? But she loved her roses (didn't that help the Armenians?) – the only flowers she could bear to see cut. (*MD*, 132–3)

Such a passage does not validate Clarissa Dalloway, especially as the poetic style of the novel encourages us to make links between its recurrent images. Here we are reminded of the roses which Moll Pratt, the Irish flower-seller, wishes she could fling in tribute at a passing wealthy car: she 'wished the dear boy well (it was the Prince of Wales for certain) and would have tossed the price of a pot of beer – a bunch of roses – into St James's Street out of sheer light-heartedness and contempt of poverty had she not seen the constable's eye upon her, discouraging an old Irishwoman's loyalty' (*MD*, 22). The associational play of images and recurrent motifs reminds us of worlds beyond Clarissa's own social circle. Clarissa Dalloway and the Irish flower-seller exist in almost separate worlds, and the novel registers this economic division, while subsuming both within its texture. And while Mrs Dalloway is certainly the 'heroine' of the novel, her feelings and memories dominating the novel, she is also seen and judged critically. Her own limitations are clearly exposed and her life is commented upon by others too: by Peter Walsh, saddened by her conformity, her absorption into a marriage defined by its 'inlaid table, the mounted paper-knife, the dolphin and the candlesticks, the chair-covers and the old valuable English tinted prints' (*MD*, 49); or by her servant Lucy, envious of the 'loveliness' of her mistress, 'mistress of silver, of linen, of china' (*MD*, 43). The marxist critic, then, might well begin by reading the text for its attention to social class, and for the ways in which ideology is expressed through individual subjects.

Clarissa Dalloway's world is held up to scrutiny within the novel, exposed often by breezily casual, but tell-tale, glimpses of the ideology of the governing class. One early example is the quick succession of bereavement followed by anxiety regarding inheritance in a sentence ostensibly setting the scene for the narrative's day: 'For it was the middle of June. The War was over, except for someone like Mrs Foxcroft at the Embassy last night eating her heart out because that nice boy was killed *and now* the old Manor House must go to a cousin' (*MD*, 7; my emphasis). The novel ventriloquizes the thoughts of Mrs Dalloway and often suggests that they are typical of her social class – is it Mrs Dalloway who worries over the old Manor House, or Mrs Foxcroft? But implicit critiques of this society are not simply censures of Clarissa Dalloway. Like the novel itself, she permits the ideologies of her class to be seen, but she is not, herself, commensurate with this ideology.

Mrs Dalloway is a product of her society (Peter Walsh sees in Clarissa 'a great deal of the public-spirited, British Empire, tariff-reform, governing-class spirit, which had grown on her, as it tends to do . . .': *MD*, 86), but she is also a victim of it. Defined by class *and* gender, Mrs Dalloway is disenfranchised from the political and cultural power which the men of her rank enjoy. Her feelings and memories include much self-satisfaction and complacency at the life she leads, a life in which cut roses are more important than the plight of Armenians (or is it Albanians?). But hers is also a life of regrets and frustrations, of awareness of the sheltered nature of her own experiences (*MD*, 38) and even, glimmering, an awareness of her own oppression. This is most powerfully represented by her sympathetic identification with Septimus Smith, whose suicide provides her party with a source of conversation, but the narrative throughout points up a doubling between the shell-shocked former soldier and the society hostess. While the novel's setting is ostensibly at the heart of political power (Big Ben tolls 'the hours' – the novel's original title – throughout), it views such power refracted through those both included and, more frequently, excluded from it. While Richard Dalloway is close to the Prime Minister and Peter Walsh is an imperial administrator in India, Clarissa herself is peripheral to political decision-making. That *Mrs Dalloway* is not overtly political, then, is because women are removed from the centres of power. In Patrick Brantlinger's terms, *Mrs Dalloway* is 'an antipolitical political novel' (1996, 230).

Thus far, then, this marxist reading has examined the ideological and class positions within the novel, drawing largely upon characterization and narrative employment (the intertwining of the stories of Septimus and Clarissa, for example). One of the most persistent criticisms of marxist interpretations of literature is their neglect of literary form. This is arguably true of work influenced by Lukács' theories of classic realism in which characterization and subject-matter tend to dominate over expression. There is also a residual suspicion among some marxists that the aesthetic and the political are somehow antithetical – that to 'tell the truth' in literature is to refuse the excesses, the performativity, the exuberance of poetry. In the terms of Jameson's always-historicizing analysis, this suspicion is itself the product of a capitalist culture which has appeared to split the poetic and the political:

> . . . one of the determinants of capitalist culture, that is, the culture of the western realist and modernist novel, is a radical split between the private and the public, between the poetic and the political . . . We have been trained in a deep cultural conviction that the lived experience of our private existences is somehow incommensurable with the abstractions of economic science and political dynamics. Politics in our novels, therefore is, according to Stendhal's canonical formulation, a 'pistol shot in the middle of a concert'. (Jameson, 1986, 69)

Jameson renews earlier debates within marxism concerning the relative merits of classic realism and modernism (identified with Lukács and Adorno respectively). In place of Lukács' rejection of modernism as an anti-political aestheticism, Jameson reads modernist texts for their repressed political contents. We have already seen how *Mrs Dalloway* might be interpreted – in a marxist reading of the novel – as an ironic portrait of an elite society from within. In Jameson's terms, *Mrs Dalloway*, like the fiction of Conrad and other modernist texts, embodies the reifications of capitalism within its very form. In his, as in

Adorno's terms, modernist expression explores and articulates the fissures in society, the experience of capitalism as characterized by confusion and fragmentariness. *Mrs Dalloway* is typical of modernist works in its refusal of pattern, its resistance to paraphrase, its attempt to evoke confusion, not to dispel it. There is no investment here in 'rationality' as the governing principle of interpretation, analogous to the 'instrumentality' of capitalism. Instead, *Mrs Dalloway* turns from and repudiates the style and values of classic realism in a form of ideological critique. At the very level of form, it refuses to guarantee meaning, refuses omniscience. In ways which are receptive to Bakhtinian analysis, *Mrs Dalloway* articulates the experiences and feelings of a wide range of characters, not just of its central heroine, as they reflect upon themselves and upon her. This polyphony engages with the voices of others without the attempt to arrogate the final word, as the narrator of classic realism tends to do. The style of *Mrs Dalloway* sets itself against the authority, the rationality, the instrumentality of other kinds of discourse, implicitly in its poetic stream-of-consciousness style, with its random and chaotic flux of ideas, and explicitly, in its condemnation of Sir William Bradshaw. In a rare passage of narrative comment, Sir William and his obeisance to proportion are scrutinized: 'Sir William with his . . . infallible instinct, this is madness, this sense; his sense of proportion' (*MD*, 110).

These attributes of *Mrs Dalloway's* style lend themselves to feminist arguments concerning the 'feminine sentence', but they are also shared attributes, held in common with other modernist texts, and, as such, are open to marxist as to feminist readings. The blaze of poetic style of Woolf's fictions is as political as it is aesthetic, political even in its aestheticism. In Jameson's terms, modernist style presupposes and reflects the fragmentation of a world self-divided by capitalism, but it also proffers a 'Utopian compensation' for everything lost in the instrumentality of capitalism: 'the place of quality in an increasingly quantified world, the place of the archaic and of feeling amid the desacralization of the market system, the place of sheer color and intensity within the grayness of measurable extension and geometrical abstraction' (1983, 236–7).

Marxist readings of literature, then, need not be confined to reflecting on ideological and subject positions, but can also be used to address the interactions between literary form and social and political contexts. Literary forms such as realism, modernism, pastoral, elegy embody and rework political ideals and implications. This is not to label literary forms according to always-already defined political categories, but to scrutinize the ways in which literature engages with traditions which are inevitably literary, social, economic and political.

QUESTIONS FOR FURTHER CONSIDERATION

1. Adorno wrote that 'art is defined by its relation to what is different from art'. How important do you think it is that we situate the literary text in a network of relations?

2. Marxism has traditionally claimed an absolute priority for the economic, in its belief that material production is the ultimately determinant factor of social existence. To what extent does this argument still hold in contemporary society and how might this principle be reconciled with the 'competing' claims of gender, race, sexuality?
3. Is a marxist criticism a task of bringing to light politics latent in the text or of politicizing the text?
4. Can a literary text such as *Mrs Dalloway* both expose and escape the ideological pressures of its own time? Of our time?
5. Can the political status of genres be determined in quite the way this reading has suggested? Is classic realism, for example, necessarily 'conservative' in its form?
6. If Mrs Dalloway's marginal status in relation to the centres of power is at the heart of the political dimension of the novel, is this then a properly 'marxist' or a 'feminist' reading? In what ways are the marxist and feminist readings of *Mrs Dalloway* in this collection complementary or conflicting?

ANNOTATED BIBLIOGRAPHY

Eagleton, Terry. *The Eagleton Reader*, ed. Stephen Regan. Oxford, 1998.
This anthology reproduces work from throughout Eagleton's career, and thus demonstrates something of the shifts in British marxist theories over the last thirty years: from early work inspired largely by Williams, through the structuralist marxism of the 1970s and early 1980s, to the critiques of postmodernism and the exploration of Irish postcoloniality of the 1990s. The writings include theoretical reflections as well as particular readings of literary texts. Regan's introduction and notes to each essay provide a useful commentary on Eagleton's work, if not a particularly critical one.
Eagleton, Terry, and Drew Milne, eds. *Marxist Literary Theory: A Reader*. Oxford, 1996.
Both this and Mulhern's (below) are good places to start, as their anthologized essays reflect the diversity of marxist approaches to literature. Eagleton's and Milne's anthology has the broader historical range: from seminal extracts from Marx and Engels to Callinocos' polemic against postmodernism (1989). Excerpts from theorists now seen as problematically 'vulgar' marxists (such as Caudwell and Goldmann) can be usefully contrasted with later structuralist marxisms, and marxist-feminist and post-colonial approaches illustrate the increasingly hybrid nature of marxist theories.
Mulhern, Francis. *Contemporary Marxist Literary Criticism*. Harlow, 1992.
Mulhern's anthology is an important supplement to that of Eagleton and Milne, as its more limited focus permits the inclusion of more contemporary and specialized topics: issues of gender (Cora Kaplan) and empire (Said) are again included, but so too are discussions of popular culture (Bennett and Denning), the avant-garde (Bürger) and film theory (Stephen Heath). Mulhern's introduction situates these readings within a discussion of the evolution of marxist literary criticism and reviews the state of Marxist theory the early 1990s.
Williams, Raymond. *Marxism and Literature*. Oxford, 1977.
This is the first book in which Williams explicitly identified his practice with marxism, but its value is primarily its ability to discuss complex and subtle theories clearly. In the first section there is a focus on the historical development of the key terms culture, language, literature and ideology; in the second Williams questions and redefines key marxist concepts such as 'base and superstructure' and 'determination', and elaborates

his most influential theory – of the 'dominant, residual and emergent' ideologies of society; in the final section Williams turns to literature as a material practice (the social character of signs, notations and conventions, for example) and concludes with the questions of commitment and creative practice.

Williams, Raymond. *Politics and Letters: Interviews with New Left Review*. London, 1981.

Through the mode of interviews, this book allows us to see both the divergences between marxist perspectives (between Williams and his interviewers from the *New Left Review*) and Williams' own revisions of his earlier work. There are substantial interviews on each of his published books, as well as biographical and political discussions, and all are highly accessible and lively.

SUPPLEMENTARY BIBLIOGRAPHY

Adorno, T. et al. *Aesthetics and Politics*. London, 1980.

Althusser, Louis. *Lenin and Philosophy and Other Essays*, trans. Ben Brewster. London, 1971.

————. *Essays on Ideology*, trans. Ben Brewster. London, 1984.

Barrell, John. *Poetry, Language and Politics*. Manchester, 1998.

Barrett, Michèle. *The Politics of Truth: from Marx to Foucault*. Oxford, 1991.

Belsey, Catherine. *Critical Practice*. London, 1980.

Bennett, Tony. *Formalism and Marxism*. London, 1979

Bennett, Tony et al., eds. *Culture, Ideology and Social Process: A Reader*. Milton Keynes, 1981.

Benton, Ted. *The Rise and Fall of Structuralist Marxism*. London, 1984.

Bewes, Timothy. *Cynicism and Postmodernity*. London, 1997.

Bottomore, Tom et al., eds. *A Dictionary of Marxist Thought*. Oxford, 1991.

Brantlinger, Patrick. *Fictions of State: Culture and Credit in Britain, 1694–1994*. Ithaca, NY, 1996.

Brown, Laura. *Alexander Pope*. Oxford, 1985.

————. *Women and Ideology in Early Eighteenth-Century English Literature*. Ithaca, NY, 1993.

Coole, Diana. 'Is class a difference that makes a difference?' *Radical Philosophy*, 77, May/June 1996.

Eagleton, Terry. *Marxism and Literary Criticism*. London, 1976.

————. *Walter Benjamin: or Towards a Revolutionary Criticism*. London, 1981.

Felski, Rita. *Beyond Feminist Aesthetics: Feminist Literature and Social Change*. London, 1989.

Gagnier, Regenia. *Idylls of the Marketplace: Oscar Wilde and the Victorian Public*. Aldershot, 1987.

Hawkes, David. *Ideology*. London, 1996.

Jameson, Fredric. *The Political Unconscious: Narrative as a Socially Symbolic Act*. London, 1983.

Jameson, Fredric. 'Third-World Literature in the Era of Multinational Capitalism', *Social Text*, 17, 1986.

Janowitz, Anne. *Lyric and Labour in the Romantic Tradition*. Cambridge, 1998.

Johnson, Pauline. *Marxist Aesthetics*. London, 1984.

Landry, Donna. *The Muses of Resistance: Laboring-Class Women's Poetry in Britain, 1739–1796*. Cambridge, 1990.

Levinson, Marjorie. *Wordsworth's Great Period Poems*. Cambridge, 1986.

Lovell, Terry. *Consuming Fiction*. London, 1987.

Macherey, Pierre. *A Theory of Literary Production*, trans. Geoffrey Wall. London, 1978.

Milner, Andrew. *Literature, Culture and Society*. London, 1996.

Sim, Stuart, ed. *Post-Marxism*. Edinburgh, 1998.

Simpson, David, ed. *Subject to History: Ideology, Class, Gender*. Ithaca, NY, 1991.

Sprinker, Michael. *History and Ideology. Proust*: A la récherche du temps perdu *and the Third French Republic*. London, 1998.

Williams, Raymond. *The Country and the City*. London, 1973.

————. *Keywords*. Fontana, 1983.

Wood, Ellen Meiksins, and John Foster Bellamy, eds. *Defense of History: Marxism and the Postmodern Agenda*. New York, 1997.

OTHER WORK CITED

Leavis, F. R. 'After *To the Lighthouse*', *Scrutiny*, 1942.

THERE IS NO SUCH THING
AS READER-RESPONSE THEORY

Martin McQuillan

READERS

In the end most of the questions we ask in the name of literary theory come down to the difficulties of reading. One of the obvious places to start from in trying to answer such questions is the role of the reader. As a student or critic of Literature this is what you are: a reader. If literary theory destabilizes assumptions about the experience of the literary then it is quite right that theory should interrogate what comes 'naturally' to literature, namely the reading process. Without reading or readers there would be no such thing as literature. Books which are not read are merely ornaments on a shelf made from paper and ink. They might as well be used as paperweights or doorsteps and certainly cannot be said to constitute the literary.

A text only becomes meaningful when it is read, when a reader interacts with the words on the page to produce meaning. What we call reading is an active participation on the part of the reader to construct meaning from a piece of writing. Reading is therefore something which the reader has a role in and something which takes places over a period of time. It is only when the reader actually reads (actively participates in the construction of meaning) that a text might be said to exist. You will notice the fine distinction we are making here between the terms 'book' or 'piece of writing' and 'text'. This will be a distinction familiar to you from your understanding of structuralism. 'Text' is the name given to the interaction between reader and writing which produces meaning. A text is the temporal experience of reading which actualizes meaning, the experience of which is specific to each individual reader. We might speak of the novel *Pride and Prejudice* but the novel only becomes a 'text' when it is read by a reader.

Accordingly, every reader will have his/her own experiences of a 'text'. I might read *Pride and Prejudice* and think it a witty satire on social manners, you might read *Pride and Prejudice* and find it a piece of reactionary propaganda which supports the subordination of women. While we could both be correct in our readings (or we could both be wrong) certainly our experiences of the text are different. The experience of the text is not solely constituted by the hour we spend in the library or on the bus reading. A reading of a text is as complex as the person who reads. The meanings that you as a reader will produce in relation to a text are affected by all the things which make you up as a person. The actual time spent reading is important but your experience of reading will also be informed by the experiences you bring to that moment of reading.

For example, the way you read is influenced by your gender (often women and men read differently). This does not just mean that women read in the garden using a treasured postcard as a bookmark while men read in the toilet using a half-eaten sandwich to mark their page. Rather, it means that the experiences which have informed you as a person and which have conditioned you socially in certain codes of masculinity and/or femininity will effect the way you respond to a piece of writing. As a post-Spice Girls woman of the early twenty-first century you might find the predicament of the Bennett sisters in *Pride and Prejudice* disturbing if not altogether alien. However, a reader in 1950s Britain with its much stricter social conventions might find Elizabeth Bennett's circumstances reassuringly (and disturbingly) familiar. Indeed, a reader from a society with altogether different ideas about the situation of women may even find the novel licentious.

It is not simply that women read in a different way from men. Certainly all women do not read in the same way. Rather the positions that are open to men and women as readers may vary within the same textual experiences. Furthermore, a text may set itself up as offering different readerly positions to men and women. For example, it would be perfectly possible for both a male and female reader to read *Pride and Prejudice* as an ideological support to patriarchy (or as a social satire) but the text itself offers different positions to the male and female reader in relation to the plot and characters. Remember the D'Arcy mania which swept Britain following the BBC adaptation of this novel. The text encourages the heterosexual female reader to collude with the romantic fantasy that Elizabeth had got her man through true love. The male reader is encouraged to identify with D'Arcy as the strong and (mostly) silent type who wins his girl through integrity and speaking his mind. These positions offered to the reader depend upon conventional ideas about masculinity and femininity and also help to perpetuate those ideas. However, it is always possible to read against the positions offered by a text. We might say that Elizabeth gets D'Arcy not by the miracle of true love but because she plays the marriage market of Regency England better than any of the other women. She gets D'Arcy, the house and the money not because she will only marry for love but because she is the most desirable commodity on the marriage market and will make D'Arcy (the man with most consumer power) the best wife.

In certain respects the various theoretical positions of feminism, postcolonialism, marxism, and queer theory are really only inflections of this interrogation of the role of the reader. These readings of *Pride and Prejudice* depend upon the ways we might read as a wo/man. Feminism is a process of reading by women in order to question the representation and construction of femininity by a text so as to ask whether that construction is an adequate response to the experiences of women as readers and thereby challenge such constructions. The text might offer us the consoling love story but we chose to read against that position. However, the gender of a reader is not the only experience s/he brings to a text. The position a reader occupies in relation to a text will also be influenced by their race and their class (as well as their sexuality, age, education, environment and so forth). A working-class reader may offer a different reading from a middle-class reader and it is not necessarily the case that it will be the working-class reader who sees Jane Austen's novel as a portrait of bourgeois normality to the exclusion of the proletariat as a class. A black woman may produce a different reading of *Pride and Prejudice* than a white woman. She could ask why she was being offered this text as a canonical representation of the nineteenth century rather than the autobiography of an enslaved woman such as Mary Prince. In this way the role of the reader is informed by present historical circumstances as well as the reading positions offered by the text.

Literary theory enables us to read against the grain of the positions offered to us as readers by a text. This is what we mean by critical thinking or critical theory, to read carefully with and against the assumptions and values a text offers to us as natural or normal. In so doing a critical reader should not come to the text with their own set of presuppositions about what the text will be about and so close off the possibilities of meaning within the text. Rather the reader ought to be sensitive to the singularity of a text, what makes it unique and what constitutes the individual relation between a particular reader and this particular text. In this way the reader responds to each individual text to produce specific critical readings, rather than take a series of theoretical terms and operations and apply them willy-nilly to a range of different texts. This is the sausage machine type of theory we as readers should always try to avoid: having a preconceived theoretical model into which we pour texts at one end and produce identical predetermined and packaged readings at the other end.

For example, not all postcolonial readings of Jane Austen novels would necessarily question the text's canonical status. A reading of *Persuasion* might respond to the references made to the places visited by the British navy which exclude any mention of the Caribbean or Indian natives living there. When reading *Mansfield Park* we might pay attention to the fact that Sir Thomas makes his money by owning slave plantations in Antigua, while a reading of *Emma* might respond specifically to a short but significant exchange between Emma and Mr Knightly in which the condition of women in England is compared to the condition of slaves in the colonies. In this last instance a postcolonial reading would necessarily become involved with questions of gender just as any reading of *Mansfield Park* must engage with issues of class and ownership. In fact it is impossible (even if we wanted to) to compartmentalize the discrete approaches offered to us as readers by something like this guide. In each singular act of reading our critical response will inevitably synthesize the different knowledges we gain from the different approaches we take to a text. For example, there is no such thing as a 'pure' postcolonial reading which takes account solely of issues of race and Empire independent from considerations such as gender, class, psychoanalytic constructs of otherness, deconstruction's understanding of knowledge and language, cultural hegemony, history and so forth.

There is then no single theoretical approach to a text as the introduction to this volume makes clear. The various knowledges which come under the term literary theory are not separated within the act of reading in the way that they are in this anthology for the pedagogical ease of categorization. Different approaches combine and relate to one another in complex ways and will do so uniquely during each individual act of reading. This is as true for one person reading two different texts by the same author as it is for two people reading the same text. If there were no difference of opinion between readers then there would be no need for critics and no need for you as a reader to attempt to express your response to a text in the form of critical thinking or in a written essay. Criticism then (we might equally use the word reading) is an act of judgement by an individual in the face of a text but not, it should be stressed, just as the reader pleases. This is literally what criticism means, it comes from the Greek word *criticos* meaning to judge. If every critical reading is a judgment in response to a text then it is the difference between judgements made by individual readers which makes criticism possible and is the very condition of a political reading of a text.

It is impossible for there ever to be a purely just judgement which could impose itself without encountering some opposition. The fact that people challenge laws is because these laws are judgments imposed upon them by others who have their own sets of interests to protect. The necessary making of laws is the condition of society, the challenging of those judgements is the possibility of politics. No judgement is ever absolutely correct and is always made from a subjective point of view to the detriment of some person or group. Therefore, criticism can be said to be political because it is an act of judgement which cannot foreclose discussion in the way it would like (my reading is correct and you are wrong) and so has to compete with other critical readings in a strategic network of relations. Thus, it is the singularity of the reader and the singularity of the readings which s/he produces which makes criticism possible and is the conditions of a 'political reading' as such.

Now – and here is the crux of the matter so pay attention – this is not the same thing as saying all readings are equally valid and, as you may have been told, there are no wrong answers in literature. I say this not because there is some innate perfect meaning lying buried in a text waiting to be extracted by a suitably qualified reader. Rather it is because as readers we come to a text not only with our own set of personal experiences to inform our reading but we also come via certain institutional paths and as subjects in history. These two things are related but let's take the first one first.

There has never been an occasion in your life, and there never will be, when you read 'innocently' or 'simply'. Whenever you read you read according to a set of institutional codes and expectations. In the past you may have read for character, theme, plot, setting, description, the author's biography, clever uses of language or what the text had to say about the human condition. None of these things are necessarily 'natural' to reading or could be described as reading 'innocently'. When you read for such things you were following a practice of reading laid down for you by the institution which policed your reading. This may have been a school, a university or media reviews of books, all of which will have guided you as to what to look for in a text, what to expect to be there when you found it, and the sorts of things to say in response to it. You may have been encouraged in the past to say things like 'this is a very effective use of language' or 'this line tells us about the poet's relation to his father' or 'Macbeth is one of the most interesting characters in English Literature'. Effective language is language which means something so that is hardly a valid criticism, if all books were merely the author's biography retold with the names changed there would be no such thing as fiction, and Macbeth was Scottish. It is not that language, biography, character, plot and so forth are not significant things to be interested in when reading, as other chapters in *Introducing Literary Theories* have shown language and plot are particularly important. Rather, the point is that when you read for these things in the past you did so not because they were the natural thing to do but because you were trained to do so by the institution in which you practised your reading. It may have been appropriate at 'A' level or 'H'-grade to have talked about character in Macbeth and wholly inappropriate to discuss the symbolic exchange of the phallus in the play.

Texts also change with history. For example, a reader of Shakespeare's *The Merchant of Venice* reading after the holocaust will not approach the play in the same way as a Renaissance reader trained to appreciate the character of the jew as a comic villain. On the one hand, a marxist or new historicist approach would suggest that through reading a reader can gain access to the historical context from which a text emerged. Reading *The Merchant of Venice* would tell us about the circumstances of Shakespeare's historical moment. Knowledge of this history informs the response of an individual reader and places that reader within a historical relation to the text. On the other hand, and as a radicaliza-tion of this marxist approach, deconstruction proposes in a memorable phrase that 'there is nothing outside of the text'. This means that even when we think that we are standing outside of a text looking in on it (for example, acceding to the historical circumstances of Early Modern England by reading Shakespeare in the twentieth century) we as readers are already caught up in a network of textual relations which condition our reading. These textual relations include the narratives of identity we bring to the text (e.g. class, gender, sexuality), the institutional rules which guide our reading, and our place in the narrative of history (e.g. being a postcolonial or postmodern reader). This is only half the story though because the text we are reading will be part of, and will have helped shape, that network of interweavings in which the reader is placed. For example, Shakespeare's writing has played a significant role in the construction of the canon of English literature and so affected ideas about national identity, femininity and masculinity, the exclusion of racial minorities from literature and so on. In other words, when we read a text there is nothing but context.

RESPONSES

This is a dizzying paradox when encountered for the first time but it goes to show that even the most difficult and puzzling aspects of literary theory often come down to the question of the reader. My task in this introduction, like the other introductions in this guide, was to introduce a specific theoretical approach, namely what is called reader-response theory. As you will appreciate from all that has been said above the problem of the reader inflects every aspect of literary theory and cannot be set apart from particular theoretical approaches. In this way I would like to suggest that there can be no such thing as a discrete theoretical approach to reading which does not take account of every other chapter in this volume (and, indeed, this was a motivating principle behind this volume). However, as we shall see there is a branch of literary theory called reader-response theory which sets out to specifically examine the role of the reader. Such a description of reader-response theory is only true up to a point. For the most part the heterogeneous theoretical approaches sometimes called reader-response theory (sometimes called reception theory) are not a unified field of thought. Very often reader-response theory is a catch-all term for a collection of writings about reading (most of which are either opposed or contradictory) which is used more for ease of categorization than to express the force of a distinctive theoretical approach. It could hardly be otherwise since the idea of the reader is so important to the whole of so-called literary theory and crosses over all the boundaries and categories of theory. I am pleased rather than apologetic when I suggest to you that there is no such thing as reader-response theory, if by theory we mean a unified body of knowledge which produces a general set of rules, practices and prescribed formulae which will operate consistently every time.

Reader response has been a concern of criticism at least since Plato and Aristotle. In *The Republic* Plato considers the ways in which the reader receives representations (or texts) in the famous parable of the cave in Book IX. In his *Poetics*, Aristotle is concerned with the effects produced on the reader by a tragic drama. Aristotle calls the feelings of pity and fear aroused in the reader (or spectator) of tragedy, catharsis. Nineteenth-century critics like Samuel Taylor

Coleridge and Matthew Arnold were also interested in the responses readers made to texts. In his lectures on Shakespeare, Coleridge identified the reader's active participation in the illusion of fiction as 'willing the voluntary suspension of disbelief', while Arnold's criticism was often concerned with the ways in which reading might affect individuals in order to make them better citizens. This was also an interest of what is frequently called New Criticism. New Criticism was a formalist approach to literary study dominant in Europe and America shortly before and after the Second World War. Most of what is known as reader-response theory is recognized as having been written in response to new criticism.

As a type of formalism new criticism emphasized the importance of the words on the page as the primary arbiter of meaning. In this type of criticism the role of the reader is secondary to the text itself which is thought of as an independent and self-contained entity. All meaning resided within the text and it was the task of the reader to uncover what was already there. This is not to say that all New Critics were not interested in the question of the reader. The British critic I. A. Richards pioneered a variety of practical criticism in which he set his students the task of analysing previously unseen poems which had the poets' names removed. Richards observed that different people produced different readings of the same text and often said that they disliked poetry written by the so-called great authors. However, he put this divergence down to the intrinsic ambiguity (and therefore cleverness) of the texts themselves rather than consider the idea that people offered different readings because their own individual experiences informed their production of meaning in different ways. The American critics W. K. Wimsatt and Monroe Beardsley went further to suggest that literary criticism should not be concerned with issues such as the reader, or the author's biography and intentions, or the historical context from which the text emerged. Such matters were extraneous to the fundamentally autonomous text and should be considered an error in reading. Wimsatt and Beardsley called the mediation of the reader's response to a text (as an outside concern) into a piece of criticism the 'affective fallacy'. The way the reader is affected by a text being a false concern, what was important was to pay attention to the form of the text. Such insistence did not always fit easily within the work of a critic like F. R. Leavis who shared both Arnold's assumptions about the improving effects of great works of literature and new criticism's assumptions concerning the formal analysis of individual texts whereby one read individual texts as distinctive experiences rather than focusing on what bound them to contexts they shared with other aspects of their culture. [While Leavis is not, strictly speaking, a New Critic in that this was a North American critical movement based in large part on the work of John Crowe Ransom, Allen Tate, R. P. Blackmur, Robert Penn Warren and Cleanth Brooks, there are considerable similarities between the New Criticism and the work of Leavis and other critics who published in the journal *Scrutiny*, especially in the shared focus on individual texts and equally shared notions of a text's organic unity discerned through the close reading of details. – Ed.]

The dominance of New Criticism and the related manifestations of practical criticism in the Anglo-American academy began to be challenged in the late 1960s by different groups of critics interested in the question of the reader. Structuralism in its French and later Anglo-American forms displaced the importance traditionally focused on the author as producer of meaning. In an extraordinarily powerful and influential essay 'The Death of the Author' the French critic Roland Barthes stressed the active involvement of the reader in the production of meaning. The Italian structuralist (later novelist) Umberto Eco also emphasized the importance of the reader in opening up the possibilities of interpretation in his book *The Role of the Reader*. Structuralist narrative theory (sometimes called narratology) also added to the debate by identifying different positions available to a listener of a story. The American narratologist Gerald Prince distinguished between the reader and the narratee, the narratee being the person who a text posits as a listener (for example, the 'you' I have addressed throughout this essay). This is not the same thing as the reader, just as the narrator of a story like *Great Expectations* (Pip) is not the same as the author (Charles Dickens). Narratology helped open up debates about the different positions open to listeners, receivers and readers but not all the reader-response theory which followed it observes the subtle distinction between reader and narratee.

The reader-response theorists (now we are talking about those critics who for ease of categorization are placed within the canon of disparate texts which is known as reader-response theory) Michael Riffaterre and Jonathan Culler are related to structuralist traditions of reading. Like Wolfgang Iser and Stanley Fish they accept that the meaning of a literary text cannot be separated from the role taken by the reader. Their work responds to new criticism's insistence that meaning rests in and with the text waiting for a reader to uncover it. Fish along with Culler was one of several Anglo-American critics influenced by ideas in European continental philosophies during the 1960s and 1970s. Fish's reader-response theory proposes that all readers are part of interpretative communities which train the reader into a shared set of expectations about how a text should be read and what it might mean. Influenced by Culler's later interest in deconstruction, Fish concludes that it is the task of the critic to examine the rules and conventions of any interpretative community which determines the outcome of a reading. The importance placed on the reader by structuralism and reader-response theory at this historical juncture is particularly significant because such an approach to reading challenged the traditional hierarchies of authority in which students were told how to read by teachers who had 'mastered' the text by cracking the author's/text's hidden code of meaning. Stressing the active participation of the reader in producing meaning rather than the importance of the author or teacher was a considerable subversion of authority. No doubt such reader-response theories were shaped by the political spirit of the 1960s and 1970s just as much as they offered intellectual support to intellectual radicals.

As an example of what reader-response theory looks like we might usefully contrast two essays by so-called 'reception theorists', which roughly treat the same subject. Michael Riffaterre's essay, 'Describing Poetic Structures: Two Approaches to Baudelaire's "Les Chats"' (*LT*, 149–61), is a good example of the crossover between structuralism (here semiotics) and formalism. This essay is a criticism of the linguist Roman Jakobson and the anthropologist Claude Lévi-Strauss's reading of a poem by Baudelaire. While Riffaterre shares Jakobson's formalist view of poetry as a special use of language he argues that the linguistic features identified by Jakobson and Lévi-Strauss could not be perceived even by informed readers and so their account of the poem is invalid because it fails to recognize that literary meaning depends upon the reader's response to the text. Instead Riffaterre proposes a reading of the poem which only takes account of those aspects of the poem which a succession of readers throughout history have responded to. The fact that various readers (including what he calls the 'superreader' such as poets, critics and translators) have responded to these aspects of language shows their significance. However, Riffaterre remains formalist enough to insist that the reader's response is only evidence of the presence of poetic meaning in a text. Meaning remains a property of the words on the page and is not constructed by the reader. The problem for Riffaterre is his inability to explain why the linguistic features noted by Jakobson and Lévi-Strauss are not evidence of poetic meaning.

German *Rezeptionstheorie* [reception theory] is only one strand of the many theories of reader response but is often thought of as a metonym for the whole field. It might be useful to think of reception theory as a moment in the history of European philosophy's interest in questions of the literary. Like deconstruction, it is informed by the European tradition of philosophical phenomenology which proposes that the object of philosophical investigation is the contents of consciousness. Phenomenology (the study of phenomena) is interested in how phenomena (that which appear) are perceived and understood. The reading process is then an obvious point of departure for such a study. The reception theory of German critics like Hans-Robert Jauss and Wolfgang Iser takes its lead from a tradition of German phenomenological interest in literature leading from the philosophers Edmund Husserl and Martin Heidegger to Hans-Georg Gadamer and the Geneva School of phenomenological criticism which included the American J. Hillis Miller (later a significant voice in deconstruction). Gadamer's version of hermeneutics (the science of interpretation) is particularly important for reception theory because it stresses that interpretations of literature arise out of a dialogue between past and present readings.

Hans-Robert Jauss's essay, 'The Poetic Text Within the Changes of Horizons of Reading' (*LT*, 162–78), is another account of a poem by Baudelaire. Like Riffaterre's reading Jauss's description of his moment-by-moment responses to the text as it opens out before him offers him a way of providing a detailed close stylistic analysis like the formalist New Critics while paying attention to the active participation of the reader in the production of meaning. In the second half of this essay we can see the emphasis Jauss places on history in the construction of literary meaning and the conditioning of a reader's response to a text. He argues that while different historical periods may have their own dominant interpretations of a text the meaning of a text lies in the fusion of these different interpretations over time. Similar to Riffaterre's version of different readers picking up on significant points in a poem and thereby singling out these points as constitutive of the poem's meaning, Jauss thinks of literary meaning as a coming together of all the points of interest remarked upon by readers at various historical moments. Once again the problem with such an approach is the difficulty it has in dealing with an idiosyncratic interpretation of a text by a single reader.

While many of the arguments made in these essays may be familiar to you from your reading of other theoretical approaches, and reader-response theory (if such a thing exists) is no longer as significant a theoretical force as it once was, these texts are still worth reading. Firstly, they are exemplary in their subtle and detailed close reading of texts. Secondly, they show the importance of the reader in the construction of meaning. Thirdly, they are pivotal texts in the development of ideas about the literary and indicate the ways in which the question of the reader has taken up a dominant place in literary theory. Fourthly, they are proof that any theoretical category is not a conceptually unified critical position but consists of conflicting knowledge which are influenced by (and influence) other areas of thought.

NOTES TOWARDS A READING OF MRS DALLOWAY

Given what I've just said about the impossibility of identifying a unified critical position, let us now attempt something risky, if not foolhardy, which is to 'apply' this so-called approach (which is not, of course, an approach as such) to one of our canonical texts, *Mrs Dalloway* by Virginia Woolf. The novel's opening will suffice to demonstrate the issues involved in reader-response theory:

> Mrs Dalloway said she would buy the flowers herself.
> For Lucy had her work cut out for her. The doors would be taken off their hinges; Rumpelmeyer's men were coming. (*MD*, 3)

What are we to make of this? Firstly, we might be puzzled about the connection or lack of a connection between these sentences. The first sentence stands as a paragraph on its own, which is unusual in a piece of prose. It is certainly not the way we would expect, say, a newspaper report to begin. The opening two words 'Mrs Dalloway' is a repetition of the title of the book; add this fact to the relative abruptness of the first paragraph and we can assume that we are experiencing certain literary conventions. The book does not explicitly state that this is a fiction but we as readers begin to piece together meaning as we proceed through the text and work on the assumption that it is both fictional and literary. Consider the opening line, 'Mrs Dalloway said she would buy the flowers herself.' Who is speaking here? Is it a third-person narrator reporting the indirect speech of Mrs Dalloway? We might assume so on first encountering the sentence. However, if we read a little further the passage quoted above is followed by 'And then thought Clarissa Dalloway, what a morning – fresh as if issued to children on a beach'. This is puzzling. We seem to have a moment of direct speech (or at least direct thought) 'what a morning – fresh as if issued to children on a beach'. However, there are none of the grammatical markers of standard prose which indicate this – there are no inverted commas for example. Re-reading the opening line we might question whether this is in fact a straightforward case of indirect speech. The confusion suggests that we are dealing with a specifically literary text and a little knowledge of the literary canon will tell us that we are reading a piece of modernist prose. This mode of writing is called free indirect style, in which the thoughts of characters are reported as part of the narratorial voice.

Piecing together this information has involved a good deal of assumption and inference (much of it unconscious) on the part of the reader. The reader draws out implicit connections in a text, constructing meaning from the gaps. To use Wolfgang Iser's term, the reader 'concretizes' the literary work, piecing language into meaning from the cues presented by the text. In order to do this the reader must draw upon his or her own knowledge of the world and of literature in general. For example, we are happy to collude with the telepathic fantasy of the narratorial voice when the unspoken thoughts of Clarissa Dalloway are reported. This is a literary convention. However, by the time we have read this opening we have also positioned Mrs Dalloway in terms of social class. She says that she will buy the flowers herself. We infer that this is not the normal situation – if she bought flowers all the time it would not be an issue. The fact that she is going to buy 'the' flowers suggests that the flowers are for a special occasion. The purchasing of flowers is itself an act of excess, demonstrating Mrs Dalloway's disposable income – she is not buying potatoes or rice for example. The opening word of the novel, 'Mrs', already suggests that she is a married woman and, depending on the historical context of the novel which we also piece together as we proceed, will have the responsibility of running a house. The fact that she does not usually buy 'the' flowers herself indicates her wealth and social position. The relationship between Mrs Dalloway and Lucy can now be worked out. It would seem that Lucy would normally buy the flowers but she is too busy today. Lucy could have been Mrs Dalloway's daughter or sister or lover but rather she has her 'work' cut out and would appear to be a servant. Such an inference is made on the basis of our knowledge of Edwardian society, even though nothing to date in this novel actually confirms that its setting is Edwardian. The fact that the 'doors would be taken off' suggests a special occasion, perhaps a party, while the informed reader will know that Rumpleymeyer & Co. was a furniture removal firm trading from 72–73 St James' Street, Westminster, London at the time the novel was written. Both of these 'cues' encourages the reader to make certain inferences about Mrs Dalloway's class and the nature of the event in preparation.

The connections between these phrases and sentences I have supplied here are, in part, derived from the unavoidable knowledge of having read the entire novel, or at least of having some prior knowledge of the text and its author. Read out of such context the reader may very well actualize these sentences in a different way. For example, the opening sentence might suggest that Mrs Dalloway was on her way to a funeral, perhaps that of Lucy's husband or other relation. Lucy could be busy preparing the house for guests at the wake. Rumpelmeyer's men might be coming to the funeral or could be thugs sent round by the notorious Rumpelmeyer to collect a debt from the dead husband and so on. So far, this reading is not inconsistent with the facts as we know them but would have to be revised as we progress through the novel, gathering more information about Mrs Dalloway and Lucy. Wolfgang Iser would argue that the reading process is always a dynamic one in which the work is made up of 'indeterminacies', moments that depend for their effect on readerly interpretation and which can therefore be read or interpreted in different and possibly conflicting ways. The more information a text gives the greater its indeterminacies. This may be the result of a complex narrative, as in the case of *Mrs Dalloway*, or as a consequence of suggestive and poetic language, as in a drama like *The Tempest*. When Prospero says 'this thing of darkness I acknowledge mine', we might infer that he is talking about Caliban. However, the richness of the language will evoke different responses from different readers, who will each read the phrase in different ways. Does Prospero refer to Caliban, his magic, his island, his specific treatment of Caliban, his colonialism and so forth? The language of *The Tempest* thus opens the text onto greater indeterminacies just as the reader attempts to close off indeterminacies (make the text more determinate) by constructing meaning from the possible different interpretations open to the reader by any given cue.

QUESTIONS FOR FURTHER CONSIDERATION

1. In what ways does a specific interest in the reader alter the traditional model of literary criticism?
2. How does reader-response theory's understanding of language differ from that of structuralism or poststructuralism?
3. What debts do other theoretical approaches (such as deconstruction or feminism) owe to reader-response theory?
4. Reader-response theorists tend to prefer prose or poetry in their writing. What challenges does a play like *The Tempest* present to reader-response theory?
5. What historical differences might exist between a present-day reading of *Mrs Dalloway* and that offered by a reader contemporaneous with the novel?
6. What are the salient features of the implied reader of *Mrs Dalloway*?

ANNOTATED BIBLIOGRAPHY

Barthes, Roland. 'The Death of the Author'. *Image-Music-Text*, trans. Stephen Heath. London, 1977.
One of the most important (and shortest – eight pages) pieces of criticism you will ever read. Barthes argues that while the reader is actively involved in the construction of meaning, the author by comparison does not control how meaning is produced in the moment a text is in general circulation. Once a text is being read by readers who interpret it in different ways the author (as a producer of meaning) is effectively dead.
de Man, Paul. *Allegories of Reading: Figural Language in Rousseau, Nietzsche, Rilke, and Proust.* New Haven, CT, 1979.
A difficult but endlessly rewarding account of how reading is figured by the play of language within a text. As such meaning is said to be arbitrary and beyond the control of the reader as well as the author. De Man's version of deconstruction offers a consideration of phenomenology and consciousness beyond reader-response theory's constrained understanding of language. See the entries on this title in the bibliographies for the chapters on deconstruction and poststructuralism.
Eco, Umberto. *The Role of The Reader: Explorations in the Semiotics of Texts.* Bloomington, IN, 1979.
Like Barthes' later work, Eco makes a distinction between 'writerly' (or closed) texts which limit the possibilities of interpretation and offer a fixed meaning to the reader (e.g. Superman comics or James Bond novels) and 'readerly' (or open) texts which depend upon the active participation of the reader in the production of meaning (e.g. *Finnegans Wake*).
Fish, Stanley. *Is There A Text in This Class? The Authority of Interpretative Communities.* Cambridge, MA, 1980.
All of Fish's reader-response essays collected in one volume. He argues that any reader is part of a community of readers and their response to a text will be determined by the conventions of reading within which he or she is educated in a given socio-historical context.
Freund, Elizabeth. *The Return of the Reader: Reader-Response Criticism.* London, 1987.
A detailed but concise and accessible account of the canon of texts known as reader-response theory. Starting with I. A. Richards and the New Critics the study goes on to introduce the work of Culler, Fish, Holland and Iser. Freund's introduction relates the question of the reader to other theoretical approaches.

SUPPLEMENTARY BIBLIOGRAPHY

Barthes, Roland. *S/Z*, trans. Richard Howard. New York, 1974.
Bennett, Andrew, ed. *Readers and Reading*. London, 1995.
Bleich, David. *Subjective Criticism*. Baltimore, MD, 1978.
Brooks, Peter. *Reading for the Plot: Design and Intention in Narrative.* Oxford, 1984.
Crosman, Inge, and Susan R. Suleiman, eds. *The Reader in the Text: Essays on Audience and Interpretation.* Princeton, NJ, 1980.
Culler, Jonathan. *On Deconstruction: Theory and Criticism After Structuralism.* Ithaca, NY, 1982.
Docherty, Thomas. *Reading Absent Character: Towards a Theory of Characterization in Fiction.* Oxford, 1983.
Gadamer, Hans-Georg. *Truth and Method*, trans. Garrett Barden and John Cumming. New York, 1975.
Holland, Norman. *5 Readers Reading*. New Haven, CT, 1975.
Holub, Robert C. *Reception Theory: A Critical Introduction.* London, 1984.
Howendahl, Peter Uwe. *The Institution of Criticism.* Ithaca, NY, 1982.
Iser, Wolfgang. *The Implied Reader: Patterns of Communication in Prose Fiction from Bunyan to Beckett.* Baltimore, MD, 1974.

————. *The Act of Reading: A Theory of Aesthetic Response*. Baltimore, MD, 1978.

————. *Prospecting: From Reader-Response to Literary Anthropology*. Baltimore, MD, 1989.

————. *Toward an Aesthetic of Reception*, trans. T. Bahti. Brighton, 1982.

Jauss, Hans-Robert. *Aesthetic Experience and Literary Hermeneutics*. Minneapolis, MN, 1982.

Miller, J. Hillis. *The Ethics of Reading: Kant, de Man, Eliot, Trollope, James, and Benjamin*. New York, 1987.

Orr, Leonard. 'Reception-aesthetics as a Tool in Literary Criticism and Historiography', *Language Quarterly*, 21: 3/4 (1983).

Prince, Gerald. 'Introduction to the Study of the Narratee', *Poétique*, 14, 1973.

Richards, I. A. *Practical Criticism*. London, 1964.

Riffaterre, Michael. *Semiotics of Poetry*. London, 1978.

Riquelme, John Paul. 'The Ambivalence of Reading', *Diacritics*, 10: 2, 1980.

Scholes, Robert. 'Cognition and the Implied Reader', *Diacritics*, 5: 3, 1975.

Thomas, Brook. 'Reading Wolfgang Iser or Responding to a Theory of Response', *Comparative Literature Studies*, 19, 1982.

Tompkins, Jane P., ed. *Reader-Response Criticism: From Formalism to Post-Structuralism*. Baitimore, MD, 1981.

Weber, Samuel. 'Caught in the Act of Reading', *Demarcating the Disciplines: Philosophy, Literature, Art*, ed. Samuel Weber. Minneapolis, MN, 1986.

Wimsatt, Jnr, W. K., and Monroe C. Beardsley. 'The Affective Fallacy', rpt. in W. K. Wimsatt, *The Verbal Icon: Studies in the Meaning of Poetry*. London, 1970.

CHAPTER

6

THE SELF, THE OTHER AND THE TEXT: PSYCHOANALYTIC CRITICISM

Jill Barker

Both literary criticism and psychoanalysis engage in the interpretation of texts – the former explicates or comments on texts which have been crafted and (usually) published. The latter uses artlessly spoken texts, which are treated by the analyst as a source of information about the unconscious mind of the speaker, and used therapeutically. Both disciplines thus seek for a meaning beyond the immediately apparent context of the texts, both seek an enhanced understanding, though with different goals.

Psychoanalysis and psychoanalytic literary criticism both pose one of the largest general questions the human race ever attempts to consider: 'Who am I?' They follow that up with a pair of subsidiary questions: 'How did I become that?' and 'What price am I paying to be that?' In answering these questions, an extensive group of analytic and critical practices can be developed. For the literary critic in particular there is a further question to address: 'What, within the text, counts as the "I" who is asking these questions?' (*The Tempest*, and Peter Greenaway's film version, *Prospero's Books*, will be especially helpful in considering this last issue.) Clearly, these three questions are not a complete description of psychoanalytic literary criticism, but if they are carefully thought through along the lines that I will sketch out, they will take any reader a long way into the analysis of any text. Later I will look at Shakespeare's *The Tempest*, but to begin with I want to demonstrate that these ways of thinking can be productive for any work of literature. Continuing to use general terms, then, we can say that psychoanalysis begins its own specific investigation of these questions along the following lines.

The first question: 'Who am I?' is a question about identity: about the nature of the self. One inevitable answer to this question is 'I am that which speaks', or (to paraphrase that) 'I am that which uses language'. Without language use, the question itself cannot be asked, so any being that asks that question is by definition a speaker (or a writer – see the section on Derrida) – at any rate, a language user. Selfhood is known as subjectivity. That answer allows us to consider the nature of language, and what language-use does to its users. Language is not needed unless something is absent but nevertheless imaginable. Following from that answer, then, is the important subsidiary perception: a being that uses language is constructed out of loss, and loss in turn is inextricably linked with desire. It is only in the absence of a desired object that language becomes necessary, and through the use of language that a self comes into existence. The form of that existence (that subjectivity) is both desiring and linguistic. Furthermore, the self is not a single, consistent entity, but a divided or multiple self located within and constructed by its many different discourses.

The answer to the second question ('How did I become that?') is for every self (i.e. every speaking subject) something like the personal history of the loss out of which both language use and desire both came. It is the personal version of a more general situation recognized by both Freud and Lacan, namely that the self appears when the infant is deprived of absolute possession of its desired object (referred to as the mother) by a figure of authority (referred to as the Father). Freud's famous 'Oedipal triangle' of mother–father–child involves a dynamic of denial and loss, compensated by the acquisition of language. Language takes the place of the lost object of desire. Lacan's essay on 'The Mirror Phase' (*Écrits*, 1977) explains this in greater detail.

The price paid for selfhood as a linguistic existence (subjectivity) is a submission to the laws and structures of language, to the loss and the resulting sense of division in the self, and to the endless unachievability of the desired object. Clearly such a cost must generate discomfort in the psyche. The price also involves the creation of an abjected other to the self: an aspect of selfhood which one finds unacceptable, and so casts out, projecting it onto some other creature. One can see Caliban in *The Tempest* as an abjected other – a creature who is perceived as containing all the characteristics that the 'virtuous' humans deny possessing. Thus our wish to see ourselves as unified subjects contains an inherent misrecognition: an act of bad faith or of repression of unwanted desires.

Freud uses the term 'screen memories' (*SE*, III, 1903) for the memories that conceal significant earlier events: within both the literary text and the discursive text of psychoanalysis, the other is displayed (screened) as in a cinema – at a distance from its origin, and also hidden (screened) from view behind the metaphoric duplicities of language. Yet the qualities of this 'other' are of great importance, since the self is projected into/onto the other and formed in relation to it. The function and significance of the divisions within the subject can be addressed using the fundamental Lacanian concepts of loss, desire and the three 'orders' of the psychic structure as they occur within language (The Real, the Imaginary and the Symbolic).

James M. Mellard, writing on Virginia Woolf, discusses Lacan's categories very clearly and helpfully in relation to *To the Lighthouse* (*LT*, 233–60). First, however, some details about Freudian therapeutic practice are necessary to understand Freud's terms when they are applied to textual analysis. The 'talking cure' developed by Sigmund Freud assumed that the patient's stream of unchecked speech ('free association'), especially including reported dreams, could provide the therapist with metaphoric clues to the discords within the unconscious mind which were causing the patient's physical (and therefore psychic) symptoms. Anxieties and repressed material could be represented metaphorically or metonymically, by processes of 'condensation' or 'displacement'. In this way dreams 'screen' the unconscious mind, in both senses of the word. Dreams also constituted a process, the 'dream work', with which the subject dealt with those conflicts by reflecting on them at a non-literal and therefore tolerable level. For Freud, and for later psychoanalysis generally, mind and body interact closely. Language thus gives a kind of oblique access not just to that area, of the mind which is outside conscious control but also to knowledge which is outside awareness, and especially to events which are lost to memory. Like a screen and like a code it both conceals and reveals the subject, hiding the history of a psychic state in language which, read subtly, narrates the events of the subject's construction. Symptoms in the present are read by Freud as a coded repetition of past traumas or frustrations, now repressed from consciousness. The fact of their repetition is an indicator of their importance in the patient's mind. Significantly, repetition is also a feature of literary language – it may occur as rhyme, as a sustained set of images or as a recurring structural motif – in any form, it can be read in a Freudian manner, as indicating something to which we as readers need to pay attention. (Greenaway, for example, picks up repeated references to the elements in *The Tempest*, and uses water to develop one aspect of his reading of the play.) The early 'analyses' were narrated by Freud in his case studies, such as 'Dora' ([1901] *SE*, XVII, 1905) and 'The Wolf Man' (*SE*, XVII, 1918), while the conceptual bases for the therapy were developed within and alongside those essays in works such as *Jokes and Their Relation to the Unconscious* (*SE*, VIII, 1905) and *Some Psychical Consequences of the Anatomical Distinction Between the Sexes* (*SE*, XIX, 1925). In publications ranging over more than thirty years, language, narrative and subjectivity are simultaneously both the object of study and the means by which psychoanalysis reaches its objective. The discourse of the unconscious is read with attention to many of the same features that literary critics consider – repetitions, metaphor (condensation) and metonymy (displacement). This textual focus by psychoanalysts has made it an appropriate resource for literary criticism: Wright (1984), Barry (1995, 96–120) and Vice (1996) discuss the similarities at greater length.

A set of more-or-less experimental therapeutic praxes and a collection of theories about the nature of the mind and of language (and their intersection) form the unstable, disputed but nevertheless hugely influential foundation of psychoanalysis. Psychoanalytic theory is itself multiple: Freud's opinions chan-ged during his lifetime, and those theories in turn were taken up with differing emphases by disciples who developed and reinterpreted them: Jungians, Klei-nians, ego psychologists, Gestalt theorists, and Lacanians are just a few of the major schools of psychoanalytic thought, each of which deserves study in its own right. All of these multiple sets of ways of reading that constitute 'psycho-analytic literary theory' are concerned with the nature of subjectivity, and with the subject's emotional orientation towards figures from the outside world, reconstituted as aspects of the mental world. Thus reconstructing the world afresh, the subject is at a remove from (an otherwise inaccessible) reality, in ways which resemble Foucauldian concepts of the social construction of mean-ing as well as feminist 'constructionist' gendering.

Although Freud used literature and his own interpretations of literary texts (notably Sophocles' *Oedipus Rex* and Shakespeare's *Hamlet*, but also E. T. A. Hoffman's 'The Sandman') to elucidate points about the organization of (and processes within) the unconscious mind, early attempts to apply Freud's theories to literature did not produce particularly sophisticated insights.

For Freud, desire and the loss of the object of desire are crucially bound up with sexuality and gendering and with emotional maturation, and these in turn with the identity of the speaking subject, again generating intersections and interactions between psychoanalytic literary criticism, feminism, structuralism and deconstruction. Psychoanalytic literary theory is involved in a ceaseless set of exchanges with each of these, as they are with one another, in ways which can be conflictual as much as cooperative. Barthesian theories of the death of the author mesh with structuralist theories of the signifier and of the text as a social product. There is no longer a clear connection between the author's intention in writing a text and the reader's interpretation of that text. For this reason the early twentieth-century psychoanalytic approach of 'psychoanalyzing' the characters or of interpreting the text as a manifestation of the original author's subjectivity, though still occasionally used, is not appropriate to a postmodern perception of the detached, contingent nature of textual interpretation. I will not discuss that kind of character analysis further here, but interested readers may refer to Barry (1995, 96–108).

A considerably more sophisticated approach is to view texts as cultural products, containing their own subjectivity which resides in the text itself. It is the text which manifests anxieties, immaturities or neuroses. Literature has been described as doing the dreaming of the culture, and as Freud observed, psychic work takes place in dreams, helping to sort out and to express that which is repressed from the conscious mind. Thus my reading of *The Tempest* (below) is not interested in any psychic investment Shakespeare may have had in 'his' text, nor in the characters as such, except as they represent aspects of the text's subjectivity. In considering the transference and counter-transference and its fluidities, psychoanalytic theory is close to Barthes' view of the *scriptible* (Barthes, 1970), where rival discourses discern various meanings within the text, depending on their own agendas. Reader-response theory, too, draws on both structuralist and psychoanalytic assumptions.

This chapter next focuses on one of the most substantial and radical rereadings of Freud: that of Jacques Lacan (1901–81), whose school of thought has been stimulating and productive for literary criticism since the mid-1970s. Lacan's re-reading focused on Freud's texts in terms of language and meaning, where previously they had been seen as to do with the mind and the body. In theorizing that the unconscious is structured like a language, Lacan brought Freud's theories into an area where they could be understood using the concepts of Saussure and the structural linguists. He thus reclaimed them for poststructuralist approaches, while never losing touch with the theoretical concerns which they also addressed. Lacan's thought was disseminated through the training Seminar for students of psychoanalysis, which he conducted from 1954 to 1980. Access to the written version of the Seminar was for long occluded, complex and disputed, and power struggles over access to Lacan's notes or to pirate copies of the Seminar delayed publication. The translation of Lacan's allusive and complex prose into English further delayed access, and the massive French *Écrits* appeared in English at less than half the length, as *Écrits: A Selection*. Other good translations, notably by Wilden (1981), give more comprehensible access to further sessions of the Seminar. Students will find a guide such as Wright (1984) or Bowie (1991) helpful for exploring Lacan's notoriously obscure writing in greater depth.

Freud had found that human development – the achievement of mature subjectivity – involved the establishment of specific objects of desire and an acceptance of loss as imposed by external constraints. Because desire both seeks its goal and is blocked from its goal, it becomes deflected towards substitute goals (objects). For Freud these objects tend to be read as real, even though the movement from one real object to another reality may be reached via a pun (that is, via language). A classic example is the well known 'glanz auf der Nase' bilingual pun where the prohibition of an English-speaking child from looking at the nursemaid's nose (glance at the nose) becomes in the German-speaking adult an eroticized desire for a woman with a shiny nose (*Glanz auf der Nase*). It is this conceptualized image of a substitute object of desire that Lacan calls the *objet petit a* (the small 'o' other, so-called because French for 'other' is 'autre'). That which opposes the subject's initial desire is the Law of the Father, which is similar to the Other (with a capital O), occasionally rather enchantingly translated as 'the big Other'. *The Tempest* involves one of the most comprehensive analyses of desire imaginable. Every character in the play is in a condition of having lost a desired object, or of being actively in search of one, and all are under the control of the massive paternalistic authority of Prospero, who creates the world which they inhabit and within which the power of their desire is used to manipulate them. For these reasons, and also because he is the teacher of Miranda and Caliban, Prospero functions as the Law of the Father and so is the source of all language and meaning on the Island. Even he, however, has a history of deprivation and loss which constructs him (in his turn) as a desiring subject. One might, only half jokingly, see the difficulties over publication of Lacan's Seminar as constructing Lacan (like Pospero) in the field of the Other, and his writings (like Prospero's created island-world) as an *objet petit a*. Ignominious as the comparison may seem, both Trinculo's drunken crew and the would-be translators and editors of Lacan, furthermore, are not unlike a primal horde as they wrangle over the masculine inheritance of the Law of the Father.

I referred above to the Oedipal triangle of mother–father–child. The mother is commonly a desired other but, because already claimed by the Father, un-attainable to the infant. Explicit desire for her must be repressed, screened from the conscious mind, for fear of the Father's retribution. She therefore becomes symbolized as an object of desire within the unconscious mind by some other term. Processes of condensation and displacement which may be experiential (looking at the beloved nurse) or linguistic (glance/*Glanz*) or both generate this alternative screening term, behind which the mother/object is concealed (the bizarrely sexy shiny nose). Recent psychoanalytic theorists indicate this psychic location by the term (m)Other, indicating both the mother (who is the initial desire both of the subject and also of the Father) and the impossibility of that desire – thus the structure of the term 'mother' contains within it the structures of denial and loss: of the necessity for the substitution of an *objet petit a* for the original object of desire. All this is contained in the sign '(m)Other', In accepting the Law of the Father there are gains as well as losses, as the infant moves out of the Imaginary state (with its deceptive oceanic sense of unity of the self) into the Symbolic order where semiotic structures (especially but not exclusively lan-guage) are possible. Narrating the difference between the Imaginary and the Symbolic as a transitional sequence can give the impression that one model supersedes the other, but ideally the three orders need to be conceptualized as coexisting and even as interpenetrating one another on occasion. The psyche has different *kinds* of access to the Imaginary and the Symbolic orders, while the Real is outside psychic experiences because exterior to representation of any kind.

It can be argued that Lacan generates a poststructuralist reading of Freud. On the one hand psychoanalysis seems to be intrinsically and originally a struc-turalist interpretation of the nature of texts, language and the subjectivities within these semiotic systems. In its use of terms of irreducible and mutually defining opposition (subject/object etc.) and its totalizing construction of the orders of the Imaginary, the Symbolic and the Real, Lacanian theory is fundamentally structuralist, no matter how far discussion may complicate and sophisticate those terms. Counter-claims are made that the Lacanian view of the Real as outside language, and of subjectivity as decentred from an 'essential' self gives it poststructuralist credentials, allowing a participation in (rather than a subjection to) the deconstructive turn. This debate is focused in *The Purloined Poe* (1988) where both Derrida and Johnson see psychoanalysis as subject to the deconstructive turn. Wright (1984) agrees. Žižek (1989) most persuasively sees psychoanalysis as poststructuralist. Lacan refers ambiguously to the 'desire of the Other': most simply, the subject's desire for the Other, but also the desire (for something else) experienced by the Other. The self thus (a) desires the other, (b) desires to be the Other, and (c) shares the desire of the Other for some object, which is a third term in the triad of desire. In its third form, the phrase 'desire of the Other' also indicates the insistence by the Law of the Father that it be heard within the Imaginary, an urgency generated by definition because the very existence of the Imaginary poses a barrier for the Other: a moment when (or a place where) it experiences lack and so, inevitably, desire. Žižek sees that one implication of what he calls 'the lack in the Other' is that an unnameable (and so extra-structural) transcendent term disrupts the apparently closed structure outlined by Lacan's three orders. Discovering such a lack depends on using the 'Other' flexibly, as a subject in its own right, as well as a force outside the subject. One might follow Žižek by seeing Prospero as the lacking/desiring Other when he seeks and is satisfied by his revenge. But if his brother Alonso's repentance can supply the 'lack in the Other', has it not also named that lack, and so reclaimed it for the structures of analysis? Paradoxes like this make psychoanalytic criticism both tricky and satisfying. In a more complex way, Prospero seems to desire Ariel's constant presence and approval – a state he achieves by naming and seemingly endlessly deferring Ariel's desire for freedom.

Lacan's strongly visual imagination is manifested in his use of elaborate diagrams which, in purporting to explain, tease the reader with the offer of clarity while actually delivering further obscurity and so a further demand for interpretation. In general these schemata of Lacan's such as the schema L (Lacan, 1977, 193) or schema R (197) are useless without extended additional explanation, thus plunging back into the linguistic condition from which they seem to hold out the possibility of transcendence and escape. Lacan's diction is often also spatio-mathematical: a psychic event may take place 'in the field' of some specified concept, where another writer might say something like 'in the context' or 'under the umbrella'. A formulation such as 'field', while sustaining that sense of physical location which pervades psychoanalytic conceptualization, additionally invokes both mathematical terminology and the idea of magnetic fields of force. Equally significantly, it recalls Jakobson's structuralist-linguistic discussion of the 'axes' along which metaphor and metonymy move. Where Freud saw a divided consciousness, Lacan sees a linguistic subject existing in and divided by language. Stephen Heath, in his essay on 'Difference' (*LT*, 211–32), is concerned with the moment of that division and the awareness of 'difference' which constitutes it, a moment narrated by Caliban's personal history. Such difference may involve gender, certainly, but also that which imposes division of the subject from the other: the phallus. Caliban's outcast condition defines him as the abjected other, and it was his attempt to wield a literal phallus (attacking Miranda) that brought the weight of Prospero's anger as the Law of the Father upon him. He is redefined in a way which focuses on his linguistic status, as he who has 'learned to curse'.

The 'gaze' is variously considered by Heath ('Difference', *LT*, 211–32), Freud and Lacan. Heath's essay begins with ways in which the relation between the subject and the other involves the gaze, and how the gaze produces conclusions of a deceptive certainty, eliding the degree to which what is seen is already contained within interpretative social structures – the viewer sees that which social structures dictate is there to be seen, in this case sexual difference. Freud had already identified the 'scopic drive' and the importance of seeing to infant psychic development (see, for example, 'The Uncanny': *SE* XVII, 1919) and had referred to the unconscious mind as 'ein andere Schauplatz' – an alternative theatre-stage). Again, Lacan's most frequently cited essay is 'The Mirror Stage' (*Écrits*, 1977), a discussion of the infantile misidentification of the self as unified, through viewing its reflection in a mirror. It is at least in part through this interpretative gaze, distinguishing field and ground, that the gazer-subject foreshadows entry into the sense of an arbitrary division from other(s) and an illusory wholeness of self which the Symbolic order, and thus language, constitutes. The theme of reflections, of concealment, of licit and illicit viewings, of *trompe l'œuil*, pervades psycho-analytic literary criticism, and produces an interpretation of the visions in dramas as continuous with verbalised language, both being capable of representing unconscious states metaphorically.

It is therefore not surprising that Lacanian theory was first transmitted to the English-speaking world through the work of film-theorists to whom it offered ways of theorising their medium at an academic and critical level of sophistication. Through the 1970s the journal *Screen* functioned as a critical forum for discussions of contemporary French philosophy and of its development within film theory. With the increasing availability of English translations of Lacan's works, discussions broadened to literary criticism more generally.

From its inception, it was apparent that psychoanalysis was not just problematic, but also productive and inescapable for feminists. Responses vary from as early as Julia Kristeva ('About Chinese Women' (in Moi, 1974), and a large corpus of writing through Mitchell (1982) and Gallop (1982) to Doane ('Woman's Stake: Filming the Female Body', in Vice, 1996). The Freudian concepts of castration and penis-envy raise problems for feminism since Freud's discussion of the process of emotional maturation is unequivocally gendered. Yet his view depends on perceiving woman as lack (of the phallus). For Lacan the phallus, though still powerfully metaphorized by the penis, has become a transcendent term: it can be whatever enforces rules, and hence the structuring of the meaning (the Symbolic order).

Heath observes what this means for Lacan when the latter uses visual modes: interpreting such objects as the Bernini statue, or the child's view of sexual organs, observing flaws in Lacan's assumption that seeing and knowing are the same thing. By definition, the entry of the (masculine) subject into the

Symbolic order involves a sight of the female as absence (as a lack), in terms of the absence of the phallus. Often it seems that, for Lacan, difference within the subject is precisely the difference between man and woman, and subjectivity depends on locating the woman as other (the object of desire) but also within the Other (the rule-giver). Lacan uses discourse which does not locate itself in relation to gender: which, in implicitly believing itself in relation to gender, ignores its own assumptions of authority and masculinity. Heath clarifies how Lacan's most significant perceptions locate the important area of difference within language, where the subject is constituted. Here the subject's lack is enacted, not in relation to biological detail, but in relation to the *idea* of a plenitude of meaning which language (and the Other) appear to promise but cannot supply. Insofar as *The Tempest* considers all characters to be both lacking (and so desiring), it places lack indiscriminately within both the masculine and the feminine domains. If the island, the Imaginary world, is a location of lack but also of the free-play of creativity, it may be read as having strongly feminine aspects. That lability in turn is masked by Prospero's apparent control of all the apparitions through spells and physical violence, and therefore through the Symbolic order, subservient to the Law of the Father. There are different ways of perceiving these relationships, each of which can be persuasively argued, as I shall show later. If the other as loss is the same as the abjected other, we are driven to associate that with Caliban, who is reviled on racial, sexual and class grounds and described as having lost his chance of humanity. Prospero also denies him the opportunity to become a father, ('I had peopled else/This isle with Calibans': *T*, I.ii, 350–1), effectively castrating him. The more firmly one can repudiate an 'other', finding it disgusting or monstrous, the more strongly one's sense of self is reassured. We must ask then, what it is in Prospero that needs to keep this abjected other always in his presence, always carrying the weight of Prospero's contempt as he carries the weights of firewood. Linguistically, Caliban's curses and lewd suggestions rebound language back at Prospero, reformed with a power which is not his, and which he cannot silence (as a symbolic castration). If Caliban is screening Prospero's psychic conflicts, as the abjected other screens the desire of the Father/Other, it would be worthwhile to analyze the content of Prospero's contempt.

The symbolizing psychic structure put forward by Lacan both depends on, and exists in tension with, that 'essential' physical feature of different genitalia which culture uses to divide masculine from feminine in terms of 'loss'. That particular interpretation is itself a cultural construct, and there are many moments in Lacan's writing where he fails to see this. An insistent return to the physical, without a perception that it too is a cultural construct (a vision), can only destabilize the theory he has built upon it of the mind in the Symbolic order. It is imperative also to reverse the chain of thought and see the phallus as a figure for, or a signifier of, that (undefined) loss which is inherently a part of humanity *as a linguistic entity*. Heath observes that the Foucauldian circumstances to do with power relations which construct a view of the female as a view of lack have been silenced. Hysteria can be seen as a refusal to take up that position of the not-male. Instead, Freudian psychoanalysis sees such symptoms as supporting and confirming its own theoretical structures. Woman is thus not construed as a speaking subject, except when producing the kinds of meaning that psychoanalysis as a dominant discourse has empowered itself to hear and to 'cure': the very meanings that it sees as direct access to the unconscious. In those terms, Caliban is in the position of the hysteric – using wild language that defies the Father and refusing to accept his construction in abjection. Lacan's linguistic theory might offer solutions to the problematic of an apparent essentialism in much of Freudian and Lacanian discussion, while acknowledging that theorizing the relationship between the body and the Symbolic order can lead to a chicken-and-egg situation: either our insertion into language depends on physical difference, or our perception of physical difference stems from our semiotic (linguistic) capacities to understand what we see. Which came first is very much a political question. As suggested above, one solution is to recognize that even the body is only present to the gaze through the culturally constructed conventions of interpretation – of, in fact, the already-existing Symbolic order.

The idea of subjectivity in the text can be taken further, using the entire text as a model of the psychic structures of the subject, such that the characters in it are metaphoric divisions within the subject. Thus in this version, Prospero *is* 'the Other' and the Father of the Symbolic order within the text's psychic structure, with the Island inhabitants representing the extra-Symbolic, otherwise known as the Imaginary, or as the female/the lack. At the same time, however, the characters are open to treatment as 'subjects' in their own right. We can turn to use Prospero as a subject within whose structure Ariel functions as *objet petit a*, thus elucidating the multidirectionality of Lacan's phrase 'the desire of the Other'.

The Imaginary for James Mellard, in his essay on Woolf's *To the Lighthouse* (*LT*, 233–60), is made up of the distinctive misrecognitions of the Mirror Phase: the fantasized sense of wholeness, whose completion takes place through an acceptance of loss/prohibition – in other words, of the Law of the Father. This is characteristic of Prospero's view of himself as absolutely powerful at the beginning of the play, achieved by accepting banishment from Milan. Mellard explicitly places the Imaginary and the Mirror Phase together in the field of the undifferentiated self and the power of the mother, the Imaginary union between infant and (m)Other flourishing pre-linguistically. Prospero's devotion to his magic involves a belief that these nurturing forces are his own, as a garment is, to be put away and taken up at will. He is thus in a state of Mirror Phase misrecognition. Representations of the genuinely maternal are notably dead, non-human and even despised: Sycorax, the 'blue-ey'd hag' is regarded by Prospero as a kind of devil, while Miranda's dead mother is reduced to a stock phrase: 'Thy mother was a piece of virtue' (*T*, I.ii, 56), and then to a bodily function: 'Good wombs have borne bad sons', says Miranda (*T*, I.ii, 120). Prospero's hesitations, however, reveal that the projection of wholeness is onto an other that is already divided and doubting – unwittingly setting up fissures even within the Imaginary which clamour to be interpreted: his postponement of Ariel's freedom is one such, and his forgetfulness over the Caliban plot is another. Only at the close of the play does he begin to consider his own status as a social and moral being, and discover that his use of magic arts has involved him in a balancing act between the Symbolic and the Imaginary, which are out of his control.

Before turning to our sketch of a reading of *The Tempest*, it is worth considering James Mellard's reading of *To the Lighthouse* somewhat. Mellard's bivalent text functions in two directions: using Woolf to explain Lacan, and Lacan to explicate Woolf. (The latter is a dangerous, almost reductive, project since he risks finding a final 'truth' in the text, and at times his discourse appears to suggest that it is Woolf who put 'meanings' in the text and not Mellard. If Mellard's search for his own *objet petit a* is illusorily satisfied, we at least should know better than to mimic him.) There is here an example of an enduring difficulty for literary criticism that the reading ends up saying less than the original while implying that it says more. More effective is his use of Woolf to explicate Lacan. Mellard's discussion, largely avoiding gender issues and focusing on the subject in the text, is especially valuable for its acute description of the orders of the Real, the Imaginary and the Symbolic. It weaves that discussion into an interpretation of Virginia Woolf's novel as a narrative of a subjectivity which matures by bringing the three orders into alignment within the field of desire, loss and mourning. Mellard expands Daniel Ferrers' perception that the 'Time Passes' section is an attempt to evade the Symbolic. He perceives the three sections of Woolf's novel as bearing a close relationship with Lacan's three orders of psychic experience, and the narrative sequencing as an enactment of a process of development of (textual) subjectivity through the three orders, to a condition of closure in which a kind of harmony or resolution is achieved.

The first section, 'In the Window', Mellard sees as the Imaginary, involved with elements of the Symbolic. For Mellard, the Real is imaged by the subject-free section of the novel, 'Time Passes'. The Real of unobserved and therefore uninterpreted decay in the edifice and fittings of the house is mapped against the human measure (and therefore Symbolic structure) of ten years, in a convincing reading which forms an immensely accurate description of the nature of the Lacanian Real.

Mellard necessarily combines his discussion of the passage through the orders with observations of the varieties of otherness which constitute the text' subjectivity. His reading shows how the other is constituted both as the Law of the Father and as the object of desire – how desire is (for) the desire of the Other. This can even take place in the Imaginary-dominated scenes of 'In the Window,' where the episode in which Mrs Ramsay responds to Mr Ramsay's need of her, at the same time precipitating an Oedipal crisis for her son James, at the moment when he loses her attention. (This has the force of a castrating impact, as he observes the Law of the Father and the desire of the Other as one and the same thing.) Ten years later in the 'To the Lighthouse' section, James experiences the same desire (in repeating the mother's desire) of/for the Other in his delight at his father's approval of his sailing skill. The *objet petit a* is both the son and Mrs Ramsay: a shifting term, depending on where the subjectivity of the text is located.

Both Mellard and Hearth are concerned with the ways in which differences (or divisions) are established in the subject – Mellard's multiple, shifting subjects face the Law of the Father in several guises – first as Mr Ramsay, denying the pleasurable trip to the lighthouse, but also (with Mr Ramsay now as subject) as the absolute loss figured by death. The death of Mrs Ramsay, who has been for so long the desire of the Other, flings the Symbolic order into conflict with the Real, at least until the desire of the Other can be transferred onto alternative objects (such as Lily Briscoe or the fine pair of boots). Imaginary relations cannot resolve difference – in other words, in the realm of the Imaginary, the Oedipal conflict is always continuing; loss is a free-floating anxiety. Even in the Symbolic difference is not so much resolved as rendered bearable. Reconciliation of the subject to the fact of lack – to the deferral of desire – is eased by the assimilation of (and participation in) the Symbolic order – not as an imposition on a subjected passive sufferer, but as a speaking subject, that is as a subject who has some ownership of the Symbolic: a right to be there. Thus, by accommodating mourning the subject comes to be able to occupy the place of the Other, albeit fitfully, and accept the temporary satisfactions of fulfilling the dictum that 'all desire is the desire of the Other'. The conclusion of Mellard's epic journey of textual subjectivity appears to be reassuring: finally, in the section 'To the Lighthouse', the task of mourning for the lost other is accomplished, and the text, by integrating its divisions, accomplishes its own Symbolic order.

There are unresolved difficulties in Mellard's analysis regarding firstly the ways in which the three Lacanian orders exist within one another (if they do), and secondly the modes whereby the sense of priority and closure associated with the 'achievement' of the Symbolic should be understood. These remain to be explored by future readings. Taking up connections between psychoanalysis and narrative theory, Mellard sees narrative as a model of the trajectories of desire, placing the reader in the position of the desiring subject, and the satisfactory conclusion of the narrative as the (achieved) *objet petit a* – that is, the mother in the field of the Imaginary. To see narrative itself as the protracted deferral of desire is to relocate the psychoanalytic discussion of a novel as a philosophical discussion about the nature of the literary text.

NOTES TOWARDS A READING OF *THE TEMPEST*

For many years, *The Tempest* has been viewed by critics and biographers of Shakespeare as his farewell to the stage before retiring home to Stratford-upon-

Avon. Prospero's magic is identified with Shakespeare's stagecraft, and the production of plots and shows with Shakespeare's theatrical career. It is now believed that Shakespeare continued to be involved in the theatre and in collaborative writings for some years after *The Tempest*, and Prospero should not be identified with him in that direct way. But there is something about the way in which this play deals with artifice and control that makes it peculiarly open to psychoanalytic interpretation, and that is certainly to do with its focus on the central figure of Prospero.

Perhaps the most difficult part of psychoanalytic criticism to come to terms with is its view of the text as having subjectivity in its own right. As such, the 'voice' of the text consists of the multiple voices of all the characters in the text, each seen as an aspect of the self. Peter Greenaway's film, *Prospero's Books*, gives an insight into this approach, which also helps to explain why the Prospero figure is so compelling. Greenaway achieves that in three phases. In the first phase we see an author, writing the text of the play at the same time as its events take place. Presumably, we are being given insight into the author's imagination. The same actor (John Gielgud) plays Prospero, and so speaks with the voice of the author, as he writes. 'The author' and 'Prospero' are clearly different characters, and are dressed differently. More striking, however, is the fact that Gielgud also speaks all the other lines as well as Prospero's. Many of the voices are accompanied: 'Miranda' consists of Gielgud's voice and the actress's voice in chorus, sustaining the multiple impressions that Shakespeare has written every part, that Prospero controls every detail, and that all the characters are part of a single complex psyche. All speech is voice-over, accompained by mime. In the second section, there is a moment when the author of the text is dressed no longer as himself, but as Prospero: suddenly, and very subtly, the two are no longer distinct. These techniques together impart a unified subjectivity to the text and display unequivocally that each of these characters/voices is neither more nor less than a part of a single, complex psyche. At this point, we are offered an island that is genuinely magic, where Shakespeare's and Prospero's arts are equivalent. The third section (the Epilogue) gives us Gielgud as a dispossessed man standing in front of a theatre curtain. He is not writing, and not 'acting' as Prospero. We see in him, to borrow a phrase from *King Lear*, 'Unaccommodated man' (III.iv, 100–1): a human being without any powers or artifice, who is dependent on the audience's approval for his survival. In a highly moving way, we are offered Gielgud as himself. It is puzzling to think why this is so moving – and proposing explanations for puzzles is the stuff of criticism. I shall look more deeply into this in a moment, but as a beginning, we might suggest that Gielgud at this point images each of us to ourselves – as helpless, but helpful, and as irrevocably social beings.

This reading can be taken further using Lacan's three orders of the Symbolic, the Imaginary and the Real, but the reading that I shall put forward is far from being the only one that might be devised. The system's usefulness is due to its peculiar flexibility: its interest and applicability depend on how the concepts can be manipulated in relation to the text.

The Symbolic order is where structuring of all kinds, particularly narrative and linguistic, takes place. One might see the island as a representation of the Imaginary: itself unnamed, it is manifestly free in many ways – free of language, for Prospero brought that to Caliban; 'full of strange noises' – sounds outside the meaningful spectrum of any human understanding, self-willed and bubbling up playfully. On the island, boundaries of reality and illusion can be crossed. Against that, the island world is interpenetrated by the Law of the Father, since the noises that fill the isle are the susurration of the mind of its creator, uninterpretable precisely to Caliban, the least competent linguist. Around Prospero, the structures created by him include Ariel's captivity and Ferdinand's log-carrying task – which suggest that he should be seen as the Other (or Law of the Father) which names and which says no – which, in fact lays down the boundaries and hence the meaning of the experienced world. Spirits function under the control of the magician, who thus fills the role of the Lacanian Father and who, imposing the Symbolic order on them, creates structure and meaning. Prospero imposes order strictly, using archaic forms of control such as captivity, threats and physical punishments. It is he who controls memory, insisting that the nature of the past must structure the present and the future. This belief is also Prospero's error, since it generates the patterns of anger, mistrust and revenge which dominate his plot-making. Prospero thus attempts to make both of the other orders subservient to himself as structuring Other.

I argue, then, that much of *The Tempest* faces us with a subjectivity dominated by the Symbolic order, where a centralized narcissistic consciousness asserts the possibility of absolute control. That this state of repression is inadequate is revealed by the need for unremitting efforts to sustain control. The Imaginary can be seen bubbling through in Ariel's poetic language and highly creative renderings of Prospero's instructions. It is Ariel, after all, who forges the storm, and Ariel who invents the story of the King of Naples' transfiguration by the sea. Notably too the songs are emanations from the spirits, in which they add their own playfulness to Prospero's structures.

Prospero himself is ambiguous: one notices that he seems feminized in his usurpation and that his holding of Ariel captive seems to be out of his own control as he keeps changing the rules and the date of Ariel's release in ways which suggest that Ariel's presence is needed. Together, Ariel and Prospero constitute a divided subject, both sides of which are involved in a dynamic of desire, and Prospero's fear of the Imaginary is clear in his endless postponements of Ariel's freedom. Further, Prospero is out of control at that much-noticed moment when time rushes on with him and he has forgotten the conspirators (*T*, IV.i, 139). He has been immersed in the delights of his own creations within the Imaginary – the masque of goddesses, Iris, Ceres and Juno. (The effects of time, as Mellard notices, are deeply implicated in the Real.) All of these are parts of a repressive subjectivity, in which delight struggles to be recognized and appears only dimly, permitted by the Law of the Father as long as it obeys the rules.

The Imaginary, however, cannot long be treated in this way. The price of controlling the Imaginary for Prospero is isolation from society. Not unlike Marlowe's Faustus, his connection with normal human society has become tenuous. The desire of the Other is signalled by Prospero's seemingly endless plotting: the play itself is in a state of desire for a lost narrative completeness. Anne Righter (Barton) (1968) detects this sense that something is hidden (16). Prospero's attempts to enforce completion involve the subservience of the Imaginary (and hence a loss to him of its vitality). His tenderness towards Ariel is displaced sorrow for his own lost capacity to access the Imaginary. The object of desire slips away perpetually. As his plot nears completion it ceases to satisfy and Prospero chooses to return to Milan, for what he must consign to the realm of loss is his magic (which is the same as his sense of omnipotence). Learning that involves a capacity to begin to learn his own mortality: 'Every third thought will be my grave' (T, V.i, 310). The play closes with Prospero proposing to tell the story of his life, in other words to formulate his life as a narrative or plot, something which he is confident he can do. He can now achieve this because desire has moved on, and must reconcile itself with a more fundamental area of loss, that of the text's own completeness outside narrative.

All along, the incompleteness of Prospero's worldview has been adumbrated by the repetition of the number 'three' as a motif. Three, being neither one (the narcissistic self) nor two (the dyad of infant/mother), stands for the way in which language is generated when the Law of the Father (one term) generates desire in the subject (a second term) for the object of desire (a third term). It also numbers/names the three orders of the psyche that must all be acknowledged. Within the play, Miranda has known Ferdinand for three hours; Prospero at several points believes he has three hours in which to work out his plan; and in Milan, every third thought will be his grave. The bell that rings for the dead in Ariel's song does so in triplets ('Ding, dong, bell'), that cut across the four-stress lines of the rest of the song (T, I. ii, 397–405). I have considered the Symbolic and the Imaginary at some length, but what of the Real, that third and most elusive order, which exists as a condition of the body, outside language or representation? It is that domain where the body, in its meaningless unglossable form takes over from all other systems of meaning. This is now the object of Prospero's desire. It is present, perhaps, as death. When Prospero attempts to think death we all know that this cannot be wholly achieved within language, but as a meditation on something beyond understanding. A third of his time is to be in contemplation of the end of all the Symbolic and Imaginary orders, and all that then remains is something transcendent and inexpressible in language: death, or the Real.

With the Epilogue the play moves beyond Prospero's concerns and focuses us on the play and on ourselves. One might ask how the Epilogue fits into my three-part pattern, but I now refuse to break such a delicate piece with the weight of the Symbolic. It is by stepping outside itself, outside its own structures, in the Epilogue that the text plays with a sense of its own wholeness and completion. By definition, any Epilogue is both inside and outside the structure of the play's composition – this one particularly so, as it images Prospero's (fictional) renunciation of magic as the author's (actual) distancing from his parts. He displays the multiplicity of the subject by his presence outside the role of Prospero.

QUESTIONS FOR FURTHER CONSIDERATION

1. If the unconscious mind is 'screened' by our language use, what problems does this raise for contextual material such as primary sources and the works of reporters and historians? Could it be seen as useful?

2. Because of the way in which it makes use of metaphor and metonymy, literature has been described as the dreams of our culture. If that is so, what kind of 'dream work' can literature do? (It may be best to focus on a particular work of literature to follow this question through.)

3. Psychoanalysis has been criticized for its masculine emphasis and its tendency to locate the abjected other and/or the desired other as female. What responses are there to this criticism that would relocate the female without losing the useful aspects of psychoanalytic theories?

4. 'Who am I, Caliban?' If language structures identity, how far can we claim that Caliban's identity is his own creation? What would undermine that claim, from a psychoanalytic point of view?

5. In what ways is Prospero divided between domination and submission? If one sees the text as a desiring subject, how does this split in Prospero illuminate it?

6. In the Notes, I see the island as representing the Lacanian Symbolic. Formulate the arguments that would attack that view, and identify the island as the Imaginary. (You might begin by considering where to locate the Symbolic order.)

ANNOTATED BIBLIOGRAPHY

Freud, Sigmund. *The Standard Edition of the Complete Psychoanalytic Works of Sigmund Freud*, 24 vols, ed. and trans. James Strachey. London, 1953–74.
This is the standard English translation of Freud's works. It contains his developing theories regarding infantile sexuality and the development of the Oedipus complex, his discovery of the unconscious mind, and his changing views of the drives towards both pleasure and death. He establishes the relationship, between linguistic ambiguity and the unconscious, especially with regard to jokes, parapraxes, Freudian slips and dreams. His discussions of case histories, such as 'The Wolf Man', 'Little Hans' and 'Dora' are essential reading, and scholarly debate especially among feminists about their conduct and status as evidence continues unabated.
Gallop, Jane. *The Daughter's Seduction: Feminism and Psychoanalysis*. Ithaca, NY, 1982.
Gallop spells out the fundamental feminist problems with psychoanalytic theory,

particular with the move that traditional psychoanalytic theory sees in the female as committed to the course of maturation – from an attachment to the mother to an attachment to the father. Gallop works from within the concepts, of the discipline, and seeks, with Lacan, to redefine the phallus as a referent-free concept, or at least having a contingent and therefore shifting referent to do with those sources of power which institute the Symbolic order. When the phallus is freed from its association with the penis in this way, a criticism of essentialism in both psychoanalytic and feminist discourses becomes possible, without sacrificing the intellectually valuable linguistic and philosophical concepts of Freud, Lacan and other thinkers.

Lacan, Jacques. *Écrits: A Selection*, trans. Alan Sheridan. London, 1977.

This is a selection of the original French version of *Écrits* (ed. Jacques Alain Miller. Paris: 1966). The short and comparatively readable essay on the Mirror Stage is widely misunderstood, and it is well worthwhile for students to form their own opinion of Lacan's views on this. Especially useful is the appended guide to Lacanian vocabulary and to reference points in the text where key terms are discussed and used.

Lacan, Jacques. *The Four Fundamental Concepts of Psychoanalysis*, trans. Alan Sheridan. London, 1977.

An extremely important and relatively readable set of articles edited from the lecture series and subsequent question-and-answer sessions. Lacan deals with the nature of psychoanalysis. In the first section he argues for the transformation of Freud's views of the unconscious mind into the Lacanian view of the unconscious as primarily linguistic. Section two on the gaze as *objet petit a* is of fundamental importance both to the visual arts and to the concept of the 'screen', discussed above. Finally, after a section on the transference as an exchange of psychic identifications between patient and analyst. Lacan moves to bring psychoanalytic practice and language theory into juxtaposition through the concepts of desire/lack.

Laplanche, J., and J. Pontalis. *The Language of Psychoanalysis*, intro. Daniel Lagache London, 1973.

This encyclopaedic dictionary of psychoanalytic terminology is an extended reference work, containing substantial discussions of key terms from a variety of schools of psychoanalysis, including American and modern French. The invaluable bibliographic references give the locations in Freud's works and elsewhere where concepts originated and thus form a guide to further reading. It is not designed for the literary critic, and some of the more arcane Lacanian formulations do not appear.

SUPPLEMENTARY BIBLIOGRAPHY

Adams, Parveen. *The Emptiness of the Image: Psychoanalysis and Sexual Differences*. London, 1996.

Barker, Jill. 'Does Edie Count? A Psychoanalytic Perspective on "Snowed Up"', in *Literary Theories: A Case Study in Critical Performance*, eds Julian Wolfreys and William Baker. London, 1996.

Bowie, Malcolm. *Freud, Proust and Lacan*. Cambridge, 1987.

———. *Lacan*. London, 1991.

———. *Psychoanalysis and the Future of Theory*. Oxford, 1991.

Brooks, Peter. 'The Idea of a Psychoanalytic Literary Criticism', in *Discourse in Psychoanalysis and Literature*, ed. Shlomith Rimmon-Kenan. London, 1987.

———. *Body Works: Objects of Desire in Modern Narrative*. Cambridge, MA, 1993.

Chase, Cynthia. 'Desire and Identification in Lacan and Kristeva', in *Feminism and Psychoanalysis*, eds Richard Feldstein and Judith Roof. Ithaca, NY, 1989.

Con Davis, Robert, ed. *The Fictional Father: Lacanian Readings of the Text*. Amherst, MA, 1981.

Ellmann, Maud, ed. *Psychoanalytic Literary Criticism*. London, 1994.

Felman, Shoshana. *Writing and Madness: Literature/Philosophy/Psychoanalysis*. Ithaca, NY, 1985.

————. *Jacques Lacan and the Adventure of Insight: Psychoanalysis in Contemporary Culture*. Cambridge, MA, 1987.

————, ed. *Literature and Psychoanalysis: The Question of Reading: Otherwise*. Baltimore, MD, 1982.

Ferrer, Daniel. To the Lighthouse', in *Psychoanalytic Literary Criticism*, ed. Maud Ellmann. London, 1994.

Gallop, Jane. *The Daughter's Seduction: Feminism and Psychoanalysis*. London, 1982.

Grosz, Elizabeth. *Jacques Lacan: A Feminist Introduction*. London, 1990.

Hartmann, Geoffrey. *Psychoanalysis and the Question of the Text*. Baltimore, MD, 1978.

Irigaray, Luce. *This Sex Which Is Not One*, trans. Catherine Porter. Ithaca, NY, 1985.

————. *Speculum of the Other Woman*, trans. Catherine Gill. Ithaca, NY, 1985.

Kaplan, E. Ann. *Psychoanalysis and Cinema*. London, 1990.

Kerrigan, William, and Joseph H. Smith, eds. *Interpreting Lacan*. New Haven, CT, 1983.

Kristeva, Julia. *Desire in Language: A Semiotic Approach to Literature and Art*, trans. and ed. Leon S. Roudiez. New York, 1980.

————. *Powers of Horror: An Essay on Abjection*, trans. Leon S. Roudiez. New York, 1982.

————. *The Kristeva Reader*, ed. Toril Moi, trans. Sean Hand and Leon S. Roudiez. Oxford, 1986.

Lacan, Jacques. 'Desire and the Interpretation of Desire in *Hamlet*', *Yale French Studies*, 55–6, 1977.

————. *Écrits: A Selection*, trans. Alan Sheridan. New York, 1977.

————. *The Four Fundamental Concepts of Psychoanalysis*, trans. Alan Sheridan. London, 1977.

————. *Speech and Language in Psychoanalysis: The Language of the Self*, trans., ed. and intro. Antony Wilden. Baltimore, MD, 1981.

MacCannell, Juliet Flower. *Figuring Lacan: Criticism and the Cultural Unconscious*. London, 1986.

Mitchell, Juliet, and Jacqueline Rose, eds. *Feminine Sexuality: Jacques Lacan and the Ecole freudienne*. London, 1982.

Muller, John P., and William J. Richardson, eds. *The Purloined Poe: Lacan, Derrida and Psychoanalytic Reading*. Baltimore, MD, 1988.

Mulvey, Laura. 'Visual Pleasure and Narrative Cinema', in *Visual and Other Pleasures*. Basingstoke, 1989.

Rose, Jacqueline. *Sexuality in the Field of Vision*. London, 1986.

Vice, Sue, ed. *Psychoanalytic Criticism: A Reader*. Cambridge, 1996.

Wilden, Anthony. 'Lacan and the Discourse of the Other', in Jacques Lacan, *Speech and Language in Psychoanalysis*, trans. Anthony Wilden. Baltimore, MD, 1981.

Wright, Elizabeth. *Psychoanalytic Criticism: Theory in Practice*. London, 1984.

Young, Robert, ed. *Untying the Text: A Post-Structuralist Reader*. London, 1981.

Žižek, Slavoj. *The Sublime Object of Ideology*. London, 1989.

————. *Enjoy Your Symptom! Jacques Lacan in Hollywood and Out*. London, 1992.

OTHER WORKS CITED

Barry, Peter. *Beginning Theory*. Manchester, 1995.

Barthes, Roland. *S/Z*. Paris, 1970.

Kahn, Coppélia. 'The Providential Tempest and the Shakespearean Family', in *Representing Shakespeare: New Psychoanalytic Essays*, eds M. M. Schwartz and Coppélia Kahn. Baltimore, MD, 1980.

James, D. G. *The Dream of Prospero*. Oxford, 1967.

Orgel, Stephen. 'Prospero's Wife', in *Rewriting the Renaissance: The Discourses of Sexual Difference in Early Modern Europe*, eds Mary W. Ferguson et al. Chicago, 1986.

Righter (Barton), Anne. 'Introduction', *The Tempest*. Harmondsworth, 1968.

Sunderland, David. 'So Rare a Wonder'd Father: Prospero's Tempest', in *Representing Shakespeare: New Psychoanalytic Essays*, eds M. M. Schwartz and Coppélia Kahn. Baltimore, MD, 1980.

CHAPTER

7

DECONSTRUCTION, WHAT REMAINS UNREAD

Julian Wolfreys

PRELIMINARY STATEMENTS (REITERATING, IN OTHER WORDS)
Deconstruction is an old French word. *Déconstruire. Déconstruction. Se déconstruire.*

It's a very old word in the French language. (Derrida, 1996, 224)

It is also an English word, derived from French: *Deconstruction*. The same as the French. Almost. The same and not the same. *Deconstruction/Déconstruction*. What a difference an accent makes. The accent and its non-translation might be said to mark economically and in a violent fashion the fortunes of deconstruction.

The first known written appearance of the word in English is in 1882. As with its French predecessor, it has legal connotations: 'A reform the beginnings of which must be a work of deconstruction'.

Deconstruction presages reform.

Deconstruction is always immanent in the conceptual languages of western metaphysics. Yet

> Operating necessarily from the inside, borrowing all the strategic and economic resources of subversion from the old structure, borrowing them structurally, that is to say without being able to isolate their elements and atoms, the enterprise of deconstruction always in a certain way falls prey to its own work. (Derrida, 1974, 24)

Deconstruction is associated with the texts of Jacques Derrida, especially his earlier publications from the 1960s, where he employs the term *deconstruction*.

The term is used on occasion as a possible translation for two German words, *Destruktion* and *abbau*, employed by Martin Heidegger.

Deconstruction is neither a concept nor a thing.

It does not name a methodology.

Deconstruction is one term among many used by Derrida in his writing. Among the other terms used are *hymen, écriture, différance, text, trace, arché-écriture*.

> Derrida had initially proposed [the word *deconstruction*] in a chain with other words – for example, difference, spacing, trace – none of which can command the series or function as a master word. (Kamuf, 1991, vii)

None of these words, *deconstruction* included, is privileged over any other. They are all used on different occasions, in different and differing contexts, without any term assuming an absolute value of use over any of the others. The use of the words is dictated by the object of analysis or text being analyzed, and according to the range of contexts – historical, philosophical, conceptual, discursive – which determine the shape and structure of the object or text in question.

> We have taken a series of terms from Derrida, who took them from texts read not according to a program or a method . . . but, at least in (irreducible) part, according to the flair and the chance of encounters with what is bequeathed or repressed by the tradition. We have said several times that these terms are singular in the sense that they remain more or less attached to the text from which they were taken, and never achieve the status of metalinguistic or metaconceptual operators. (Bennington, 1993, 267)

They, and others, constitute what Derrida calls non-synonymous substitutions. That is, they do not mean the same thing, nor do they serve the same purpose, yet they operate in the performance of Derrida's writing in a similar dislocating fashion to describe the unfolding of the functioning structure of a concept.

The purpose in exploring the structure of the structure – its structurality – is to show how all structures rely on a centring or grounding principle, idea, concept which, though never examined as such, guarantees the identity, meaning, value of the structure.

> . . . the concept of structure and even the word 'structure' itself are as old as . . . Western science and Western philosophy . . . Structure – or rather the structurality of structure – although it has always been at work, has always been neutralized or reduced, and this by a process of giving it a center or of referring it to a point of presence, a fixed origin. The function of this center was not only to orient, balance, and organize the structure . . . but above all to make sure that the organizing principle of the structure would limit what we might call the *play* of the structure. (Derrida, 1978, 278)

The text, a structure, an idea, an institution, a philosophy, all contain in themselves that which disturbs and is in excess of the serenity of the full, simple identity as such.

To show the structurality of structure is not to deconstruct a text.

You cannot deconstruct a text.

Derrida does not offer us a method of reading called 'deconstruction' which, once learned can be applied to anything we choose to read.

Deconstruction does not name an analysis which allows you to make the text mean anything you like, nor can you ignore either that which the text imposes on you or the structures which determine the singularity of the text.

Derrida provides us with exemplary discussions of text, of a word, a structure, a concept, the structuring principles of a concept. In these exemplary discussions, he has occasionally used the word 'deconstruction'.

Exemplary readings and discussions are faithful to the singularity of that which is being discussed.

Derrida's writing has on a number of occasions performed the exemplary tracing of the contours of whatever it takes to be its object of analysis. In this gesture of tracing, which doubles the writing being delineated in a transformative fashion, Derrida alights upon a single theme, term, word, concept. In so doing, he transforms the structure of the text – concept, institution, theme – through examining how that single figure operates in the structure as a whole, in excess of the structure. At the same time, Derrida does not only analyze this word or figure, standing back at a critical distance. He also puts it to work as a figure for determining the function of that which is being discussed.

The figure in question, far from calming down the production of a single meaning in the overall economy of the text, troubles that logic, making the univocal meaning undecidable. In unfolding the structurality of the structure, Derrida thus makes plain the *aporia* within the structural logic, on which the structure depends for its transmission, yet which it suppresses everywhere. In opening the structure's play to its own movement – already installed in the structure and not imposed from some supposed 'outside' – beyond the centre which the text is conventionally assumed to approve, or on which it is otherwise grounded, Derrida's discussion performs in other words the textual oscillation always already within the structure.

It is such oscillation which conventional and institutional acts of reading seek to damp down, often through institutionally approved methods and techniques of reading that aim to emphasize the harmony of identity, at the cost of difference and undecidability.

So, to reiterate: on the one hand, the exemplary reading cannot be rendered as a methodology, a technique, because, in being faithful to the contours of what is being analysed, the exemplary critique or analysis never applies a theory. On the other hand, the analysis is always already applied, in that it applies itself responsibly to its text. It offers the rigorous delineation of that which is in question, which, when performed, transforms the text, concept, institution, through the focus on that which moves the structure but which is not necessarily logical within the economy of the structure.

SUPPLEMENTARY STATEMENTS
(DECONSTRUCTION, SPEAKING FOR ITSELVES)

Let us turn our attention to a number of commentaries concerning deconstruction, as a way of constructing or construing a provisional analysis or explanation of this term which avoids the positivist or constructivist tendencies implicit in conventional critical determination.

> You know the programme; [deconstruction] cannot be applied because deconstruction is not a doctrine; it's not a method, nor is it a set of rules or tools; it cannot be separated from performatives . . . On the one hand, there is no 'applied deconstruction'. But on the other hand, there is nothing else, since deconstruction doesn't consist in a set of theorems, axioms, tools, rules, techniques, methods. If deconstruction, then, is nothing by itself, the only thing it can do is apply, to be applied, to something else, not only in more than one language, but also with something else. There is no deconstruction, deconstruction has no specific object . . . Deconstruction cannot be applied and cannot *not* be applied. So we have to deal with this *aporia*, and this is what deconstruction is about. (Derrida, 1996, 217–18)

On the one hand . . . on the other hand . . . This formula is, it might be said, that which formulates the law of undecidability which is irreducible to any programme of analysis other than the programme which states that there is no programme to, or programming of, the idea of deconstruction. Thus when Derrida remarks 'you know the programme', there is an ironic distancing at work.

Derrida's careful exposition of deconstruction turns on what appears to be a formal or structural paradox in his statement. Logically, a statement such as 'deconstruction is . . .' should not be able to accommodate two diametrically opposed positions, particularly where one is 'deconstruction is . . .' while the other formula begins 'deconstruction is not . . .' (or any other variation of such a formula). Conventionally speaking, logic requires a decision of an either/or nature, an identification being put in place which resolves matters through the establishment of a proposition or identity which is homogeneous, self-contained, having a hermeneutically closed totality within the structure of which there is no element at odds with the elements of the structure.

For example, something is said to exist or not to exist; it is either present or absent, living or dead, true or false. When a character in a novel, such as the narrator of John Banville's *Ghosts*, remarks 'I am there and not there' (Banville, 1994, 39), strictly speaking such a statement should be impossible, and not simply because of logic, but because, ontologically, any consideration of subjectivity should remain consistent, not merely linguistically, but as a comprehension of the condition of Being.

Yet here, in this statement of Derrida's, 'deconstruction', inasmuch as this word names anything, names two conditions which take place simultaneously, if I can put it like this (and I'm not altogether sure that I should), pertaining at the structural and semantic level of inscription to the formal contradiction of the written utterance, while at the same time also commenting on the equally simultaneous, seeming impossibility of two identities within the same identity which differ from each other, and both of which defer the totality or completeness of either. A spacing, an opening of a concept takes place as the very condition of its expression, its writing.

The condition that I am describing, this spacing-deferring or structural differentiation, does not require that I or anyone else observe it in order that it take place. It always already does, and does so, moreover, as the condition of what Derrida calls *writing, text, différance*, and, of course, *deconstruction*. It is an opening within identity (structural, conceptual, ontological, epistemological), whereby the very thought of that identity is possible only through its necessary incorporation of the signs of its non-identity, its other, which informs every aspect of the structure as structure. Moreover, these elements, for want of a better word, are not separable, nor identifiable as absolutely separable terms; instead they are mutually enfolded, each into the other at every moment, and everywhere irreducible to a single concept, idea or key term, the self-identity of which might be shown were I to seek to 'regress' in such an act of reading 'back' towards the single atomic element. Thus deconstruction is not a structural term simply speaking, nor is it a means of analyzing structure so as to identify an originary or grounding principle or centre within a structure, whether one speaks of a narrative, a philosophical, conceptual or theological discourse.

There is not, then, and never can be, any such thing as an applicable reading method called deconstruction because whatever deconstruction can be said to name, it does not name, nor should it be taken that this name suggests, a method or the tools, the ensemble of procedures, protocols or devices, by which to pursue or otherwise put in place a method. And yet deconstruction takes place; insofar as we cannot help but fall into an ontologically oriented discourse by referring to an 'it' or, implicitly, an 'it-ness', as though deconstruction were possessed of an ipseity, we have to say, as does Derrida, that deconstruction is already applied, it is already at work. *There* it might be said is deconstruction, and yet this *there* locates no object as such. Here, once more, is the paradox, which emerges as a result of reaching a limit of definition; or rather the two sides of the limit named by the very thought of de*finition*; or, rather, let me remark the redoubling, and with that, the deferring, differing, two sides of two limits at least (*on the one hand . . . on the other hand . . . 'Deconstruction cannot be applied and cannot not be applied'*), which Derrida has already remarked, and which is always already remarked in any deconstruction, taking place prior to any observation or commentary and as that without which there could be no commentary, no discernment of what is called, all too loosely, meaning.

Thus language is found falling into the ruins it already is and that which remains as the remains of language is the experience in this attempt at definition of the aporetic. Here it might be suggested, is the work of deconstruction, and here is deconstruction at work. It is this which one must seek to read. Therefore,

> Deconstruction – which is never single or homogeneous, but which can here, at least provisionally, be identified with 'the work of Derrida' – is concerned with the lucid, patient attempt to trace what has not been read, what remains unread or unreadable within the elaboration of concepts and workings of institutions. (Royle, 1995, 160)

Here, Nicholas Royle addresses both the question of reading which I have been at pains to unfold and the concomitant recognition that the matter of reading is irreducible either to a single mode of analysis or a process the stratagems and motions of which remain the same throughout its space. Moreover, and as a provisional definition, this heterogeneous multiplicity of the unread, not-read, the unreadable and yet-to-be-read that is named deconstruction is discernible within both discourse and, as Royle puts it, 'the workings of institutions'. The question is therefore not only of tracing or attempting to trace patiently that which inhabits language or writing narrowly defined, but also that which makes possible the practical, political and historical operation of, for example, a university. There is that which 'has not been read, what remains unread or unreadable', in the articulation of social and political organization, whether one speaks of the university, the government, the idea of government or democracy, the notion of nation, to which attention needs to be given.

However,

> No doubt the success of deconstruction as a term can be explained in part by its resonance with *structure* which was then, in the 1960s, the reigning word of structuralism. Any history of how the word deconstruction entered a certain North American vocabulary, for instance, would have to underscore its critical use in the first text by Derrida to be translated in the United States, 'Structure, Sign, and Play in the Discourse of the Human Sciences.' [Derrida, 1978, 278–93] . . . As used here 'de-construction' marks a distance (the space of a hyphen, later dropped [from the word 'deconstruction']) from the structuring or construction of discourses . . . that have uncritically taken over the legacy of Western metaphysics. If, however, it cannot be a matter of refusing this legacy . . . then the distance or difference in question is in the manner of assuming responsibility for what cannot be avoided. Deconstruction is one name Derrida has given to this responsibility. It is not a refusal or a destruction of the terms of the legacy, but occurs through a re-marking and redeployment of these very terms, that is, the concepts of philosophy. (Kamuf, 1991, viii)

There is, as you can see from this passage, a certain history to the fortunes of deconstruction, as this term arrives from France in the text of Jacques Derrida and is received, translated and put to work or made to work within the Anglo-American university. Necessarily, to understand deconstruction in this context one must return to its first translation in order to comprehend as fully as possible the transport and transformations undergone by deconstruction. As Jacques Derrida has remarked apropos a too hasty act of reading, there is 'no excuse for contenting oneself with flying through a text . . . the effects of thus skimming . . . on the fly are not limited to the hastily formed impression' (Derrida, 1999, 228), and that return to the first translation on the part of Peggy Kamuf signals the need to resist 'reading on the fly'.

This is the responsibility that reading entails, a responsibility good readers have to this word, deconstruction, and the responsibility which Kamuf announces as a sign of Derrida's use of the word in relation to the very terms, the 'concepts of philosophy'. In returning to begin a reading of Derrida, Kamuf's text thereby re-marks in its own act a responsibility already at work, and thereby is not content merely to look to a prior text and to read that patiently (one aspect of the question of responsibility), but to issue an injunction to responsibility in and as the future of readings, of reading to come.

Thus, reading Kamuf – and Derrida – as responsibly as possible in so brief a space as this essay, and realizing all the while the dangers of haste in this space, I respond by noting the redoubling and displacement of the times of reading and/ as responsibility; we note that even as Kamuf reiterates that by which Derrida's text is marked, so too does her own text enact or perform the very same question and yet in a different manner. In this fashion, what remains as yet unread is that deconstruction is not simply a thing of the past, on which one dutifully comments; for as the form of Kamuf's performative commentary gives one to understand, deconstruction is untimely; deconstruction is also deconstruction to come, while always already having been remarked, and remarking itself in different times; as it cannot be assigned to a single time, a single instance, deconstruction remains – and comprehending this remains the good reader's responsibility. And this is why, more than ever, it remains to be remarked once more, in order to resist the 'hastily formed impression' that

> Deconstruction is not a theory or a project. It does not prescribe a practice more or less faithful to it, nor project an image of a desirable state to be brought about. (Bennington, 1988, 7)

It may of course be remarked that in citing yet another source, I am merely repeating myself. This recitation is all the more necessary, however, in the very face of impatience, of a desire to get on and to reach some point where the reader can come to terms with deconstruction and, in so doing, apprehend its operation within critical discourse as being of service in the production or projection of a meaning, an identity, or what Geoffrey Bennington terms 'a desirable state'. No doubt this would be the desirable state of affairs: to have done with deconstruction by assuming its functioning as a theory or project for the purpose of projecting the desirable state. But the reader's responsibility is to see that this must not happen, and so, if only for this reason, it must be reiterated that, from one perspective at least

> Deconstruction is not a dismantling of the structure of the text but a demonstration that it has already dismantled itself. (Miller, 1991, 126)

Of course, you know the programme. However, in the face of that which remains to be read, that which has not been read, it is equally necessary to state, in the words of J. Hillis Miller, that

> Sentences of the form 'Deconstruction is so and so' are a contradiction in terms. Deconstruction cannot by definition be defined, since it presupposes the indefinability or, more properly, the 'undecidability' of all conceptual or generalizing terms. Deconstruction . . . can only be exemplified, and the examples will all differ. (Miller, 1991, 126)

Miller refines the comprehension of deconstruction by defining another aspect of the impossibility which all attempts at definition as acts of reading in the name of deconstruction encounter. One cannot define, that is to say read, deconstruction in any general, conceptual, totalizing or theorizing fashion (the good, the responsible reader cannot render it as either a theory or project, much less a theoretical programme) given that the understanding of deconstruction proposed here involves a recognition of deconstruction's irreducibility to a stable, single meaning.

Furthermore, given the fact that such irreducibility demonstrates that deconstruction is 'never single or homogeneous', it follows that every instance of what I choose to name deconstruction is, to paraphrase Miller, exemplary. One does not utilize deconstruction to demonstrate the exemplarity of, for example, a literary text; one attempts, as part of the act of responsible reading, to trace patiently that in the rhythms of the text which remains unread as its exemplary instance, as that which in the text in question marks that text in its singularity and recognizing that such singularity is, paradoxically, what it shares with other literary texts.

In coming to terms with such irreducible singularity and the reiteration of singularity as the exemplary feature of every literary text *qua* the literary, the reader can thus begin to grasp how every so-called instance of deconstruction must perforce be exemplified and that, in Miller's words, 'the examples will all differ'. Which is why, to turn back to Bennington

> All of Derrida's texts are already applications, so there is no separate 'Derrida' in the form of theory who might *then* be applied to something else. Insofar as 'Deconstruction' tends to become a method or a school, we might say that it has forgotten this, and has begun at least to make Derrida into a theory which it wants to put into practice . . . we cannot simply be content to claim that Derrida (sometimes) applies his own theory, or

unites theory and practice, or performs theoretical practice . . . (Bennington, 1996, 17)

Doubtless, this question of forgetting has played a huge part in the fortunes of deconstruction in the history of its reception, transmission and translation within the Anglo-American university of the last thirty-five years. Forgetting in these historical instances – and they are more than one, it cannot simply be assumed that the question of deconstruction has been addressed in the same fashion on either side of the Atlantic; nor, furthermore, that the question has remained the same throughout the period in question; each encounter remains to be exemplified, and, as is well known, or should otherwise be admitted, the examples will all differ – amounts in very specific ways to forms of resistance, to acts of repression as so many symptoms of the technics of the institution in the projection of the illusion of an identity or 'desirable state'. Which is why, in the face of so much forgetting, the reader would do well to let Derrida comment once more on the question of the incommensurability between, on the one hand, deconstruction and, on the other, method:

> I am not sure that deconstruction can function as a literary *method* as such. I am wary of the idea of methods of reading. The laws of reading are determined by that particular text that is being read. This does not mean that we should simply abandon ourselves to the text, or represent and repeat it in a purely passive manner. It means that we must remain faithful, even if it implies a certain violence, to the injunctions of the text. These injunctions will differ from one text to the next so that one cannot prescribe one general method of reading. In this sense deconstruction is not a method. (Derrida, 1983, 124)

Derrida's remark echoes the second comment from Miller, cited above, as well as issuing both a caution and an injunction concerning reading. There can be no single method of reading because every text is exemplary and singular.

This, to reiterate, is how one knows, paradoxically, that one is in the presence of the literary, so called; and this, to reiterate again, is the *aporia* with which the reader has to deal in the name of a responsible literary criticism, a name, by the way – *literary criticism* – which gathers together countless acts of reading and yet which cannot be reduced to a method.

However, one cannot simply read as one chooses because there is that question of responsibility, already announced by Peggy Kamuf and named here by Derrida as the act or responsibility of remaining faithful. For these very reasons, one cannot pretend to summarize or to seek to encapsulate meaning, function or purpose. The responsible reader cannot determine the literary simply as a range of effects, anymore than he or she can hope to do this with the name deconstruction. Were the reader to seek to do so, he or she would be seeking to produce the overly hasty impression, to read 'on the fly', to provide potted versions of thought, and to put things, as the phrase has it, *in a nutshell*:

> The very idea of a nutshell is a mistake and a misunderstanding, an excess – or rather a defect – of journalistic haste and impatience, a ridiculous demand put by someone . . . everything in deconstruction is turned toward opening, exposure, expansion, and complexification . . . toward releasing unheard-of, undreamt-of possibilities *to come* . . .
>
> The very meaning and mission of deconstruction is to show that things – texts, institutions, traditions, societies, beliefs, and practices of whatever size and sort you need – do not have definable meanings and determinable missions, that they are always more than any mission would impose, that they exceed the boundaries they currently occupy . . . A 'meaning' or a 'mission' is a way to contain and compact things, like a nutshell, gathering them into a unity, whereas deconstruction bends all its efforts to stretch beyond these boundaries . . . Whenever deconstruction finds a nutshell – a secure axiom or a pithy maxim – the very idea is to crack it open and disturb this tranquillity . . . cracking nutshells is what deconstruction *is*. In a nutshell. (Caputo, 1997, 31–2)

What could possibly be said about John Caputo's commentary, which in some manner he has not already said in other words, and which is not already anticipated in the various other citations? Except to say, of course, that this excerpted passage is, itself, performative, in as much as it explores both the paradoxical and exemplary in its own articulation of all that is inimical to the figures of the opening and the possibilities *to come* which deconstruction figures. In a nutshell, so to speak, the passage encapsulates that concerning deconstruction which cannot be gathered into a nutshell, whether one speaks of the production of a meaning or mission – either an interpretation of deconstruction or the interpretation which such an interpretation of deconstruction would then make possible.

Such gatherings and the rush to gather things up is figured in this metaphorical figure, 'in a nutshell', on which Caputo plays as he demonstrates, on the one hand, how the figure operates, through both its own example and the exemplary instance of deconstruction, while, on the other hand, demonstrating how, *in a nutshell*, deconstruction exposes, in every singular instance, how the idea of the nutshell, when considered properly, no longer gathers, but opens onto other considerations. Hence the passage economically operates around its own figure and the paradox of a simultaneous contrapuntal movement of closing *and* opening, gathering *and* displacing.

In short – and in a nutshell – the passage, when read carefully, teaches us to attend to the contradictory ebb and flow of language, and its production of meaning, in a performative fashion: not through a consolidation of elements into a single meaning (the figure of the nutshell), but through the operation of deferral and differentiation, a spacing and, once again, a doubling of figuration, a disfiguration if you will.

Which leads me to another comment of Derrida's, which he opens by allusion to the demand for the 'nutshell' approach to thought with the phrase 'in short':

> In short, deconstruction not only teaches us to read literature more thoroughly by attending to it as *language*, as the production of meaning through *différance* and dissemination, through a complex play of signifying traces; it also enables us to interrogate the covert philosophical and political presuppositions of institutionalized critical methods which generally govern our reading of a text . . . It is not a question of calling for the destruction of such institutions, but rather of making us aware of what we are in fact doing when we are subscribing to this or that institutional way of reading. (Derrida, 1983, 125)

this or that institutional way of reading . . . this phrase perhaps sums up most economically what it means to seek to provide a meaning in a nutshell. The institutional way of reading is of course necessary, from one perspective, for the functioning of the institution itself. After all, there are students, there are teachers, there are examinations, and then . . . there are more students, and the assessment of quality which is undertaken in Britain, by, for example, the Higher Education Funding Councils of England or Scotland, is predicated in part on the repeated transmissibility of ideas and what are nebulously termed 'values' while at the same time, inculcating in the student body (as though this were capable of being placed in a nutshell) transferable skills for 'use' in workplaces other than the university.

Not that there is necessarily anything pernicious or repressive in this. *Not necessarily.* It is not a question of calling for the destruction of such processes, to borrow from Derrida's remarks. However, what the maintenance of such procedures and the overseeing of the repeated functioning of the institutional machinery implicitly keeps in place is, if not a conscious willingness, then at least a more or less organized compliance with the idea that one ought to 'go with the flow', to subscribe to such procedures without necessarily being aware of it, and without interrogating 'the covert philosophical and political presuppositions of institutionalized critical methods which generally govern our reading of a text'.

This in part serves to begin to explain the historical transformation, translation and subsequent transmission of deconstruction as a *method* with goals and outcomes. By providing for deconstruction a meaning, by placing it in a nutshell, making it in short into an institutional way of reading with its own presuppositions, institutional reception could – and has in certain cases – fashioned deconstruction after its own image, for epistemological and political purposes which operate on a scale much larger than the example of Higher Education. Again, this is not a question of a deliberate plan on the part of some 'evil empire'; it is, however, a necessity of the economic functioning of institutions and the philosophical discourses which underpin them. In the immediate example of the university, deconstruction can best function if it can be transformed into a reading method operating more or less like other reading methods with the ability to be abstracted, taught as a set of theorems and procedures which, in turn, can be applied to a range of texts, and, in the process, producing another competent set of analyses all of which generate yet one more set of final meanings.

It is perhaps a sign of how inappropriate so-called deconstruction is to such procedures that it has resulted in so many vehement responses both within and outside the university. Despite the efforts to transform deconstruction into a discernible method with a finite number of protocols in place, deconstruction remains as so many instances of resistance, and for this reason:

> As a transformative strategy without finality, as the destabilizing differential effects always already at work everywhere, deconstruction is never single but necessarily multiple and incomplete. (Royle, 1995, 128)

While it is the case that the careful reading for which Derrida calls does not involve the overthrow or destruction of institutions, nonetheless, the openness, undecidability and ongoing multiplicity by which Nicholas Royle provisionally defines deconstruction is, or at least can be seen as being, quite disturbing.

To begin, and to recall an earlier point, if the process in which one is involved does not come to a rest, then every act of reading must be all the more vigilant, constantly, and the reader must assume a commensurately constant responsibility for that vigilance.

Also, the very question of incompletion and undecidability which the recognition of deconstruction forces upon readers throws them back on the questioning of the implicit assumptions to which they subscribe institutionally, philosophically and ideologically.

Once more, there is not simply a question here of responding or attending to that which has taken place in the past, but that which continues to take place, that which will continue to take place and to come within future situations. And so, as readers, we are confronted with the endless question of response and responsibility, in short with the question of the ethics of reading. It is perhaps for this very reason that Derrida has occasion to define deconstruction in the following fashion:

> I have often had occasion to define deconstruction as that which is – far from a theory, a school, a method, even a discourse, still less a technique that can be appropriated – at bottom *what happens or comes to pass* [ce qui arrive]. (Derrida, 1995, 17)

That which arrives, that which is always arriving is, of course difficult, if not impossible, to pin down or otherwise locate. So, to recall the point yet again – and it does need making, repeatedly, as the 'history of deconstruction' (by which I mean the institutional and political vagaries of this name since the 1960s in the context of higher education) shows – one needs to understand how,

> Concerning the institution that is the university put in question by the PC debate, the term 'deconstruction' is most often presumed to refer to a

theory, a method, a school, perhaps even a doctrine, in any case, some identifiable or localizable 'thing' that can be positioned – posed and opposed – within that institution, but also that can be excluded from this defined enclosure. (Kamuf, 1997, 141)

The question of deconstruction is therefore a political one; or, more accurately, the question of deconstruction raises from a number of places many questions, not least those which have been articulated from distrust, distaste, fear, hostility, allergic reaction or even, simply, incomprehension and a lack of willingness 'to interrogate the covert philosophical and political presuppositions' of those very questions, which it would be a question of deconstruction to begin to think, in order to begin to make 'us aware of what we are in fact doing when we subscribe to' such questions.

Therefore, deconstruction – 'which is never single or homogeneous' – should be 'concerned with the lucid, patient attempt to trace what has not been read, what remains unread or unreadable within the elaboration of concepts and workings of institutions', as Derrida makes clear in this following discussion. As he argues, the premises of a discourse:

> . . . are not absolute and a historical . . . They depend upon socio-historical conditions, hence upon nonnatural relations of power that by essence are mobile and founded upon complex conventional structures that in principle may be analyzed . . . and in fact, these structures are in the process of transforming themselves profoundly and, above all, very rapidly (this is the true source of anxiety in certain circles, which is merely revealed by 'deconstruction': for before becoming a discourse, an organized practice that *resembles* a philosophy, a theory, a method, which it is *not*, in regard to those unstable stabilities or this destabilization that it makes its principal theme, 'deconstruction' is firstly this destabilization on the move in, if one could speak thus, 'the things themselves'; but it is not negative. Destabilization is required for 'progress' as well. And the 'de-' of *de*construction signifies not the demolition of what is constructing itself, but rather what remains to be thought beyond the constructivist or destructionist scheme). What is at stake here is the entire debate, for instance, on the curriculum, literacy, etc. (Derrida, 1988, 147)

OBJECTIONS, HISTORIES, AND METHODS: SO-CALLED DECONSTRUCTION

Of course, I can hear the voices already. I've slanted the evidence in favour of the idea that deconstruction is neither an analysis, nor a critique, even less a method, a programme, a doctrine, a school of thought. Look at the names: Miller, Kamuf, Bennington, Royle, Caputo, Derrida himself, several times, on several occasions. Defending what he does by saying that he doesn't do it, and saying that he's never said this is what you do (even though he hasn't and he doesn't). As for the others, well, they're all deconstructionists (aren't they?),

they all practice the methodology (more or less, now and then); they, and others like them . . . well, that's deconstruction for you. It's all very slippery and its practitioners are among the slipperiest. Imagine: an introduction to 'deconstruction' in something called *Introducing Literary Theories: A Guide and Glossary*, in a chapter, moreover, which addresses, under the heading 'Deconstruction', three essays, by Jacques Derrida, J. Hillis Miller and Nicholas Royle, some of those very 'deconstructionists' who have already been quoted, which insists that there is no such thing as a deconstructive approach to literary studies, no such thing as a methodology or school of thought. Imagine. Why, *I* can imagine one of the voices saying, indignantly, I expect whoever's writing this, being a deconstructionist, has even written things like this before. (You're wrong, I'm not, for all the reasons above; but you're right, I have; 1996, 179–244; 1998a; 1998b, 1–49).

Deconstruction has to exist. It has to have an identity. It has to be identifiable, at least for some (see Kamuf, 1997, 141). And, usually, introductions, especially when they are introductions to what we call literary theory, are conventionally obliged to suppose that what is being introduced does, in fact, exist. Deconstruction is taught. It is taught, in universities, as a method of reading and analysis, even while it is given an institutional history. Usually these histories suggest that 'deconstruction' is a French mode of thought, originated by Jacques Derrida, then translated and imported, into the US and UK, into American-English and English-English, and established as a critical practice, especially in the US, in Departments of English (see Adamson, 1993, 25–31). Certainly, Derrida has commented on a number of occasions about the fortunes of deconstruction in North America in these terms, even though he dissociates himself to greater or lesser extents with those manifestations of 'deconstruction'.

Part of the history of 'deconstruction' is to suggest that it flourished as a critical methodology in the early 1970s, particularly at Yale University, where it was championed by four critics in particular, J. Hillis Miller, Geoffrey Hartman, Harold Bloom and Paul de Man (see Rorty, 1995, 178–9). This 'gang of four' were, along with Derrida, who was a visiting professor at Yale during these years, subsequently referred to, usually in the media, and elsewhere, among academics hostile to the idea of deconstruction (even though they never showed signs of really ever having understood 'it'), as the Yale School. These critics practised deconstruction, it was claimed. They allegedly showed through readings of canonical and classical texts that there was no meaning in a work. You could talk about these texts endlessly because the texts could mean anything you chose. The critical discourse of these and other critics was assumed to rely on word play, on puns, on esoteric and obscurantist prose, on an inmixing of literary analysis, a neo- or quasi-Nietzschean renunciation of value and moral worth, and an importation of hard-to-read continental philosophers (especially Hegel and Heidegger!), which assaulted the value of literary masterpieces.

I may be accused of parodying here, but then it's hard to see how one can parody a range of misrepresentations which, themselves, not only verge on but often, and unintentionally, go right over the edge of parody. I have used the words 'claimed' and 'assumed' above to suggest that, in bad journalistic fashion – though a fashion not restricted to journalists alone, but adopted, often all too readily by certain academics – nothing much was *read*. Nothing is clearer, if you take the time to do the research, that, on these and other occasions (about which Nicholas Royle speaks 'On Not Reading: Derrida and Beckett', *LT*, 298–309), many have not read either the texts of Derrida or those who are aligned with the word *deconstruction*. (The reader is also referred to Peggy Kamuf's discussion of a review from the *New York Review of Books*, and a letter which the review subsequently drew forth (1997, 141–5).) If there are similar concerns between the work of Jacques Derrida and that of, say, Paul de Man, or Peggy Kamuf, Geoffrey Bennington, Hillis Miller or Philippe Lacoue-Labarthe, then there are also marked dissimilarities, which remain unread and which are equally as strong as the similarities, if not more so. However, the attempt to define deconstruction as a practice partakes of that tendency in the history of thought to assign resemblances between disparate things: conventionally, one erases the difference between thinkers, between texts, in the effort to domesticate the textual ground shared between them, producing a likeness into which all can be subsumed, at the cost of difference. Producing a theory is, therefore, producing what Derrida has described as a 'family atmosphere' (1989, 7), or tailoring a theoretical equivalent of the 'one-size-fits-all' garment.

However, there is neither the time nor the space, unfortunately, to do much more than to gesture, in a highly schematic manner, in the direction of the 'history of institutionalized deconstruction'. What the response to 'deconstruction' tells us is that 'deconstruction' whatever it may have or have not meant, had to be invented and given an institutional, unified identity, which, once defined and domesticated, could then be signalled, gestured towards, and often attacked, as merely one example of 'radical' thought 'infecting' 'our' – detractors and critics just love the bullying power which that plural pronoun affords them; they give themselves credit to speak for others, even though others haven't been consulted, and may even hold differing views – universities and colleges. I have yet to describe the conventional view of what deconstruction as a methodology might be, free from all critical attacks. Two brief examples will have to suffice, bearing in mind all the while Derrida's caveat concerning reading too hastily.

The misreading or not-reading of Derrida emerges chiefly from responses to his *of Grammatology*, where, among other things, he examines and calls into question the operation of meaningful structures of binary opposition as these pertain throughout the history of western metaphysics. This assessment of what Derrida termed at the time 'logocentrism' – the conceptual movement of thought which calms movement in favour of locating centres, origins, essences – was part of the work of *Of Grammatology* to expose how any system, structure, form or concept, in orienting itself according to some centre or truth, necessarily suppresses that which remains undecidable according to the logical economy of the structure. Yet that which is undecidable, or that which contradicts the logic and identity of the subject, is also that which serves to articulate the structure. This 'movement' if you will, this trace of the undecidable, is not something foreign to the structure. It is always already of it and in it as a necessary feature of the structure or concept's identity, yet always in excess of that which is deemed proper to the identity in question.

Derrida's discussion was taken to be part of a general method, and this method was called by critics deconstruction. From such acts of translation, translating from the specific to the general, come the tendencies to theorise deconstruction and, in so doing, to give deconstruction the 'it-ness' of a discernible identity, to create for it the 'family resemblance', and to assign 'it' 'its' institutional home. Such gestures in this direction can be found in discussions of deconstruction which attempt to come to terms with 'it' by Christopher Norris and Terry Eagleton. Norris suggests that:

> To deconstruct a text is to draw out conflicting logics of sense and implication, with the object of showing that the text never exactly means what it says or says what it means. (Norris, 1988, 7)

Clearly for Norris, deconstruction is an activity, available for the critical reader's mastery, and reliant upon that reader's active imposition of the method of analysis. Although the remark can be read as subject-sensitive (one could always draw out conflicting logics according to the peculiarities of the text), it is all too easy to see how such a remark, which is by no means untypical of definitions of deconstruction, can be amplified and otherwise worked up into a general programme for a critical purpose. Mistaking the drawing out of conflicting logics for what Derrida does or, worse, all that Derrida does, it is only another step to suggesting that this is what deconstruction does (as Norris in fact implies in the opening of the sentence). Eagleton offers a similar definition. Despite the fact that, in 1981, he had described deconstruction as a kind of 'left reformism' (1981, 133), giving it a provisional political identity, and subsequently made it plain that deconstruction was not 'of course, a system, or a theory, or even a method' (1981, 135), two years later here is Eagleton on the subject of deconstruction once more:

> 'deconstruction' is the name given to the *critical operation* by which . . . [binary] oppositions can be partly undermined, or by which they *can be shown* partly to undermine each other in the process of textual meaning . . . *The tactic of deconstructive criticism . . . is to show* how texts come to embarrass their own ruling systems of logic; and *deconstruction shows this* by fastening on the 'symptomatic' points, the *aporia* or impasses of meaning, where texts get into trouble, come unstuck, offer to contradict themselves. (Eagleton, 1983, 132, 133–4; emphases added)

Eagleton's view is similar to Norris's; phrases such as 'critical operation' and 'the tactic of deconstructive criticism' invent the possibility that one can deconstruct. The phrases I've highlighted all nod in the direction of a weary pedagogy, a quasi-scientifism of teaching by example. The implication, obviously, is that the reader can study Derrida's texts with the purpose of extracting a critical practice and then, having gained control over the niceties of this form of criticism, rendering it, that is, as a theory or method, can go away and apply the extracted model to whichever text he or she wishes.

This is not the case, however. If you spend some time with the texts of Jacques Derrida, or with critics whose work has been associated with that of Derrida, such as Nicholas Royle or J. Hillis Miller, you will find that there is no method, no reproducible structure of critique, except the act of responsible attentiveness.

EXEMPLARY ESSAYS:
TRANSLATION, TRANSFERENCE, TRANSPORT

I wish to consider now three essays by Derrida ('Letter to a Japanese Friend', *LT*, 282–7), Miller ('Thomas Hardy, Jacques Derrida and the "Dislocation of Souls"', *LT*, 288–97) and Royle ('On Not Reading: Derrida and Beckett', *LT*, 298–309) as being exemplary of the patient attentiveness to aspects of conceptual and literary structures which remain unread. Each of the essays deals in some sense with the movement between languages, between texts, even within the same language. Such movement is necessary and inevitable as that which makes meaning possible, even though the attempt to read after meaning is one which aims to still the movement. The three essayists do not work with a common theory of language and its effects. Derrida employs the occasion of the possible translation of *deconstruction* into Japanese to translate *deconstruction* from its translated, transformed institutional reception in the university. Miller reads a poem by Thomas Hardy to consider issues of communication and transference, where the transmission determines the identity of the addressee ahead of its arrival. Royle considers the tripartite relationship between the trope of not reading in Derrida, the not-reading of Derrida within the academy, and Derrida's professed inability to read Samuel Beckett. Each essay differs from every other essay, except in the respect paid to the singularity of that which is being read. There is no method here, no applied theory as such. Yet Royle, Miller and Derrida each share a similar attentiveness and patience to that which interests them.

As just mentioned, the occasion of Derrida's letter is the discussion of the possibilities of translating 'deconstruction' (see Bennington, 1993, 166–79). Immediately, Derrida turns the discussion of translation to the desire to avoid negative connotations for 'deconstruction', initiating a clearing of the ground by indicating that the significance of 'deconstruction' is best approached by considering what it ought not to be. At the same time, Derrida stresses that one cannot simply say what deconstruction is or is not because no univocal or unequivocal meaning pertains to the word, even if one stays in the same language, French (*LT*, 282). The sense of the word is always multiple within itself, and it cannot be traced to a single sense or source. Also, the word changes its meaning according to use. Thus, there is already a translation effect at work within one language and within one word. Moreover, Derrida points out, the meanings of 'deconstruction' have been translated or transferred according to the contexts of use (282). Here, Derrida is speaking of that translation which 'deconstruction' undergoes in the conceptual, technical and institutional (as, for example, in the transformation of 'deconstruction' into a technical name for a critical operation practised in an institutional guise).

For Derrida the question of deconstruction is always one of translation within the history of western thought. Deconstruction *qua* translation is the movement which inhabits and informs the 'conceptual corpus' of western thought (282). The question is one of how we effect the movement in thought between conceptual structures, other than by translation. Moreover, what is taken with us, what is transformed, and what remains untranslatable? To put this final question another way, what are the remains of deconstruction? What remains to be read in 'deconstruction' which the Anglo-American translation of 'decon-struction' has left unread? Derrida continues, explaining how the word imposed itself upon him in his search for the adequate translation, from German to French, of those terms used by Heidegger already mentioned, that avoided negative connotations (282–3). Derrida's opening advice in his correspondence is recalled, transferred, as he returns to an anterior moment of confrontation over the issue of translation. Explaining his choices, enumerating the linguistic, semantic and technical possibilities of 'deconstruction', Derrida re-presents the variety of meanings available in the family of words which, while offering 'models', do not represent 'the totality of what deconstruction aspires to at its most ambitious'. Furthermore, each 'model' cannot merely be accepted; its conceptual structure must first be questioned (283).

Remaining 'deconstruction', deconstruction nonetheless becomes translated. Derrida points to certain translations of 'deconstruction' which have occurred as a result of more obvious lexical meanings. From this he proceeds to elaborate the sense of 'deconstruction', not in some general, abstract or conceptual fashion (for that is impossible). Instead, he insists on discussing the possibility of the word's possible significations only within certain contexts. It should be clear from this that 'deconstruction' is not to be thought of as a conceptual term which arrives 'ready-made' to determine the meaning of a situation (such as the terms True/False might conventionally be said to do). Derrida grounds his use of the word by sketching a brief history of the emergence of 'deconstruction' as, initially, a 'structuralist' gesture, but also as a response to structuralism (284). Importantly here, 'deconstruction' is signalled as naming in part the compre-hension and reconstruction or reformation of the structural 'ensemble' of, say, a concept. As Derrida puts it, deconstruction names a 'genealogical restoration' (284).

Deconstruction cannot therefore be 'reduced to some methodological in-strumentality or to a set of rules and transposable procedures' (285), because that which is read as deconstructive, what remains elsewhere unread and yet translated into the language of the system, is intrinsic to the structurality of the structure. As Derrida says in this piece, deconstruction is neither 'an *analysis* nor a *critique*' (284). Furthermore, it is not a method, even if it appears to have suffered a history of translation aiming at the wilful reinvention of the term as a 'technical and methodological' metaphor for a process or procedure (285).

Derrida continues, pointing out that we should also avoid thinking of deconstruction as an act awaiting application to a text, object or theme (see Norris and Eagleton, above). If deconstruction *is* anything, it is an 'event'. It takes place, as the French reflexive verb suggests, everywhere, *in* every structure, theme, concept, conceptual organization, ahead of any consciousness (285). Its event is not the same every time but is a condition of or (we might say) translated by the structure in which it insists. Reading the taking place of deconstruction gives us to understand the operation of the structure, allowing the possibility of comprehension and reform. In effect, this comprehension and reformation (both terms requiring a patient analysis of their conceptual constitution) is what Derrida imagines as he sketches the possibility of translating deconstruction. His own text gestures towards the performance, if we can put it this way, of the deconstruction of deconstruction. This is not because Derrida's letter is a deconstructive reading, but because he analyses, within the limits of a specific use and reception, a specific history, the 'incapacity of the word to be equal to a "thought"' (285). Thus, this letter addresses itself, in anticipating its addressee and the future transmission of deconstruction, to deconstruction's previous communications.

J. Hillis Miller's essay also concerns the possible effects of transmission and communication. In presenting a reading of Thomas Hardy's poem 'The Torn Letter', Miller situates his discussion, providing a 'line of communication' (*LT*, 288), via Franz Kafka and Jacques Derrida, in order to consider the performative effects of a letter on the addressee as this is given exemplary expression through Hardy's text. Writing, Miller points out, citing Kafka, dislocates (289). It spaces addresser and addressee, not only from one another, but also from themselves, within themselves. The self is translated in the event of writing into 'multiple simultaneous selves' (296), or 'many different selves' (295), all of whom are phantom fragments of a supposedly stable identity. And this is what writing effects, this is the performative condition of writing: to spectralize the self. Furthermore, writing is not simply an act in which I engage, that act then producing a dislocated other self, or other selves consequent on my act of writing. To think in this fashion would still, in effect, be to locate my self, my presence or identity as the centre or origin of that writing. When Derrida says in 'Letter to a Japanese Friend' that the word 'deconstruction' 'imposed itself' on him (282), he signifies a certain arrival from some other place. Similarly, when Miller remarks that Hardy's poem, 'The Torn Letter' with which he is concerned in the essay in question, appears 'to have been written with foresight of Jacques Derrida's meditations on July 9, 1979' (291), he signals a transport, translation, or transference of particular traces which have no particular origin as such, and thus are, strictly speaking, phantomatic. There appears to be in writing what Derrida calls the 'figures of *dictation*' at work, an 'experience of the other . . . that commands a certain writing, perhaps all writing', and thereby installs in writing 'forms of originary alienation' (Derrida, 1995, 238). I do not merely become these different selves in writing, I am dictated to from multiple, simultaneous places which remain unidentifiable. Writing haunts and thus disorganizes any sense of location, temporality, priority or identity. Writing marks a differentiation, a spacing, as well as always having the power to transform 'you' into the 'you' which it addresses. This is not Miller's theory, and neither is it Derrida's, even though both men have, on numerous occasions, discussed the temporal and spatial dislocations, deferrals and differentiations traced in writing. It is precisely not a theory, as Miller's essay economically demonstrates, because this understanding of writing is effectively performed by both Kafka and Hardy, ahead of and in anticipation of any so-called 'theory of deconstruction'. For Miller, writing, even as it seeks to communicate and to connect, only serves in its very movement to displace by the very rhythm and spacing of its transport and transference. Indeed, displacement, dislocation, are always already the movement *of* and *in* writing, ahead of any transference or communication.

In situating his discussion of the performative haunting and fragmenting, ruinous effects of writing, particularly the act of writing a letter, Miller has recourse to Derrida's 'Télépathie'. In this essay, Derrida, Miller asserts and shows, discusses the possible performative effects of the letter on its recipient. As Miller puts it, the letter is capable, unintentionally, of creating the identity of the addressee (289). The performative power of the letter is in its ability to 'bring into existence an appropriate recipient', as Miller suggests in paraphrasing aspects of Derrida's essay, (289). The letter, before the event of its transference, carries in it the anticipated translation of the self, 'just as poor Boldwood, in Thomas Hardy's novel *Far from the Madding Crowd*, becomes the bold lover Bathsheba's valentine seems to tell him he is' (290). In drawing out the logic of Derrida's commentary on the performative capability of epistolary acts, Miller effectively shows how Hardy's poem, quite unintentionally, anticipates Derrida's argument (290–1), as has already been remarked, and even as Derrida's essay seems to have been written uncannily in anticipation of Miller's present argument (289). Derrida, writes Miller, 'has been programmed by the poem to write an interpretation of it before, beside, or after the letter, so to speak, in displacement from any conscious encounter with it' (291). Derrida's essay does not therefore invent a theory of epistolary transmission; he merely responds to that which the epistolary performs, 'translating' what is already there in writing, without ever having read Hardy's poem. Hardy's poem for Miller makes the same claims concerning transmission and performativity as Derrida's essay, albeit in a highly different, singular manner. Opening the lines of communication, Miller shows how, in a certain way, writing operates upon the reading self, who becomes not the 'I' who speaks, who thinks, who writes this poem letter, a letter in fragments, in ruins, but the self who becomes instead that 'you' to whom the poem addresses itself. Taking this to be the case, we should return to 'Letter to a Japanese Friend' in order to comprehend how the letter assumes the identity of a 'you' who we become if we receive its address carefully, no longer seeking to think of 'deconstruction' as a theory or method, but instead as that which traces all articulation of identities.

If there is a question here of reception and the construction of identity, then it must also be acknowledged, as does Nicholas Royle, that 'a writer's work can be received without being read: texts can have effects without being read' (*LT*, 299). Once more, though in a manner significantly different from either Miller or Derrida, the emphasis here is on communication, transmission, translation. Indeed, Royle, in beginning his essay, stresses a certain translation of Derrida's work as an effect of having not read Derrida. Royle's interest in having not read Derrida, Derrida not reading, and not reading in Derrida's work all concern Royle's principal interest in the 'spectral character of writing'(301). Miller, as already acknowledged, speaks of the ghostly as an effect of writing, of writing's ability to produce ghosts. This interest is pursued as Royle traces the relationship between Derrida's 'professed inability to write about' Samuel Beckett and the ways in which Beckett's work might be read so as to illuminate the questions of reading and writing after Derrida.

Thus the critic employs a reading of Beckett, much as Miller had provided a reading of Hardy, to address issues raised by these writers, but which they share with Derrida, albeit articulated in a manner very different from Derrida's own explorations. (Once more, the point here, in passing, is that Derrida's concerns do not originate with him, nor do they amount to a theory. They are, often, the concerns of literature but, within the conventional and even, in some cases, current horizon of expectations of literary analysis, remain unread.) Royle's concern in so doing is to move from conventional wisdom on Derrida – that his work is either 'philosophical' or 'literary' – in order to suggest that in part, because of the constant enunciation of authority vested in the articulation of 'I', Derrida is not sufficiently literary enough (299, 303).

Royle draws on Derrida's work on citationality and iterability as a condition of writing, the possibility that for writing to be readable, it can be transferred, transmitted, translated, outside its context or initial inscription (see Derrida, 1982, 309–30; 1991, 11–48). Take briefly the form of the proper name. Although the proper name is supposedly unique, in order that it be meaningful or readable, it must operate as does language in general: it must be capable of retransmission outside of its supposedly original occasion, unique status or authoritative inscription (see Bennington, 1993, 104–14, 148–66; also, see Bennington on title, 241–58). In being iterable, the proper name is not proper, but is wholly typical of writing's movements and translations. This quality of iterability pertains to all language, determining the fact of its readability. For Royle, that writing is iterable suggests that, far from having been read, definitively, it remains as a possible future iteration, still to be read, not yet having been read. The iterable movement of writing dissolves all authority, and specifically that, in this essay, of 'I'. 'I', that which 'I' write as a sign of my authority and control, also as an iterable re-mark bears in it in the possibility of its function and comprehension, the iteration beyond me, beyond my death (Bennington, 1993, 110). Thus, *in* the articulation of what Royle calls 'identity-as-authority' is traced the displacement of authority, not read, not yet read, awaiting reading (304). In short, the effects of writing.

Taking Derrida's professed feeling of intimate proximity of Beckett as the instance of not reading in Derrida (301), Royle turns to Beckett's text. Beckett's writing enacts for Royle this displacement of authority, where 'I' is not attributable to any source, but is, instead, the articulation of the spectral as the space of what is called the literary. The critic traces the instances of pronominal markers across the text of Beckett as the dislocation of authority through the written trace, which remains (as) unattributable. In this reading, the 'space of literature . . . disables and dissolves the very possibility of "one's own position"' (303). Derrida's writing, on the other hand, is, unlike Beckett's, marked by numerous signs of 'identity-as-authority', especially, as Royle shows, in their opening gambits of numerous essays where 'I' appears everywhere, centre-stage, apparently seeking to control the scene (303).

For this reason, Derrida's writing may be tentatively understood, the critic warily proposes, as not literary enough. From the perspective of the reading of Beckett, and juxtaposing Beckett with Derrida, the latter's writings are seen to 'deploy and rely on authority effects', which subsequently are 'dissolved and dispossessed' in the space of literature and by the effect of writing (304). Thus writing deconstructs the sovereign 'I'. 'I', in being written, deconstructs the assumption of it-self as a univocal location. *Se déconstruire*: it (itself) deconstructs (itself). In this understanding, if the literary is that which dispossesses one of all authority, Derrida's writing, which is taken as performing the deconstruction of the subject, in assuming the subject position only to displace that, does not go far enough, and needs 'to be further radicalized' (305). Realizing the 'folly' (305) of such a proposal, Nicholas Royle concludes by imagining a future moment of not reading Derrida, where Derrida is no longer cited, but is, in Royle's term *ex-cited*; quoted nowhere, but having passed spectrally into the language (305).

To the extent that deconstruction is still termed a method or a school of thought, the communication has not yet reached its destination. Having gone awry through the passages of translation, deconstruction remains unread in its guise as that which names an identity. The conventional narratives of so-called deconstruction leave deconstruction unread in their constructivist or determinist efforts to introduce 'deconstruction', to produce for 'it' a stable identity, to offer it up as one more, somewhat idiosyncratic yet nonetheless typical conceptual structure in the family atmosphere of western metaphysics, and thereby hope to keep at bay the spectrality which deconstruction barely names as the potential for making the invisible visible, through performative acts of reading that which has, thus far, remained unread. What can be said therefore is that, if, as a provisional definition after Royle, deconstruction is that multiplicity of traces which remain unread in the structurality of any text, structure, institution or concept, then deconstruction, we might say, is also that, precisely, which remains unread, in the texts of Jacques Derrida. Hence the need and the inescapable double-bind (not) to (not) read this signature, Jacques Derrida, as the authorising source of deconstruction.

NOTES TOWARDS A READING?

If, as I claim above, there is no such thing as deconstruction, no such thing as a deconstructive methodology or approach to the literary and, furthermore, no such thing as deconstruction, for want of a better word, other than that which is always already at work in various structures that we name, for example the literary or institutional, how can I, in all justice, present you with 'notes towards a reading' of whichever literary text I might choose from those which are addressed as the canonical works-in-common to which all the contributors have turned their attention?

Moreover, if, as so many critics (who find themselves described as 'deconstructionists') have claimed that there is no such thing as a final or a complete reading, that reading remains always to come, and not as something to be completed at a future date but as an impossible horizon always receding, to which we have an inescapable responsibility, knowing all the while that we will never have done with reading (and that this, furthermore, is the responsibility which the very idea of reading in all its impossibility imposes upon us), how can I then propose, under the rubric of some 'notes towards a reading' (which after all might be taken to be some excuse, more or less, for not reading at all or reading on the fly with all the implications which such a hasty act entails), to pretend that where we're heading might in fact resemble a reading?

These questions, far from resembling what might be called the so-called typical gesture of deconstructive or deconstructionist rhetoric (as though there were such a thing), are, in fact, both necessary and urgent. They point to the need to take our time, to read carefully, with patience and with diligence, being attentive to whatever text is before us, even, *especially*, the texts of Jacques Derrida. If I were to proceed in a wholly conventional manner, and pretend for the moment that all I had said above had not been written, and that, furthermore, that there *were* a methodology or analytical mode or procedure named deconstruction, I might then be able to offer something described as a reading. How would I do this? I would take from Derrida's work some instance of analysis and, having laid out its procedures; having then claimed that these singular procedures were typical of what Derrida does elsewhere (which I could show by turning to those texts that conveniently supported my hypothesis, which then could be proven with a combination of textual sleight of hand and arm wrestling, whereby in ignoring the difference of those other texts, the difference between the ways in which each text will proceed and therefore differ from every other text, could *therefore* be shown (and look, *there*, there it is, in that *therefore*, the autocratic tyranny of the logical inference in the guise, in the place of reading), I would continue then to take this procedure and 'apply' it to whatever text I cared to choose.

I could do that, but I'm not going to. Or, I could still recognize deconstruction as a form of reading, a school of critical discourse, a movement, and claim, with adequate support, that it's a well-known fact that deconstruction, so called, is one branch or subset of so-called poststructuralism, as though poststructuralism were itself the collective noun for a group of more or less easily definable discourses and critical practices . . .

– but wait a minute; doesn't the following chapter discuss poststructuralism?

– Yes, you're absolutely correct.

– And – and I'm sorry for jumping ahead like this, I know it's very bad reading practice, skipping over pages in order to get to the next section . . .

– That's quite alright, it's much more interesting than this one anyway.

– Anyway, where was I? Oh yes, in the next chapter, Mark Currie discusses poststructuralism and, in his discussion, he cites both Jacques Derrida and J. Hillis Miller, in pointing to the salient traits of poststructuralism. For example, he takes Derrida's commentary on Swiss Linguist Ferdinand de Saussure as an example of a poststructuralist analysis, doesn't he?

– Yes, but what does he then go on to say?

– Well he argues that Derrida reads in the text of Saussure an attempt to escape a realist discourse but that this 'anti-realist tendency' becomes implicated, as an example of a paradoxical instance in Saussure's thought, in the realism from which it strives to escape.

– You're right so far; I don't see the problem.

– There's no problem, but this appears to be a definition of poststructuralism . . .

– or one of its tendencies.

– Exactly.

– So, you're suggesting here is evidence of the existence of poststructuralism and that my own remark, which suggested that poststructuralism was a collective noun for a more or less discernible group of discourses is, in some measure, flawed.

– You appeared to be on the verge of repeating yourself . . .

– that's a personal problem which has nothing to do with deconstruction . . .

– as if you were going to say that poststructuralism doesn't exist.

– What does Mark Currie go on to say, in the same paragraph?

– He points out that there's a misconception concerning both structuralism and poststructuralism that they are based on radical new premises concerning language and its reality effects, when in reality, if you'll pardon the expression, such concerns go all the way back to Plato.

– so what does this tell you about 'poststructuralism' (and, perhaps, by the way, about 'deconstruction')?

– That these are names given to concerns and effects which, in different manifestations, have been around for much longer than the names themselves in their current use appear to acknowledge?

– Precisely. And, furthermore, you'll notice that, in the chapter on reader-response theory . . .

– in which Martin McQuillan claims that there's no such thing . . .

– McQuillan makes a statement to the effect that interest in the reader or audience has been around in critical discourse since Plato. So, on the one hand, we have to deal with the fact that recent critical discourse, of the last forty years or so, has a habit of wanting to create identities, of wanting to assign proper names to what, in the words of Martin McQuillan, comes down to reading. What this habit seeks to achieve is to call an end to the attention to detail in the name of identification and of getting on with business. However, on the other hand, what both Currie and McQuillan help us to realize is that there are certain critical concerns which persist and which have to do with the singularity of particular texts. As in the example provided by Currie, of Derrida reading Saussure, and paying attention to the fissure which opens in Saussure's discourse when, in striving to define the anti-realist condition of the sign, by being focused on the spoken, rather than the written, word, Saussure's language falls back into the mimetic or realist functions (that which is spoken of in a different context by K. M. Newton, above, as the resistance to empiricism in the criticism of Roland Barthes). In this, Derrida has an interest in what *in* language, specifically writing, undermines or disrupts the apparent logic or transparency of language. Such an interest, in the paradoxical, in the destabilizing, that are silent or overlooked and yet which one may find everywhere in structures, of logic, discourse, novels, epistemologies, institutions (and one can find these everywhere), is apparently typical of poststructuralism. And yet poststructuralism, so called, and deconstruction (if by this name, for one last time, we appear to mean not only the work of Derrida, but also Miller, Kamuf, Bennington, Royle and others), so-called, cannot be reduced to this interest.

– So Mark Currie is wrong?

– No; what he identifies in Derrida is one aspect of Derrida's work incommensurable with and irreducible to that name – poststructuralism – which is an economic, epistemo-institutional marker, symptomatic of larger tendencies as old as western thought, the signs of which remain unread. Currie, along with others in this volume, employs terms such as deconstruction and poststructuralism, in a manner symptomatic of institutionally organized activities which read in particular ways, for particular purposes, and thereby leaving behind that which remains unread. There is, in Currie's essay, a general tendency towards an institutional normalization, if I can put it this way. On the one hand, it operates by reading Derrida's quasi-concepts such as *différence* as metaphors which destabilize our conception of how language works, and, in doing so, gathers 'poststructuralist criticism as a whole' (arguing a similarity between the work of metaphor and the work of poststructuralism, as though one were a metonymic figure for the other); on the other hand, he passes over comments such as those of Paul de Man's, where, in the very essay Currie discusses, de Man remarks that 'the deconstruction is not something we have added to the text but it constituted the text in the first place' (*LT*, 339). It is exactly a remark such as this which we have seen already in this chapter, and it is precisely the kind of remark which the normative discursive, epistemological gesture must, like Wittgenstein, pass over in silence. What de Man has pointed out, prior to this remark – and we should turn to this if only so that we can move away from this awkward and misleading term, *deconstruction* – '[t]he reading is not "our" reading, since it uses only the linguistic elements provided by the text itself' (*LT*, 339). Even if we remain in the realm of the linguistic and the literary, supposing for the moment that it were possible to divorce the semantic from the epistemological, the metaphorical from the ideological, the narratological from the philosophical, it should be noted that the 'reading' takes places ahead of our analysis; reading of this kind is not imposed but at work as the dislocating condition of structures of meaning. And it is precisely that, which, in Currie's reading of de Man, remains unread.

So, if, simply for the sake of convenience, we employ a term such as poststructuralism, it is as part of a more complex process by which reading comes to an end because we have to be able to get on with things, or at least so we're told. Moreover, Currie's approach is not wrong but, to oversimplify, a process wholly consonant within epistemo-institutional imperatives, if we comprehend the extent to which the Derrida who is read, that is to say the strand followed by Currie in Derrida's text which is traced, is one in which a certain resistance to realism and mimeticism within language offers, among the many interests of Derrida which remain unread, a way of addressing narratological concerns counter to the mimetico-humanist interests of traditional criticism, such as New Criticism. Thus poststructuralism is produced as a necessary oppositional, and yet still institutional, countersignature, operating dialectically through the very identification by which it may be read as assuming oppositionality. Poststructuralism becomes identified as simply this process of reading which emphasizes the fragmentary and discontinuous rather than the organic, the unified and the homogeneous. Difference is named as that which is being read in the name of poststructuralism (and deconstruction), but it is precisely difference – by which, let's say, deconstruction may be identified in the first place, however mistakenly – which remains unread. And this is the very thing of which we should be wary, to stress this once more, this very same institutionalization of the insurrectionary text.

– But Currie also includes J. Hillis Miller, specifically Miller's reading of *Mrs Dalloway*, as an example of a poststructuralist reading which takes 'the received formalist view of the system of indirect discourse . . . showing it to be rather more complicated', particularly as this concerns what Miller terms the 'irreconcilability' between the individual and the universal. There is an attention in Miller's reading to elements of Woolf's novel which don't cohere in an organic, undifferentiated whole. That's rather like the tension observed by Derrida between the anti-realist tendency in Saussure's theory of language and the slippage into realism.

– Like, but not the same as.

– Yes.

– So there's a difference?

– Yes.

– And would you say that the difference is at least as important as the alleged similarity?

– Now that you mention it.

– So, while both Miller and Derrida complicate our understanding of the texts they choose to read by pointing to elements which cannot be resolved and therefore contain and are articulated by incommensurate difference by which the very idea of meaning is made possible in the first place, thereby unveiling that which is undecidable in any system or structure, neither does so in the same manner; each responds to a particular aspect which is peculiar to the text being discussed, and which, furthermore, can be said to announce the singularity of that text; while, at the same time, letting us know that we're engaged with the question of text by being marked, and remarking, that which is the same but not quite, the same and yet not the same; in short, we might say it's a question of repetition with a difference.

This is what Derrida, in *Limited Inc.*, terms iterability with its 'alogical logic' (1988, 119). Iterability does not, Derrida points out, signify repetition simply; it does not signify 'repeatability of the same, but rather alterability of this same idealized in the singularity of the event . . . It entails the necessity of thinking *at once* both the rule and the event, concept and singularity. There is thus a reapplication . . . of the *principle* of iterability to a *concept* of iterability that is never pure' (1988, 119). Something which is *like* something else (whether we are talking about texts, concepts or reading processes and effects) is not *the same as* that to which it has a resemblance. But normative acts of reading pass over and silence the difference that is already at work. This is the effect of (not)reading which is operative within the naming of reading as either deconstruction or poststructuralism, or, indeed, the former as a subset of the latter.

But then, it might be argued once more, that, in saying this, I am myself a deconstructionist or poststructuralist critic. This is the limit with which we have to deal, and which remains to be read. What I would say for now is that we only recognize the difference and the singularity by being able to note that which reiterates from text to text and which is irreducible to the self-same. So, if the question of reading comes down to this, to noticing that which remains to be read and yet having to read this every time in another manifestation as the alogical logic of the notion of reading, it has to be said that such reading is not very helpfully served by giving it a name such as 'deconstruction' or 'poststructuralism' (or, indeed, 'literary theory'). The act of reading is, itself, irreducible to a finite, determinable set of concerns which, once understood, will remain the same for every text we approach and for all time.

With this in mind, let's turn to Tennyson's *In Memoriam A.H.H.*, remembering all the while that this sketch, in its consideration of the work of the trope of faith as an instance of iterability, and in its acknowledgement of matters of translation and transport, neither amounts to a 'deconstruction' of the text (except in that this is to observe the work of deconstruction in the motions of iterability, supplement and transference within the structures of the text), nor to a *reading*, in the sense that I could produce an articulation of *In Memoriam* which leads towards a unitary meaning or which assumes that there is no remainder. As Geoffrey Bennington has put it, there is no end to reading because 'no one reading will ever be able to claim to have exhausted the textual resources available in the text being read' (2000, 11). Thus the figure of *towards* in the phrase

NOTES TOWARDS A READING OF *IN MEMORIAM A.H.H.*

should be read not as indicating a 'convergent movement' (Bennington, 2000, 11) towards a determinable horizon named as 'a reading'; instead, we should consider this gesture as naming what Bennington describes as a 'dispersive perspective' (11). The temporality of this *towards* (which, by the way, is arguably, what concerns Tennyson apropos the matter of faith) is that of 'an always-yet-to-come' (Kamuf, 1997, 171).

Articulated through irregular though frequently recurring tropes, the question of Tennyson's faith resists as much as it encourages inquiry and analysis. *In Memoriam*'s faith is made manifest through indirection, anamnesis and a specifically Christian 'analogy of apperception or appresentation' (Husserl, cited in Ward, 1995, 151), rather than through conventional Christological representations predicated on the promise of presence or the locatability of some logocentric origin. Tennyson's is not a negative theology, though, even though many of the lyrics proceed by negation. Tennyson's faith is expressed through something like a quasi-theology which comes from within and yet exceeds theology in its comprehension of the limits of language to express the unknown, the other, and to allow the other to manifest itself as a haunting spirit through a language expressing that limit. There are limits, after all, to what can be expressed in words (*IM*, 74.9–10; 75.13, 16). Words halt on the brink of representation, instead bearing witness to the unrepresentable. Thus the poet halts, saying that he cannot say. *In Memoriam* is a fragmented, self-fragmenting text which seeks to find ways of speaking of God indirectly, and attempting to do so through the constant acknowledgement of an undecidability which haunts even the most assured figures of speech pertaining to the matters of faith, as though speech were itself the constant remarking of the border of apperception. Admitting that one cannot see, that one cannot put into words what one can see, and that one's responsibility is to leave 'unexpress'd': this is to articulate one's faith in other words; it is to give oneself over to the incorporate, immanent spirit within which one dwells and which haunts one from within and which yet is to come.

Tennyson makes this clear in the following qualification: 'No visual shade of some one lost, / But he, the Spirit himself, may come' (*IM*, 93.5–6). The distinction is made between the ghost and the spirit, though not explained. At most, one might comprehend the limit at which Tennyson speaks through a fragmenting temporality within the line. The ghost, the revenant, is not our concern here, Tennyson tells us. That is merely the phenomenal, anthropomorphized representation of 'some one' returning from the past. The Spirit is different from the ghost in that it is remarked as the haunting possibility of something other which may or may not make itself apparent, from a temporal moment to come. The analogy of apperception makes the two forms of haunting distinct, broken off from one another by the play on similarity or resemblance which is itself troubled as the limit of representation, and further disjointed through the temporal distinction formally marked between the two lines. And the distinction is enforced further in that implicit rejection of what may be seen in favour of what may be hoped for: or, in other words, that possibility, the articulation of which expresses faith. However, faith, to be faith, has also to be spirited away, read as the experience of *only* the supplement-without-origin, refiguring itself if it is to operate for Tennyson within *In Memoriam*.

It therefore seems necessary to make the point that while faith is the principal focus of this sketch, it is not to be mistaken as the figure *par excellence* of supplementary tropological play in *In Memoriam*. Faith is but one of many figures which operate the troping machinery of the text. It is possible to name only a few of these tropological devices which haunt Tennyson's poem: haunting, light, illumination, dust, veil, ghosts, phantoms, flashes, spirit, spectre, love, tract, type. None of the figures remain stable in Tennyson's use, even as they all serve in the illumination of faith, or as they enlighten the reader as to faith's power to illuminate, addressing also faith's spectrality. Nor are they rooted in some originary figure.

With regard to the tropological work of *In Memoriam*, matters are never articulated unequivocally. Although the poet's 'prospect and horizon' (*IM*, 38.4) has vanished, there remains a 'doubtful gleam of solace' (*IM*, 8). It is significant in the context of Tennysonian tropes relating to the question of faith that the adjectival form ('doubtful') modifies, and is modified by, a questionable illumination ('gleam'), which is both figurative *and* literal. While the effect of the line is to put doubt into doubt even as it is expressed, the undecidability of the figure puts into doubt the certainty of the reading to decide how the trope's movement may be calmed. Elsewhere 'doubt' is again related to the disappearance of light, a conventional enough Christian, specifically Broad Church configuration for the loss of faith (*IM*, 41.19; 95.49). Yet, this is rendered complicated by the repeated insistence on the spectrality of doubt. We read of 'a spectral doubt' (*IM*, 41.19), the 'slender shade of doubt' (*IM*, 48.7) and 'doubts', we are told, are 'spectres of the mind' (*IM*, 96.13, 15). Doubt is therefore doubtful and difficult to read. Tennyson casts a shadow on the unequivocal projection of doubt as that which is absolutely distinguishable from faith.

Tennyson makes this plain when he remarks: 'There lives more faith *in* honest doubt / Believe we, than in half the creeds' (*IM*, 96.11–2; emphasis added). Faith is incorporate: a spectral figure without presence it nonetheless *lives on*, incarnate in doubt itself. And this is a matter of faith ('Believe we'). Faith persists uncannily in the articulation of doubt with more vitality than in any theological system or programme. Read as a quasi-concept, destabilized through figural reiteration, faith, instead of remaining stable as an idealized figure or stable concept, marks, to recall Derrida's words on iterability, 'an aconceptual concept' as Tennyson employs it: 'heterogeneous to the philosophical concept of the concept', faith is, in Tennyson's translation of the term, 'a "concept" that marks both the possibility and the limit of all idealization and hence of all conceptualization' (1988, 118). Tennyson's affirmation of doubt is also then, simultaneously, an affirmation of faith. There is in Tennyson's figures the reading of faith's survival as a process of transformations, transportations and translations *within* and *despite* the idea of systems.

A tension between translation and transcendence which opens onto the aporetic experience of faith can be read in constant attention to transport, from one state to another, which also figures a blending. This double movement is described by Tennyson in the poem as 'the same, but not the same' (*IM*, 87.14). Such double-writing is figured in a number of places, employing the formula *from_to_* (*IM*, [Prologue] 25, 35; 21.19; 41.2; 44.14; 46.7; 72.6; 89.33; 123.6; 126.10) as a transformative trope which, reworked some thirty or more times, establishes the iterability of faith's faith as that which is simultaneously unrepresentable, unprogrammable and yet which is immanent in all forms, all phenomena. Furthermore, these reiterated figures operate in a manner resistant to any but the most basic systematization. Redoubling and moving elsewhere, they speak to a constant disinterrance within the same.

There is another way to comprehend the double work of this figure, a doubling which interrupts any straightforwardly discernible structure. *From_to_* is marked by, and remarks, both spatial and temporal transition, regardless of what comes to fill those blank spaces. We read the implication of a motion from one place, one event, one condition, state of being or emotion to another. We also read temporal transition, inasmuch as, conventionally speaking, one may be said to move from the past to the future. Yet the formula in question completes each phrase by a kind of figural palindrome, so that the motion appears to recirculate, to return to its beginning point, to disrupt and thus paradoxically double itself in its own process. This brings me back to the analogy of apperception or appresentation, that troping wherein is figured, in Tennyson's words, 'the same, but not the same'. Each figure is thus invested with the possibility of a reading-to-come which is, in the words of Werner Hamacher, 'still not yet what it already is' (1998, 3). Yet, we can only read the process of analogy indirectly through the basic formal resemblance which its reiteration makes possible. This analogical formula appears to build as it reiterates, and yet it resists unity and coherence. The 'building', if it can be called this, is already disrupted by the dissimilarity on which it also relies. There is none but the most basic structural similarity between 'from state to state' or 'from place to place' and 'From flower to flower, from snow to snow' (*IM*, 22.4) or 'From April to April' (*IM*, 22.7). Nor could one draw out distinctly that which echoes from these lines to 'From orb to orb, from veil to veil' (*IM*, 30.28).

Faith is not coherent then, it never can be comprehended as such. Faith maintains itself and its precarious possibility by always already having moved on, by having spirited itself into an other manifestation, whereby faith is recognized in the articulation of belief: '. . . we, that have not seen thy face,/ By faith, and faith alone, embrace, / Believing where we cannot prove' (*IM*, [Prologue], 2–4). Embodying and even, as the poet puts it, embracing contradiction (the absence of proof is taken as 'proof', if not of Christ, but faith's faith in the other's revenance), faith, distinguished from knowledge, appears as the result of illumination and as illumination itself, illumination of faith illuminating itself from within the darkness that we name doubt, and which, mistakenly, we believe to be separate from faith, not a necessary condition for the revenance of faith.

In Memoriam struggles with the very grounds of any conventional Christology which operates through mimesis. It struggles at the limit of representation so as to apprehend the Christological spectre, the invisible other within the conventions of form. This invisible, haunting other is faith, which is precisely that which 'we cannot know' (*IM* [Prologue], 21). The impossibility or, more accurately, the undecidability concerning the 'Strong Son of God, immortal Love' (*IM* [Prologue], 1), is exactly the precondition of faith. Faith, like the son of God, cannot be represented because it is not available to sight or representation. And, as if to make this point as clearly as possible, Tennyson opens the poem with the line just quoted, whereby, through a process of translation, Christ is disembodied, anthropomorphic representation resisted, in being named 'immortal Love'. Thus, from coming to terms with the impossibility of Christological representation, faith grows. It is invisible and yet illuminates ('seeing' its very invisibility enlightens), a light emanating from the Son of God as a 'beam in darkness' (*IM* [Prologue], 24). Moreover, in recognizing this, we apprehend how not only is Christ Love, but also illumination. There is no body of Christ here. Christ illuminates, but faith also illuminates, and what it brings to light is the light of the other. Such enlightenment, while coming from an other place, also comes from and dwells within, collapsing distinctions such as inside/outside. What therefore has to be negotiated through the revelation of faith-as-incarnation is a kind of spectral onto-theology which, to paraphrase and cite Derrida on onto-theology, is that which dismisses or rejects religion as a 'little system', the 'petty cobwebs we have spun' (*IM*, 124.8), while, paradoxically, being that which also 'perhaps . . . informs . . . the theological and ecclesiastical, even religious, development of faith' (Derrida, 1998, 15).

QUESTIONS FOR FURTHER CONSIDERATION

1. If deconstruction names neither an analysis nor a method, to what extent is it useful, or even possible, to retain the word within critical discourse? If the word and all that is invoked by it is not employed, what remains?
2. How might you begin to discern the workings of deconstruction within institutions?
3. In the light of the discussions of the texts of Derrida and others, how do we comprehend a statement such as 'I am there and I am not there'?
4. Do any of the 'themes' of *In Memoriam* have any meaning outside the textual systems ('philosophical', 'cultural', 'ideological', 'theological') of the poem? Are such systems themselves complete, or do they belong to other structures and systems?
5. Consider the figure of 'Arthur Hallam' in *In Memoriam* as another manifestation of the tropological work of the poem.
6. Is there any aspect or figure of, or concept in, *In Memoriam* which remains stable, in the light of what has been said of the question of faith?

ANNOTATED BIBLIOGRAPHY

de Man, Paul. *Allegories of Reading: Figural Language in Rousseau, Nietzsche, Rilke, and Proust.* New Haven, CT, 1979.
The essays collected here demonstrate the author's fascination with European Romanticism and its legacy, the rhetoric of identity and the relationship between figural language and reality. Paul de Man takes language as a form of reflection, which for him is a fraught and problematic process. The author works through a series of close readings, demonstrating how the relationship between word and thing is conventional, not phenomenal. See the references to this text in the bibliographies to reader-response theory above and Poststructuralism below.
Derrida, Jacques, and John D. Caputo. *Deconstruction in a Nutshell: A Conversation with Jacques Derrida.* New York, 1997.
The first part of this book is a roundtable discussion with Derrida, in which he responds to questions concerning deconstruction, improvising and elaborating points concerning philosophy, justice, responsibility, the gift, the idea of messianism, community and his writings on James Joyce. From the roundtable discussion, Caputo elaborates on issues raised in the roundtable in seven chapters, which do double service as a commentary on the discussion and a lucid introduction to certain major topics in the text of Jacques Derrida, without reducing Derrida's text to a systematic or formulaic methodology.
Derrida, Jacques. *Of Grammatology*, trans. Gayatri Chakravorty Spivak. Baltimore, MD, 1974.
Divided in two sections, the first considers the nature of writing in relation to the concept of Being. It proposes through its own practice or performance a critical or 'grammatological' reading which examines the aporetic in metaphysical thought. Derrida posits the idea that metaphysics relies on the suspension of logical movement and the hierarchical manipulation of binary oppositions which support such thinking. Derrida

examines the oppositions 'voice/writing' and 'presence/absence' to consider how in the history of western metaphysical thought the former term is always privileged over the latter. The idea of writing is examined for the lack of attention paid to its operations in philosophy and for the way it is distrusted as a form of communication. Derrida works with a number of terms which have subsequently been considered by those who insist on the idea of deconstruction as a critical methodology as essential to the lexicon of deconstruction: trace, inscription, logocentrism, reserve, gramme, *différance*, supplement, logocentrism.

Derrida, Jacques, *Aporias*, trans. Thomas Dutoit. Stanford, CA, 1993.

Two essays, 'Finis' and 'Awaiting (at) the Arrival', comprise this publication, in which Derrida considers the aporia between singularity and the general, while also addressing various modes of specificity of experience. The aporetic obligation involved in playing host to the foreign while respecting its foreignness is considered. Derrida's interests are articulated around a critique of various cultural histories and theorizations of death.

Kamuf, Peggy. *The Division of Literature or the University in Deconstruction*. Chicago, 1997.

Kamuf offers a sustained historicization of the development of literary studies in the university, while looking also at the political aspect of debates concerning the perception of 'deconstruction' and its assumed relationship to the question of 'political correctness' among academics and within institutions. Kamuf pursues this discussion also through a consideration of the figure of 'credit' in, among others, Herman Melville and G. W. F. Hegel.

Lacoue-Labarthe, Phillippe. *Typography: Mimesis, Philosophy, Politics*, intro. Jacques Derrida, trans. Christopher Fynsk et al. Cambridge, MA, 1989; rpt. Stanford 1998.

A selection of essays from the French edition; the English-language edition is introduced by Derrida, whose discussion of Lacoue-Labarthe's work focuses on the latter's analysis of mimesis. Concentrating on both philosophy and poetics, particularly in the texts of Hölderin, the essays offer radical reappraisals of questions of subjectivity, paradox and mimesis, politics, mimesis and supplementarity, and the logic of identity, demonstrating the indirect yet powerful influence of Derrida on certain aspects of philosophical thought in France today.

SUPPLEMENTARY BIBLIOGRAPHY

Beardsworth, Richard. *Derrida and the Political*, London, 1996.

Bennington, Geoffrey. 'Deconstruction is Not What You Think', in *Art & Design*, 4: 3/4, 1988.

————. *Legislations: The Politics of Deconstruction*. London, 1994.

————. 'X', in *Applying: to Derrida*, eds John Brannigan, Ruth Robbins and Julian Wolfreys. Basingstoke, 1996.

————. *Interrupting Derrida*. London, 2000.

———— and Jacques Derrida. *Jacques Derrida*, trans. Geoffrey Bennington. Chicago, 1993.

Brandt, Joan, *Geopoetics: The Politics of Mimesis in Poststructuralist French Poetry and Theory*. Stanford, CA, 1997.

Brannigan, John, Ruth Robbins and Julian Wolfreys, eds. *Applying: to Derrida*. Basingstoke, 1996.

Caputo, John D. *The Prayers and Tears of Jacques Derrida: Religion without Religion*. Bloomington, IN, 1997.

Caruth, Cathy. *Unreclaimed Experience: Trauma, Narrative, and History*. Baltimore, MD, 1996.

Clark, Timothy. *Derrida, Heidegger, Blanchot: Sources of Derrida's Notion and Practice of Literature*. Cambridge, 1992.

Critchley, Simon. *The Ethics of Deconstruction: Derrida and Levinas*. Oxford, 1992.
Derrida, Jacques. *Writing and Difference*, trans. Alan Bass. London, 1978.
———. *Dissemination*, trans. and intro. Barbara Johnson. Chicago, 1981.
———. *Margins of Philosophy*, trans. Alan Bass. Chicago, 1982.
———. 'Deconstruction and the Other: Interview' Richard Kearney, *Dialogues with Contemporary Continental Thinkers: The Phenomenological Heritage*. Manchester, 1983.
———. *Glas*, trans. John P. Leavey, Jr and Richard Rand. Lincoln, NE, 1986.
———. *The Post Card: From Socrates to Freud and Beyond*, trans. Alan Bass. Chicago, 1987.
———. *The Truth in Painting*, trans. Geoff Bennington and Ian McLeod. Chicago, 1987.
———. *Limited Inc.*, trans. Samuel Weber et al. Evanston, IL, 1988.
———. *The Ear of the Other: Otobiography Transference Translation*, trans. Peggy Kamuf. Lincoln, NE, 1988.
———. *Of Spirit: Heidegger and the Question*, trans. Geoffrey Bennington and Rachel Bowlby. Chicago, 1989.
———. 'At this very moment in this work here I am', trans. Ruben Berezdivin, in *Re-Reading Levinas*, eds Robert Bernasconi and Simon Critchley. Bloomington, IN, 1991.
———. *Given Time: I. Counterfeit Money*, trans. Peggy Kamuf. Chicago, 1992.
———. *The Other Heading: Reflections on Today's Europe*, trans. Pascale-Anne Brault and Michael B. Naas, intro. Michael B. Naas. Bloomington, IN, 1992.
———. *Specters of Marx: The State of the Debt, the Work of Mourning, and the New International*, trans. Peggy Kamuf, intro. Bernd Magnus and Stephen Cullenberg. New York, 1994.
———. *Archive Fever: A Freudian Impression*, trans. Eric Prenowitz. Chicago, 1995.
———. *The Gift of Death*, trans. David Wills. Chicago, 1995.
———. *On the Name*, ed. Thomas Dutoit, trans. David Wood, John P. Leavey, Jr and Ian McLeod. Stanford, CA, 1995.
———. *Points . . .: Interviews*, 1974–1994, ed. Elizabeth Weber, trans. Peggy Kamuf et al. Stanford, CA, 1995.
———. 'The Time is Out of Joint', trans. Peggy Kamuf, in *Deconstruction is/in America*, ed. Anselm Haverkamp. New York, 1995.
———. '"As if I were dead": An Interview with Jacques Derrida', in *Applying: to Derrida*, eds John Brannigan, Ruth Robbins and Julian Wolfreys. Basingstoke, 1996.
———. *The Politics of Friendship*, trans. George Collins. London, 1997.
———. *Resistances of Psychoanalysis*, trans. Peggy Kamuf, Pascale-Anne Brault and Michael Naas. Stanford, CA, 1998.
Hart, Kevin. *The Trespass of the Sign: Deconstruction, Theology and Philosophy*. Cambridge, 1989.
Hobson, Marion. *Jacques Derrida: Opening Lines*. London, 1998.
Howells, Christina. *Derrida: Deconstruction from Phenomenology to Ethics*. Cambridge, 1999.
Kamuf, Peggy. 'Preface', in *A Derrida Reader: Between the Blinds*, ed. Peggy Kamuf. New York, 1991.
Kronick, Joseph G. *Derrida and the Future of Literature*. Albany, NY, 1999.
Johnson, Barbara. *The Critical Difference: Essays in the Contemporary Rhetoric of Reading*. Baltimore, MD, 1980.
Johnson, Christopher. *System and Writing in the Philosophy of Jacques Derrida*. Cambridge, 1993.
Miller, J. Hillis. *Fiction and Repetition: Seven English Novels*. Cambridge, MA, 1982.
———. *Theory Now and Then*. Hemel Hempstead, 1991.
———. *Topographies*. Stanford, CA 1995.
Nancy, Jean-Luc. *The Birth to Presence*, trans. Brian Holmes et al. Stanford, CA, 1993.
Plotnitsky, Arkady. *Complementarity: Anti-Epistemology after Bohr and Derrida*. Durham, NC, 1994.

Ronell, Avital. *The Telephone Book: Technology, Schizophrenia, Electric Speech*. Lincoln, NF, 1989.

Royle, Nicholas, ed. *Afterwords*. Tampere, 1992.

————. *After Derrida*. Manchester, 1995.

Sartilliot, Claudette. *Citation and Modernity: Derrida, Joyce, and Brecht*. Norman, OK, 1993.

Smith, Robert. *Derrida and Autobiography*. Cambridge, 1995.

Steigler, Bernard. *Technics and Time, 1: The Fault of Epimetheus*, trans. Richard Beardsworth and George Collins. Stanford, CA, 1998.

Wolfreys, Julian. *Deconstruction • Derrida*. London, 1998a.

————, John Brannigan and Ruth Robbins, eds. *The French Connections of Jacques Derrida*. Albany, NY, 1999.

Wood, David, ed. *Derrida: A Critical Reader*. Oxford, 1993.

OTHER WORKS CITED

Banville, John. *Ghosts*. New York, 1994.

Derrida, Jacques. 'Introduction: Desistance', trans. Christopher Fynsk, in Philippe Lacoue-Labarthe *Typography: Mimesis, Philosophy, Politics*, trans. Christopher Fynsk et al. Cambridge, MA, 1989.

————. 'The Rhetoric of Drugs', in *Points . . . Interviews*, 1974–1994, ed. Elisabeth Weber, trans. Peggy Kamuf et al. Stanford, CA, 1995.

————. 'Faith and Knowledge: The Two Sources of 'Religion' at the Limits of Reason Alone', trans. Samuel Weber, in *Religion*, eds Jacques Derrida and Gianni Vattimo. Stanford, CA, 1998.

————. 'Marx & Sons', in *Ghostly Demarcations: A Symposium on Jacques Derrida's Specters of Marx*, ed. Michael Sprinker. London, 1999.

Hamacher, Werner. *Pleroma: Reading in Hegel*. Stanford, CA, 1998.

Ward, Graham. *Barth, Derrida and the Language of Theology*. Cambridge, 1995.

Wolfreys, Julian. 'An "Economics" of Snow and the Blank Page, or, "Writing" at the "Margins": "Deconstructing" "Richard Jeffries"?', in *Literary Theories: A Case Study in Critical Performance*, eds Julian Wolfreys and William Baker. London, 1996.

————. 'Justifying the Unjustifiable: A Supplementary Introduction, of Sorts', *The Derrida Reader: Writing Performances*, ed. Julian Wolfreys. Edinburgh, 1998b.

CRITICISM AND CREATIVITY: POSTSTRUCTURALIST THEORIES

Mark Currie

The most controversial moment in Paul de Man's essay 'Semiology and Rhetoric' (*LT*, 328–41) is an aside in his final sentence which claims that the difference between literature and criticism is delusive. I want to use this as a point of entry to poststructuralist literary theory. In different ways it is a proposition which takes its place in the work of many of poststructuralism's key thinkers from Barthes's formula that there are no more critics, only writers, to the inventive critical styles of Derrida and other deconstructors. Its explanation opens up other questions, such as the genealogy of poststructuralism, the issue of reference in language, the possibility of scientific objectivity, and the knowability of the past. It also helps to define the legacy of poststructuralism, particularly in terms of the destruction of literary theory as we knew it, and the rise of storytelling as a critical activity, both in the novel and in the new historicisms.

There is nevertheless something quite obnoxious about a critic demolishing the boundary between literary and critical writing. It seems to involve an unjustified self-elevation on the critic's part, from the secondary and derivative role of a commentator to that of a primary creative producer, and in the same stroke it drags literature down by implying that its importance lies in the critical knowledge that it yields about itself and literature at large. Both of these tendencies are evident in poststructuralist approaches. There is an attitude of apparent self-importance, a feeling that the reading is more important than the thing read, and a recurring claim that valued literary texts speak only of themselves, no matter how strong the illusion that they are capable of reference to something else. Given these apparent aspirations to literariness, it is ironic that the language of poststructuralist discourse sets new standards of ugly complexity, pretentious neologism and puerile over-abstraction. Perhaps the real delusion lies in this chippy rearrangement of an established hierarchy.

But de Man was not blowing his own trumpet in this way, nor expecting *Allegories of Reading* to displace Proust in the canon. He was responding to a kind of reciprocity between literature and criticism in the twentieth century that seemed to set them on a convergent course. A useful rubric under which to describe this convergence is the notion of the decline of realism, a process which can be traced in parallel through literary modernism and formalist criticism. There is a clear sense in which the modernist novel draws much of its experimental energy from the rejection of realistic conventions established in the eighteenth and nineteenth centuries. On one hand there is the ironization of those conventions, a kind of illusion-breaking candour about fictional techniques, a baring of devices, which foregrounds the illusory and constructed nature of the realistic effect. This species of illusion-breaking irony includes techniques such as dramatizing the process of fictional production, parodying past styles, the use of surrogate authors and readers, the poeticization of prose style and narrative self-commentary. It is a kind of literary self-referentiality which seems to incorporate critical distance in a novel, and gives it a critical function in relation to its own history of rules and procedures. On the other hand there is the assertion of a different kind of reality: a more subjective, interior and contingent reality than the stable social, physical and external world of the conventional novel. To this tendency we could attribute technical innovations such as multiple narrators, sustained focalization, stream of consciousness, an increasingly suggestive symbolism and the use of outside worlds as metaphors for inner landscapes. In short, the modernist novel contributes to a growing doubt over the viability of realism as a concept by highlighting its artificiality and its fluidity.

There are two points to be made here about the decline of realism and the ascent of reading. The first is that novels like this tend to generate more ambiguous and multiple meanings than those rooted in the faithful representation of a pre-existing reality, placing a greater burden on reading as a process of rendering the text intelligible. The second is that if reality is seen as contingent and constructed, there is a sense in which realism itself is a reading, one possible reading among others, or a collective agreement over what constitutes reality. To view realistic literature as a kind of reading is to emphasize that reality is not prior to language and interpretation but a product of it, as well as to massively extend the scope of the term *reading*. There is a feeling that realism is a kind of sham: a discourse that effaces its own techniques, language and role in projecting structure onto experience which has no shape *per se*. And this feeling is in evidence in much of the literary criticism of the first half of the twentieth century, which seemed to accept the critical insights of the modernist novel and incorporate them into their own critical readings. So, for example, in Russian formalism and early structuralism, one of the main concerns is to expose the sham of realism by baring its devices and revealing its role in projecting shape and form onto the world.

If the critique of realism was underway within the novel itself in the modernist period, it was only a part of more widespread awareness of the role of language and convention in structuring reality. At around the same time, Saussure was making a similar claim not only for realistic fiction, but for the conditions of linguistic reference in general: that words are capable of reference only because they project their system of differences onto the non-linguistic world. Like literary realism, then, the language system at large generates an illusion that words can refer directly and objectively to reality, but their ability to do so depends on the hidden conditions – conventions, codes and differences – which make reference possible. In the light of this proposition, the role of the critic shifts from being a commentator on the illusion generated by language (say the fictional world) to that of someone who unveils these hidden conditions, revealing the underlying structural relationships that enable meaning.

There is clearly a common philosophical denominator between these approaches to realism and reference, and therefore a reciprocity between them. But the contemporaneity of Saussure's *Course* and the modernist critique of fictional realism can be slightly misleading. There may well have been unseen historical forces contributing to this climate of scepticism, relativism and anti-realism, forces also at work in the emergence of scientific relativity, existential philosophy or psychoanalysis. But the actual reciprocity between fictional and structuralist critiques of realism was not apparent, especially in the Anglo-American tradition, until much later in the twentieth century, when Saussure's work was taken up in the humanities and the anti-realist tendencies in criticism found their theoretical underpinnings. But if Saussure's account of the sign acts as a kind of linguistic premise for structuralist thought, the same can not really be said of poststructuralism. If we take Derrida's dealings with Saussure as an example, we do not find him paying homage to structural linguistics as an origin of anti-realist thinking. His reading of Saussure's account of the sign in *Of Grammatology* is as a symptom of something much larger, namely the tendency in anti-realist thinking to remain implicated with realism no matter how hard it may strive to escape. In his early work, Derrida calls this inescapable condition the 'metaphysics of presence', which he describes as an ineluctable desire to ground general explanations and theories in some form of presence To the extent that this desire is at work in Saussure, it is worth pointing out that for Derrida, Saussure is just one example of the anti-realist tendency with a much longer history, not its origin, and that it is considerably easier to find proclamations in Derrida's work of the foundational influence of modernist writers on his thinking than of *The Course in General Linguistics*. I say this partly to support the idea of the convergence of literature and criticism that de Man advances, but also to correct a wide misconception often spread by critical commentators that structuralism was based on some radical new premise about language, and that poststructuralism found a way of making it more radical still. As Derrida is always reminding us, questions about realism, or the ability of language to refer to an extra-linguistic reality, have been with us at least since Plato, and can be traced throughout the history of western metaphysics, including literature.

Returning for a moment to Derrida's relation to Saussure, we find him talking of the sign not as some radical new hypothesis but as a concept inherited from the old dualist tradition of metaphysical thinking, the key characteristic of which was to separate the form and the content of language. But the radical impact of Saussure's thesis lay in the proposition that in language 'there are only differences without positive terms', a proposition taken by most structuralists to mean that the content of a word was a kind of illusion, a referential illusion, and that its real content was in fact the hidden system of differences which enabled that illusion to occur. Derrida's claim is that this proposition is undermined by the fact that Saussure still understands the sign as a two-sided entity, a *signifier* and a *signified*. If Saussure was attempting to articulate a monistic theory of the form and content of language and argue for their inseparability, the distinction of signifier and signified is unnecessary. It is nothing more than a residue of dualistic metaphysics which subverts the monism which the *Course* proposes. Worse than that, it installs an ambiguity in the premise of structuralist thought which can be traced through literary structuralism as a kind of slippage between two markedly different attitudes to linguistic analysis. Does a structuralist critic deny the presence of content in language or merely ignore it? Many commentators give the impression that the radical reputation of structuralist criticism was founded on the outright denial of referential content in language, and that structural linguistics provided the hypothesis that, however powerful the referential illusion, language could only ever refer to itself. But this kind of hypothesis is not easily found in the work of structural linguists.

If we take Roman Jakobson, whose work on the question of reference and self-reference was enormously influential on this kind of commentary, we find no such denial of referential content. In 'Closing Statement' in 1960, he argued that any utterance or act of communication had several distinguishable aspects or functions occurring simultaneously in different degrees. For example, it is possible for an utterance to convey meaning about the outside world, the language system and the message itself at the same time, or in his own terminology, to be at once referential, metalingual and poetic. Some discourses, he argues, seem more orientated towards one of these functions than others. Poetry, for example, foregrounds the poetic function of language by drawing attention to the way in which things are said, to the point where reference seems like a lesser consideration; prose, on the other hand, seems to use language in a more transparent way and so foregrounds the referential function. But if the poetic function seems to dominate in poetry, this does not mean that the referential function is negated or absent, nor that the poetic function of prose is absent. A linguistic analysis can focus on any aspect of the communication that it pleases – the poetic function of prose for example – so that the analyst has some input into which aspect of the communication to foreground. In other words, foregrounding is not something determined only by the nature of the language under analysis: it is also an active process on the part of the analysis, the critic or the reader. Put simply this means that if you ask a question about the metalingual aspect of an utterance, you get a metalingual answer, but this doesn't mean that the referential aspect dissolves or that the outside world ceases to exist. Sometimes it seems that the radical reputation of structuralism is based on a mistake or an exaggeration, and the occasional commentator dares to say so. 'The student who says in a university seminar that Lawrence is splendidly true to life will be answered with smiles of conscious superiority as if he had committed some mild *bêtise*,' notes A. D. Nuttall in his discussion of Jakobson's similarly uncontroversial argument in 'Realism in Art'. The mistaken assumption according to Nuttall is 'that modern literary theory has exploded the idea that literature is in any way authentically true to life' (Nuttall, 1983, 54). If this is a mistake, and the radical reputation of literary structuralism rests on nothing more than a claim that realism has a conventional element, the ambiguity in structuralist approaches to reference has a lot to answer for.

The ambiguity between bracketing off and denying the referential dimension of language is the starting point for de Man's essay: 'By an awareness of the arbitrariness of the sign (Saussure) and of literature as an autotelic statement "focused on the way it is expressed" (Jakobson), the entire question of meaning can be bracketed, thus freeing the critical discourse from the debilitating burden of paraphrase' (*LT*, 330). For de Man, then, the epistemological issue of meaning is merely side-stepped by semiology, whereas any radical critique of reference will focus on referential meaning in conjunction with its formal and figural aspects. Later in *Allegories of Reading*, to which this essay serves as an introduction, he finds this critique in Rousseau, whose 'radical critique of referential meaning never implied that the referential function of language could in any way be avoided, bracketed or reduced to being just one contingent linguistic property among others, as it is postulated, for example, in contemporary semiology' (de Man, 1979, 204). In other words, semiology implicitly denies reference by ignoring it and transforming form into the primary content of a discourse, but de Man is looking for a less ambiguous position capable of bringing referential meaning into confrontation with other aspects of language in a way which will more explicitly purge language of its referential content. It is clear in the discussion of Yeats (*LT*, 334–5) that de Man rejects any Jakobsonian sense of an easy co-presence of different aspects of language or of any decision to give priority to one aspect over another. There is also an unmistakable revulsion to the idea of reference which is imaged variously as a trickster, a disease or the victim of some horrible collision.

The argument against reference in *Allegories of Reading* can be summarized like this. If Jakobson sees the total meaning of a discourse as the sum of the six functions he identifies, the bracketing-off of reference in the name of *poetics* produces a partial reading of that discourse. No matter how much scientific attention is poured onto the formal and self-referential aspects of that discourse, the referential aspect is still there, lurking but ignored, in happy coexistence with the other functions. De Man argues instead that reading should sustain the contradiction between different aspects of language. If semiology gives the impression that form *is* the *total* meaning of a discourse, it does so by ignoring its other aspects and allowing a partial reading to present itself as a total reading. This is *totalization* – the great enemy of deconstruction – or *synecdoche*, whereby a part stands for the whole. This is a useful preliminary way of understanding the impact of deconstruction in literary theory: a deconstruction reads a narrative for contradictions, aims to sustain them, and not reduce the text to a stable, single structure or meaning.

One of the interesting aspects of de Man's attitude to reference is that he cannot express it theoretically: it is 'a difficulty which puts its precise theoretical exposition beyond my powers' (*LT*, 333). It is only by reading texts that a critique of referential meaning emerges, so that the linguistic theory is always embedded in the reading of a particular text and remains unextractable from that context. In his two examples here, of ambiguous rhetorical questions, and in the more extended analyses later in *Allegories of Reading*, there is a clear sense that ambiguity is a much more catastrophic condition than we would normally assume, that literary language exists in this condition more than most, and that the victim of the catastrophe is referential meaning. Characteristically, de Man tends to move from readings which emphasize the collision of different aspects of linguistic meaning into general claims about the nature of language, its self-referentiality, its inability to refer to the outside or the impossibility of separating the literal from the metaphorical. Simple as the strategy may seem, it represents a profound shift for literary theory. For Jakobson, the linguistic model is a foundation or a premise for the analysis of a literary text. For de Man, the text is the premise which yields linguistic knowledge. In other words the direction of the relationship between linguistics and literature has been reversed. The linguistic model in structuralism tended to reduce the rich diversity of literary texts to some bland common denominator, as instances of grammatical rules, or as abstract structures illustrating the enabling conventions of meaning. Poststructuralist readings tend to use the complexity of individual texts to demolish the neat categories and methods which the linguistic model brings to texts. Or to use Barthes's language, the relation of the linguistic model to literature has shifted from one of *deduction* to one of *induction*, no longer moving from general rules about language to the analysis of particular texts, but from the analysis of texts towards a negative knowledge of those general rules.

If my account a moment ago of the impact of poststructuralism in criticism was that it refused the view of a text as a stable structure, there is now an important qualification. The text is not only something that can't be pinned down by scientific (semiological) analysis. By being unpindownable, it destabilizes the model of analysis and in this sense yields its own linguistic knowledge. For de Man, one model of analysis at stake is what he calls the inside/outside model in literary studies. The main characteristic of the inside/outside model is that nobody knows which is which. The opposition of form and content implies that form is external, yet in another sense the form of a work is within it while its content is often something which is pointed to outside the work. For this reason the opposition of intrinsic and extrinsic criticism has never been clear. Intrinsic criticism in the hands of new criticism was formalist while extrinsic brought external information such as historical, biographical or referential perspectives to bear. Many critics after the new criticism began to express the relationship between the outside of literature and formalism the other way around. Here is A. D. Nuttall again: 'There are two languages of criticism, the first "opaque", external, formalist, operating outside the mechanisms of art and taking those mechanisms as its object, the second "transparent", internal, realist, operating within the world presented in the work' (1983, 80). This confusion is really a facet of the ambiguity surrounding structuralist attitudes to reference, as well as being de Man's version of Derrida's engagement with Saussure: 'The recurrent debate opposing intrinsic to extrinsic criticism stands under the aegis of an inside/outside metaphor that is never being seriously questioned' (*LT*, 330). The problem with literary semiology, for de Man, is that even if it seems to understand reference, on Saussurean lines, as a purely internal effect of language, it still imports the inside/outside model by distinguishing between, for example, the referential and the autotelic. If Derrida saw the distinction of signifier and signified as a residual dualist presupposition, this is exactly the problem for de Man with the inside/outside model. Speaking of Saussure's justification to base his study of language on speech – the pure inside of language – as opposed to writing which is merely an external representation of speech, Derrida characterizes the new relationship between the poles: 'The outside bears with the inside a relationship which is, as usual, anything but simple exteriority. The meaning of the outside was always present within the inside, imprisoned outside the outside, and vice versa' (1976, 100).

Derrida's engagements with linguistic theory are often humorously complex: they illustrate that language itself does not cooperate with any model which seeks to stabilize it, reduce it, or close down its infinite complexity. Linguistic terminology in Derrida's work tends to take on ironic force, no longer naming some feature of language, but naming some problem in a prior theory or tradition. *Différance* is a good example of a term which does its utmost not to designate anything except the unstoppable motion of language in the face of attempts to keep it still for a moment; or, to put it another way, if it designates anything it is the inadequacy of the Saussurean term difference. Simple terms such as writing, metaphor and signifier are used by Derrida in ironic ways to upturn and collapse the oppositions to which they belong in linguistic theory at large, designating the presuppositions of former accounts of meaning without asserting anything about the nature of language: language will always undermine the categories and distinctions by which linguists attempt to define and totalize it.

Perhaps the most famous misrepresentation of Derrida's engagement with language theory is the way that critics and philosophers have interpreted the slogan *Il n'y a pas de hors-texte*. If I am right in the paragraph above that Derrida never attempts to say anything of his own about language, but only to show that it disrupts, exceeds and resists its own analysis, the slogan does not mean there is nothing outside of the text as most commentators have taken it. It is closer to *there is no outside-text*. Derrida does not mean that reality does not exist except as an illusion foisted on us by language, but that it is not possible to distinguish categorically between what is within and what is outside. So, for example, the idea often associated with Derrida that all language is metaphorical is a problem in the definition of literal meaning, not an ontological claim. Those who claim that poststructuralism rests on a theory of language which denies reference to the outside world are mistaken on two grounds. First, they assume that the linguistic model comes first, like a premise which is then applied to instances – the realistic novel for example – of language. As I have said, theoretical knowledge, however negative, comes if anything from reading narratives against the grain of any linguistic model for analysis. Second, they assume that poststructuralism is a knowledge of language when it would be safer to see it as an argument against the knowability of language which shifts attention away from knowledge of language towards the language of knowledge.

This shift points to the real cataclysm of poststructuralist thought, which emerges from a glaring contradiction in structuralist thought. I began this discussion with the argument that the impetus behind structuralism derived from a view that language constructed rather than reflected the world, created rather than revealed the structures that we think of as reality. And yet the structuralist seems to assume, on the whole, that a metalanguage such as linguistics is capable of describing language from a stance of scientific objectivity. If language creates, rather than reveals, the world surely metalanguage also creates, rather than reveals, the structures of language. Reference to language is after all no different from reference to the so-called outside world. There can surely be no position outside of language from which language can be viewed objectively. Derrida calls this a repetition and a redoubling of structuralism's basic insight.

If structuralist thought is to remain true to its own basic insight, the idea of metalingual distance on which most literary criticism is dependant is no longer viable. How can criticism deny the transparency of language in general only to assume the transparency of its own descriptions? This conundrum takes us back into the conflation of literature and criticism from which we started, since the boundary between literary and critical writing disappears as a consequence of the impossibility of metalingual distance. Much of the notorious difficulty of poststructuralist writing derives from this collapse of metalingual distance. Criticism moves into a phase in which it can no longer posit the objectivity of its insights and abounds instead with new creative practices. De Man's formula for an allegory of reading is typical of the way that such practices ambiguously divide responsibility for an insight between the critic and the text itself: is he speaking of an allegory about reading within the text, or is the allegory a property of the reading? There is one line of argument in de Man that indicates that allegory is not an intentional structure but a kind of translation performed by the critic according to his own interests; and yet there is another which claims that the deconstruction 'is not something we have added to the text, but it constituted the text in the first place' (*LT*, 339). Either way, the consequence is that poststructuralist critics characteristically translate some of our best-loved literary works into unrecognizable metalingual tracts: for example, Proust's *A la Recherche du Temps Perdu* becomes, in the hands of Gilles Deleuze, a meta-language better capable of exploring the semiotics of narrative than any critical language, or in Paul de Man's, a deconstruction of the distinction between metaphor and metonymy.

An equally apparent consequence of the collapse of metalingual distance is the increasing opacity of poststructuralist critical writing, that jargonesque and neologistic tendency about which I was so rude at the start of this piece. It is possible to defend this kind of opacity and difficulty as a kind of self-conscious awareness of the role of critical language in projecting structure onto the language under analysis. This is certainly true of a neologism such as Derrida's *différance*, a term which precludes any easy transparency to its analytical objects and foregrounds its graphic materiality by transposing Saussure's 'e' to an 'a'. This may sound like the death of critical reason, and many have argued that it was. It certainly compels a different definition of literary theory and criticism. Writing four years after his attempts to evangelize his readers on behalf of the objectivity of the linguistic model, Barthes provides a useful alternative when he proposes that 'theoretical does not of course mean abstract. From my point of view it means *reflexive*, something which turns back on itself' (1973, 44). If a theoretical discourse is one which turns back on itself, reflects upon itself, the canon of literary theoretical texts is suddenly opened up to hundreds of literary texts, especially modernist and postmodernist novels, but equally the Canterbury Tales, Shakespeare plays, Romantic and modernist lyrics, not to mention television advertisements, sitcoms, cartoons and films. Contemporary criticism is awash with such claims, that theory is no longer a discourse about critical discourse, no longer a set of propositions about propositions, but a kind of knowledge yielded by discourses everywhere. Or to use the most influential terminology, theory and criticism are no longer constative (truth-telling) discourses, but performatives, or discourses which enact and perform their views rather than state them. Theory as reflexivity, then, is a way of avoiding what Derrida calls the 'platitude of a supposed academic metalanguage' (Derrida, 1992, 60), or what Barthes sees as the 'hypocritical distance of a fallacious metalanguage' (1973, 44) and ensures that criticism begins, in de Man's words, to practise what it preaches, namely writing.

There are many places where this new performative criticism has led since its inception in the 1970s, and not all of them in my view are positive. If I had to point to negative outcomes, I would gesture in the direction of new historicist anecdote (see John Brannigan's chapter in this volume), which often strikes me as a retreat from theory into a metaphorical discourse bristling with theoretical suggestivity but without the faintest idea of what it is suggesting. On the other side of the traditional borderline, I think there are negative outcomes for literature. The ascendance of metafictional self-contemplation, for example, into the orthodoxy of historiographic metafiction – fiction which endlessly highlights the artificiality of its own retrospect – seems to me a kind of dumbing-down of poststructuralist approaches to historical reference. But I don't have the space to argue these cases at length here. At any rate, the theorization of fiction and the aestheticization of theory both seem to stand or fall on a principle more akin to the traditional vagaries of aesthetic value than the rules of critical reason. But on a more positive note, I agree with de Man when he asserts that 'metaphors are much more tenacious than facts', and that the 'apparent glorification of the critic-philosopher in the name of truth is in fact a glorification of the poet as the primary source of this truth' (*LT*, 339). If we look at Derrida's output since the mid-1980s, there is a clear acknowledgement of the power of metaphor to outstrip that of conventional reason, and his work presents a litany of theoretical metaphors such as postcards, gifts, various forms of technology and ghosts which scrupulously avoid the platitude of a meta-language.

The use of figurative language in criticism can be rationalized as a kind of performativity, an acknowledgement of the creativity of criticism and a refusal of the critical distance assumed by traditional metalanguages. But this is a tendency in criticism that is not without its critics, particularly when the values of argumentation are displaced by the kind of associative logic by which figurative language tends to operate. J. Hillis Miller, for example, has identified a tendency in new historicist reading towards what he calls the problem of the biological synecdoche, or a kind of argument in which a small detail is seen to bear within it the pattern of a complex whole. Usually this is an objection to the scale of a generalization which derives from the analysis of a particular detail, as if the properties of the detail had the explanatory power of DNA. It is a basic methodological objection that can also be found in the work of Dominic La Capra, who cautions against what he calls world-in-a-grain-of-sand arguments in the new historicisms: those paralogical methods of argument which imply universals by means of analogy and association, and so replace the value of logic with the importance of being interesting. La Capra sees this kind of critical synecdoche as a way of allowing a detail, either from a text, or from the cultural historical context of a text, to resonate with a paralogical suggestivity, an implicit universalism, while remaining free of the need to formulate the theoretical connection between part and whole. There is a deep reluctance to take responsibility, a kind of hostility to critical and theoretical formulations, which links new historicist criticism to modernist literature in a relation of aspiring similarity to the modes of aesthetic production, or to the performativity of fragments, rather than to the values of critical distance.

There is a danger that the kind of paralogical suggestivity which thrives in poststructuralism has diminished the credibility of criticism. Over-suggestive, aestheticized modes of criticism have become something of a target both from the inside and the outside of the critical establishment. Consider, for example, Richard Dawkins's lampoon of the literary critical mind in *Climbing Mount Improbable*:

> I have just listened to a lecture in which the topic of discussion was the fig. Not a botanical lecture, a literary one. We got the fig in literature, the fig as metaphor, changing perceptions of the fig, the fig as emblem of pudenda and the fig leaf as modest concealer of them, 'fig' as an insult, the social construction of the fig, D. H. Lawrence on how to eat a fig in society, 'reading fig' and, I rather think, 'the fig as text'. (1997, 2)

Dawkins continues to lampoon the literary mind for its markers of provisionality and metaphoricity (somehow, if you will, at some level, in some sense, if I can put it this way), fixing finally on the closing sentence in which the fig is installed as the unnamed forbidden fruit in the story of Genesis, thereby acquiring in one stroke the kind of significance lacking in an otherwise miscellaneous collection of associations and paralogical links. Of course Dawkins is using this as a preamble to his own, superbly theorized, actually biological synecdoche, in which the DNA of a fig bears within it the whole story of human evolution. I don't think it would be right, at this point, to make fun of Dawkins's own central metaphor – a mountain called improbable which we all have to climb in search of our own brains – and prefer to acknowledge that there might be some truth in his satire, a recognizable species of contextualism in which the metaphoricity of miscellaneous objects and details is allowed to resonate freely without the tenor of the metaphor ever being explicitly stated. If this is a kind of historicism, it is a new kind. Or perhaps it is an old kind with a new inflection. There are elements of the old historical scholarship, a division of academic labour so deep that expertise was an isolated and untheorized knowledge of some cultural atom. But the new inflection saves the procedure from images of batty, purposeless expertise exactly because it still communicates with theory, or with the end of theory, or with the deconstruction of theory. Just as for the deconstructionist, a literary text was invariably construed as an allegory of deconstruction itself, of the impossibility of theory, so too, the isolated object is often construed as a theoretical metaphor of historicism itself, a microcosmic emblem of a historiographical issue which need not be stated – a kind of post-symbolist theorizing which installs William Empson's first type of ambiguity (in which a detail is effective in several ways at once, by comparison with several points of likeness or antithesis with several points of difference) at the heart of critical analysis.

Whether viewed positively or negatively, this mutual contamination of the critical and the literary discourse seems to represent a point of convergence for several different strains of criticism. The transition from a scientific literary structuralism to a more playful and creative poststructuralism is only one way of telling this story. Derrida, for example, tends to point to modernist literature rather than structuralism as the key influence on his critical practice, so that when he comes to write on Joyce there is a strong sense of the reciprocity between the critical act and the literary object. But these tendencies can also be located in the marxist tradition. This is how Eagleton describes Benjamin's new style of microscopic sociology:

> In this kind of microanalysis, the individual phenomenon is grasped in all of its overdetermined complexity as a kind of cryptic code or riddling rebus to be deciphered, a drastically abbreviated image of social processes which the discerning eye will persuade it to yield up. (Eagleton, 1990, 362)

He goes on to say a little later:

> What this method then delivers, is a kind of poetic or novelistic sociology in which the whole seems to consist of nothing but a dense tessellation of graphic images; and to this extent it represents an aestheticized model of social enquiry . . . The literary styles of Benjamin and Adorno themselves are among the finest examples of this mode.

And elsewhere we find Marjorie Levinson pointing to Romantic literature as a possible source for the new aestheticized criticism when she remarks that 'our new and scandalous criticism is therefore a reprise of our critical object: the Romantic ideology'. In each case it is, above all, the metaphor or synecdoche that seems to do this work of conflating the subject and the object: the dialectical quality of the metaphor, its ability to bring two separate realms into cognitive and emotional relationship, but not as Max Black and Ezra Pound, I. A. Richards and Paul Ricoeur would have it, as a kind of synthesis of two semiological fields. It is rather the oscillation between two apparently incompatible claims that metaphor brings to the new criticisms: the ability to make claims about the past which are both constative descriptions of the past as past, and performative inventions of the past as projections from the present. This is what G. B. Madison describes as the is/is-not character of metaphorical statements. He argues:

> The meaning of a metaphor is not like the meaning of a straightforward referential proposition or a constative utterance; it is not what is apparently said, but is, rather, what the utterance shows in transcending itself towards what is not said in the saying, and it is what the utterance does when it leads another person to recreate for himself a meaning analogous to the intended by the maker of the metaphor.

If metaphor can be characterized like this, so too can poststructuralist criticism as a whole, as a kind of is/is not structure, in which critical insights are offered in the same breath as they are taken away. While this may often be a source of difficulty, it is also a gateway into a new critical universe, in which the relationship between performative and constative language, or between literature and criticism, is irreversibly reformulated.

NOTES TOWARDS A READING OF *MRS DALLOWAY*

Poststructuralist readings are, as I have said, often concerned with the difficulties of reading. They are often orientated towards the undoing of very systematic readings, or present the view that the complexity of a text is not reducible to any easy scheme that such a reading advances. For this reason, poststructuralist readings are highly conscious of preceding readings, or of dominant views which have shaped a particular text around certain preoccupations and interests. In the case of *Mrs Dalloway*, we could say that the dominant preoccupations are aesthetic and narratological, which is to say that the novel has been constructed by critics as a kind of aesthetic or narratological experiment.

To put it oversimply, critical response to *Mrs Dalloway* fell into quite distinct phases in the twentieth century. Initially it was viewed as a highly poetic, as opposed to realistic, novel in which the outside world, or the novel's characters, are indistinct, and subordinated to poetic, aesthetic and narratological projects. Like many responses to modernist fiction, there was a feeling that the novel was poetic and experimental in style because it was trying to meet the new demands of an inner landscape, or the representation of experience as filtered through a mind. In the mid-twentieth century the emphasis was placed more squarely on narrative structure as they related to questions of realism. *Mrs Dalloway* was a text which received a lot of attention from critics interested in narrative point of view, in stylistics or in structural linguistics, and in these cases was analyzed from a rigorously formalist point of view, and as an ordered system. Poststructuralist approaches can be understood as a challenge to this dominance of formal and aesthetic considerations, and tend to emphasize instead the active role of the reader in the reading and interpretation of the text. Sometimes this has entailed the deconstruction of ideas of ordered narrative structure, and more recently has involved an attention to the historical specificity and content of a novel traditionally viewed in aesthetic terms. This sketch will outline some of these developments as they relate to the description of poststructuralism above.

Broadly, formalist approaches to *Mrs Dalloway* would explore the system of indirect discourse by which the novel is narrated. This would mean attempting to define the relationship between the narrative voice and those interior monologues of characters which dominate the novel. A stylistician, for example, would view the novel as a third-person omniscient narration in which the use of indirect thought and free indirect thought pervades the narrative. This means that, though there is a third person narrator, that narrator rarely talks to the reader directly for very long, and spends much more time reporting the thought of characters. One of the preoccupations of formalist criticism was to analyze this movement between narrative voice and the interiority of a character in as exact and scientific a way as possible. Hence, there is a tendency to resort to linguistics as a place where the categories of indirect thought and free indirect thought have a very precise description. The poststructuralist reading of Mrs Dalloway will often be a response to this attempt at neat and ordered description of narrative structure. Hillis Miller, for example (Miller, 1982), explores the same issue of voices in the novel, but without trying to present the system as in any way ordered and intelligible. For Miller there is a feeling that the movement between narrator and characters is a source of confusion and illogicality. He presents the omniscient narrator's voice as a kind of collective, telepathic, universal perspective in which all the characters' thoughts are embedded. He also spends much of his analysis showing difficulties in the transition from one voice to another, for example in the odd and inconsistent shifts between the narrator's present and the retrospect of reporting other minds, so that the narrator is sometimes temporally distanced from characters and sometimes contemporaneous with them.

Miller's reading, then, is taking the received formalist view of the system of indirect discourse and showing it to be rather more complicated: a disquieting mode of 'ventriloquism' as he calls it. His reading constantly homes in on irreconcilable difficulties that emerge from the formalist systematization, presenting them as conflations, confusions and aporias. The novel is for Miller 'based on an irreconcilable opposition between individuality and universality', and it is concluded that 'narration in indirect discourse, for Woolf is repetition and merging at once' (Miller, 1982, 187).

Part of Miller's point in this discussion is to show that, where there is no linguistic clue which can resolve these confusions of voice, the reader is all the more actively involved in the generation of meaning, or making decisions on meaning that the text itself does not assist. It is the kind of text which demands a certain level of creative invention on the part of the reader. This idea of the reader's input into the sense of the text can be found in many different forms, and particularly in recent readings which seek to oppose the traditional aesthetic and formalist readings. Miller's reading may be moving away from the idea of a scientifically describable objective structure in the novel, but it remains within the orbit of linguistic science and formalist analysis, and gives the impression that the text is in some way *about* the use of indirect discourse. In this way it does not differ significantly from the earliest responses to *Mrs Dalloway* which viewed it primarily as an aesthetic experiment with so-called 'stream of consciousness' narration.

Other critics have sought a different kind of input from the reader, and in recent years this has particularly involved the input of historical specificity, or of background context which seems deliberately repressed in the novel. Jeremy Tambling (1993) and Trudi Tate (1998), for example, are critics who have read *Mrs Dalloway* more rigorously in relation to its 1923 setting, and particularly in relation to the state and the First World War. The interesting thing about these readings is that they are not so focused on the text as such, and often depend on glimmers of social context which can then be expanded critically with historical knowledge. Readings such as these often depend of strategies which derive from the notions of critical synecdoche described above. One small detail in a text can be used to make a case against traditional aesthetic readings, that the novel is in fact a satire of the attitudes that underlay the First World War.

If these historicist readings are poststructuralist in the sense that they are orientated against the dominant formalist readings that have shaped *Mrs Dalloway*, they can also seem to be orientated against the text itself. They are readings which view the excluded historical background of the text as somehow constitutive of the text. This has much in common with the structuralist account of the sign, which views the meaning of words as comprised by words which are not there, absent and excluded. There is also the Foucauldian sense of meaning as a structure of exclusion, in which deconstruction would be a process of readmitting excluded material on which meaning invisibly depends. But there is of course also a dimension of creativity involved in the construction of context for a reading. If the critic can focus on what is absent, rather than merely present, in the text, there is in theory no limit to the concerns that can be brought to bear on a reading. Whether historicist readings are anchored in some barely visible cultural/historical detail in the text or not, there is a clear sense here of the critic bringing extrinsic information to the text, and so of the critic as inventor of the text in relation to a particular set of interests. Sometimes contemporary criticism seems to be inventing perverse, unintended and unexpected ways of viewing a novel, and can seem to be working against the grain of the text itself. These are indications of the kind of creative freedom which poststructuralism has introduced in criticism. The precise ways in which they interact with questions of the metaphoricity of textual details or with the creative styles of critical discourses themselves differs from critic to critic. The rejection of objectivity, and of systematic formalism, presents a range of problems which arise from the idea of deconstruction and various new historicisms as performative acts: creative acts which generate the text in the act of reading according to the position and the interests of a given reader.

QUESTIONS FOR FURTHER CONSIDERATION

1. How is the idea of a critic as a creator of a literary text underpinned theoretically? Do you think that constitutive theories of criticism, in which a critic is seen to generate a text in the act of reading, can underpin a creative critical practice which rejects the distinction between literary and critical writing?
2. What does it mean for a critical text to be realistic in relation to a literary one? Is there any sense in which a literary text has objective properties, or any obligation for a critical text to represent such characteristics faithfully?

3. Would it be possible, or desirable, to rid critical discourse of metaphorical and metonymic language? Is it legitimate for critical discourse to adopt a position of creative suggestivity in relation to its literary objects?

4. What is the status of cultural/historical details in the reading of a literary text such as *Mrs Dalloway*? Do you think that a detail can contain within it the pattern of a whole entity as complex as a novel?

5. Would it be possible to view *Mrs Dolloway* as a text which takes language itself as its primary topic? If so, what importance do you attach to its specific setting and the historical moment to which it refers?

6. Do you consider that things which are not represented in *Mrs Dalloway* actually inhabit the text as a kind of unconscious? If so, is there any limit to the scope of topics which a critic might bring to bear on the text?

ANNOTATED BIBLIOGRAPHY

Culler, Jonathan. *Literary Theory: A Very Short Introduction*. Oxford, 1997.
Probably the best short introduction to contemporary theory, and particularly useful on the critical trend towards performativity.
de Man, Paul, *Allegories of Reading: Figural Language in Rousseau, Nietzsche, Rilke, and Proust*. New Haven, CT, 1979.
Somewhat bossy, complex and logically slippery, a fascinating account of 'figural' language in literature and the way it often yields knowledge of what de Man describes as the 'impossibility' of pinning language down with linguistic terminology. A stunning display of deconstruction as allegorical interpretation. See the entry for this book in the bibliographies to the chapters on deconstruction and reader-response theory, above.
Derrida, Jacques. *Acts of Literature*, ed. Derek Attridge. New York, 1992.
An anthology of Derrida's writings on literature, useful for the illustration of performative readings after the collapse of metalingual distance in criticism, particularly in 'Ulysses Gramophone'. The collection contains an introductory interview concerned with the relation of literature and criticism.
Nuttall, A. D. *A New Mimesis: Shakespeare and the Representation of Reality*. London, 1983.
A lucid counter-argument to poststructuralist critiques of realism, sometimes wrongheaded, but touching usefully on Jakobson and other structuralist approaches to realism.
Young, Robert, ed. *Untying the Text: a Post-Structuralist Reader*. London, 1981.
A stimulating collection including Barthes's 'Theory of the Text' containing his critique of criticism as a metalanguage, and a useful introduction on the same subject.

SUPPLEMENTARY BIBLIOGRAPHY

Barthes, Roland. 'Introduction to the Structural Analysis of Narratives', in *Image-Music-Text*, trans. and ed. Stephen Heath. London, 1977.
Deleuze, Gilles. *The Logic of Sense*, trans. Mark Lester with Charles Stivale, ed. Constantin V. Boundas. New York, 1990.
de Man, Paul. 'The Epistemology of Metaphor', *Critical Inquiry*, 5: 1, Autumn 1978.
———. *Allegories of Reading: Figural Language in Rousseau, Nietzsche, Rilke, and Proust*. New Haven, CT, 1979.

————. *Blindness and Insight: Essays in the Rhetoric of Contemporary Criticism*, 2nd edn. London: Methuen, 1983.

————. *The Resistance to Theory*. Manchester, 1986.

Derrida, Jacques. *Of Grammatology*, trans. and intro. Gayatri Chakravorty Spivak. Baltimore, MD, 1976.

————. *Writing and Difference*, trans. Alan Bass. Chicago, 1978.

————. 'White Mythology: Metaphor in the Text of Philosophy', trans. F. C. T. Moore, *New Literary History*, 6: 1, Autumn 1974; rpt. Derrida, *Margins of Philosophy*, trans. Alan Bass. Chicago, 1982.

Gasché, Rodolphe. *The Tain of the Mirror: Derrida and the Philosophy of Reflection*, Cambridge, MA, 1986.

Hutcheon, Linda. *A Poetics of Postmodernism: History, Theory, Fiction*. New York, 1988.

Jakobson, Roman. 'Closing Statement: Linguistics and poetics', in *Style in Language*, ed. Thomas A. Sebeok. Cambridge, MA, 1960.

————. 'On Realism in Art'. *Readings in Russian Poetics*, eds L. Matedjka et al. Ann Arbor, MI, 1978.

MacCabe, Colin. *James Joyce and the Revolution of the Word*. London, 1978.

Melville, Stephen. *Philosophy Beside Itself: On Deconstruction and Modernism*. Minneapolis, MN, 1986.

Riffaterre, Michael. *Fictional Truth*. Baltimore, MD, 1990.

Ronell, Avital. *Crack Wars: Literature, Addiction, Mania*. Lincoln, NE, 1992.

Saussure, Ferdinand de. *Course in General Linguistics*, trans. Roy Harris. London, 1972.

OTHER WORKS CITED

Eagleton, Terry. *The Ideology of the Aesthetic*. Oxford, 1990.

Dawkins, Richard. *Climbing Mount Improbable*. Harmondsworth, 1997.

Miller, J. Hillis. *Fiction and Repetition: Seven English Novels*. Cambridge, MA, 1982.

Tambling, Jeremy. 'Repression in Mrs Dalloway's London', in *Mrs Dalloway and To the Lighthouse*, ed. Sue Reid. London, 1993.

Tate, Trudi. *Modernism and the First World War*. New York, 1998.

HISTORY, POWER AND POLITICS IN THE LITERARY ARTIFACT: NEW HISTORICISM

John Brannigan

THE HISTORY AND THEORY OF THE NEW HISTORICISM

In the late 1970s and early 1980s literary critics seemed to become more interested in the relationship between literature and history. In Britain and the USA the contents of literary journals, the subject of critical books, university courses and the titles of academic conferences were reflecting a growing interest in examining how literature reflected, shaped and represented history. Although feminist, marxist and postcolonial critics were at the forefront of this development in literary criticism, it was a group of American critics known as the new historicists who were responsible chiefly for the prominence of historicist approaches to literature in the 1980s and 1990s. Where many previous critical approaches to literary texts assumed that texts had some universal significance and essential historical truth to impart, new historicist critics tended to read literary texts as material products of specific historical conditions. New historicism approached the relationship between text and context with an urgent attention to the political ramifications of literary interpretation. In the eyes of new historicist critics, texts of all kinds are the vehicles of politics insofar as texts mediate the fabric of social, political and cultural formations. This view is evident in the work of new historicist critics who read historical context through legal, medical and penal documents, anecdotes, travel writings, ethnological and anthropological narratives and, of course, literary texts.

An important realization of the new historicism is that literature and history are inseparable. History is not a coherent body of objective knowledge which can simply be applied to a literary text in order to discover what the text does or does not reflect. Literature is a vehicle for the representation of history, and it does contain insights into the formation of historical moments. It reveals the processes and tensions by which historical change comes about. But it does not behave passively towards history; it does not, in other words, reflect history as a mirror. Literature shapes and constitutes historical change. Literary texts can have effects on the course of history, on the social and political ideas and beliefs of their time. For new historicism the object of study is not the text and its context, not literature and its history, but rather literature *in* history. This is to see literature as a constitutive and inseparable part of history in the making, and therefore rife with the creative forces, disruptions and contradictions, of history.

The issues with which new historicist critics are most concerned are the role of historical context in interpreting literary texts and the role of literary rhetoric in mediating history. Louis Montrose argued that the key concern of new historicist critics was 'the historicity of texts and the textuality of history'. He explained that by 'the historicity of texts' he meant that all texts were embedded in specific social and cultural contexts, and by 'the textuality of history' he meant that all of our knowledge and understanding of the past could only exist through the 'surviving textual traces of the society in question', the very survival of which suggested that they were subject to 'complex and subtle social processes of preservation and effacement' (Montrose, in Veeser, 1989, 20). Literature and history, in Montrose's view, were fully interdependent, and no knowledge existed outside of the realms of narrative, writing or discourse.

The work of these critics follows from, and develops further, the interests and beliefs of previous generations of marxist and historicist critics who re-evaluated the stories that past societies had told of themselves. Historicist critics introduced a degree of scepticism concerning the construction of historical narratives, and the place of the critic or historian within those narratives. Historicism understands the stories of the past as society's way of constructing a narrative which unconsciously fits its own interests. marxist critics, borrowing from the lessons of historicism, see history as the procession of stories favourable to the victor, the ruling class, with literary texts as much as historical texts taking part in that procession. On a simple level marxism fractures the idea that history is singular and universal by positing that all history is rife with class struggle, in which the interests of the dominant economic group are represented as the interests of society in general while the interests of the proletariat, those who sell their labour for wages, are not represented, or are represented as those of a particular minority. One direct consequence of this view is evident in the work of marxist historians who have revisited conventional accounts of the past with a view to telling stories of how the working or labouring classes lived. New historicists have followed a somewhat similar path in revisiting the literature of the past in order to tell stories about women, the colonised, the insane, the heretics and the persecuted. There is a significant difference between the work of marxists and new historicists, however. Marxists tend to think of their critical practice as, in some ways, emancipatory, of liberating the story of the oppressed from being lost to history. New historicists return to stories of the oppressed only in order to discover how these stories mark the effectiveness of the apparatus of oppression.

In her explanatory essay on the relationship between 'Marxism and New Historicism' (*LT*, 428–38), Catherine Gallagher traces the history of left-wing criticism in the US, and in particular the debt of new historicist critics to the radical campaigns of the new left in the 1960s and early 1970s. She situates the new historicism within left-wing criticism, despite the problems which marxists have with the political quietism of new historicist practice. Gallagher explains the evolution of the central concerns and characteristics of new historicism from the influences of marxism, feminism and deconstruction on literary studies, and defends the reasons why new historicists found themselves in the position whereby 'we could neither renew our faith in marxism nor convert to deconstruction' (*LT*, 433). The questions with which she follows this defence indicate the differences between new historicism and the political agendas of other literary theories:

> Was it possible, we asked, that certain forms of subjectivity that felt oppositional were really a means by which power relations were maintained? Was a politics organized by the discourse of liberation inevitably caught inside modern America's terms of power? Was it theoretically possible even to differentiate the individual subject from a system of power relationships? (*LT*, 433)

In part, new historicism is an analysis of the failure of the left-wing politics of student radicalism in the 1960s and 1970s to instigate social and political change, hence the questions which Gallagher asks all suggest the bewilderment of someone disillusioned by the rhetoric of oppositionality, liberation and individual subjectivity. The answers to these questions are all gloomy, from the point of view of an emancipatory practice: certain forms of 'oppositional' subjectivity do help to sustain power relations, discourses of liberation were indeed informed by and trapped within America's 'terms of power', and no, it was not possible to distinguish the individual subject from power relationships.

Gallagher suggests some ways in which new historicism is a direct challenge to some comfortable illusions of contemporary literary studies – various notions of the political and ideological imports of literature – and she defends new historicism against its detractors. She attempts to rescue it from the charge of being complicit in the power relationships it describes by arguing that it is instrumental in introducing to the classroom a whole range of non-canonical texts and compelling political issues. She fails to address the most serious concern of left-wing opponents of the new historicism, however, which is the political import of what it teaches students. In ranging through the history of western imperialism and the ideological discourses of gender oppression, new historicism teaches students that resistance plays clumsily and helplessly into the hands of existing power relationships, that struggle is merely the most visible sign of co-option, and that power seeps into every facet of routine, daily life. Moreover, by refusing to define the location or specific, localizable nature of power relationships, and by insisting 'that power cannot be equated with economic or state power', new historicists might also be accused of going beyond deflating the utopian project of marxism to embracing the politics of conservatism.

For new historicists, literary texts have specific functions within a network of power relations in society. Literature can serve to persuade us of the justice of particular causes, or can police the dominant ideas of a particular time by representing alternatives or deviations as threatening. In Shakespeare's time, for example, the idea prevailed that the ruling order was sanctioned by religious providentialism, and it was maintained by a wide range of representations which formed a consensual discourse, of which literary texts were a part. In our own time, the idea that individuals should be free to choose between competing products and services is widely accepted as of universal benefit, and this is maintained by representations as diverse as television advertise ments, legal documents, literary texts and company reports. These representations serve to ratify the existing social order, by participating in a consensus which margin-alises or alienates any form of dissent from the social order.

New historicists were influenced by Claude Lévi-Strauss's recognition that culture is a self-regulating system, just like language, and that a culture polices its own customs and practices in subtle and ideological ways, as they were influenced also by the anthropological studies of cultural systems by Clifford Geertz and Abner Cohen. For new historicists this recognition has been extended to the 'self', particularly in Stephen Greenblatt's early and seminal study, *Renaissance Self-Fashioning*. What makes the operations of power particularly complex is the fact that the self polices and regulates its own desires and repressions. This removes the need for power to be repressive. No physical or military force need be deployed or exercised for power to have operated effectively in the interests of dominant ideological systems when the self, ideologically and linguistically constructed, will reproduce hegemonic operations. In this respect, representations and discourses are involved more heavily in policing and bolstering the authority of the social order than the physical or military apparatus of the state.

This kind of approach to literature did mark a significant turn away from the humanist idea that literature could teach human beings valuable lessons in moral and civil behaviour. New historicists replaced this notion of literature as the benevolent, kindly teacher with the view that literature was rather a loyal watchdog, patrolling the fences of a conservative social order. Shakespeare was not the teacher of morals, but the guardian of the state. To show this is the case, new historicist critics have examined the ways in which Shakespeare's plays performed vital roles in support of state and church ideologies. The Renaissance period, and Shakespeare in particular, has been an important object of study for new historicists, partly because it marks the beginnings of the modern era of history, but partly also because of the canonical status of Shakespeare and some of his contemporaries in twentieth-century literary studies. New historicists have sought to politicize Shakespeare, not least because this would reveal that even the most revered literature is implicated in the grubby business of power relations and state ideology.

THE CRITICAL PRACTICE OF NEW HISTORICISM

New historicism emerged as a recognizable practice in 1980, when Greenblatt published *Renaissance Self-Fashioning* and Montrose published his essay, 'Eliza, Queene of Shepheardes', on state ideologies in Elizabethan pastoral forms, both of which are seminal works in the formation of a distinct critical practice. Greenblatt gave this critical practice the name of 'new historicism' in 1982, although he later claimed that he was amazed at how the name acquired currency. There are significant differences between the various new historicist critics in how they read literature in relation to history, and in how they see literature behaving towards and within the social order. Stephen Greenblatt, Louis Montrose, Catherine Gallagher, D. A. Miller, Joel Fineman and Walter Benn Michaels have all pursued very different critical approaches and focused on different themes and interests. But they do share common practices and assumptions, particularly concerning methodological issues and the nature of power relations. They had succeeded in drawing attention to a turn towards history in literary studies, and, although many of them were not always comfortable with the label 'new historicism', they shared some common theoretical assumptions which made them identifiable loosely as a group. In his anthology of essays on the new historicism in 1989, H. Aram Veeser summarized these common assumptions as follows:

1. that every expressive act is embedded in a network of material practices;
2. that every act of unmasking, critique, and opposition uses the tools it condemns and risks falling prey to the practice it exposes;
3. that literary and non-literary 'texts' circulate inseparably;
4. that no discourse, imaginative or archival, gives access to unchanging truths nor expresses inalterable human nature;
5. finally . . . that a critical method and a language adequate to describe culture under capitalism participate in the economy they describe. (Veeser, 1989, xi)

Veeser's list of common theoretical assumptions is general enough, which is to say non-specific enough, to allow for the wide range of differences in new historicist ideas, practices and applications. These are the assumptions which underpin the thought and practice of new historicism, but they also share common strategies of reading and analyzing texts. There are, in general, four characteristics which I want to suggest are common to new historicist critics.

Firstly, new historicists tend to examine widely different texts in order to show that those texts play a key role in mediating power relations within the state. Secondly, they treat literary texts as inseparable from other texts and forms, and inseparable from the social and political contexts in which they are embedded. Thirdly, they share the view that literature, like other written sources, raises the possibility of subversion against the state only to contain, and make safe, that subversion. Fourthly, it is common to all new historicist analyses to study a range of texts in the same epoch, and to assume, or argue, that each epoch has its own mode of power.

We can examine how these reading strategies and theoretical assumptions work by analyzing exemplary essays by new historicist critics. Let us take, firstly, Louis Montrose's essay ' "Shaping Fantasies" ' (LT, 439–56), which appeared in the second issue of *Representations*, the flagship journal of the new historicism which was launched in 1983. The subject of Montrose's essay is the construction of a powerful mythical identity for Elizabeth I through narratives and dramas which played out the 'shaping fantasies' of Elizabethan culture. Shakespeare's *A Midsummer Night's Dream* is the principal subject of Montrose's essay, but he also examines a dream recounted in the autobiography of Simon Forman, a popular Elizabethan medical guide, a colonial travel narrative by Sir Walter Raleigh and other travel tales of the Amazon. Montrose shows how these texts share common images, themes and metaphors which have a direct bearing on the representation of power in Elizabethan society. Although he devotes much of his discussion to Shakespeare's play, he does not privilege the play with greater insight or understanding of its time than the other texts. Nor is it any less implicated in political representations. Montrose examines Shakespeare's play in relation to these medical, colonial and travel narratives in order to explain how the persona of Elizabeth I was invented and disseminated. In this essay, then, literary texts and other texts are interdependent, and they are not only produced by social and political discourse, but are also in fact the makers of this discourse, as Montrose sees *A Midsummer Night's Dream* playing a vital role in shaping the cult of Elizabeth.

Shakespeare's play does so not at the behest, or under the express authority, of the Queen, for as Montrose argues 'the Queen was as much the creature of her image as she was its creator . . . her power to fashion her own strategies was itself fashioned by her culture and constrained within its mental horizon' (LT, 455). Subjectivity is shaped by power relations as much as it has any effect on their outcome. Montrose's conception of the relationship between power and subversion is slightly more complex than that of Stephen Greenblatt. For Greenblatt, texts of all kinds offer us glimpses of subversion, but only in order to contain subversive elements effectively. Power requires the representation of subversion at some level in order to justify its own practices, and so subversion is always exposed only to be made safe. For Montrose, however, representations of Elizabethan forms of power are less effective in containing subversive possibilities than Greenblatt allows. Montrose shows that Elizabeth was precariously placed as a woman at the head of a strongly patriarchal society, and her power was then a series of contradictions and complications which had to be manipulated and managed, both on a bureaucratic and a symbolical level, in order to secure her interests as a flawless head of state. Shakespeare's play threatens to subvert the powerful image of the Queen as mother of the state by instating male prerogatives, and marks a point of transition in which the iconography of a virgin Queen as head of a patriarchal state begins to become precarious. Montrose entertains a more complex and inherently unstable notion of power than does Greenblatt or, indeed, D. A. Miller. On our final criterion, that each epoch is characterised by its own mode of power, this is true of Montrose's argument too. The subject of his analysis is the specific modes and media of power which shape the reign of Elizabeth I, and the texts which he analyzes in relation to each other are all from that same epoch. This suggests that these texts, in circulation with each other at a particular time, come together to form a common discourse of power relations in that time. In suggesting that Shakespeare's play joined with others in the later decades of the sixteenth century to mark the growing instability of representations of the virgin Queen, Montrose is also indicating that there is soon to be a change of epoch, and with it new set of relations and modes of power.

We can compare the work of Montrose with D. A. Miller to see what new historicists share in common. D. A. Miller's essay, 'Discipline in Different Voices', takes up Foucault's (and, less directly, Baudrillard's) interest in the carceral and looks at the way in which Dickens's *Bleak House* represents and makes visible the carceral in mid-nineteenth-century England. Miller's emphasis in this essay is on one novel, and therefore is not interested in tracing the shift in power relations or in the mode of representation of power through widely different texts and contexts, as is the common practice of Greenblatt and Montrose. The essay focuses almost exclusively on Dickens's novel alone, and therefore doesn't deal with a discursive formation constituted by several texts of various genres, as is evident in Montrose's essay. Miller's essay is then more of an application of a Foucauldian idea to a literary text than a genealogy of power.

Miller resembles Montrose in the sense that he treats literary texts as inseparable from their contexts and indeed the very idea that *Bleak House* acts as a vehicle for the carceral in Victorian Britain demonstrates his belief that literary texts are embedded in social and political discourses. According to Miller the novel has a precise function within these discourses, to comfort readers with the illusion of a difference between the penal or institutional space in which power acts repressively against individuals and the liberal society 'outside' which is free, private and safe, and is usually regarded as the home of the happy family. Although Miller makes no explicit comment on the possibilities of subversion in this society, it is implicit in his argument that power works through the medium of cultural forms like Dickens's novel in order to secure its own interests against subversion. *Bleak House*, he argues, serves to remind its readers and their families that outside the comfort and security of home awaits the violence of the prison, the workhouse and the mental hospital, and therefore warns against any disruption of the cosy economy and values of the home and the family. In a simplification of Foucauldian notions of the social function of the text, Miller argues that the novel bears a message for society to reform its institutions and for the family to avoid disruption and conflict. It is also clear in the essay that the relationship between the novel and the carceral is a product of the particular forms which both took in the Victorian period, and that this Victorian period therefore has its own particular mode of power. With the exception of the first of our criteria, Miller's essay broadly shares the characteristics of new historicist critical practice as defined above, and perhaps the most important similarity is that all regard literary texts, and texts of all kinds, as vehicles of power.

CRITICISMS AND PROBLEMS

If new historicism emerged in opposition to types of literary criticism and of historical investigation which failed to theorise cultural and historical differences in their own work, and failed to recognize the temporal and generic specificity of texts and events, new historicism was also subject to the same criticisms by the mid-1980s. From that time onwards, the criticisms of new historicism have proliferated and become stronger. In particular, these criticisms have focused on the new historicist tendency to reduce all representation of history to the same basic model of power relations, and the tendency to subject texts to a superficial and generalised reading, locating the ostensible positions of texts in the grid of discursive formations without interrogating the interpretability of those texts.

To take the first criticism, Carolyn Porter has articulated this particularly well in her article from 1988, 'Are we being historical yet?':

> New historicism projects a vision of history as an endless skein of cloth smocked in a complex, overall pattern by the needle and thread of Power. You need only pull the thread at one place to find it connected to another. (Porter, 1988, 765)

Porter argues that new historicism has succeeded in displacing the grand narrative of progress which dominated the old historicism, and indeed which shaped the development of empirical history, only to replace it with another grand narrative, that of power. Moreover, she suggests that the effect of this model of power relations in new historicism is to consider all historical events the subject of an elusive but generalized and universal condition of power. To Porter it seems ironic that a practice which claims to be historicizing texts and events ends up making them the product of an ahistorical, universal and apparently omnipotent force. Frank Lentricchia attributes the centrality of this ill-defined and seemingly rampant and universal 'power' in new historicist analyses to the influence of Foucault, whose 'depressing message' of a power 'saturating all social relations to the point that all conflicts and "jostlings" among social groups become a mere show of political dissension' is repeated uncritically by the new historicists (Lentricchia, in Veeser, 1989, 235).

It is certainly the case that, whether examining pastoral poems in the Elizabethan period, confessions of an Italian heretic in the sixteenth century, the realist novel in Victorian England or the encounters between colonizers and natives in the New World, new historicists seem to find the same model, whereby power produces its own subversion in order to contain and control subversion more effectively. Power is everywhere, in every facet of western society and culture, but nowhere is it clear what power is, how it is made, where it fails or ends, what is outside of power, or even how power emerges. The new historicist conception of power is borrowed from Foucault's *History of Sexuality*, Volume One. Lentricchia's claim that it is accepted uncritically by the new historicists is shared by Lee Patterson, who sees the new historicist interest in circularity demonstrated in their critical practice when he writes: 'There is no space outside power because power is the only term in the analyst's arsenal' (Patterson, in Ryan, 1996, 96). Power is everywhere, because it is sought for everywhere, and at the same time it erases the specificity of the historical moment. Effectively, new historicism silences dissent and subversion, and eradicates difference, by looking only for power.

The second major criticism of new historicism is that it tends to subject texts to the most superficial and generalized readings as a result of an interest in the function rather than the interpretability of texts. If Louis Montrose can make texts of various genres, from medical to travel narratives, from a Shakespeare play to an essay justifying colonial expansion, perform the very same function in a general discourse, and make them repeat the same formulation, it is easy to see why new historicism has been criticized for a lack of sensitivity to the complexity of literary texts. When this criticism has been expressed by formalist critics we might choose to regard it as the result of an opposition to historical criticism. But when J. Hillis Miller rebuked new historicism as 'an exhilarating experience of liberation from the obligation to read' (Miller, 1991, 313), as a flight of fancy away from an ethical obligation to the other, even to the otherness of the past, we may expect his opposition to be based on more than a desire to return to an ahistorical practical criticism. And when the historicist critic Kiernan Ryan argues that new historicism 'is undoubtedly the poorer for its reluctance to meet the complex demands of a text's diction and formal requirements' (Ryan, 1996, xviii), he does so from the desire to see a radical historical criticism which engages with the detail of the text in order to show even more clearly the historical and political implications and locations of the text.

We can trace the new historicist focus on the function of a text rather than its interpretability to Foucault. Foucault focuses on the position of texts and statements within discursive formations. Texts are, in Foucault's conception, pawns in the game of discursive transformations, and are therefore subject to an interrogation of what position they occupy, but not of what they mean. Foucault's archaeological analysis seeks to uncover the participation of texts and statements in discourse, not to scrutinize the varieties of meaning which may be produced from texts and statements. Reading the text is not, it seems, a necessary part of this process, and is certainly not as necessary as a knowledge of how texts connect with other texts, how the textuality of history forms a kind of discursive fabric. If new historicism fails to read literary texts, and seems to be completely insensitive to the differences between texts, between genres and indeed between textual and historical events, it is a product of following, perhaps too rigidly, the Foucauldian model of discursive analysis.

THE USES OF NEW HISTORICISM

Primarily through the work of new historicists, Foucault brought to the discipline of literary studies an emphasis on the function and condition of texts within a network of power relations, on the positions of subjectivity within those texts, and on the contests for meaning and control of meaning displayed in the reception and criticism of texts. New historicists have contributed to literary studies a close attention to the effects and functions of literature in history, and to how literature plays a part in constructing a society's sense of itself. As a critical practice, it is useful principally in showing how literary texts circulate with other texts in a particular period to construct and shape the power relations of that society. By adopting new historicist strategies, and abiding by its theoretical assumptions, we can explore the relationship between literature and colonialism, gender oppression, slavery, criminality or insanity. We can examine the degrees to which literature participates in forming the dominant ideological assumptions of a particular time.

Of course, new historicists differ on how we might do this. Miller adopts Foucault's writings on incarceration and discipline to reveal the part that Dickens's *Bleak House* plays in policing and disciplining mid-Victorian society. Montrose reconstructs a network of myths and writings of the Elizabethan period to show how these various texts circulated with each other to produce a discourse of Elizabethan power. In each case, the focus is the same – the relationship between literature and the power relations of the past. Miller's essay is simpler than Montrose's in that it tends towards a method of applying Foucault's ideas on the carceral and on discipline to a literary text in an attempt to show how penal discourses are refracted through the text. Montrose's method, on the other hand, juggles with a variety of literary genres to fashion a discourse of power, which itself is complex and fraught with contradictions and conflicts. Montrose shows how one text jars against another, producing the possibility of incoherence or instability, and explores the extents to which discourses of power are always shifting, insecure and rife with tensions.

New historicist essays enable us to see how literary texts which may be read as entertainments, as character studies, or as complex, formal and linguistic structures, can also be read for their comprehension of cultural manifestations and mediations of power and political control. They are useful not in helping us to locate the specific political position of a text, but in formulating the ways and means by which literature is complicit in the operations of power. New historicism is the most important indication of a turn to history in literary studies, and although it may be criticised for exercising a kind of violence to the specificity of historical events in constructing what appear to be seamless narratives of power through long periods of time, it is also responsible for revealing the capacity of literary texts as political acts or historical events. New historicist strategies of reading enable us to construct alternative political and historical stories out of the relationship between literature and other forms of representation, to fashion alternative histories of oppression and power through the surviving textual traces of the past.

NOTES TOWARDS READINGS OF
THE TEMPEST AND *IN MEMORIAM A.H.H.*

The object of study for a new historicist critic is the way in which a culture represents itself. For new historicists, written texts are the products of social, cultural and political forces, not solely the creation of an individual author, and so texts reflect and engage with the prevailing values and ideologies of their own time. Accordingly, if written texts are embedded in their own historical contexts, then it is possible for the critic to reconstruct the ways in which any text interacted with and shaped the society, culture and politics of the past. One of the most common methods used by new historicist critics to do this is to situate literary texts in relation to other texts of the same period, and to construct a kind of dialogue between a wide range of texts. In part, this method shows that literary texts share common assumptions and values with more mundane writings, such as religious pamphlets, medical records, travel anecdotes and confessional narratives, hence arguing that literary texts are rooted in particular contexts, and are not free of ideological or historical constraints. This method is particularly common in studies of Renaissance literature, especially of Shakespeare's plays.

To perform such a reading in relation to *The Tempest*, for example, would reveal that Shakespeare's play was deeply embedded in the values and debates of its own time. Firstly, the play would have to be linked to other kinds of texts written in the same period. Such texts are not selected at random. Usually, it requires some knowledge of the immediate biographical or historical contexts of the play. It is believed, for instance, that Shakespeare based the events of the play on an account he had read of a ship that was wrecked in the Bermudas on its way to the English colony in Virginia in 1609. Although *The Tempest* is set on an island somewhere between Tunis and Naples, the similarity of his setting to the account of the Bermudan shipwreck has prompted a number of historicist critics to argue that *The Tempest* is an allegory of the colonial encounter between Europeans and the native peoples they subjugated. The relationship between Prospero and Caliban is central to this reading of the play. Prospero is represented as the learned, magical master of the island, in common with many of the colonial narratives of Shakespeare's time which reported that native Americans often believed that the European colonizers possessed strange magical powers (which were often technological inventions). Caliban, on the other hand, is represented as treacherous, foul-smelling, violent, savage, ignorant and, in Prospero's words, 'got by the devil himself' (*T*, I.ii, 321–2), in common with colonial stereotypes of the native.

Caliban, although he is not properly a native to the island, claims that it is his home: 'This island's mine, by Sycorax my mother, / Which thou tak'st from me' (*T*, I.ii, 333–4). Prospero is thus represented as the colonial usurper, although he and his daughter Miranda represent themselves as benevolent masters. Miranda denounces Caliban as an 'abhorred slave', who, when she and her father have attempted to civilize him, has ill-treated and betrayed them in return. Prospero accuses Caliban of raping Miranda, which he does not deny, and Caliban plots against his master, attempting to turn his own allies and subordinates against him. Miranda attributes Caliban's failings to 'vile race', which 'had that in't which good natures / Could not abide to be with' (*T*, I.ii, 353–62). Here, Miranda reflects the prevailing representations of the colonized as savage races, who betrayed the trust put in them by their benevolent masters whose only intentions, it seems, are to bring education and civilization to the natives.

The Tempest might thus be seen to represent and reflect the ideologies of colonialism, a reading which could be reinforced by comparing the views expressed in the play with such colonialist writings as Harriot's *A Briefe and True Report of the New Found Land of Virginia*, Raleigh's *The Discovery of the Large, Rich, and Bewtiful Empyre of Guiana*, Spenser's *A View of the Present State of Ireland* and Rich's *Newes from Virginia: The Lost Flocke Triumphant*. All of these texts were written and circulated in Shakespeare's lifetime, and together form a powerful set of colonial representations and stereotypes. It is the routine assumption of new historicist critics that the similarities between such an array of texts form a discourse, which regularly shapes and determines the views, values and actions of the society and culture in which it is fostered. For new historicists, all forms of power and control operate through the medium of textual representations, a point which is itself at the heart of *The Tempest*. Prospero is master over Caliban because of his books, 'for without them', Caliban tells his co-conspirators, 'He's but a sot' (*T*, III.ii, 91–3). Language and textuality are constitutive of subjectivity and power, and Caliban knows that in order to subvert Prospero's power over him he needs to counter Prospero's mastery of the art of representation. Thus, *The Tempest* illustrates a theoretical argument which is central to the critical practice of new historicism.

New historicist analyses do not necessarily involve constructing relationships between a wide range of texts, however, and often focus on how a specific literary text (usually one which enjoys considerable status or prestige in literary history) represents or negotiates power relations. The aim of such an analysis is to identify the ways in which literature acts as a vehicle for power relations, and the ways in which we can read the possibilities both for subversion and containment in the literary texts of the past. Tennyson's *In Memoriam* should serve as a good example. It was published first in 1850, the same year in which Tennyson became the Poet Laureate, and the poem became popular with the Victorian reading public, and especially, it seems, with Queen Victoria, who is reputed to have helped Tennyson revise the poem. The poem occupies a site of considerable power and prestige in Victorian culture, therefore, particularly as it articulates the feelings of private grief and mourning with which Victoria herself became associated after the death of her husband, Prince Albert.

For a poem so easily associated with the symbolic sites of political power in nineteenth-century England, however, *In Memoriam* also poses a threat to the established social order. The poem was written in grief for the death of Tennyson's friend, Arthur Hallam, and at various points the poem suggests that Tennyson and Hallam were lovers. It figures the poet's grief for Hallam as that of a widower for his wife, and recalls the intimacies shared between them. Occasionally the poem figures the love in friendly or spiritual terms, but the analogies which Tennyson draws upon to explain their relationship frequently turn to sexual desire: 'My spirit loved and loves him yet, / Like some poor girl whose heart is set / On one whose rank exceeds her own' (*IM*, 60.2–4). Tennyson imagines the ghost of Arthur Hallam above him, and beckons him as before to 'Descend, and touch, and enter' (*IM*, 93.13). These sexual analogies or images recur throughout the poem, even after Queen Victoria reputedly changed the gender of the poet's lover, which, as Alan Sinfield has argued, simply confirmed the suggestion that the relationship featured a shared bed (Sinfield, 1986, 127).

That a poem of such symbolic significance should celebrate same-sex relations threatens to subvert the sexual and moral order of Victorian culture, since it runs counter to the moral stereotypes of the degeneracy associated with homosexuality and the natural and spiritual sanctity of heterosexual marriage. *In Memoriam* suggests the potential for subversion, but the poem resolves its apparent departure from the dominant moral order of Victorian society by concluding with a homely, pastoral image of heterosexual love. The poem concludes with the happy marriage of Tennyson's youngest sister, and with the poet's renewed sense of hope and faith. The final stanza of the poem restates his faith in 'One God' too, 'to which the whole creation moves' (*IM*, 131.142–4), and thus the poem resolves not merely its suggestions of sexual subversion, but also the numerous doubts it expresses about religious faith and social stability. Against the threat of secular science, *In Memoriam* closes with faithful optimism.

This is only one of the ways in which the poem contains the threat of subversion and reinforces the social and political order of Victorian society. It celebrates the virtues of English civilization over 'the blind hysterics of the Celt' (*IM*, 109.16) and 'the red fool-fury of the Seine' (*IM*, 127.7). It also confirms the role of poetry as the public expression of private emotions (in contrast to the eighteenth-century model of public satire), and thus attempts to depoliticize the role of poetry within the Victorian ethos of individualism and bourgeois liberalism. But the most significant function of the poem, from a new historicist approach, is that it opens up the possibility of sexual subversion, only in order to contain it more effectively in its recapitulation of heterosexual morality. The poem retreats away from homosexuality, as if homosexual love could only have existed in youthful immaturity, not with the passage of time. For a new historicist critic, this type of closure at the end of the poem marks the ideological resolution of a social problem or contradiction, and typifies the conservative function of powerful representations in our culture.

QUESTIONS FOR FURTHER CONSIDERATION

1. If, as new historicists contend, subjectivity is inseparable from power-ful social and cultural discourses, how might this affect the way we read 'character' in literary texts?
2. Lee Patterson argues of new historicist analyses that 'There is no space outside power because power is the only term in the analyst's arsenal.' To what extent does this hinder new historicism in interpreting literary texts?
3. One of the most common methods of new historicist analyses is to consider literary texts as one among many forms of representation and to treat literature in relation to other kinds of discourse. What are the advantages and disadvantages of this practice?
4. In the notes towards a reading of *The Tempest* above, the argument is that the play reflects the ideologies of colonialism. Construct the counter-arguments to this view, and suggest criticisms of the ways in which *The Tempest* is interpreted by new historicist critics.
5. In what ways are Prospero and Caliban in *The Tempest* shown to be constructed and shaped by language and discursive formations?
6. How does *In Memoriam* help us to understand mid-Victorian society and culture? Does the reading sketched above help us to understand the past, or is it more attuned to the concerns of the present?

ANNOTATED BIBLIOGRAPHY

Greenblatt. Stephen. *Renaissance Self-Fashioning: From More to Shakespeare*, Chicago, 1980.
Although this was not Greenblatt's first book, it was the first in which he employed the concepts of power, discourse and subjectivity to analyze literary texts, a practice which became known subsequently as new historicism. Greenblatt argues in this book that in the Renaissance period there was a transformation in the social and cultural structures which changed the character of subjectivity. He analyzes the ways in which writers and individuals like Thomas More, William Tyndale, Thomas Wyatt, Edmund Spenser and Christopher Marlowe fashioned their self-identities through a network of social, psychological, political and intellectual discourses.
Greenblatt. Stephen. 'Invisible Bullets: Renaissance Authority and its Subversion'. *Glyph*, 8, 1981: 40–61.

One of the most influential new historicist essays, by which I mean that it has been widely discussed and widely anthologized. Greenblatt begins with an anecdote about an Italian heretic, Menocchio, whose radical subversiveness got him burned at the stake on the authority of the Inquisition. Greenblatt uses this anecdote to explain his argument that subversiveness is necessary in order for power to become visible and fearsome, and to extend his argument to suggest that seemingly orthodox texts generate subversive insights which are an integral part of a society's policing apparatus. He then proceeds to examine this argument in relation to Thomas Harriot, the author of a report on England's first colony America, and to Shakespeare's *I Henry IV*. He finds in each case that power produces the appearance of subversion in order to contain and police subversion more effectively.

Miller. D. A. *The Novel and the Police*. Berkeley, CA, 1988.
Miller differs from the new historicists in Renaissance studies, like Greenblatt and Montrose, in that he applies Foucault's concepts directly and explicitly to literary texts, rather than owing some of his implicit assumptions to Foucault. Miller takes Foucault's work on discipline, punishment, policing and incarceration and explores what kind of readings emerge from the application of those concepts to Victorian novels. Miller focuses on Charles Dickens, Anthony Trollope and Wilkie Collins in his study.

Vesser. H. Aram, ed. *The New Historicism*. London, 1989.
The first of Veeser's collections of essays on the new historicism, in this volume Veeser gathered together essays on the emergence, reception and criticism of new historicism, which include contributions from prominent practitioners like Louis Montrose, Joel Fineman, Catherine Gallagher and Stephen Greenblatt to critics like Brook Thomas, Frank Lentricchia, Vincent Pecora and Hayden White. Veeser's introduction attempts to define the characteristics of the new historicism, and in general this anthology is useful for reading debates on what the new historicism represents in literary studies, including its shortcomings and weaknesses.

Vesser. H. Aram, ed. *The New Historicism Reader*. London, 1994.
Whereas the first of Veeser's collections published essays about the new historicism, the second anthology published examples of the critical practice of new historicism. It included classic new historicist essays by Stephen Orgel, Stephen Greenblatt, Louis Montrose, Joel Fineman, Walter Benn Michaels, Catherine Gallagher and many others. Some of the essays included, such as the essays by Brook Thomas and Eve Kosofsky Sedgwick, do not follow the classic new historicist formula, which Veeser usefully describes as the process of 'converting details into knowledge' by five measured operations: 'anecdote, outrage, resistance, containment, and the critic's autobiography – all in a tight twenty-five pages' (5).

SUPPLEMENTARY BIBLIOGRAPHY

Armstrong, Nancy. *Desire and Domestic Fiction: A Political History of the Novel*. Oxford, 1987.
———— and Leonard Tennenhouse, eds. *The Violence of Representation: Literature and the History of Violence*. London, 1989.
Brannigan, John. *New Historicism and Cultural Materialism*. Basingstoke, 1998.
Boyarin, Daniel. ' "Language Inscribed by History on the Bodies of Living Beings": Midrash and Martyrdom', *Representations*, 25, Winter 1989.
Brown, Marshall, ed. *The Uses of Literary History*. Durham, NC, 1995.
Bruster, Douglas. 'New Light on the Old Historicism: Shakespeare and the Forms of Historicist Criticism', *Literature and History*, 5: 1, Spring 1996.
Cox, Jeffrey N. and Larry J. Reynolds, eds. *New Historical Literary Studies: Essays on Reproducing Texts, Representing History*. Princeton, NJ, 1993.
Dimock, Wai-Chee. 'Feminism, New Historicism and the Reader', *American Literature*, 63: 4, 1991.
During, Simon. 'New Historicism', *Text and Performance Quarterly*, 11: 3, July 1991.

Foucault, Michel. *The Archaeology of Knowledge*, trans. A. M. Sheridan Smith. London, 1972.

―――. *Discipline and Punish: The Birth of the Prison*, trans. Alan Sheridan. London, 1979.

―――. *The History of Sexuality, Volume 1: An Introduction*, trans. Robert Hurley. London, 1981.

Gallagher, Catherine. *The Industrial Reformation of English Fiction: Social Discourse and Narrative Form 1832–1867*. Chicago, 1985.

Geertz, Clifford. *The Interpretation of Cultures*. London, 1993.

Goldberg, Jonathan. *James I and the Politics of Literature: Johnson, Shakespeare, Donne and their Contemporaries*. Baltimore, MD, 1983.

―――, ed. *Queering the Renaissance*. Durham, NC, 1994.

Greenblatt, Stephen. *Learning to Curse: Essays in Early Modern Culture*. New York, 1990.

―――. *Marvelous Possessions: The Wonder of the New World*. Oxford, 1991.

Hamilton, Paul. *Historicism*. London, 1996.

Hawthorn, Jeremy. *Cunning Passages: New Historicism, Cultural Materialism and Marxism in the Contemporary Literary Debate*. London, 1996.

Howard, Jean. 'The New Historicism in Renaissance Studies', *English Literary Renaissance*, 16, 1986.

Michaels, Walter Benn. *The Gold Standard and the Logic of Naturalism: American Literature at the Turn of the Century*. Berkeley, CA, 1987.

Miller, D. A. 'Discipline in Different Voices: Bureaucracy, Police, Family and *Bleak House*', *Representations*, 1:1, 1983; rpt. in *The Novel and the Police*. Berkeley, CA, 1988.

Miller, J. Hillis, 'Presidential Address 1986: the Triumph of Theory, the Resistance to Reading, and the Question of the Material Base', *Theory Now and Then*. Hemel Hempstead, 1991.

Montrose, Louis Adrian, ' "Shaping Fantasies": Figurations of Gender and Power in Elizabethan Culture'. *Representations, 1:2*, Spring *1983*.

―――. 'Renaissance Literary Studies and the Subject of History', *English Literary Renaissance*, 16, 1986.

―――. ' "Eliza, Queene of Shepheardes", and the Pastoral of Power', *The New Historicism Reader*, ed. H. Aram Veeser. London, 1994.

Newton, Judith. 'History as Usual? Feminism and the "New Historicism" ', *Cultural Critique*, 9, Spring 1988.

Porter, Carolyn. 'Are We Being Historical Yet?', *The South Atlantic Quarterly*, 87: 4, Fall 1988.

―――. 'History and Literature: "After the New Historicism" ', *New Literary History*, 21, 1990.

Ryan, Kiernan, ed. *New Historicism and Cultural Materialism: A Reader*. London, 1996.

Tennenhouse. Leonard. *Power on Display: The Politics of Shakespeare's Genres*. London, 1986.

Thomas, Brook. *The New Historicism and Other Old-Fashioned Topics*. Princeton, NJ, 1991.

―――. 'Walter Benn Michaels and the New Historicism: Where's the Difference?' *Boundary 2: An International Journal of Literature and Culture*, 18: 1, Spring 1991.

Wilson, Richard, and Richard Dutton, eds. *New Historicism and Renaissance Drama*. Harlow, 1992.

OTHER WORK CITED

Sinfield, Alan. *Alfred Tennyson*. Oxford, 1986.

CONFLICT AND CONTRADICTION: CULTURAL MATERIALISM

John Brannigan

Cultural materialism emerged in Britain in the 1980s as a critical approach to literature which understood and read literary texts as the material products of specific historical and political conditions. Its central concerns are in the ways in which literature relates to history, and what interpretations of a literary text might result from analyses which privileged historical contexts as the key to understanding the meanings and functions of literature. An important realization of cultural materialism is that texts produce different meanings and interpretations when read in different times and in different locations. Shakespeare's *The Tempest* might have been understood in very different ways in late sixteenth-century England than it has been read and performed in the Caribbean in the twentieth century, for example. The most prominent practitioners of cultural materialism – Alan Sinfield, Jonathan Dollimore, Catherine Belsey – share much in common with new historicists in the USA, particularly in treating literary texts as agents in making sense of a culture to itself. They also share with new historicists a common preoccupation with the Renaissance period, and with the roles which literature and theatre played in interpreting and explaining Renaissance society to itself. Cultural materialists participated with new historicist critics in the radical reinterpretation of Shakespeare and his contemporaries, shifting the focus of Shakespeare studies away from traditional emphases on the bard's universalism and humanism and towards a study of how Shakespeare's texts functioned in Elizabethan society to articulate specific cultural, gender or sexual identities, or indeed to highlight the ways in which power was deployed, distributed and manipulated in sixteenth-century England. But cultural materialists have also gone further than new historicists in emphasizing the political functions of literary texts in our own time, and in critiquing the ways in which literature is often appropriated in conservative political discourses to shore up notions of national heritage or cultural superiority. Accordingly, cultural materialists tend to read literary texts in ways which frustrate conservative interpretations, either by interpreting texts as the vehicles of radical critiques of conservative politics, or by exposing the means by which texts do serve the interests of conservatism.

The roots of cultural materialism lie in the work of prominent left-wing academics of the 1960s and 1970s who challenged 'traditional' approaches to literature by, firstly, contesting the ways in which certain kinds of texts were privileged as 'literary' and others dismissed as 'popular', and secondly, debating the validity of the idea of literature as embodying timeless, universal human values. The work, for example, of Stuart Hall, Raymond Williams and Richard Hoggart in extending literary analyses to the broader domain of 'culture' exposed the ways in which literary criticism had conventionally scorned the value of popular forms of entertainment and reading as tasteless, mass consumption and privileged the reading of a select canon of 'literary' texts as an index of sophistication. Hall, Williams and Hoggart, each in their own ways, suspected that what lay behind such distinctions between the popular and the literary was a class distinction whereby the working classes were conveniently represented as slavishly following mass-market trends while the middle and upper classes were seen to be improving their minds and morals by reading 'high' literature. Culture was, however, shown to be more complex than this in the work of these left-wing critics, for whom examples abounded of the ways in which popular expressions could mean as much, and function in similar ways, as a literary text. 'We cannot separate literature and art from other kinds of social practice', wrote Raymond Williams, because those who enjoyed classical music and Shakespeare's plays were no more sophisticated, privileged or special than those who preferred 'The Beatles' or Mills & Boon novels (Williams, 1980, 43). Cultural studies was not so interested in making the icons and fashions of popular culture equivalent to high art and literature, however, as it was preoccupied with studying the ways in which cultures told stories about themselves through all forms of media and artistic representation. It was predominantly marxist in its critique of the ideological functions of 'culture', and suggested that culture was inseparable from politics. Walter Benjamin had argued in his definition of *historical* materialism that since history was written by the rulers and conquerors, accordingly the 'cultural treasures' of the world were the spoils of conquest and oppression, remarking: 'There is no document of civilization which is not at the same time a document of barbarism' (1992, 248), which in practice means that we must take care when we encounter stories of genius writers and great art to analyze the material circumstances which enable art and literature to be so highly acclaimed. Thus, in cultural materialist terms, the claim that Shakespeare is a universal writer is also a claim that English literature can make sense of and explain the world to itself, a claim which is then uncomfortably close to the boast of English imperialism. That

Shakespeare's reputation as a universal genius gained considerable ground in the eighteenth and nineteenth centuries, when English imperialism reached its height, should alert us to the historical circumstances in which 'greatness' is celebrated and promoted.

Implicit in Benjamin's explanation of historical materialism is a radical reversal of the assumption of progressive humanism that the road to civilization leads away from the barbarism of the past. Benjamin proposes instead that civilization depends on barbarism, that in order for the middle classes to become civilized the working classes must be made barbaric, or in order for the English to be civilized, there must be a barbaric 'other' in the colonies against whom the English can define themselves. One can see in Benjamin's thinking the significance which he attributes to 'representation'. Conventional marxist analyses emphasized the economic means of control which the middle classes exerted over the working classes, but for Benjamin, as for Antonio Gramsci, the ideological or representational means of control were even more important. The 'bourgeois' class may dominate the workers by economic means, but their dominance is made plausible and is perpetuated at the level of representation. For Gramsci the task of marxist criticism is then to engage with capitalism on an ideological level, representing the interests of the working and peasant classes and exposing the contradictions and 'false consciousness' of the bourgeoisie. Indeed the possibility of all social and political change relies upon the outcome of this ideological struggle – as Gramsci explains in his *Prison Notebooks* 'men acquire consciousness of structural conflicts on the level of ideologies' (Gramsci, 1971, 365). According to the view which sees economics as the sole determining factor, ideology is a delusion which conceals the real, and therefore need only be dismissed as false while the real task of transferring the means of economic production to the proletariat is conducted. But this is to miss the point that bourgeois ideology succeeds in holding the captive attention and support of all classes. Gramsci referred to this condition as hegemony.

The influence of marxist ideas and approaches is one of the key factors in distinguishing between the practices of cultural materialism and those of new historicism, for new historicists were more influenced by Michel Foucault's historicist model of power relations than by marxist cultural studies. For Sinfield, Dollimore and other cultural materialists, however, the emphases which marxists such as Gramsci, Benjamin and Williams placed on the function of literature as an agent of bourgeois ideology and power suggested the need for an interpretative approach to literature which could accommodate marxist analyses of the politics of representation. Sinfield and Dollimore published what amounted in effect to a manifesto of cultural materialism as a foreword to an edited collection of essays entitled *Political Shakespeare* in 1985, a collection which represented and celebrated the arrival of radical new historicist perspectives in Renaissance studies. In their preface, the editors acknowledged a debt to Raymond Williams for the term 'cultural materialism', which he had used to describe his own work in *Marxism and Literature*:

It is a position which can be briefly described as cultural materialism: a theory of the specificities of material cultural and literary production within historical materialism . . . it is, in my view, a Marxist theory, and indeed . . . part of what I at least see as the central thinking of Marxism. (1977, 5–6)

In acknowledging the debt to Williams, Sinfield and Dollimore were declaring that cultural materialism was in many senses the progeny of marxist literary and cultural studies. It shared with marxism the notion of history as perpetual struggle between social and cultural factions, and it shared too the idea that representations of all kinds played a part in the cultural politics of their time. Dollimore and Sinfield set out the key principles of cultural materialism in the foreword to *Political Shakespeare*:

Our belief is that a combination of historical context, theoretical method, political commitment and textual analysis offers the strongest challenge and has already contributed substantial work. Historical context undermines the transcendent significance traditionally accorded to the literary text and allows us to recover its histories; theoretical method detaches the text from immanent criticism which seeks only to reproduce it in its own terms; socialist and feminist commitment confronts the conservative categories in which most criticism has hitherto been conducted; textual analysis locates the critique of traditional approaches where it cannot be ignored. We call this 'cultural materialism'. (1985, vii)

The four key principles in this statement are not particularly descriptive of the method or critical practice of cultural materialism, but they are general indications of the conditions in which cultural materialists see themselves operating. The principles proposed by Sinfield and Dollimore are designed to displace what they call 'traditional' approaches, the main features of which are implied in the definition of each of the principles. Cultural materialism, accordingly, is defined as a reaction against criticism which treats texts as possessing 'transcendent significance', which interprets a text 'in its own terms' and within 'conservative categories', and which grounds its understanding of a text solely within close textual analysis. In contrast to the liberal and conservative critical approaches suggested in this foreword, cultural materialists registered a new phase of political and ideological conflict, in which literary criticism could not remain neutral. While the liberal political beliefs and practices of postwar Britain, realized in the form of the welfare state, the NHS (National Health Service), scholarships, nationalized industries and local government, were steadily, often swiftly, eroded by the new right-wing ideologies of Thatcherism, literary critics like Dollimore, Sinfield, Belsey, Barker and Holderness scrutinized how literary texts played their part in sustaining and perpetuating conservative ideologies. Sinfield, for example, has shown how Shakespeare has been pressed into service to teach reactionary social norms, to justify imperialist ideology, even to sell military weapons, but in reply Sinfield has offered dissident readings of Shakespeare's texts which challenge traditional conservative and humanist readings. Cultural materialists have sought to change the terms in which writers such as Shakespeare are read and interpreted. Instead of the humanist focus on issues of character, morality and 'timeless' human values, cultural materialists have asked questions of texts which are concerned with power and resistance, race and gender, ideology and history.

Jonathan Dollimore's *Radical Tragedy* is exemplary of cultural materialist approaches. Dollimore analyzes Jacobean tragedies for the ways in which they relate specifically to two major ideological constructs – establishment providentialism (which held sway in Renaissance times as the explanation of monarchical power as the product of divine will, therefore justifying the union of church and state and discouraging possible rebellions or criticisms of either institution), and the autonomous, essential individual (which posits the idea of an unchanging human nature, symbolized in the individual soul). Dollimore's study is partly recovering the ideological contexts in which Jacobean texts were produced and read, but partly also a self-consciously twentieth-century return to those contexts to challenge humanists ways of reading them. So, for example, in the case of providentialism, Dollimore shows how texts such as Marlowe's *Dr Faustus* and Jonson's *Sejanus* not only foreground providentialist explanations of Renaissance politics and society but also provoke disquieting and challenging questions about the limits and contradictions of providentialism. At stake in his analyses is not just a concern to discover how such texts interacted with their own historical contexts, but Dollimore is also keen to show that literature acts in subversive as well as conservative ways, that literary texts can expose the limitations and faults of conservative political orthodoxies as it can reinforce them. Thus Dollimore's book demonstrates the value of analyses of historical context, as well as highlighting the political commitment of cultural materialism to discovering the ways in which texts go against the grain of conservative interpretations and values.

In *Political Shakespeare*, Dollimore and Sinfield brought together the work of new historicist critics like Leonard Tennenhouse and Stephen Greenblatt and the work of cultural materialists, largely, although not exclusively, represented by themselves. The title is polemical to begin with, advertising the commitment to politicizing literature which has become characteristic of cultural materialism. In the foreword the editors articulated their dislike of criticism which disguises its political agenda, and which pretends to be politically neutral:

> Cultural materialism does not, like much established literary criticism, attempt to mystify its perspective as the natural, obvious or right interpretation of an allegedly given textual fact. On the contrary, it registers its commitment to the transformation of a social order which exploits people on grounds of race, gender and class. (Dollimore and Sinfield, 1985, viii)

This is quite different to the work of new historicism, almost invariably focused on the past as belonging to a different epoch, ideologically and politically, to our own. Cultural materialists are committed to interpretations and investigations which have overt political ends in the contemporary world. Perhaps the best example of this commitment is Sinfield's synthesis of literary analysis, historical investigation and political engagement in *Literature, Politics and Culture in Postwar Britain*, in which he traces the emergence of consensus politics in postwar England, with its promises of full employment, comprehensive free education, and welfare and healthcare for all, and charts also the destruction of the welfare state under Mrs Thatcher's governments in the 1980s. Sinfield studies the ways in which the literature of the period foregrounds and contributes to these historical shifts, finding in the working-class writing of the 1960s, for example, that such writers as Alan Sillitoe, John Braine and John Osborne did not represent the genuine interests and aspirations of the working class, but instead reflected the process of *embourgeoisement* which the consensus politics of the 1950s and 1960s seemed to effect. The emergence of working-class writing does not indicate for Sinfield an improvement in the lot of the working class, merely that the working class have become the object of closer cultural scrutiny, in which service a handful of writers came to prominence. However authentic the class credentials of the writers, the fate of the working class cannot be changed, according to Sinfield, if the oppressed social position of the writers has no effect on the form in which they are working. Sinfield argues that writing itself was an inherently conservative act: 'There were writers of lower-class origin, it was acknowledged, but in the very act of becoming writers they were co-opted to middle-class forms' (Sinfield, 1989, 40). The premise of Sinfield's argument is that the act of writing itself in the 1950s was a middle-class act, and that the readers and audiences for literature in the 1950s were largely middle class. The representation of working-class life apparently achieves no dramatically radical position when performed to a middle-class audience already hungry for representations of 'the other' anyway. Such an analysis of the conservative cultural politics of working-class writing is offered up in Sinfield's study as part of an explanation for the state of Britain in the 1980s, which for left-wing intellectuals was a dramatic shift away from the promises of the Labour government of 1945 to provide for the poor and disenfranchised of British society. Sinfield has been the most prominent cultural materialist to engage so actively in diagnosing contemporary political problems in the course of interpreting and explaining literary texts and their functions within society. Reading literature for cultural materialists is a political activity. It reflects and shapes the meanings which we as a society assign to texts and cultural practices, and it is therefore also a site of contest between competing political ideologies.

This sense of reading as political conflict can also be seen in Sinfield's *Faultlines*, in which he states that his intention is 'to check the tendency of *Julius Caesar* to add Shakespearean authority to reactionary discourses' (1992, 21). Literary texts acquire and are assigned cultural authority to different degrees and at different times in each society, and can be appropriated and co-opted to speak for one or more political ideologies. The meanings of these texts will always be contested, but what cultural materialists are interested in showing is that where meanings are contested there is almost always more at stake than insular aesthetic or artistic principles. Sinfield summarizes his argument in *Faultlines* as the following: 'Dissident potential derives ultimately not from essential qualities in individuals (though they have qualities) but from conflict and contradiction that the social order inevitably produces within itself, even as it attempts to sustain itself' (1992, 41). In new historicist accounts of the operations of power, power seems to function as a flawless, perfectly efficient and effective machine. Sinfield disputes this, however, and offers a reading of power which reveals its faults, or more correctly the conflicts and contradictions within power which may reveal dissident perspectives and which Sinfield calls 'faultlines'. It is through these 'faultlines', Sinfield claims, that we can read the alternative identities and values, and dissident ideas, of a given society.

In *Faultlines* Sinfield argued that the motivation for cultural materialist readings lay in the conservative and reactionary uses to which literary texts had been put. Cultural materialism as a practice necessarily reacts against the appropriation of literature in conservative political discourses:

> Conservative criticism has generally deployed three ways of making literature politically agreeable: selecting the canon to feature suitable texts, interpreting these texts strenuously so that awkward aspects are explained away, and insinuating political implications as alleged formal properties (such as irony and balance). (1992, 21)

In order to counter these conservative readings, and in order to make texts politically *dis*agreeable, cultural materialists can adopt the same strategies, or turn them against traditional or reactionary texts. If, as cultural materialist critics assert, Shakespeare is a powerful ideological tool in our society, there are ways of reading which can counter the authority which Shakespeare lends to reactionary discourses.

In an essay published in 1983 Sinfield explained that there were four principal ways of dealing with a reactionary text: (1) Rejection 'of a respected text for its reactionary implications . . . can shake normally unquestioned assumptions . . .' (2) 'Interpretation . . . so as to yield acceptable meanings . . . is, of course, available to the socialist critic . . .' (3) 'Deflect into Form(alism): One may sidestep altogether . . . the version of human relations propounded by the text by shifting attention from its supposed truth to the mechanism of its construction . . .' (4) 'Deflect into History':

> [T]he literary text may be understood not as a privileged mode of insight, nor as a privileged formal construction. Initially, it is a project devised within a certain set of practices (the institutions and forms of writing as currently operative), and producing a version of reality which is promul-

gated as meaningful and persuasive at a certain historical conjuncture. And then, subsequently, it is re-used – reproduced – in terms of other practices and other historical conditions. (Sinfield, 1983, 48)

The last method is a preferred method of cultural materialists in general, of putting the text in its contexts, whether the contexts of production or the contexts of reception, so as to expose the process by which it has been rendered in support of the dominant culture. Once this process has been exposed then the text can be interpreted by dissident critics 'against the grain'. Examining literary texts in their historical contexts is, for cultural materialists, a process of estranging those texts from the naturalized conservative readings to which they have been routinely treated. To show that Shakespeare's plays were inseparable from the ideological struggles of their time is, firstly, to dismiss the idea that his plays are timeless and universal, but it is also to alert us to the ways in which Shakespeare serves ideological functions in our own time too. In this case, historically situated and contextualized readings taught cultural materialists that the past could lend radically different meanings to canonical literary texts.

In the 1980s both new historicism and cultural materialism were interested in stressing the extent to which the past differs from contemporary uses of the past, the extent to which the past is alien or 'other' to our own modern episteme, and, borrowing from Michel Foucault and Clifford Geertz, they were at the same time aware of the structural similarities between this historical difference and the cultural differences being emphasized by postcolonial critics, feminists, gay theorists and race theorists. Increasingly in the late 1980s and throughout the 1990s, cultural materialist critics extended their analyses into the domains of 'queer' theory, postcolonialism and feminism. Jonathan Dollimore published *Sexual Dissidence* in 1991, while Alan Sinfield examined the representations and figures of effeminacy in twentieth-century culture in *The Wilde Century* in 1994. Both studies extended and deepened the ways in which cultural materialist critics read literature and culture through concepts of 'difference', focusing in particular on the cultural politics of sexual difference. Do gay and lesbian sexualities pose a radical challenge to the prevailing norms and values of our societies, or are they merely the same as 'straight' sexualities? This is a question which concerns both Sinfield and Dollimore in their respective studies, and it indicates the extent to which their recent work builds on their early work as cultural materialists. Both critics have extended the analyses of earlier concepts of dissidence, faultlines and deviance by focusing more particularly on the specific cases of sexual dissidence, and the dissident strategies of lesbian and gay subcultures.

Cultural materialism, like new historicism, has succeeded in literary studies in displacing earlier formalist concerns with textual unity and humanist concerns with character and authorship, and changing the ways in which we approach literary texts and their meanings. Although there are very few critics who identify themselves explicitly as 'cultural materialist', the influence of cultural materialism on literary studies in Britain has been pervasive, most notably in the current centrality of historicist approaches, the suspicion of texts with 'canonical' or cultural authority, and the importance of concepts of 'difference' in analyses of the cultural politics of texts. Arguably too, cultural materialism has been instrumental in encouraging self-reflexivity in our critical practices, and a wider concern for the way in which literary studies interacts with, and learns from, the study of culture, society, history, politics and other disciplines. Cultural materialism has enriched literary studies by probing the relationship between literature and social, cultural, political and sexual power, and giving literary criticism a sharper political focus on the present as well as the past.

NOTES TOWARDS READINGS OF
THE TEMPEST AND *IN MEMORIAM A.H.H.*

As the above essay suggests, Shakespeare became a major source of debate and conflict for literary critics in England in the 1970s and 1980s. Shakespeare had become a cultural icon of considerable symbolic significance in England, and his plays were conventionally represented as timeless works of genius which revealed transcendent truths about the human condition. Cultural materialist critics argue, in contrast, that Shakespeare's works are embedded in specific historical and material contexts, and perform particular, usually conservative, functions in our society. For a cultural materialist, then, Shakespeare is so central to contemporary English culture not because of any transcendent messages in his writings, but because his work is continuously made the vehicle of conservative cultural ideologies. By making it compulsory to study his plays in schools, and by teaching those plays in ways which foreground apolitical issues of character, plot and theme rather than more contentious and pertinent political issues such as race, gender, sexuality or corruption, Shakespeare is made to represent and convey conservative political and cultural values.

Cultural materialist readings of Shakespeare, therefore, have usually tried to show one of two things. One could either demonstrate that Shakespeare's plays emerged out of heated political and cultural controversies of his own time, and thus diminish the extent to which the plays could be celebrated as free from the ideological constraints of history (this is very similar, of course, to new historicist analyses of Shakespeare's plays). Or, alternatively, one could read the plays in relation to the controversies of our own time, and foreground the ways in which Shakespeare's plays can be read subversively, to support dissident political or cultural causes in our society, for example. In both cases, cultural materialist analyses work to counter the tendency to read canonical texts in conservative ways simply by demonstrating that all texts are inseparable from specific material and historical conditions.

To show how this kind of analysis would work in relation to Shakespeare's

The Tempest, for example, we would need to examine the ways in which this play foregrounds particular debates and issues from the time in which it was written and produced. A cultural materialist interpretation of *The Tempest* would follow much the same kinds of arguments as a new historicist interpretation, but with one important difference. New historicists tend to examine the processes whereby a literary text reflects and constitutes the dominant ideologies or discourses of its time. Cultural materialists, on the other hand, argue that such ideologies are fraught with conflicts and contradictions, which are in turn reproduced and explored in literary texts. While new historicists might argue, then, that *The Tempest* reflects a powerful set of colonial stereotypes and representations, a cultural materialist reading would illustrate how *The Tempest* reveals the contradictions and faultlines of colonial discourses in Shakespeare's time.

The Tempest, as we saw in the new historicist reading above, was written at a time when England was engaged in various colonial projects in the 'New World', and may have been based on the story of one voyage to the Americas which was shipwrecked in the Bermudas. This has prompted a number of contemporary historicist and materialist critics to read the play in relation to early modern colonial discourses. But while new historicists would draw attention to the ways in which the play replicates the terms of colonial ideology, cultural materialism would emphasize the conflicts and debates inherent in colonial ideology which are explored in the play. One such debate concerns the conflict between a utopian and a materialist conception of colonialism. The most prominent conceptions of colonial ventures in Elizabethan society seemed to be utopian. They emphasized the mythological and mystical aspects of the New World, and thus represented it as a virginal, edenic territory of magic and wonder, giving it such names as 'Virginia', 'Arcadia' and 'Fairyland'. Accordingly, Shakespeare represents his colonizer, Prospero, as a man of magical powers who holds court over an island in which he can make wondrous things happen.

Caliban's dreams illustrate his magical view of the island. He is enchanted by its appearance and its noises, and believes that the island has an abundance of treasures which will simply fall into his hands.

> *Caliban*: The isle is full of noises,
> Sounds, and sweet airs, that give delight and hurt not.
> Sometimes a thousand twangling instruments
> Will hum about mine ears, and sometimes voices
> That if I then had waked after long sleep
> Will make me sleep again; and then in dreaming
> The clouds methought would open and show riches
> Ready to drop upon me, that when I waked
> I cried to dream again.
>
> (*T*, III.ii, 138–46)

The Tempest does not reflect this utopian view of colonialism, however, for it represents such an anti-materialist approach to the colonial project as doomed to failure. Caliban's dreams of treasures falling from the sky are indicative of the idealism of many contemporaneous colonial ventures, but *The Tempest* shows that such dreams are sent to distract Caliban. He is eventually led by his dreams not to fall into riches, but into a cesspool of horse-piss instead (*T*, IV.i, 182, 199). Similarly, although Prospero attempts to rule over the island with his magical powers, he also comes to articulate the view that there is no substance to the dream of bountiful riches. 'We are such stuff as dreams are made on', he tells us:

> *Prospero*: . . . These our actors . . .
> were all spirits, and
> Are melted into air, into thin air;
> And like the baseless fabric of this vision,
> The cloud-capped towers, the gorgeous palaces,
> The solemn temples, the great globe itself,
> Yea, all which it inherit, shall dissolve;
> And, like this insubstantial pageant faded,
> Leave not a rack behind.
>
> (*T*, IV.i, 148–56)

The dreams of riches and magical powers which fuelled the fire of colonial ambitions in early seventeenth-century England, then, appear to be mocked in *The Tempest* as 'baseless' and 'insubstantial'. They are dreams which drive their followers to distraction and torment, but not to success. Perhaps the play's most potent symbol of colonial adventure is the shipwreck, since it signifies the fate of all such idealism, that, as the ship master says in the opening scene, 'we run ourselves aground' (*T*, I.i, 4). As Jeffrey Knapp argues, however, it is not just the dreamers who fail in *The Tempest*, but also the more materialist expansionists such as Alonso, who is, of course, shipwrecked (Knapp, 1992, 225). It is possible to argue that *The Tempest* is suggesting that all such ventures are destined for failure, perhaps because of the corrupt motivations of the adventurers, but what is more clearly evident in the play is the clash of two ideologies of colonial expansion. *The Tempest*, according to a cultural materialist reading, represents the conflicts and contradictions inherent in early seventeenth-century colonial discourse itself, and explores and contributes to debates about the nature of colonialism. The idea that Shakespeare's plays are connected to, and indeed participate in, debates about the conduct and nature of colonial expansion is, of course, deeply antithetical to humanist approaches to Shakespeare. Instead of lauding Shakespeare as a universal genius, cultural materialists attempt to situate his works within specific political and cultural frameworks, and to argue that Shakespeare lived in a time of turbulent change in which it is foolish to assert that the playwright was unconcerned with and disengaged from the most serious social and political issues of his time. For cultural materialists, literary texts help to shape the way in which a culture makes sense of itself, which means that we can read texts for their interactions with history, but we must also be aware that texts participate in history and help to mould an image of that history which is both partial and partisan.

Another important realization of cultural materialism, however, is that literary texts are not fossils or artifacts, but are active constituents of meaning in our time. This means that texts perform particular functions in our own society, for example in the way in which Shakespeare is taught in schools as the vehicle of universal humanism. Cultural materialists tend to read literary texts against the grain of prevailing conservative or humanist interpretations, and in support of dissident or marginal social identities in our society. In the case of Tennyson's *In Memoriam*, for example, it is indisputably a poem of its time, and reflects Victorian concerns about the clash of religion and science, as well as the interactions between individual desire and social conventions. But it can also be read to reflect ideas of sexuality which are controversial and subversive now.

To read Tennyson's elegiac love poem for his friend, Arthur Hallam, is to become conscious of potentially challenging notions of homosexual love. The love between Tennyson and Hallam is controversial because it seems to suggest a continuum between homosociality and homosexuality, and the poem oscillates between metaphors of friendship and metaphors of marriage. As with the reading of *The Tempest* above, there would be many similarities between a cultural materialist reading of *In Memoriam* and a new historicist one, and indeed Alan Sinfield's book on Tennyson borrows heavily from new historicist modes of analysis (Sinfield, 1986). But one principle difference is that cultural materialism tends to read literary texts not only for the subversion they may have opened up in the past, but also for their subversive potential in contemporary culture. Thus, Sinfield also focuses on the construction of gender and sexuality in *In Memoriam*, and argues that Tennyson's poem elevates gender and sexual identities which are marginalized in our societies into socially symbolic roles. *In Memoriam*, on close inspection, holds up the sexual love between two men as a symbol of hope and optimism for the future, and takes the love between them as symbolic of the possibility of an idyllic afterlife. It is possible to argue, therefore, that a poem which is central to our vision of Victorian England, which is stereotyped for us in images of heterosexual family and community life, is also a poem which exalts homosexual love as an ideal. Sinfield advances such an argument in his book in order to proffer the notion that Tennyson threatens to present us with a reversion to the Greek ideal of homosexual love. To read controversial notions of gender and sexual identities into this canonical Victorian poem, then, is not simply to offer an alternative perspective on the Victorian period (although it certainly does that), but also opens up the possibility that literary texts can function to support dissident and subversive ideas in our society too.

Cultural materialism frequently functions, then, as an oppositional criticism, reading against the grain of prevailing cultural and political orthodoxies in order to enlist the support of powerful literary and cultural texts for dissident causes.

QUESTIONS FOR FURTHER CONSIDERATION

1. To what extent is cultural materialism a marxist theory of literary and cultural production? What role does 'political commitment' play in cultural materialist criticism?
2. Kiernan Ryan criticizes cultural materialism for being too concerned with a political agenda to engage with the literary text as a complex linguistic form. In what ways might a politically committed criticism be antithetical or contradictory to literary analysis?
3. 'We cannot separate literature and art from other kinds of social practice' (Raymond Williams). Consider the implications of this statement for the study of literary texts. What would such a critical practice involve?
4. 'In education Shakespeare has been made to speak mainly for the right' (Alan Sinfield). In what ways might *The Tempest* be read to support or speak for left-wing politics?
5. 'It is the task of cultural criticism to decipher the power of Prospero, it is equally its task to hear the accents of Caliban' (Stephen Greenblatt). To what extent would a cultural materialist reading of *The Tempest* achieve what Greenblatt suggests?
6. In the notes towards a reading of *In Memoriam* above, sexuality is the main source of dissident or subversive potential in the poem. Consider the ways in which the poem articulates other forms of dissidence, and situate these in relation to the poem's historical and cultural contexts.

ANNOTATED BIBLIOGRAPHY

Belsey, Catherine. *The Subject of Tragedy: Identity and Difference in Renaissance Drama*. London, 1985.
Belsey contends that modern understandings of human subjectivity derive from the Renaissance period, and demonstrates the emergence of the individual subject in her readings of Renaissance texts. The book is divided into two parts, the first dealing with 'Man', the second with 'Woman'. Belsey argues that this was the period in which 'Man' became the 'common-gender noun', failing to include women, and defining 'Woman' as having meaning only in relation to 'Man'.
Dollimore, Jonathan. *Radical Tragedy: Religion, Ideology and Power in the Drama of Shakespeare and his Contemporaries*. Hemel Hempstead, 1984.
Dollimore examines the ways in which Renaissance drama represented crises in contemporary ideas of order, religion and subjectivity. He discusses a wide range of important changes in Renaissance society, including changes to concepts of law, theology, identity, providence, cosmos, class, virtue and sexuality. He also situates these discussions of Renaissance society in relation to twentieth-century debates about literature, subjectivity and society.

————, and Alan Sinfield, eds. *Political Shakespeare: New Essays in Cultural Materialism*. Manchester, 1985.

The appearance of this volume marked the emergence of cultural materialism as a major new critical approach in British literary studies. The essays contained in the volume are divided into two parts. All of the essays in Part One examine Shakespeare in the contexts of Renaissance culture and society. The second part, 'Reproductions, Interventions', examines the twentieth-century contexts of Shakespeare's plays, and how Shakespeare has been deployed in education, cinema and theatre.

Sinfield, Alan. *Faultlines: Cultural Materialism and the Politics of Dissident Reading*. Oxford, 1992.

Sinfield's largest and most ambitious book to date brings together and refocuses some earlier work on Shakespeare and the early modern period in general, and addresses the debates arising from cultural materialist and new historicist work. It contains ten chapters and a brief photo-essay, all of which address questions of cultural authority and dissident readings ('dissidence' is Sinfield's preference over the new historicist term 'subversion'). Like almost all cultural materialist work, Sinfield's book is primarily interested in challenging the function of literature in the present day, even when it is engaged in reading and interpreting the historical contexts of early modern texts.

SUPPLEMENTARY BIBLIOGRAPHY

Barker, Francis. *The Tremulous Private Body: Essays on Subjection*. London, 1984.

Brannigan, John. *New Historicism and Cultural Materialism*. Basingstoke, 1998.

Belsey, Catherine. *The Subject of Tragedy: Identity and Difference in Renaissance Drama*. London, 1985.

Drakakis, John, ed. *Alternative Shakespeares*. London, 1985.

Hawkes, Terence, ed. *Alternative Shakespeares Volume 2*. London, 1996.

Hawthorn, Jeremy. *Cunning Passages: New Historicism, Cultural Materialism and Marxism in the Contemporary Literary Debate*. London, 1996.

Holderness, Graham, ed. *The Shakespeare Myth*. Manchester, 1988.

Milner, Andrew. *Cultural Materialism*. Carlton, 1993.

Prendergast, Christopher, ed. *Cultural Materialism: On Raymond Williams*. Minneapolis, MN, 1995.

Ryan, Kiernan, ed. *New Historicism and Cultural Materialism: A Reader*. London, 1996.

Sinfield, Alan. *Literature in Protestant England 1560–1660*. London, 1982.

————, ed. *Society and Literature 1945–1970*. London, 1983.

————. *Alfred Tennyson*. Oxford, 1986.

————. *Cultural Politics – Queer Reading*. London, 1994.

Wilson, Scott. *Cultural Materialism: Theory and Practice*. Oxford, 1995.

OTHER WORKS CITED

Benjamin, Walter. *Illuminations*, ed. Hannah Arendt, trans. Harry Zohn. London, 1992.

Dollimore, Jonathan. *Sexual Dissidence: Augustine to Wilde, Freud to Foucault*. Oxford, 1991.

Gramsci, Antonio. *Selections from the Prison Notebooks*, trans. Quentin Hoare and Geoffrey Nowell Smith. London, 1971.

Knapp, Jeffrey. *An Empire Nowhere: England, America, and Literature from* Utopia *to* The Tempest. Berkeley, CA, 1992.

Sinfield, Alan. 'Four Ways with a Reactionary Text', *Journal of Literature Teaching Politics*, 2, 1983.

Sinfield, Alan. *Literature, Politics and Culture in Postwar Britain*. Oxford, 1989.

Sinfield, Alan. *The Wilde Century: Effeminacy, Oscar Wilde and the Queer Moment.* London, 1994.
Williams, Raymond. *Marxism and Literature.* Oxford, 1977.
————. *Problems in Materialism and Culture.* London, 1980.

POSTCOLONIALISM AND THE DIFFICULTY OF DIFFERENCE

Gail Ching-Liang Low and Julian Wolfreys

> The telling of colonial and postcolonial stories . . . demands a more naked relation to the ambivalence represented by the greater mobility of disempowerment. To tell the history of another is to be pressed against the limits of one's own. (Sara Suleri)

One significant aspect of the modern world has been the impact and legacy of imperialism, colonial territorial acquisition and control – particularly of European imperialism. Part of this impact and legacy, a part which remains with us, is the production of what Sara Suleri defines as acts of 'cultural articulation' (1995, 111), including the narratives in which such articulation is embedded and the kinds of language, the specific discourses of colonialism, race and otherness which have developed and which serve to generate those narratives.

This is not simply a one-way process. Rather, it also involves a more complex, frequently ambivalent procedure of cultural transition, whereby the narratives and other forms of cultural articulation of non-western cultures have assumed and assimilated aspects of colonial and imperial culture. On the subject of such a legacy, Kwame Anthony Appiah has remarked that 'all aspects of contemporary African cultural life including music and some sculpture and painting . . . have been influenced – often powerfully – by the transition of African societies *through* colonialism' (1995, 119). From the nineteenth century, European powers started a major scramble for territory so much so that by 1914, more than three-quarters of the world was controlled by Europeans. The processes associated with European modernity emerged on the back of imperialism and, in many ways, represents its darker underside. Postcolonial theory has emerged from an interdisciplinary area of study which is concerned with the historical, political, philosophical, social, cultural and aesthetic structures of colonial domination and resistance; it refers to a way of reading, theorizing, interpreting and investigating colonial oppression and its legacy that is informed by an oppositional ethical agenda. In relation to colonial history, some of the basic questions that preoccupied critics include: Are there common structures to colonial domination across different geographies and different histories? What is the relation between material and hegemonic forms of oppression, between power and representation in specific situations? Is power total? What kinds of challenges are possible and what forms do they take? If official history is the history of the powerful, how do we recover these anti-colonial oppositions? How, and in what way, have some of the founding assumptions of the Enlightenment such as rationality, progress, beauty and taste been produced by colonial history? Questions relating to political independence – to the *post*-colonial (even though Appiah and others argue that, despite the historical withdrawal of colonial powers, there is a sense, because of the persistence of the material and immaterial traces and effects of colonial culture in African life, that some African nations are not yet postcolonial) – are equally important: What is at stake in the articulation of cultural or national identity? Can one hope to recover or create identities, artistic and representational forms and culture which are not overdetermined by that imperial legacy? Is writing in a colonial language and tradition a form of 're-' rather than 'de-'colonization? Who is postcolonial when global capitalism contributes to a neocolonial world? Finally, because of its commitment to interrogate structures of domination, postcolonial theory has had of necessity to address institutions, intellectuals and the role they play in the network of power and knowledge. Accordingly, especially recently, postcolonial theory has been more critical and self-reflexive of its own theoretical presumptions and its institutional location in perpetuating an unequal global exchange.

The publication of Edward Said's *Orientalism* (1978) emerges as a key moment in the development of postcolonial theory within the academy. Drawing on Foucault and Gramsci, Said's monograph is a polemical and critical study of the ways in which the Occident has sought to objectify the Orient through the discourses of the arts and the human and social sciences. For Said, there are two distinct aspects to his use of the term *Orientalism* which inform his study. First, it is the generic term employed 'to describe the Western approach to the Orient; Orientalism is the discipline by which the Orient was (and is) approached systematically, as a topic of learning, discovery and practice' (1978, 73). Additionally, *Orientalism* designates in Said's study 'that collection of dreams, images and vocabularies available to anyone who has tried to talk about what lies east of the dividing line' (73). His definition of Orientalism as a 'discourse' was distinctly enabling for the emerging field of postcolonial theory because it enabled critics to see how different sorts of cultural and representational texts contributed to the formation of structures of power. Said sees an intimate connection between systems of knowledge and strategies of domination and control; hence his critique is an interdisciplinary interrogation of western intellectual, aesthetic, scholarly and cultural traditions. Methodologically, Said differs from Foucault in that, in defining Orientalism, in reading its forms and manifestations, Said does not take texts *en masse* but, instead, considers individual texts to be exemplary. Thus, he combines close textual analysis 'whose goal is to reveal the dialectic between individual text or writer and the complex collective formation to which his work is a contribution' (1978, 24). Such an approach may be seen through the attention given to Kipling in Gail Ching-Liang Low's essay, which we discuss below in more detail (*LT*, 481–98).

The Essex Sociology of Literature conference for 1984, which Edward Said attended, was entitled 'Europe and its Others' and provided a forum for an international collection of scholars to address colonial issues. The Essex conference also provided the venue for introducing two other leading figures, Homi Bhabha and Gayatri Spivak, who together with Said have been hailed somewhat cheekily by Robert Young as the 'holy trinity' of postcolonial theory. While there are significant differences between the work of Spivak and Bhabha (their work is fully explored, alongside that of Said, in Young, 1990, and Moore-Gilbert, 1997), they share, as Robert Young puts it, 'the assumption [as does Said] that imperialism was not only a territorial and economic but inevitably also a subject-constituting project' (1990, 159). Bhabha's work, informed by psychoanalysis, enunciation theory and deconstruction, and latterly by post-modern theory, emerged from the space of *Orientalism* but was also framed as a distinct challenge to its representation of colonial hegemony as omnipotent and uniform. Bhabha's essay, 'The Other Question' (1983) interrogates racism and racial stereotyping through a theory of racial fetishism (further developed in Bhabha's 1986 critical introduction to Fanon's *Black Skins/White Masks*). As Bhabha argues, from a partial rereading of Said in which he also takes issue with Foucault:

> The fetish or stereotype gives access to an 'identity' which is predicated as much on mastery and pleasure as it is on anxiety and defence . . . This conflict has a fundamental significance for colonial discourse . . . The stereotype . . . as the primary point of subjectification in colonial discourse, for both colonizer and colonized, is the scene of a similar fantasy and defence – the desire for an originality which is again threatened by differences of race, colour and culture. (Bhabha 1994, 75)

In 'Of Mimicry and Man' (1984) he develops the idea of ambivalence:

> Within the conflictual economy of colonial discourse . . . the demand for identity, stasis . . . and the counter-pressure of . . . change, difference . . . mimicry represents an *ironic* compromise . . . the discourse of mimicry is constructed around an *ambivalence* . . . the *ambivalence* of mimicry ([that

which shows itself as] almost the same, *but not quite*) does not merely 'rupture' the discourse, but becomes transformed into an uncertainty which fixes the colonial subject as a 'partial' process. (1994, 85–6)

'Signs Taken for Wonders' (1985) elaborates ambivalence and mimicry through a new term 'hybridity', which is defined by Bhabha as 'the revaluation of the assumption of colonial identity through the repetition of discriminatory identity effects . . . the colonial hybrid is the articulation of the ambivalent space where the rite of power is enacted on the site of desire' (1994, 112), while 'DissemiNation' (1990) develops their implicit conceptual critique of origins in the direction of national identities and narratives of the nation. Later essays will explore the difficulty of (theorizing) agency, given Bhabha's post-structuralist approach. Bhabha's account of the conflictual economy of colonial discourse has been enormously productive for the field of colonial literary criticism, even though his writing often appears wilfully dense and resistant to any easy comprehension (Moore-Gilbert 1997, 114ff.).

Gayatri Spivak's work is immensely influential in the field of colonial historiography, feminist studies, cultural studies and postcolonial studies and her writing has always sought to bring together the insights of poststructuralism, deconstruction, marxism, psychoanalysis and feminism in active collision. Sceptical of grand, ambitious and overreaching explanatory frameworks, she points out the usefulness of these theories and critiques their limitations. Spivak is concerned with what she calls the 'epistemic violence' of imperialism; she is also noted for her relentless questioning of institutions, institutional power and the role of intellectuals in institutions (*Outside in the Teaching Machine*, 1993). Her critique of the Subaltern Studies project of recovering peasant – as opposed to elite – history is emblematic of the necessity and the impossibility of speaking for/or on behalf of oppressed groups ('Subaltern Studies: Deconstructing Historiography', 1985). While Spivak is wary of this strategic project, nonetheless the term *subaltern* is crucial in Spivak's work as a 'model for interventionist practice' (Young, 1990, 159), and is usefully defined by Robert Young. Drawn from the work of Italian marxist Antonio Gramsci, *subaltern* defines class groups of ' "inferior rank" ' and is, moreover, 'particularly well suited to describe the diversity of dominated and exploited groups' (Young, 1990, 160).

Critical of western feminism's humanist assumptions, Spivak also poses the question of what it means to address woman (femininity, sexual difference) as a unifying universal analytic category, especially when different cultures, histories and political-legal contexts have produced very different notions of the 'sexed' subject ('French Feminism in an International Frame', 1981; 'Three Women's Texts and a Critique of Imperialism', 1985; 'The Political Economy of Women as seen by a Literary Critic', 1989). 'Can the Subaltern Speak?' (1988), Spivak's most influential and controversial early essay, suggests that one particular 'regulative psycho-biography' for women is *sati* or sanctioned suicide, a site of contradictory subject positions assigned to women in India by both indigenous patriarchal and British colonial regimes.

The Essex conference also provided the impetus for the emergence of the Group for the Critical Study of Colonial Discourse and its occasional bulletin, *Inscriptions*, based at the University of California, Santa Cruz. The group's aim was to foster contact between scholars and researchers on representation and colonialism; some of the figures who participated in the group and contributed papers, such as James Clifford, Caren Kaplan, Lata Mani, David Lloyd, Peter Hulme, Mary Louise Pratt and Trinh Minh-ha, from adjacent disciplinary backgrounds, were later to become established critics in postcolonial studies. Special numbers and guest editors in prestigious academic journals in this period of the 1980s consolidated the influence of colonial discourse and postcolonial theory, and also its crossovers into other aspects of literary theory; Henry Louis Gates' guest editorship of *Critical Inquiry* in 1985, entitled 'Race, Writing and Difference', contains influential figures like Jacques Derrida on apartheid, Edward Said on the reassessment of Orientalism, Abdul JanMohamed on Manichean aesthetics, Mary Louis Pratt on travel narratives, Patrick Brantlinger on empire and fiction, Homi Bhabha on ambivalence in colonial discourse and Gayatri Spivak on imperialism and feminism. The American special number was joined, on the British side of the Atlantic, by the 1988 *Oxford Literary Review* special number on colonialism and postcolonialism. OLR includes Gauri Viswanathan's well-known work on English education in India and Benita Parry's influential critique of Bhabha, Spivak and JanMohamed. Parry criticizes Spivak's 'deliberate deafness to the native voice' which, she argues, is 'at variance with her acute hearing of the unsaid in modes of Western feminist criticism', suggesting, furthermore, that Spivak's writing 'severely restricts . . . the space in which the colonized can be written back into history' (Parry, 1995, 40). While acknowledging the differences between Bhabha and Spivak's critical practices, Parry's critique focuses on their shared indebtedness to 'high theory', particularly so-called deconstruction, combined with what she describes as an 'incuriosity about the enabling socioeconomic and political institutions and other forms of social praxis' (1995, 43).

In retrospect, this criticism may be read as marking a sea-change in the analysis and methodologies of postcolonial criticism, as part of the more general turn in the late 1980s away from discursive and philosophically or conceptually oriented analyses towards a more ostensibly politicized criticism which, in the name of politics, returned to a mimetic and representational epistemology in the field of literary and cultural criticism. Parry's turn to the revolutionary Fanon, as opposed to Bhabha's earlier psychoanalytic Fanon, signals the inclusion of theories of colonialism from a different time and history to its fold, and the intense contestation over the work of the revolutionary theorist, activist and psychoanalyst. Parry's recuperation of nationalism, 'Resistance Theory/Theorising Resistance or Two Cheers for Nativism', is supported by Neil Lazarus' positive but critical review of the place of intellectuals in 'National Consciousness and the Specificity of (Post)-colonial intellectualism'. Both essays are collected in *Colonial Discourse/Postcolonial theory* (1994) and present an important alternative strand to what is sometimes seen as a celebratory 'hybridity' and anti-essentialism in some significant domains of postcolonial theory.

Another genealogy of postcolonial theory is possible if one also incorporates the work done in postcolonial criticism and Commonwealth writing. This position is argued by critics associated with the development of 'Commonwealth literature' or 'new literatures in English' in Britain and the Commonwealth. Alan Lawson, Leigh Dale, Helen Tiffin, Shane Rowlands, Stephen Slemon and Bart Moore-Gilbert all contend that the work done by creative writers like Raja Rao, Wilson Harris and Wole Soyinka foreshadows colonial discourse theory. The Leeds' conference of 1964 is marked as a key moment in the establishment of Commonwealth teaching, with writers such as Chinua Achebe and R. K. Narayan contributing lectures; some of its themes and issues such as identity, nationality, landscape, pedagogy and language would be taken up over the next decade. In their recent collective introduction to a comparative survey of postcolonial literatures and theories in English, Lawson, Dale, Tiffin and Rowlands argue for overlaps between what is sometimes taken to be two separate genealogies. 'Commonwealth post-colonialism', a term they coin, initially focused more on creative efforts and channelled energies, especially in the 1970s, into anti-colonial criticism and the writing and teaching of national or regional literatures. The African presence is particularly strong in this period of the 1970s with Chinua Achebe's *Morning Yet on Creation Day* (1975), Wole Soyinka's *Myth, Literature and the African World* (1976) and Ngugi Wa Thiongo's *Homecoming: Essays on African and Caribbean Literature* (1972) following the setting up of Heinemann's African Writers Series. (This period also witnessed the creation of Dangaroo Press based in Denmark publishing critical, theoretical and literary work from the Commonwealth.) Slemon and Moore-Gilbert argue that concepts like creolization and hybridization in Carribean writers and the work of theorists such as Edward Brathwaite and Wilson Harris anticipate the ambivalence that will surface with Bhabha's work in the 1980s. Bill Ashcroft, Gareth Griffiths and Helen Tiffin's *The Empire Writes Back* (1989) would provide a landmark teaching text where postcolonial Commonwealth literary criticism takes on board more self-consciously postcolonial theory. The publication of anthologies of postcolonial theory and criticism, notably Laura Chrisman and Patrick Williams's *Colonial Discourse and Post-Colonial Theory* (1993). Bill Ashcroft, Gareth Griffiths and Helen Tiffin's *The Postcolonial Studies Reader* (1995) and the more US-oriented *Contemporary Postcolonial Theory: A Reader* (1996) by Padmini Mongia, also marks the canonization and commodification of the field in academic studies.

The recent critical and sometimes hostile reassessment of postcolonial theory and its impact marks a phase in which the theory has come of age; Vijay Mishra and Bob Hodge's 'What is Post(-)colonialism?' (1991) points out the limitations of the all-embracing nature of *The Empire Strikes Back*, while Ella Shohat's 'Notes on the Post-Colonial' (1992) attempts a reflexive archaeology of the term post-colonial. Aijaz Ahmad's *In Theory* (1992) attempts to rejuvenate marxist connections and, like Arif Dirlik's *The Postcolonial Aura* (1997), warns against a lack of historical specificity and objects to the radical chic of metropolitan theorizing, a caution already sounded in Spivak's early work. Dirlik's academic connections are to China Studies as is Rey Chow's work; this is just a small indication of how widespread the current disciplinary affiliations and geographical concerns are in the area of postcolonial theory, and how much these disparate bases have added to, problematized and reshaped what has previously taken to be the central ground. Crossovers with the field of cultural studies and cultural theory have also been particularly productive with Stuart Hall and Paul Gilroy's interrogation of racism and representation, ethnic absolutism and nationalism. Gilroy's recent monumental study of the African Diaspora, *The Black Atlantic* (1993), argues for an ethnohistorical approach to modernity. His charting of transnational and intercultural flow of ideas about ethnicity and identity in black vernacular culture and nationalist thought develops one of the central tropes of postcolonial migration. Rey Chow's study of Chinese cinema, *Primitive Passions* (1995), Ella Shohat and Robert Stam's *Unthinking Eurocentricism: Multiculturalism and the Media* (1994), which explores the central role of the media and popular culture in shaping both Eurocentric thinking and an oppositional aesthetics of resistance, are good examples of the current willingness to apply theory to more popular forms to see how this revises and revitalizes terms and concepts.

The articles by Bhabha, Low and Chow to be considered represent, in our mixed metaphor, moments in the vast terrain and hybrid concerns of post-colonial theory and its applications. Bhabha's 'Of Mimicry and Man' (*LT*, 474–80) belongs to the early phase of Bhabha's work which is concerned with how stereotyping, imitation and mimicry all reflect an ambivalence and hybridity in colonial discourse that troubles its smooth delivery. Bhabha argues that Orientalism is as much about the colonial production of knowledges as it is about projection of fears and desires; Said acknowledges this split in his appropriation of the Freudian terms of dream analyses, manifest and latent, but understandably focuses exclusively on Orientalism's disciplinary power and effectivity. In an effort to avoid the reification of colonial power, history and subjectivity, Bhabha's arguments will question precisely the effectivity of colonial authority at the level of discourse. Consequently, his reading will emphasize the vacillation between Orientalism as the authoritative discourse of knowledge, learning and information and Orientalism as fantasy; such a vacillation renders a much more fractured and ambivalent discourse than *Orientalism* puts forward.

One significant pole of Bhabha's arguments then relies on psychoanalytic theories of identity formation, and the adoption of the mirror as the figure for discussing how vision and difference contributes to self-image. Accordingly, the colonial situation provides the opportunity for narcissistic identification in the image of the colonized as 'a reformed, recognisable Other' (475); such figures can be found in the image of the anglicized native, which in Thomas Macaulay's words, form the 'class of persons Indian in blood and colour, but English in tastes, in opinions, in morals and in intellect' (475). But this reformed image of the other is also a product of the colonial gaze which must insist on difference – not quite/ not white, not English but anglicized – in order to justify continued colonial rule. The discriminatory discourse must also produce the other as poor imitations of the self because these 'mimic men' (476) cannot ever arrive at the threshold of humanity that is identified with the colonizer; hence, the ambivalence, indeterminacy and self-contradictory nature of colonial discourse which 'must continually produce its slippage, its excess, its difference (475) in order to be effective. Here Bhabha also draws on the psychoanalytic theory of fetishism as avowal and disavowal of castration. (Bhabha makes no apologies or concessions for invoking the gendered bias in the equation of castration with lack and femininity). Racial fetishism is argued to possess a similar dynamic of avowal and disavowal in its primal encounter with the difference of skin colour; racial stereotyping is an 'arrested, fixated form of representation' based on the subject's denial of difference and desire that 'all men have the same skin/colour/race' (478).

The reformed other has the potential to unsettle and threaten the self precisely because it resembles the image of the self. Like Freud's uncanny, which catches the ease by which the self can be alienated (literally estranged or made strange) through the double, colonial mimicry is at once resemblance and menace. Colonial mimicry produces another knowledge of the self by producing a vision of the self from (an)other place; for example, in Charles Grant's treatise on the morality and necessity of Christian education and reform, the civilising mission is mirrored as an immoral form of social control. Mimicry need not be restricted to colonial history but can be also found in postcolonial literatures. For example, in *The Enigma of Arrival*, V. S. Naipaul's ambivalent mediations on Englishness, it is the narrator's loving (mis)identification with the English and veneration of things English that also enable him to see it as an invention of tradition – the handiwork of impresarios. The investment in origins is precisely what enables an intimate knowledge of its production.

The disruption of colonial discourse can also be traced, deconstructively, on a more historical front. An understanding of the discursive economy of fetishism as posed between the twin poles of metonymy and metaphor provides the link. Bhabha uses the term 'metonymy of presence' to signal the distance between the metropolitan point of articulation and origination, and the colonial periphery to which that colonial discourse has to travel. In this theory, metaphor, which presumes an identity of meaning across boundaries, is supplemented by metonymy, which registers different social, cultural and political displacements. Discourse as it is translated into a colonial context brings about hybridization and ambivalence, and points to the lie of universalism that underwrites colonial authority. The insertion into colonial discourse of beliefs, assumptions and languages that are deemed foreign to it enables a resistance or blockage; it is also employed as a strategy by postcolonial writers who work within a metropolitan literary tradition, but who want also to insist on their difference, and their resistance to a master(ing) discourse.

Bhabha's insights into the conflictual nature of colonial subjectivities is helpful for its refusal of the easy binary polarities of colonizer/colonized and colonialist/nationalist, and claims to a stable, whole and unitary identity on both sides of the divide. The ambivalence of colonial discourse opens up a space to think about how power and paranoia are linked, and paves the way for a less reductive reading of colonial texts. But Bhabha does not differentiate between the different positions the critic, the text and the context occupies in the production of ambivalence; his vacillation between all three fields makes it difficult to assess what kinds of resistance are possible to colonial authority and the status of such resistance. Also, Bhabha's psychoanalytic and deconstructive approach enables the more troubled and conflictual reading but, as Robert Young in *White Mythologies* has pointed out, it is by no means certain if this is the distinct mark of the colonial situation, or is, following deconstruction and psychoanalysis, a characteristic of all texts and all psyches.

Gail Low attempts a more nuanced reading and assessment of two key figures in imperial myth-making of the late nineteenth century; her work is enabled by the spaces opened up by Bhabha's exploration of ambivalence of colonial texts, and by the literary theoretical turn to psychoanalysis to explore questions of power, desire, pleasure, displeasure, mastery and defence in the representation of colonial relations. Contrary to the conventional dismissal of Kipling's writing as simple imperial proselytising, she asks the question: 'What kind of jingoism and what kind of effectivity?' (*LT*, 436). She discovers in Kipling's early writing a fascination with figures who cross cultural and social boundaries, especially white men 'gone native', whose transgressive status is sometimes recuperated for the colonial state, and sometimes shunned as 'beyond the pale'. Unlike the 'mimic men' of Bhabha's piece, who are figures of comedy and estrangement, the white man who can pass for native is invested with extraordinary energy within the stories. To use the psychoanalytic term, they are 'subjects who presume to know'; their distinctive status resides in their being subjects outside the circuit of desire. Hence, their fascination and power as imperial symbols lies not in the figures themselves but transferential dynamics. Here Low follows the line of Peter Brooks in arguing for the similarity between the psychoanalytic and narrative structures; the transferential dynamics of the analytic situation are similar to the transferential dynamics of storytelling and its seduction.

In particular, in 'Loafers and Story-Tellers', Low is concerned with the 'Loafer' or vagrant in what is sometimes taken to be the quintessential parable of empire, 'The Man Who Would Be King' (*LT*, 463–98). Positive responses to the loafers have often taken the line that the tale's moral lies in its expression of 'universal desire for power and domination'; these readings have remarked on the loafer's breathless daring and impudence. But Low argues that such readings of what is a much more open tale is only possible after transference has taken place; the 'truth' or moral of the tale in this way is understood to be more a retroactive product of desire than internal to the text. Focusing not on the central characters of the tale, but their relationship to each other and critics' relationship to them, Low reads in Kipling's elaborate use of various frame-narrators and focalization his sense of his own role as writer, his awareness of contemporary culture and a canny understanding of how narration is built on voyeurism, novelty and seduction. For Low, the strengths of the tale lies not in its audacious representation of conquest but in its understanding of the impudent processes of imperial mythologizing. The artist as loafer represents the flip side to the traditional portrait of Kipling as imperial bard, 'responsible for some of the founding legends of Empire' (485); Low's Kipling emerges as an opportunistic, a figure who fantasizes about crossing cultural boundaries, and a writer who turns others into narrative and commercial profit.

The difficulty of cultural crossings in a postcolonial world that bears the legacy of imperialism is at the heart of Rey Chow's work on the (re)presentation of Chinese cinema both within and without its national boundaries. The questions she asks are very much central to postcolonial theory: How do postcolonial cultural and artistic endeavours in cinema engage with the epistemic violence of colonialism, and what do they have to offer us on different sides of the cultural divide? How should a western(ized) critic discourse on non-western expressive cultures? How should a non-western critic discourse on cultural forms that are enabled by 'western' technologies? What kinds of institutional politics are involved in such cross-cultural problems and how do we circumvent their more oppressive and repressive effects? How do non-westerners deal with the post-modern extension of an Orientalist legacy? Chow's essay, 'Film as Ethnography; or Translation between Cultures in the Postcolonial World', is a calculated intervention for cross-cultural exchanges against the mutual hostilities of cultural essentialism and the guilt-ridden anxieties of the liberal western intellectual in an age of postcolonialism. To this effect, she employs the term ethnography for her model of cultural exchange. Here, ethnography is divested of its disciplinary claims to truth and knowledge, and read as 'autoethnography', which is fully cognizant of its subjective origins. Chow follows Mary Louise Pratt's definition of these forms of self-representation by colonized others which appropriate and engage with the traditions of their colonizers, but her interrogation of subject/object split in the Orientalist gaze leads her to focus on visuality both literally and metaphorically. Revising Laura Mulvey's theorization of the male gaze, Chow argues, in autoethnography 'the experience of being looked at' and the 'memory of past objecthood' (*LT*, 500) is 'the primary event in cross-cultural representa-tion' (500). Hence, the anthropological impasse of a world divided between subject and object, seer and seen, active and passive, us and them, is no longer tenable: ' "viewed object" is now looking at "viewing subject" looking' (501). Chow's autoethnographic exchanges are forms of cross-cultural narrative by which the non-Western cultures engage actively in their own acts of reflexive autoethnographization (500). Reading Gianni Vattimo alongside Walter Benjamin's radical rethinking of the concept of translation in the light of commentary by Jacques Derrida and Paul de Man, Chow argues that such exchanges are contradictory fabular forms by which the previously ethnographized survive in the media marketplace by engaging with, amplifying ironizing and displaying the terms of their subjection, calling attention to the interplay of power, myth and image. In doing so, their subversive gaze focuses upon 'a weakening Western metaphysics . . . [which, according to Vattimo, constitutes] a turning and twisting of tradition away from its metaphysical foundations, a movement that makes way for the hybrid cultures of contemporary society' (*LT*, 510–11). Furthermore, and in this Chow recalls Benjamin's emphasis on the mass culture aspect of the arcade, what is revealed is 'the weakened foundations of Western metaphysics as well as the disintegrated bases of Eastern traditions' (515).

In reading New Chinese Cinema (associated with the Fifth Generation film directors) as autoenthographic and a fabular form of ethnography, she disrupts the disciplinary professionalism which claims a truth or documentary function for the genre, and aligns herself with the postmodernist scepticism of 'metaphysical truth claims and metaphysical systems of logic' (Vattimo, 1988, xiii). But, more importantly, reading narrative cinema as (auto)ethnographic allows her to read the concept of national cinema differently: as inscriptive cultural record of images, sounds and stories, as a translation between cultures and, with postmodern hindsight, as the transformation of culture through the media. Autoethnographic forms of representation address questions of identity, ethnicity, sexuality, gender, authenticity, elite and popular, by situating the national within a transnational global traffic of mixed media and commodity capitalism. This form of culture writing engages with the hybridity, mediation, 'contamination' and 'corruption' of postcolonial forms of expression (*LT*, 509). In their content and narrative structure, distribution and reception, they enable an interrogation of the myth of authentic native and the exotic primitive within nationalistic and Euro-modernist discourses by showing them to be the structural product of displacement and identification. Correspondingly, and here Chow's text shows the influence of 'deconstruction', the critic's task is not to reinstate the deep-seated prejudice and privilege of depth, originality and fidelity which governs critical conventions; 'we [have to] take seriously the deconstructionist insistence that the "first" and "original" as such is always already difference – always already translated' (510). The desire to return to one's origin is shown to be a paradoxical desire to remove it from the very structuration that renders it 'original' in the first place. Chow argues that the 'dismantling' of the notion of origin and alterity both within and without the western world allows one to open one's eyes to – and take responsibility for – the 'coevalness of cultures' in the contemporary world:

> This notion of the other – not as idealised lost origin to be rediscovered or resurrected but as our contemporary – allows for a context of cultural

translation in which these 'other' cultures are equally engaged in the contradictions of modernity, such as the primitivization of the under-privileged, the quest for new foundations and new monuments, as so forth . . . The coevalness of cultures, is not simply the peaceful co-existence among plural societies but the co-temporality of power structures . . . that mutually support and reinforce the exploitation of underprivileged social groups, nonhuman life forms, and ecological resources *throughout the world*. (511)

The focus on film in postcolonial discourse analysis is particularly welcomed, for the terrain of postcolonial critiques has tended to focus more on the literary than on popular media forms; yet, in a transnational world, it is the latter which increasingly and more complexly impact on our feelings of belonging and exclusions. In this, we see also see the merits and the limitations of her study. Textual analysis of film offers the joys of 'close reading' and allows discussion of the spectacle of postmodern consumer culture; but the claims for a quintessential postcolonial subversiveness for the Fifth Generation is perhaps weakened by the relative exclusion of even more popular media forms and by the absence of what Ella Shohat and Robert Stam have called the different and multiple registers of spectatorship.

Nevertheless, Chow's criticism, which is a good example of the domain of postcolonial discourse analysis, intersects productively with the preoccupations and insights of deconstruction, poststructuralism, postmodernism, psychoanalysis and feminism, and is careful to take note of the relentless migrations of her subject between cultures, histories and media. Her reading of the work of the Fifth Generation of Chinese film directors shows the enormous difficulties and rewards of the postcolonial critic who takes seriously the task of cross-cultural exchange. For her critiques interrogate not only the construction of images and narratives, their attendant aesthetic and political histories, but are also aware of the processes of identification and displacement that signal a critic's location and investment in the subject matter. The difficulty and rewards of postcolonial theory and criticism is, to use Said's phrase in *Culture and Imperialism* (1993), nothing less than an attempt to come to terms with 'overlapping territories and intertwined histories'.

NOTES TOWARDS READINGS OF
THE TEMPEST AND *THE SWIMMING-POOL LIBRARY*

One fruitful articulation of postcolonial critical discourse's political engagement with the literary is to reread those texts which evoke or are otherwise encrypted or overdetermined by 'particular colonial histories, narratives and ideologies' (Hodgdon, 1998, 42). Plays such as *Othello* and *The Tempest* offer rich textual forms for the consideration of such issues, and both academic critics and theatre producers have sought to transform readers' and audiences' cultural perceptions and assumptions of these plays (see Hodgdon's account of Robert Lepage's

1992 production of *A Midsummer Night's Dream* at the Royal National Theatre: 1998, 172–90).

Critics have addressed the questions of coloniality and postcoloniality through the histories of *The Tempest's* performance. Trevor R. Griffiths and Rob Nixon, in ' "This Island's Mine": Caliban and Colonialism' (1983 – see Childs, 1999, 39–56) and 'Caribbean and African Appropriations of *The Tempest*' (1987 – see Childs, 1999, 57–74), both speak to these matters. The former looks at the history of British production from the nineteenth century onwards and the various colonial codes of representation by which the productions maintain and disseminate images of the empire and its others; the latter addresses the range of productions and other forms of appropriation from the 1950s onwards on the part of Caribbean and African intellectuals, in order to consider the question of articulating that which dominant presentations silence or otherwise downplay.

In 1985, two essays were published, Paul Brown's ' "This thing of darkness I acknowledge mine": *The Tempest* and the Discourse of Colonialism' (Brown, 1985, 48–71) and Francis Barker and Peter Hulme's 'Nymphs and Reapers Heavily Vanish: The Discursive Con-texts of *The Tempest*' (Barker and Hulme, 1985, 191–205), which specifically addressed the relation between *The Tempest* and the question of colonialism in the Early Modern period, while also building the critique of colonial discourse on the politicized critical analysis provided by cultural materialism. Subsequently, Ania Loomba and Martin Orkin edited a collection of essays, under the title *Post-Colonial Shakespeares* (1998), which volume represents a significant intervention in what Ato Quayson terms the *postcolonializing* of Shakespeare (2000, 159). Such an intervention concerns itself with the critical tracing of the discourses and manifestations of colonial and racial vocabularies, along with considerations of matters of national identity, otherness and difference. At the same time, many such readings are also interested to discern what we might legitimately call the historicity of persistence from the early modern period to the present day.

Quayson argues that *The Tempest* has received significant attention from postcolonial critics because there is an 'implicit mimeticism' which 'enters into postcolonial analyses' (165; on the question of mimeticism and the hegemony of representation in the poetics of the identity politics associated with post-colonial studies, among other methodologies, see Tom Cohen's critique, cited by Kenneth Womack below); while this suggests that there has been something of a rush to read *The Tempest* 'as representing processes of colonialism', this also suggests for Quayson that such mimeto-political acts of reading 'foreclose the possibility of extending a [more] radical postcolonial reading' (165). It would therefore be a valuable process in the space available to explore certain features of the range of postcolonial commentary on *The Tempest*, including those essays already mentioned by Brown, Brotton, and Barker and Hulme.

Bill Ashcroft, Gareth Griffiths and Helen Tiffin focus briefly on *The Tempest* in considering postcolonialism as a reading strategy, beginning with George Lamming's subversive rewriting of the play in his *The Pleasures of Exile* (1960). As they argue Lamming's reworking 'dismantles the hierarchy of Prospero, Ariel, and Caliban', in part by giving Caliban 'human status . . . denied by the European claims to an exclusive human condition':

> Along with this goes a rereading of the political allegory of *The Tempest* in which the text's concern with the issue of 'good government' is extended to encompass Lamming's sense of the injustice of Prospero's dispossession of Caliban's inheritance – 'this island's mine, by Sycorax my mother'. Finally, this reading shows the duplicity and hypocrisy by which this dispossession is effected . . . (1989, 189)

For Ashcroft and his co-authors the significance of Lamming's retelling is clearly in its politicizing redirection of our attention to elements already in the play which a western, European humanist perspective in the service of excusing or justifying colonialism has tended to explain away as natural (Caliban is a 'natural creature'), as belonging to the internal logic of the play based on supernatural elements (Caliban is the son of a witch and, therefore, not necessarily human) or otherwise kept silent. Moving on from Lamming to other readings which also rely on implicit mimeticism, Ashcroft, Griffiths and Tiffin remark in passing the emphasis given to the hierarchical binarism of colonial/marginal, self/other, European/non-European, high culture/popular culture, rationality/non-rationality.

Such binarisms, pairings and oppositions, and others like them (civilized/ savage, master/servant, human/inhuman), clearly punctuate *The Tempest* in a number of ways which direct our view of Prospero's 'colonial' position in relation to the island. Yet, if you turn to Jonathan Dollimore's argument concerning the paradoxical centrality of supposedly marginal figures in western thought, presented in the chapter on gay studies and queer theory by Jane Goldman and Julian Wolfreys, you should begin to see that, in the context of *The Tempest*, such structures are neither natural nor inevitable, but belong to the discursive and ideological effects by which one culture comes to dominate another, valorizing its own violence (often through allusion to culture and civilization) at the expense of its other, that culture which is unlike it and which therefore appears as threatening. Yet this otherness is, as Dollimore argues, the very difference by which, in the case of Shakespeare's play in particular and colonialism in general, a colonizing power defines and justifies itself.

However, it would be a mistake to read *The Tempest* as merely a play which replays the colonial imperative unequivocally through what Helen Gilbert and Joanne Tompkins summarize as its 'figuration of racial binaries and the threat of miscegenation; its representation of the New World "other" as opposed to the European "self", troped as a form of the nature/culture dichotomy; and its pervasive interest in power relationships involving dominance, subservience, and rebellion' (1996, 25). Importantly, Gilbert and Tompkins argue, the play can also be read as offering 'several sites for potential intervention in the imperial process through politicised readings and reworkings of the text' (1996, 25), and it is this which led Paul Brown to speak of the play as an 'intervention in an ambivalent and even contradictory discourse' (Brown, 1985, 48). Indeed, it is perhaps worth considering that the play's ambivalence concerning matters of race and colonization, and the various disruptions brought about by the contradictions which mark it as a riven text, which draws postcolonial critics to it so often.

One remark in particular, Caliban's to Prospero – 'You taught me language, and my profit on't / Is I know how to curse. The red plague rid you / For learning me your language' (T, I.ii, 365–7) – may be read as focusing the ambivalence, if not the potential violence at the heart of all power struggles between colonial forces and the subaltern groups which the colonialists seek to oppress. There is the enforced monolinguism of the colonial power which its subjects are forced to learn, against which is registered the polyvocality of the island itself ('the isle is full of noises'; T, III.ii, 138). As Paul Brown correctly argues, Prospero's

> 'gift' of language also inscribes a power relation as the other [Caliban] is hailed and recognises himself as a linguistic subject of the master language. Caliban's refusal marks him as obdurate yet he must voice this in a curse in the language of civility, representing himself as a subject of what he describes as 'your language' . . . Whatever Caliban does with this gift announces his capture by it. (Brown, 1985, 61)

We may, moreover, read this line and the ambivalence it articulates in the light of Homi Bhabha's thinking on the subject of colonial mimicry:

> Colonial mimicry is the desire for a reformed, recognizable Other, *as a subject of difference that is almost the same, but not quite* . . . the discourse of mimicry is constructed around an ambivalence; in order to be effective, mimicry must continually produce its slippage, its excess, its difference . . . Mimicry is, thus the sign of a double articulation; a complex strategy of reform, regulation and discipline . . . [and yet] also a difference or recalcitrance . . . [that] poses an immanent threat to both 'normalized' knowledges and disciplinary powers. (*LT*, 475)

While Paul Brown explores the various aspects of ambivalence of Shakespeare's play alongside the signs of 'contemporary British investment in colonial expansion' (Brown, 1985, 48) through a reading of the play's relation to the question of colonial holdings in the Americas in the early seventeenth century, ultimately arguing that *The Tempest* 'serves as a limit text in which the characteristic operations of colonialist discourse may be discerned – as an instrument of exploitation, a register of beleaguerment and a site of radical ambivalence' (68), Francis Barker and Peter Hulme also argue for the centrality of colonial discourse to the play. Whereas earlier historicizing forms of criticism had read early modern colonial experience as merely the context or background, inconsequential except as an excuse for the play's setting, Barker and Hulme foreground the trace of the colonial as one of the play's 'dominant' discursive concerns (1985, 198). Indeed, it is the very idea of discourse, as opposed to any simply defined notion of context or historical event, which drives this particular 'historico-political critique' (Barker and Hulme, 1985, 196); thus, in this reading, colonialism as a particular strand of language marks the very fabric of the play's text.

As the critics argue, the colonial moment must always legitimize the violence of its actions by telling its own story concerning the necessity of controlling 'native violence: Prospero's play performs this task within *The Tempest*' (201). Yet central to this project is the question of ambivalence once more, as Barker and Hulme argue when they urge upon their readers the significance of registering '*both* the anxiety and the drive to closure' which mark colonial discourse and which becomes manifest in the play (204). If Prospero's play within the play announces the necessity of role-playing, or, effectively, another articulation of mimicry, then between drama and politics (or, perhaps, colonial politics *as* drama or theatre) we find announced the fact that there is no *true* or *originary* location from which discourse springs: colonial discourse, as its own narrative and excuse, is as much an act of mimicry as that which colonialism enforces on its colonized other.

At first glance, it might seem difficult to justify an analysis of Alan Hollinghurst's *The Swimming-Pool Library*, a novel detailing the lives and sexual experiences of two gay men, William Beckwith and Charles, Lord Nantwich, in a narrative which stretches across the twentieth century (for further précis of the novel, refer to the discussions in the essays on gay studies and queer theory, and cultural studies). It is neither an overtly colonial tale, as *The Tempest* may be read, nor is it a postcolonial narrative, such as George Lamming's retelling of *The Tempest*. There are, however, a number of narrative details which we might mistakenly pass over as marginal, were we to focus solely on the questions of gay sexuality and desire. Indeed, in addressing these fleeting and liminal moments in *The Swimming-Pool Library* from the perspective of postcolonial critique as a reading strategy, and the discursive ambivalence which this reveals in Hollinghurst's text, we are able to gain insight not only into issues of colonial representation but also into normative assumptions and representations of marginal groups, such as the gay men of the novel.

Part of the narrative involves the narrator, William Beckwith, rewriting the memoirs of Lord Nantwich, in order to produce the octogenarian's biography. In reading the memoirs (which are reproduced onto the pages of the novel for the reader), Beckwith discovers that Nantwich was a colonial administrator in Africa at one point in his life. As Goldman and Wolfreys point out elsewhere in this volume, Lord Nantwich is, ironically, in the service of the very power by which his own sexuality is marginalized, a power which employs him to police and, in various other ways, marginalize the empire's colonial subjects. The uncomfortable concerns with power relations involved here concerning self/

other, hetero/homosexual, colonizer/colonized are available to critique through a consideration of the very structures and limits by which such binary oppositions operate; we are being asked obliquely to consider the ways in which the idea of a homosexual other and the idea of a colonial other are, within particularly overdetermined cultures of oppression (in the case of the novel, the same English culture of oppression at home and abroad), placed in similar, though not necessarily synonymous, relations to hegemonic normative institutions, practices and discourses.

This is further complicated in that Nantwich's language concerning his colonial subjects, though mixed with desire, nonetheless replays particular tropes typical of Anglo-Saxon perceptions of African otherness. Nantwich's language, simply put, is that of the colonizer, though brought into paradoxical sharp relief and tension by those linguistic manifestations of desire. At one instance in his memoirs, Charles reverts to racial stereotype when in Egypt, describing 'a handsome young man with the immemorial flat broad features of the Egyptian . . . [he looked] like an exotic afterthought of Tiepolo' (*S-P L*, 213). At one and the same time, this anonymous Egyptian is dehumanized through the crudest of racial typologies while being aestheticized. Importantly, this line 'produces' the young man, rather than simply representing him as a colonial subject, as other. This idea of production is crucial to Edward Said's concept of Orientalism (1978, 1–30). The act of production takes place through a powerful discursive combinatory which speaks to the question of western colonial need to exercise its power through such representations. Thus Nantwich's language is not 'his' in any simple sense, but the result of what Said describes as belonging to 'a created body of theory and practice in which, for many generations, there has been a considerable material investment' (1978, 6). Though handsome (a mark of aesthetic appreciation), the man is also 'exotic' (a sign of his orientalism). The 'immemorial' flatness of features conjures an ancient or even prehistoric figure, certainly someone outside or not belonging to 'history' (a conveniently western concept). Finally, there is that last aestheticization, the reference to the paintings of Tiepolo. The young Egyptian is simply a foreign exotic type known throughout the cultures of the West by artistic representations. Thus Nantwich's representation comes to him, as Said has it, through the material investment of many generations.

Were we limited to Charles' memoirs, we might believe that the novel were merely providing us with a certain historical accuracy, just an instance of the registration of colonialism's history, in its representation of Lord Nantwich and his memoirs, rather than touching on the persistence of certain discursive and cultural features. The issue of representation of cultural and racial identity occurs in Beckwith's own narrative. The novel opens with Beckwith's observation of a London Underground worker, referred to as 'a severely handsome black' and '[t]he black', whose work is 'invisible' (*S-P L*, 3), and who sports an air of 'scarcely conscious competence' (*S-P L*, 4). There is a marked tension in this: inasmuch as the anonymous figure works in the underground and is, to that extent, invisible, such comments serve to announce a kind of marginality; however, at the same time, his anonymity is not merely an effect of his work, but he is, again to use this figure, produced by the narrator's discourse as *only* the colour black (with, again, that brief aestheticizing touch, 'handsome'). Dehumanized by this representation, he is only '[t]he black', and implicit in the figure of 'scarcely conscious competence' is, I would argue, a tendency towards a further removal of the figure from culture, in that his ability is intimated as being part of his nature.

There is also the image of the 'dal-coloured Indonesian boy with strong yellow teeth, enormous hands and an exceptionally extensile cock' (*S-P L*, 193). Between food and sex – is there to be read here an encrypted post/colonial fantasy of consumption and incorporation of the desired body, whereby our anticipated desire of the oriental or subaltern other prefigures the psychic relocation of the other within? – the boy is fetishized in the brief representation of the most obvious metonymic details pertaining to his racial identity, as the eyes of the narrator, after having taken in the overall impression of colour first, then move in a downwards direction, strong teeth and enormous hands being typical features in representations of the colonial other; it goes without saying that the description of the boy's penis plays into the most blatantly clichéd Anglo-Saxon discourses concerning the persistence of a supposed non-western 'threat' of rampant sexuality.

Then there is Abdul, the African chef at Beckwith's health club, the Corinthian. When first introduced through the narrator's eyes, we are once again witness to processes of metonymic fetishization of the corporeality of the other, with the concomitant dehumanization. Abdul is 'a very black man . . . well built, with fierce, deep-set eyes . . . a subtle violence . . . thick lips' (*S-P L*, 46–7). The discursive production is once again typical, the representation clearly belonging to that colonial admixture, identified by Said apropos Flaubert and Conrad, of the other's attractiveness *and* danger (1978, 186). This is further accentuated when Beckwith describes Abdul carving a leg of pork (once again, the food–sex dyad): 'His hands were enormous . . . as he concentrated the lines of his face deepened, and he poked out his pink tongue' (*S-P L*, 47). Fetishization through body part in a grim, ludicrous climax of representation seems to invite comparison with late nineteenth- and twentieth-century caricatures of minstrel entertainers, as well as other racist caricatures which traverse high and low western culture. What connects Beckwith's descriptions of the Underground labourer, the Indonesian boy and Abdul, and what further links these to Nantwich's biography, is summarized in another context by Gail Low, when speaking of H. Rider Haggard's novels:

> Such a narrative moment . . . belongs to the movement of the Orientalist gaze . . . which lingers on the physical surfaces of the black man's body . . . By returning the black man in the image of white men's desires, it panders to a male narcissism . . . The discourse of primitivity sanctions the

sexual fantasy by producing the black body as animal-like, sexually savage and regressive. The . . . homoerotic desire exists . . . by reimagining the black body, within the conventions of romanticism and aestheticism, as noble savage. (Low, 1996, 53)

This is not Abdul's only appearance in *The Swimming-Pool Library*. He returns at least two more times, the first in a moment of drugged stupor for Beckwith, which might be read as suggestively intimating the account of Dorian Gray's visit to an opium den in Wilde's *The Picture of Dorian Gray*; as with that earlier novel, here there are assumptions of relation between the discourses of Orientalism and debauchery filtered through the post/colonial imagination. Abdul returns again (*S-P L*, 306–7), leading Beckwith down a dark alleyway into the kitchen of the Corinthian, where Beckwith is undressed and placed on the chopping table in a brief scene of rough sex. With Beckwith's earlier references to the kitchen's aura of 'the discipline of institutional life' and its order being compared to that of an Edwardian country house (*S-P L*, 306) just prior to the moment of sex, we may perhaps not be going too far if we suggest that a curious encryption of the novel's concerns with the colonial past, ambivalent concerns over pleasure and punishment and a certain postcolonial 'overturning' all come together here. Is this scene with Abdul readable simply as the projection of the white man's desires onto the non-white, non-European other? Is there a symbolic, if not phantasmic reworking taking place? Does Abdul and his kitchen domain – readable as a locus of low otherness, marginal and yet necessary to the maintenance of the Corinthian club – somehow reconfigure and invert the historically prior colonial moments encoded by Nantwich's memoirs? Is Hollinghurst's text available to us as attempting to engage in a momentary postcolonial working out of desire and guilt? How are we to read it and what clues might we believe it gives us?

We cannot pretend to answer these questions in this short space. Certainly, there is a colonial and postcolonial frame of references which resonates in complex and ambivalent ways in relation to the question of gay identity and sexuality throughout the novel. A more thorough analysis should, for example, focus on the question of the different principal temporal trajectories, those tracing the lives of Nantwich and Beckwith, as these trajectories cross into one another through the references to E. M. Forster, whose own fictional and historical narratives intertwined the colonial, the homosexual and the homoerotic. There are Beckwith's brief mentions of Ronald Firbank's 1924 novel *Prancing Nigger* to be considered. Finally, one should pause to consider the scene where William Beckwith visits a council estate – he describes the experience tellingly as 'culture shock' (*S-P L*, 197) – with its tower blocks named with 'surreal bookishness' after towns from the novels of Thomas Hardy (*S-P L*, 198). (A brief digression: this, in itself, should point us towards the notion that Hollinghurst realizes, even if Beckwith does not, that in relation to the discourse of colonialism Englishness is not some truth from which other cultures are viewed, but a manifest production or projection, with a self-mythologizing history of its own. This is, perhaps, a surreptitious admission that the novel engages in a postcolonial project, at least in small part, involving techniques of distancing, denaturalization, demystification and estrangement.) First encountering National Front graffiti (*S-P L*, 200), he then runs into a group of skinheads, who beat him up because, as one of them puts it, '"You can tell he's fuckin' poof"' (*S-P L*, 202). Just prior to the beating, the skinheads decide that Beckwith must be a '"Fuckin' nigger-fucker"' (*S-P L*, 202). The extreme violence of the language and the actions which follow provide a startling insight into ever more thinly veiled protocols concerning social marginalization based on the assumption of a normative model to which certain images of race and same-sex desire do not accord. And perhaps what Beckwith fails to comprehend is that his own language, inflected as it is by a colonial inheritance, is different only by degree and not in kind from the zero-limit of the skinhead's pejorative violation.

QUESTIONS FOR FURTHER CONSIDERATION

1. Consider the roles of fetishism and otherness in postcolonial discourse.
2. To what extent does the installation of ambivalence within representational strategies and structures forestall the possibility of producing a definitive reading?
3. To what extent and in what ways might the 'implicit mimeticism' of certain aspects of postcolonial studies problematize its political goals or agendas?
4. Consider Caliban in the light of the postcolonial emphasis on the figure of the subaltern.
5. Do the representations of Caliban in *The Tempest* or Abdul in the *Swimming-Pool Library* conform in particular ways to Edward Said's definition of Orientalism?
6. Taking Homi Bhabha's concept of mimicry, consider the ways in which this notion might be employed as a reading strategy for considering and comparing the roles of gay men and men of colour in *The Swimming-Pool Library* within a dominant, normative culture.

ANNOTATED BIBLIOGRAPHY

Ashcroft, Bill, Gareth Griffiths and Helen Tiffin, eds. *The Post-Colonial Studies Reader*. London, 1995.
Commendable attempt to come to terms with the diversity and heterogeneity of postcolonial theory and criticism. This reader sacrifices some detail and depth for a comprehensive sweep; it is also perhaps more deliberately focused on the literary and literary teaching than other social and political issues. Yet its sampling of work from influential metropolitan theorists from the past and the present, and its willingness to include major non Euro-American writers and thinkers offers much by way of an introduction to both the student and teacher.
Bhabha, Homi K. *The Location of Culture*, London, 1994.
Collected essays which enable one to chart Bhabha's work on colonial subjectivity,

narratives of origin, ambivalence and authority, and his postcolonial interrogation of western modernity over a ten year period. In grappling with the problem of cultural and racial difference, Bhabha consistently attempts to think beyond the binary boundaries and homogenous categories of race, nation and class to consider the interstitial and the interlocutional. His terms, the 'third space', the space of cultural translation where subject-positions are continually shifting and mutating, is just such an outcome.

Childs, Peter, ed. *Post-Colonial Theory and English Literature: A Reader*. Edinburgh, 1999.

A singularly impressive, highly focused reader. Addressing specifically literary representations and mediations of colonialism and postcolonialism through a diverse range of critical readings which speak from all perspectives and political situations of postcolonial critical discourse, the essays collected by the editor offer in eight sections consideration of literature from the early modern period to the late twentieth century, with analyses of the following texts, their contexts, histories and appropriations: *The Tempest, Robinson Crusoe, Jane Eyre, Heart of Darkness, Ulysses, A Passage to India, The Satanic Verses*.

Said, Edward. *Orientalism*. London, 1978.

Ambitious and seminal work on race, empire and representation which has influenced postcolonial literary theory and criticism significantly over the last twenty years. Said argues that the invention of the Orient as the object of study and representation goes hand in hand with imperial domination and control. He looks at major European traditions on Africa, Asia and the Middle East but the focus of the discussion is on the Middle East and Islamic cultures. Said's discussion of individuals does not always fit easily into the introductory monolithic model of Orientalism and there are tensions and contradictions in its attempt to marry a humanist vision with an anti-humanist critique, but the basic argument holds true.

Shohat, Ella, and Robert Stam. *Unthinking Ethnocentrism: Multiculturalism and the Media*. London, 1994.

Ambitious interrogation of Eurocentrism as formed and challenged by popular media and film that is concerned to explore the connections between history, literature, film and theory. Shohat and Stam's essays range from classical Hollywood films to some of the influential Third (World) cinema of resistance and their discussions encompass film as documentary and as entertainment. In arguing for a 'polycentric' multiculturalism and an ethnography of spectatorship, Shohat and Stam attempt to come to terms with contemporary transnational global capitalism in terms of its impact and its resistance.

Spivak, Gayatri Chakravorty. *Outside in the Teaching Machine*. London, 1993.

Challenging collection from Spivak which follows on from her earlier influential volume of essays, *In Other Worlds*. In her forward, Spivak describes the shift in her work from 'strategic essentialism' and anti-essentialism, to a preoccupation with agency and rethinking marginality in relation to the 'teaching machine'. She advocates breaking down the barriers of discipline, languages and canons in the academic agenda in order to deal seriously with the complexity of the transnational study of culture. Essays also interrogate the role of intellectuals (academic and artistic) and the relation between migrancy and postcoloniality; with the lessons of marxism, deconstruction and feminism in mind, she repeatedly warns us of the historical problems inherent in (re)presenting the oppressed which does (yet again) not render them silent.

SUPPLEMENTARY BIBLIOGRAPHY

Achebe, Chinua. *Morning Yet on Creation Day*. London, 1975.
————. *Hopes and Impediments: Selected Essays 1965–1987*. London, 1988.
Adam, Ian, and Helen Tiffin, eds. *Past the Post: Theorizing Post-Colonialism and Post-Modernism*. Hemel Hempstead, 1991.
Ahmad, A. *Theory: Classes, Nations and Literatures*. London, 1992.

Anderson, Benedict. *Imagined Communities*. London, 1983.

Appiah, Kwame Anthony. *My Father's House: Africa in the Philosophy of Culture*. London, 1992.

————. 'The Postcolonial and the Postmodern', in *The Post-Colonial Studies Reader*, eds Bill Ashcroft et al. London, 1995.

Ashcroft, Bill, Gareth Griffiths and Helen Tiffin, eds. *The Empire Writes Back: Theory and Practice in Post-Colonial Literatures*. London, 1989.

————, Gareth Griffiths and Helen Tiffin, eds. *The Post-Colonial Studies Reader*. London, 1995.

Aziz, Firdous. *The Colonial Rise of the Novel*. London, 1993.

Barker, Francis, Peter Hulme, Margaret Iversen and Diana Loxley, eds. *Europe and its Others*, 2 vols. Colchester, 1985.

————, Peter Hulme and Margaret Iversen, eds. *Colonial Discourse/Postcolonial Theory*. Manchester, 1994.

Bhabha, Homi K., ed. *Nation and Narration*. London, 1990.

————. *The Location of Culture*, London, 1994.

Brantlinger, Patrick. *Rule of Darkness: British Literature and Imperialism 1830–1914*. Ithaca, NY, 1988.

Brathwaite, Edward. *The Development of Creole Society in Jamaica 1770–1820*. Oxford, 1971.

————. *History of the Voice: The Development of National Languages in Anglophone Caribbean Poetry*. London, 1984.

Brooks, Peter. *Psychoanalysis and Storytelling*. Oxford, 1994.

Césaire, Aimé. *Discourse on Colonialism*. New York, 1972.

Chambers, Iain, and Lidia Curti, eds. *The Post-Colonial Question: Common Skies, Divided Horizons*. London, 1996.

Chow, Rey, *Writing Diaspora: Tactics of Intervention in Contemporary Cultural Studies*, Bloomington, IN, 1993.

————. *Primitive Passions: Visuality, Sexuality, Ethnography and Contemporary Chinese Cinema*. New York, 1995.

Chrisman, Laura, and Patrick Williams, eds. *Colonial Discourse and Post-Colonial Theory*. Hemel Hempstead, 1993.

Clifford, James. *The Predicament of Culture*. Cambridge, MA, 1988.

Coetzee, J. M. *White Writing: On the Cultures of Letters in South Africa*. New Haven, CT, 1988.

Dirlik, Arif. *The Postcolonial Aura: Third World Criticism in the Age of Global Capitalism*. Boulder, CO, 1997.

Fabian, Johannes. *Time and the Other: How Anthropology Makes its Object*. New York, 1983.

Fanon, Frantz. *The Wretched of the Earth*. Harmondsworth, 1983.

————. *Black Skins, White Masks*. London, 1986.

Frankenberg, Ruth and Mani, Lata. 'Crosscurrents, Crosstalk: Race, "Postcoloniality" and the Politics of Location', *Cultural Studies*, 7: 2, 1993.

Fuss, Diana, 'Interior Colonies: Frantz Fanon and the Politics of Identification', *Diacritics*, 23: 2/3, 1994.

Gates, Henry L., ed. *'Race', Writing and Difference*, special issue of *Critical Inquiry*, 12: 1, 1985.

Gilbert, Helen, and Joanne Tompkins. *Post-Colonial Drama: Theory, Practice, Politics*. London, 1996.

Gilroy, Paul. *There Ain't No Black the Union Jack*. London, 1987.

————. *The Black Atlantic: Modernity and Double Consciousness*. London, 1993.

Guha, Ranajit, and Gayatri Chakravorty Spivak, eds. *Selected Subaltern Studies*. New Delhi, 1988.

Hall, Stuart. 'Cultural Identity and Diaspora', in *Identities*, ed. Jonathan Rutherford. London, 1990.

————. 'When was the Post-Colonial?', in *The Post-Colonial Question*, eds Iain Chambers and Lidia Curti. London, 1996.

Harris, Wilson. *Tradition, the Writer and Society*. London, 1973.

————, *The Womb of Space*. Westport, CT, 1983.

Hulme, Peter. *Colonial Encounters: Europe and the Native Caribbean 1492–1797*. London, 1992.

JanMohamed, Abul. *Manichean Aesthetics: The Politics of Literature in Colonial Africa*. Amherst, MA, 1983.

Joshi, Svati, *Rethinking English: Essays in Literature, Language, History*. New Delhi, 1991.

Lamming, George. *The Pleasures of Exile*. London, 1960.

Landry, Donna, and Gerald MacLean, eds. *The Spivak Reader*. London, 1996.

Loomba, Ania, *Gender, Race, Renaissance Drama*. Manchester, 1989.

————. 'Dead Women Tell No Tales: Issues of Female Subjectivity, Subaltern Agency and Tradition in Colonial and Post-Colonial Writings on Widow Immolation in India', *History Workshop Journal*, 36, 1993.

Low, Gail Ching-Liang. *White Skins/Black Masks: Representation and Colonialism*. London, 1996.

Lazarus, Neil, *Resistance in Postcolonial African Fiction*. New Haven, CT, 1990.

————. 'National Consciousness and Intellectualism', in *Colonial Discourse/Post-colonial Theory*, eds F. Barker, P. Hulme and M. Iverson. Manchester, 1994.

Lawson, Alan, Leigh Dale, Helen Tiffin and Shane Rowlands, eds. *Post-Colonial Literatures in English: General, Theoretical and Comparative 1970–1993*. New York, 1997.

Kaplan, Caren. *Questions of Travel: Postmodern Discourses of Displacement*. Durham, NC, 1996.

McClintock, Anne. 'The Angel of Progress: Pitfalls of the term "Post-Colonialism"', *Social Text*, 31/32, 1992.

————. *Imperial Leather*. London, 1995.

Mani, Lata. 'Contentious Traditions: The Debate on Sati in Colonial India', in *Recasting Women*, eds K.K. Sangari and S. Vaid. New Delhi, 1989.

————. 'Cultural Theory, Colonial texts: Reading Eyewitness Accounts of Widow Burning', in *Cultural Studies*, eds L. Grossberg, C. Nelson and P. Treichler. New York, 1992.

Mohanty, Chandra Talpade. 'Under Western Eyes', *Feminist Review*, 3, 1988.

Moore-Gilbert, Bart. *Postcolonial Theory: Contexts, Practices, Politics*. London, 1997.

Parry, Benita. 'Problems in Current Theories of Colonial Discourse', *Oxford Literary Review*, 9: 1–2, 1987.

Nandy, Ashish. *The Intimate Enemy: Loss and Recovery of Self under Colonialism*. New Delhi, 1983.

Ngugi Wa Thiongo. *Homecoming*. London, 1972.

————. *Decolonising the Mind: The Politics of Language in African Literature*. London, 1986.

Parry, Benita. 'Problems in Current Theories of Colonial Discourse', *The Post-Colonial Studies Reader*, eds Bill Ashcroft et al. London, 1995.

Pratt, Mary. *Imperial Eyes*. New York, 1992.

Quayson, Ato. *Postcolonialism: Theory, Practice or Process?* Cambridge, 2000.

Said, Edward. *Culture and Imperialism*. New York, 1994.

Sharpe, Jenny. *Allegories of Empire: The Figure of Woman in the Colonial Text*. London, 1993.

Shohat, Ella. 'Notes on the Post-Colonial', *Social Text*, 31/32, 1992.

Slemon, Stephen. 'Post-Colonial Allegory and the Transformation of History', *Journal of Commonwealth Literature*, 23: 1, 1988.

————. 'Reading for Resistance in Post-Colonial Literatures', in *A Shaping of Connections: Commonwealth Literature Studies – Then and Now: Essays in Honour of A. N. Jeffares*, eds Hena Maes-Jelinek, Kirsten Holst Petersen and Anna Rutherford. Mundelstrup, 1989.

————. 'The Scramble for Post-Colonialism', *De-Scribing Empire: Post-Colonialism and Textuality*, eds Chris Tiffin and Alan Lawson. London, 1994.

Spivak, Gayatri Chakravorty. *In Other Worlds*. London, 1988.

————. *The Post-Colonial Critic: Interviews, Strategies, Dialogues*. London, 1990.

Suleri, Sara. *The Rhetoric of English India*. Chicago, 1992.

————. 'The Rhetoric of English India', *The Post-Colonial Studies Reader*, eds Bill Ashcroft et al. London, 1995.

Taussig, Michael. *Shamanism, Colonialism and the Wild Man*. Chicago, 1987.

Tiffin, Helen. 'Lie Back and Think of England: Post-Colonial Literatures and the Academy', in *A Shaping of Connections: Commonwealth Literature Studies – Then and Now: Essays in Honour of A. N. Jeffares*, eds Hena Maes-Jelinek, Kirsten Holst Petersen and Anna Rutherford. Mundelstrup, 1989.

Viswanthan, Gauri. *Masks of Conquest*. London, 1990.

Young, Robert. *White Mythologies: Writing, History and the West*. London, 1990.

————. *Colonial Desire: Hybridity in Theory, Culture and Race*. London, 1995.

OTHER WORKS CITED

Barker, Francis, and Peter Hulme. 'Nymphs and Reapers Heavily Vanish: The Discursive Con-texts of *The Tempest*', in *Alternative Shakespears*, ed. John Drakakis. London, 1985.

Brown, Paul. ' "This thing of darkness I acknowledge mine": *The Tempest* and the Discourse of Colonialism', in *Political Shakespeares*, eds Jonathan Dollimore and Alan Sinfield. Ithaca, NY, 1985.

Hodgdon, Barbara. *The Shakespeare Trade: Performances and Appropriations*. Philadelphia, 1998.

Loomba, Ania, and Martin Orkin, eds. *Post-Colonial Shakespeares*. London, 1998.

CHAPTER

12

WORKS ON THE WILD(E) SIDE – PERFORMING, TRANSGRESSING, QUEERING: GAY STUDIES/ QUEER THEORIES

Jane Goldman and Julian Wolfreys

The manifold formulations of 'gay studies' and 'queer theory' owe much to the work of Eve Kosofsky Sedgwick, Jonathan Dollimore and Judith Butler. It is difficult to find a writer in this field who does not invoke and engage with one, if not all three, of these theorists. The field, however, would not be as it is without the achievements of two others: Oscar Wilde and Michel Foucault. Wilde's writings, his life and his iconic 'queer' status, and Foucault's founding work on sexuality, are touchstones in the work of Sedgwick, Dollimore and Butler and many other gay and queer theorists. In his *History of Sexuality*, Foucault demonstrates, among other things, the nineteenth-century cultural emergence and construction of 'the homosexual' as 'a species' (1979, 43), while also creating a discourse of affirmative resistance: through an epistemo-political reformulation of the very terms of identification, the notion of homosexuality is resisted in Foucault, if not actually rejected, as a limiting, coercive form of subjection 'bound to an identity defined in the nineteenth century' (Simons, 1995, 97). The resistance involves affirmation for Foucault, in that identifying oneself as 'gay' involves a transgression of the limits of scientific or sociological determinations of identity according to some aspect of human sexual nature, while serving, in Foucault's words, 'to try to define and develop a way of life' (Foucault, 1989, 206). Oscar Wilde, in the twentieth century, has come to personify for many a transhistorical and transcultural model of homosexual or queer identity, at once both enabling and limiting. When Alan Sinfield remarks:

'Our interpretation [of sexual identity] is retroactive; in fact, Wilde and his writings look queer because our stereotypical notion of male homosexuality derives from Wilde, and our ideas about him' (Sinfield, 1994, vii), there is acknowledged an ambivalence, at least implicitly, concerning the complex of historically and culturally driven narratives around 'queerness' that mark the twentieth century after Wilde. To be *after* Wilde chronologically, and to consider oneself gay or queer is to be caught in acts of representation, albeit unconsciously, whereby one still finds oneself pursuing, chasing *after* a certain projection of Wildean images as the articulation of an unfulfillable desire. Gay studies and queer theory address the political ramifications, the advantages and dangers, of culturally 'fixed' categories of sexual identities and the ways in which they may, in the terms given such potent currency by Sedgwick, Dollimore and Butler, be performed, transgressed and queered.

Before considering the work of Sedgwick, Dollimore and Butler it is worth considering some of the broader claims and definitions, positionings and criticisms, of gay studies and queer theory. Both of these interrelated theoretical spheres are enmeshed in the material politics of their time – from Stonewall to ACT UP and Queer Nation – and caught up in the politics of identity where declaration (or confession) of one's own positionality is almost *de rigeur* for any author contributing to its debates. The slash in 'gay studies/queer theory' communicates both the progressive consolidation of these categories – queer theory, a dominant force in the 1990s, may be understood as a legacy of earlier (1970s on) gay studies (itself in complex alliance with feminist and gender studies) – and the tensions between them – there is a sense in which queer theory undoes (queers) the orthodoxies, however recently established, of gay studies. 'Gay studies' may be taken to both embrace and elide 'lesbian' studies, just as 'queer theory', in turn, has simultaneously subsumed, expanded and undone gay studies, not least by marking 'a disturbing *mobility* or non-fixity between diverse sexualities' (Luckhurst, 1995, 333). If even the *naming* of this field, or fields, of study seems excruciatingly and preciously provisional (suggested also in the tendency to resort to scare quotes for whatever our chosen terms), it is because the fraught politics of naming and categorization are so much its very business.

'Queer theory' has been claimed and refuted as the field in which we might most productively explore what is at stake for politics and people identified in terms of a range of sexualities, troubling not only the oppositional categories of heterosexuality/homosexuality, but also those of the apparently stable 'same-sex' labels of gay and lesbian too. 'Queer theory' has been claimed as giving voice to those elided or marginalized by 'gay' and 'lesbian' studies – bisexuals, transsexuals, sado-masochists, for example – and yet also refuted for silencing such voices. Queer theory is alive to its own paradoxes, playing on the tensions between its emergence as a naming, and therefore fixing category, and the possibilities opened up by its own catachrestic – *misnaming* – semantics. 'The minute you say "queer"', it has been remarked, 'you are necessarily calling into question exactly what you mean when you say it . . . Queer includes within it a necessarily expansive impulse that allows us to think about potential differences within that rubric' (Harper, White and Cerullo, 1993, 30). With such positions and contradictions in mind, queer theory intervenes in – *queers* – already familiar debates: particularly the projects preoccupying feminist and gender studies to separate gender and sexuality, and involving the delicate and vexing issues of the politics of subjectivity (essentialist/constructionist), of identity/ difference, of modernism/postmodernism, of sexuality and textuality, of margins and centre, of race, class, representation and so on.

If we can say anything provisionally about that which 'queer' mobilizes, it concerns the particular reading effects both of and at the limits of identity politics, and, especially, what remains both at stake in ascribing limits to an identity, while also opening to our experience the aporetic and the other *within* any construction of identity. While it was and continues to remain historically significant as initial acts of affirmation and resistance to normative social and cultural constructions of sexual identity that the 'lesbian and gay liberation movements . . . so culturally concertized and elaborate[d] . . . the tenets and values they represented [so that they] came to be seen as hegemonic', as Annamarie Jagose puts it (1996, 58), the limits involved in such acts of identification have themselves been resisted subsequently. The 'dissatisfaction with the categories of identification themselves and a questioning of their efficacy in political intervention' (Jagose, 1996, 71) brought with it a 'suspicion strengthened by influential postmodern understandings of identity, gender, sexuality, power and resistance. These provide the context in which queer becomes an intelligible – almost, one might say, an inevitable – phenomenon' (Jagose, 1996, 71).

However, to back up a little. It was as a possible way out of a theoretical *impasse* located in many of these issues that one of the earliest formulations of queer theory made its mark. Teresa de Lauretis, in 'Queer Theory: Lesbian and Gay Sexualities', a special issue of the journal *differences* (1991), considers how queer theory might negotiate and transcend the racism and sexism evident in gay and lesbian communities of the previous two decades. She proposes that:

> rather than marking the limits of the social space by designating a place at the edge of culture, gay sexuality in its specific female and male cultural (or subcultural) forms acts as an agency of social process whose mode of functioning is both interactive and yet resistant, both participatory and yet distinct, claiming at once equality and difference, demanding political representation while insisting on its material and historical specificity. (1991, iii)

De Lauretis's use of a colon, in her title, to separate 'queer' from 'lesbian and gay', marks for Sally O'Driscoll 'an ambiguity in the multiple meanings of *queer* as it is currently used', and played out in the tension between its semantic poles of identity and anti-identity:

The existence of queer theory would be unimaginable without the preceding decades of work in lesbian and gay studies and politics; yet the goal
of queer theory as defined by many critics is precisely to interrogate the
identity positions from which that work is produced. Using the same word
to refer to both fields has produced confusion and even some bitterness on
the part of those who fear that queer theory's critique of the subject
undermines their visibility and political ground. (1996, 30)

It seems from O'Driscoll's summation that we might easily read 'queer theory'
as 'postmodernism', for they seem to share the same good intentions and
pitfalls. Queer, 'irreducible, undefinable, enigmatic, winking at us as it flouts
convention', has become, according to Suzanne Walters, 'the perfect postmodern trope, a term for the times, the epitome of knowing ambiguity. Good-bye
simulacra, adios panopticon, arrivederci lack, adieu jouissance: hello *queer*!'
(1996, 837).

Whether or not queer theory is a resolution to, or merely a restatement of,
familiar difficulties remains to be seen. De Lauretis's definition, according to
Brett Beemyn and Mickey Eliason, 'is built on the very dualisms that much of
queer theory purports to disrupt or dismantle (female and male, equality and
difference), and De Lauretis never provides evidence to prove that queer theory
actually does transcend lines of difference. For instance, how does queer theory
address issues of racial and gender oppression?' (1996, 164). Beemyn and
Eliason are themselves somewhat nebulous in introducing their (1996) collection, *Queer Studies: A Lesbian, Gay, Bisexual, and Transgender Anthology*,
with the promise that queer theory 'allows us to view the world from perspectives other than those which are generally validated by the dominant society; we
can put a queer slant, for example, on literature, movies, television news reports,
and current events. Such queer(ed) positions can challenge the dominance of
heterosexist discourses.' Their collection sets out to fulfill queer theory's
'*potential* to be inclusive of race, gender, sexuality, and other areas of identity
by calling attention to the distinctions between identities, communities, and
cultures' (1996, 165). They point up the conscious exclusion of the category of,
and essays on, bisexuality from an earlier conference anthology (Dorenkamp
and Henke's *Negotiating Lesbian and Gay Subjects*, 1995, 1), and suggest that
queer theory can redress such omissions and others: 'by including the voices of
people whose lived experiences involve non-normative race, gender, and sexual
identities/practices, queer theory can stretch the limits of current thought and
possibly revolutionize it' (1995, 166). Yet this is possibly to stretch the limits of
queer theory to the point of rendering it an ineffectual catch-all, cure-all,
universalizing term. Michael Warner in his introduction to *Fear of a Queer
Planet*, as Beemyn and Eliason recognize, also comes close to this point in
defining queer theory, by virtue of its very performativity, as 'elaborating, in
ways that cannot be predicted in advance, this question: What do queers want?'
(1993, vii). Beemyn and Eliason worry that 'from this definition . . . queer

theory is almost anything and everything that the author wants it to be' (1996, 163).

Using queer theory to examine heterosexuality, Lynne Segal, in *Straight Sex: The Politics of Pleasure* (1994), seems to want it to be merely a denotation of dissident catachresis (Luckhurst, 1995, 335). 'Straight feminists', she concludes, 'like gay men and lesbians, have everything to gain from asserting our non-coercive desire to fuck if, when, how and as we choose' (1994, 318). The inclusivity of such broad definitions of queer and queer theory has not pleased other feminists (Sheila Jeffreys, Biddy Martin and Suzanne Walters, for example) since it so often, paradoxically, elides lesbian experiences, work and theories in favour of those of male gays. Terry Castle regards both 'queer' and '*gay*' as 'pseudo-umbrella terms' to be avoided when 'speaking of lesbianism'. She understands the popularity of the term queer to be in part 'precisely because it makes it easy to enfold female homosexuality back "into" male homosexuality and disembody the lesbian once again' (1993, 12). Adrienne Rich's (much earlier) definition of 'the lesbian continuum' (a concept indebted to the work of Carroll Smith-Rosenberg) has attracted similar criticism for building too broad a church. Just as 'the lesbian continuum' risks subsuming and homogenising lesbian and 'straight' women's experience, so the queer continuum, we might say, risks subsuming and homogenizing, even as it boasts of celebrating and foregrounding, a broad range of same-sex and dissident sexual identities. Walters is concerned about 'the implications involved in claiming "queerness" when one is not gay or lesbian' (1996, 841), and while half-jokingly observing that in academy 'you don't have to be gay to do [queer theory], in fact it is much better if you're not', points up a sinister

> kind of reigning dogma in progressive and postmodern academic circles these days that constructs an 'old-time' feminism in order to point out how the sex debates, postmodernism, and queer theory have nicely superseded this outmoded, reformist, prudish, banal feminism of old. Is it possible that queer theory's Other is feminism, or even lesbianism, or lesbian-feminism? (Rich, 1987, 842)

Much has been made of authorial positionality in these contexts. There is, for example, 'a rumorology [a Sedgwick coinage] that surrounds' Butler and Sedgwick, as Roger Luckurst observes: 'Butler, the lesbian, does her theory "straight", with demanding and rigorous close readings; Sedgwick, the "straight" who cross-identifies with gay men, does her theory in a highly camp and digressive style' (1995, 334). Walters satirizes the extremes to which identification and confession of positionality have been taken in academic discourse where for some (she exempts Sedgwick and Butler) 'we are what we do in bed' (1996, 863), and points up the potential for 'relentless narcissism and individualism' in 'narratives of queer theory'. She continues:

'I pack a dildo, therefore I am.' It is sort of like, let us make a theory of our own sexual practices (e.g., 'I'm a cross-dressing femme who likes to use a dildo while watching gay male porn videos with my fuck buddy who sometimes likes to do it with gay men. Hmm, what kind of a theory can I make of that?') (Walters, 1996, 857)

Yet queer (theory) has its uses even for some of its sceptics (including Walters); but perhaps, like postmodernism, one of its few defining qualities *is* scepticism. Alan Sinfield confesses to using the term in his book title, *Cultural Politics – Queer Reading* (1994), 'only after considerable hesitation'. Although 'male gayness' dominates his discussion – 'because it is part of [his] argument that intellectuals should work in their own subcultural constituencies' – he invokes lesbian texts and theories, writing 'inclusively of lesbians and gay men wherever that has seemed plausible – but this signals a proposed political alignment, not an assertion that "we" are "the same" (indeed, not all gay men are the same).' He succumbs, then, to the collective term 'queer' in his title, aware both that 'it may be too limiting – yielding up too easily the aspiration to hold a politics of class, race, and ethnicity alongside a politics of gender and sexuality', and that 'it may be over-ambitious' since 'many people outside activist circles still find "queer" too distressing for reappropriation; and there is still the danger that inclusion will lead to effacement' (Sinfield, 1994, x). On the other hand, Sinfield's usage of 'queer' and 'gay' in another book of the same year, *The Wilde Century: Effeminacy, Oscar Wilde and the Queer Moment* (1994), depends on a historicized account of the terms: 'for the sake of clarity' he writes 'queer' for that historical phase when, after Wilde, 'that stereotype . . . prevailed in the twentieth century . . . not contradicting, thereby, its recent revival among activists'; and he writes "gay" for post-Stonewall kinds of consciousness' (Sinfield, 1994, 3). 'Gay', he points out, 'was established as a way of moving on from' the earlier 'Wildean model' of 'queer', before being superseded by the newly reappropriated 'queer' in the 1990s. The selection of such terms is strategic:

> The aggression and ambition in the readoption of 'queer' are directly proportionate to the degree to which its use proposes to overturn the historic, hostile meaning. It plays for much higher stakes than if we tried to reinstate, say, 'the third sex'. . . . 'Queer' says, defiantly, that we don't care what they call us. Also it keeps faith with generations of people, before us, who lived their oppression and resistance in its initial terms. (Sinfield, 1994, 204)

This book has on its cover a picture of Oscar Wilde collagistically sporting a 'Queer as Fuck' T-shirt, an emblem of 1990s queer politics. The political ramifications of this anachronism inform Sinfield's 'constructionist' argument 'about the emergence of a queer identity around Wilde' which 'holds that sexualities . . . are not essential, but constructed within an array of prevailing social possibilities.' He takes up Diana Fuss's observations, in *Essentially Speaking: Feminism, Nature and Difference*, that 'homosexuality is not a transhistorical, transcultural, eternal category but a socially contingent and variant construction' (1989, 107–8), to chart its construction in the nineteenth century. 'It is not that our idea of "the homosexual" was hiding beneath other phases,' Sinfield concludes, 'or lurking unspecified in the silence, like a statue under a sheet, fully formed but waiting to be unveiled; it was in the process of becoming constituted. The concept was *emerging* around and through instances like . . . Wilde' (Sinfield, 1994, 8). It is not necessarily helpful, therefore, to read Wilde or Shakespeare, for example, or figures in their work, transhistorically as 'homosexual' or 'gay' or 'lesbian' or 'queer', but it is certainly productive to consider how these writers, and readings of their lives and works, contribute to the cultural constitution of such terms and identities.

Sedgwick, in 'Tales of the Avunculate: Queer Tutelage in *The Importance of Being Earnest*', which follows 'Queer and Now' (*LT*, 537–52) in her collection of essays, *Tendencies*, moves beyond the raft of Derridean-influenced readings of Wilde's play which celebrate Wilde 'for being Derrida or Lacan *avant la lettre*' (1993, 55) and which are (understandably) preoccupied with 'the Name of the Father' in its denouement, to consider how that term has been 'superseded, in a process accelerating over the last century and a half, very specifically by what might be termed the Name of the Family' (1993, 72). Typical of her general *modus operandi*, which Dollimore in *Sexual Dissidence* calls 'a unique integration of insightful literary analysis and persuasive cultural critique' (1993, 29), Sedgwick's reading of *The Importance of Being Earnest* opens out into explorations of contemporary lesbian and gay concerns with legal, social and political definitions of 'the family'. Also typical of her work, particularly in *Tendencies*, are 'the performance strategies of autobiographical "personal criticism"' (Luckhurst, 1995, 334). Sedgwick's activism in queer politics and AIDS campaigns, her bereavements to AIDS, her chemotherapy for breast cancer, her vilifying treatment by the right-wing press – for the notorious essay, 'Jane Austen and the Masturbating Girl' (also in *Tendencies*), for example – all inform her writing. Her first book, *Between Men: English Literature and Male Homosocial Desire*, is credited with breaking new ground for gay studies in introducing readings of nineteenth-century literature with an analysis of homosexuality, homosociality and homophobia in terms of 'erotic triangles'. She examines here the 'special relationship between male homosocial (*including* homosexual) desire and structures for maintaining and transmitting patriarchal power' (1985, 25). Sedgwick's 'arrangement of social and sexual relations', as Joseph Bristow observes in his helpful book, *Sexuality*, 'has one profound point to make: it remains difficult indeed to keep this particular cultural order intact. For the privilege granted to male-male relations stands in dangerous proximity to the very homosexuality that patriarchal fellowship is obliged to condemn' (1997, 205).

Sedgwick's second book, *Epistemology of the Closet* (1990), remains a landmark for queer theory. Here she argues 'that an understanding of virtually any aspect of modern Western culture must be, not merely incomplete, but damaged in its central substance to the degree that it does not incorporate a critical analysis of modern homo/heterosexual definition; and . . . assume[s] that the appropriate place for that critical analysis to begin is from the relatively decentred perspective of modern gay and antihomophobic theory' (1990, 1). Following Foucault's 'axiomatic' findings on the privileged relation of sexuality 'to our most prized constructs of individual identity, truth, and knowledge' (1990, 3), Sedgwick suggests that 'the language of sexuality not only intersects with but transforms the other languages and relations by which we know' (1990, 3), and draws attention to

> performative aspects of texts, and to what are often blandly called their 'reader relations,' as sites of definitional creation, violence, and rupture in relation to particular readers, particular institutional circumstances . . . The relations of the closet – the relations of the known and the unknown, the explicit and the inexplicit around homo/heterosexual definition – have the potential for being peculiarly revealing, in fact, about speech acts more generally. (1990, 3)

Epistemology of the Closet, as she explains in her foreword to *Tendencies*, explores minoritizing/universalizing views of homo/heterosexuality and hypothesises 'that modern homo/heterosexual definition has become so exacerbated a cultural site because of an enduring incoherence about whether it is to be thought of as an issue only for a minority of (distinctly lesbian or gay) individuals, or instead as an issue that cuts across every locus of agency and subjectivity in the culture' (1993, xii). *Epistemology of the Closet* has met with both acclaim and consternation. Sedgwick's 'redefinition of the closet as an epistemological predicament rather than a logistical strategy', as Eric Savoy remarks, 'has galvanized subsequent queer theory, and disturbed activists, through the deployment of two axiomatic constructions: her emphasis on closetedness as performative, and her suggestion that it can never be finally disrupted' (1994, 138). The academic critic's and reader's delight in Sedgwick's virtuoso queer deconstructive readings of literary texts is here set against the often very different aspirations and experiences of those engaged in queer politics on the street.

Tendencies makes for Sedgwick 'a counterclaim' against the 'obsolescence' of queer: 'a claim that something about *queer* is inextinguishable.' Demonstrating once more a certain indebtedness to the work of so-called deconstruction, she elaborates on the term *queer* by drawing on the term's etymology:

> Queer is a continuing moment, movement, motive – recurrent, eddying, *troublant*. The word 'queer' itself means *across* – it comes from the Indo-European root-*twerkw*, which also yields the German *quer* (transverse),

Latin *torquere* (to twist), English *athwart* . . . The *queer* of these essays is transitive – multiply transitive. The immemorial current that *queer* represents is antiseparatist as it is antiassimilationist. Keenly, it is relational, and strange. (1993, xii)

Certainly 'Queer and Now' performs queerly in its traversing of several different spheres of personal and political experience, individual and collective, from the troubling statistics on adolescent gay and lesbian suicides, and thoughts on sexual identity and familial formations, to the status of academic and intellectual work of queer theorists. Sedgwick takes stock of her achievements and sets out prospectuses for new work – on transgendered desire and identifications, on 'Queer Performativity', and on the 'politics explicitly oriented around grave illness'. Perhaps the most significant passage in the essay is where Sedgwick, overlapping with Butler's work in some ways, proposes that part of the 'experimental force [of "queer"] as a speech act is the way in which it dramatizes locutionary position itself. Anyone's use of "queer" about themselves means differently from their use of it about someone else (*LT*, 543). In this account, to declare oneself 'queer' is almost like bearing witness in a charismatic faith:

A hypothesis worth making explicit: that there are important senses in which 'queer' can signify only *when attached to the first person*. One possible corollary: that what it takes – all it takes – to make the description 'queer' a true one is the impulse *to* use it in the first person. (543)

As Luckhurst explains:

Queer is a performative signifier, in that it does not identify and represent a group 'prior' to its naming, but *enacts* a sodality through its very enunciation, in that sense the dissonance of the groups it nominates is productive in the unforseeability of the political 'bodies' it produces. (1995, 333–4)

Sedgwick's point is that its force derives from its performance in the first person (whether singular or plural she does not specify here, which performative evasion is, of course, readable as being to the point, concerning the affirmative resistance that 'queer' names and enacts, inasmuch as there is registered, silently, an openness, if you will, beyond the identification of either singular or plural, but instead, the simultaneous and undecidable possibilities of either and both). O'Driscoll argues that Sedgwick's hypothesis

elides a real difference between the chosen and the imposed. In practical terms, *queer* has the *same* sense when used in the first and second person, when it refers to lesbians and gay men; the difference between choosing to call oneself queer and being attacked on the street by people who call one queer is evident. This indicates the difference between a category that constitutes identity and one that does not. (1996, 34)

'Queer', she continues, 'as used by theorists is not an identity category' like 'woman', 'black', 'white', 'male', in that it is not 'contingent on cultural recognition (1996, 34). Sedgwick's project, however, recognizes the strategic, and contestive, political force of constructing and performing a new category of identity that itself transgresses and overturns identity categorisation.

In his outline to *Sexual Dissidence: Augustine to Wilde, Freud to Foucault*, in which his essay, 'Post/modern: On the Gay Sensibility, or the Pervert's Revenge on Authenticity – Wilde, Genet, Orton and Others', appears, Dollimore, citing *Between Men* and the pilot essay, 'Epistemology of the Closet' (1988), pays tribute to Sedgwick whose 'ongoing project' he 'share[s] and strongly endorse[s]' (1991, 29). He coins the term 'sexual dissidence' to describe

> one kind of resistance, operating in terms of gender, [that] repeatedly unsettles the very opposition between the dominant and the subordinate . . . The literature, histories, and subcultures of sexual dissidence, though largely absent from current debates (literary, psychoanalytic, and cultural), prove remarkably illuminating for them. (1991, 21)

Much of the material considered above, of course, is testimony to the many critical correctives to such an absence emerging in the period since this observation was made.

In what might be termed a Derridean move, whereby binary figures of 'subversion/containment' and 'dominant/marginal' or 'centre/margin' are inverted so as to see the epistemological and semantic reliance of one term on the other, Dollimore recognizes

> that dissidence may not only be repressed by the dominant (coercively and ideologically), but in a sense actually produced by it, hence consolidating the powers which it ostensibly challenges. This gives rise to the subversion/ containment debate, one of the most important areas of dispute in contemporary cultural theory. (1991, 26–7)

Subsequently, his discussion of homosexuality explores

> why in our own time the negation of homosexuality has been in direct proportion to its symbolic centrality; its cultural marginality in direct proportion to its cultural significance; why, also, homosexuality is so strangely integral to the selfsame heterosexual cultures which obsessively denounce it, and why history – history rather than human nature – has produced this paradoxical position. (1991, 28)

Anticipating simultaneously the performative self-consciousness of queer theorists to come and also the transgressive fluidity and destabilization of fixed identity in the mobilization of terms, Dollimore explains his use of 'homosexual' as 'always provisional and context dependent'. Instead of scare quotes he 'resort[s] again to the occasional use of a typographically pretentious "/" as a reminder that the construction of homo/sexuality emerges from a larger discriminatory formation of hetero/sexuality which it continues to be influenced by, but cannot be reduced to' (1991, 32). More significantly, however, than the provocative reflexiveness (announcing the inscribed pretension, so-called, is but one more gesture designed to draw our attention to effects which otherwise remain silent) is Dollimore's quasi-Derridean act of implicit decentring (which gesture also informs his work on matters of power and ideology in early modern tragedy; see Dollimore 1984) through the reading of the paradox of the crucial centrality, the significance, of the culturally enforced marginality of homosexuality in western discourse and culture. The power of the margin or noncentre thus becomes affirmed in any conceptual framework.

The figure of Wilde is dominant in Dollimore's work. The first part of *Sexual Dissidence* considers an 'encounter' between Wilde and André Gide in Algiers in 1895 (and the book returns to a similar scenario at its close). Dollimore's reading of this event and of various writings by both authors, leads him to contrast Gide's essentialism with Wilde's anti-essentialism, 'a contrast which epitomizes one of the most important differences within the modern history of transgression' (1991, 11). It follows that Gide's (essentialist) transgressive aesthetic is 'obviously indebted to, yet also formed in reaction against, Wilde's own' (1991, 17). Citations from Wilde and Gide also inform 'Post/modern: On the Gay Sensibility, or the Pervert's Revenge on Authenticity – Wilde, Genet, Orton and others' (*LT*, 553–69), which appears in a section of the book entitled 'Transgressive Reinscriptions, Early Modern and Post-modern', as the post-modern counterpart to the preceding essay, 'Early Modern: Cross-Dressing in Early Modern England'. This section explores these two different instances of 'transgressive reinscription' which Dollimore defines in terms of 'the perverse dynamic', signifying 'that fearful interconnectedness whereby the antithetical inheres within, and is partly produced by, what it opposes' (1991, 33). In keeping with the 'dangerous proximity', identified by Bristow in Sedgwick's account, of patriarchy's privileged 'male-male' relations to the homosexuality it is obliged to condemn, Dollimore shows that 'the significance of the *proximate*' in 'metaphysical constructions of the Other', is that 'the proximate is often constructed as the other, and in a process which facilitates displacement. But the proximate is also what enables a tracking-back of the "other" in the "same"' (1991, 33). This is Dollimore's 'transgressive reinscription, which, also provisionally may be regarded as the return of the repressed and/or the suppressed and/or the displaced via the proximate' (1991, 33). The 'Early Modern' essay is concerned with how the female transvestite of that period 'appropriated, inverted, and substituted for, masculinity – in a word, perverted it. This was primarily a question of style rather than sexual orientation.' Similarly the 'Post/modern' essay below considers how

> the elusive, probably non-existent, gay sensibility perverts the categories of the aesthetic and the subjective, restoring both to the cultural and social domains which, in the modern period, they have been assumed to

transcend, but which in the early modern period they were always known to be a part of. (1991, 34)

The 'Post/modern' essay begins with a critique of Susan Sontag's and George Steiner's work on homosexual sensibility which Dollimore counters with the view that 'the very notion . . . is a contradiction in terms', but that there is possibly an aspect of it which may be understood 'in terms *of* that contradiction – . . . a parodic critique of the essence of sensibility as conventionally under-stood' *LT*, 554). He reads Wilde, Genet and Orton through this model while identifying similarities with and departures from postmodernist and poststructuralist models of pastiche and parody. Not surprisingly, Dollimore draws on Butler's ground-breaking work on gender as performance in *Gender Trouble: Feminism and the Subversion of Identity* (1990), which makes much of parody, cross-dressing and repetition in its exploration of so-called deconstructive models of subjectivity. As Dollimore summarizes, Butler 'sees deviant sexualities . . . as parodic subversive repetitions which displace rather than consolidate heterosexual norms' (564), and cites her much quoted dictum 'gay is to straight *not* as copy is to original, but, rather as copy is to copy' (Butler, cited in Dollimore, *LT*, 564). Attending to Butler's emphasis on the 'importance of *repetition* in the process of resistance and transformation', Dollimore underlines how gay subcultures are both a crucial enabling condition of, and constituting force for, the transgressive reinscription of gender.

Dollimore, in a more recent essay, 'Bisexuality, Heterosexuality, and Wishful Theory' (1996), critiques some of Butler's assertions on homo/hetero/sexuality in an essay published after *Gender Trouble* (in Fuss's collection), where she posits heterosexuality's 'profound dependency upon the homosexuality that it seeks fully to eradicate' (1991, 23). Dollimore underlines this as 'something generally missed by those who have mis/appropriated her work for a facile politics of subversion':

> In Butler's account gay desire usually figures *in an intense relationship to* heterosexuality – so much so that it might be said to have an antagonistic desire *for* it; reading Butler one occasionally gets the impression that gay desire is not complete unless somehow it is installed inside heterosexuality. [This] generalized description of how homosexuality and heterosexuality relate [is, to Dollimore] obviously and verifiably wrong. (1996, 535)

In *Bodies that Matter: On the Discursive Limits of 'Sex'*, the last chapter of which is 'Critically Queer' (*LT*, 570–86), Butler clarifies, defends and elaborates on her propositions in *Gender Trouble*, particularly with regard to criticisms of her notion of gender performativity and cross-dressing which was mistakenly understood to suggest the existence, prior to performance, of 'a willful and instrumental subject . . . who decides *on* its gender . . . and fails to realize that its existence is already decided *by* gender' (1993, x), and of a perceived lack of attention in her thesis to 'the materiality of the body' (1993, ix). She sets out to find 'a way to link the question of the materiality of the body to the performativity of gender' while taking into account 'the category of "sex" . . . within such a relationship' (1993, 1), and, drawing on Derrida's work on the reiterative qualities of 'performative utterance' as 'citation', puts forward a model of performativity as citationality. Butler asks:

> To what extent does discourse gain the authority to bring about what it names through citing the conventions of authority? And does a subject appear as author of its discursive effects to the extent that the citational practice by which he/she is conditioned and mobilized remains unmarked? Indeed, could it be that the production of the subject as originator of his/her effects is precisely a consequence of this dissimulated citationality? (1993, 13)

She considers the ramifications of this model for 'subjection to the norms of sex': 'the norm of sex takes hold to the extent that it is "cited" as such a norm, but it also derives its power through the citations that it compels' (1993, 13). In 'Critically Queer' Butler suggests that 'the contentious practices of "queerness" might be understood not only as an example of citational politics, but as a specific reworking of abjection into political agency that might explain why "citationality" has contemporary political promise' (1993, 21).

Of related significance in the essay is Butler's exploration of drag as an allegory of 'heterosexual melancholy, the melancholy by which a masculine gender is formed from the refusal to grieve the masculine as a possibility of love; a feminine gender . . . through the incorporative fantasy by which the feminine is excluded as a possible object of love' (*LT*, 580). Butler offers the somewhat startling observation that 'the "truest" lesbian melancholic is the strictly straight woman, and the "truest" gay male melancholic is the strictly straight man'(580). She describes the resultant 'culture of heterosexual melancholy' which 'can be read in the hyperbolic identifications by which mundane heterosexual masculinity and femininity confirm themselves' (*LT*, 580). Dollimore, in 'Bisexuality, Heterosexuality, and Wishful Theory', remarks that this is 'such a theoretically exquisite irony that it seems churlish to wonder whether it is true', or whether Butler is not herself partaking of that hyperbole she has just discerned in that 'mundane heterosexual masculinity and femininity' (1996, 537). Savoy's concerns over the work of both Butler and Sedgwick are echoed here: 'the rich ironies that accrue at the site of such deconstructive operations permit fine analysis of representation, but they infuriate activists . . . who see theory as having an increasingly attenuated relationship to the risks and exigencies experienced by actual lesbians and gay men' (1994, 139).

Butler is tentative about the longevity of the term 'queer'. As a

> site of collective contestation . . . it will have to remain that which is . . . never fully owned, but always and only redeployed, twisted, queered from a prior usage and in the direction of urgent and expanding political

purposes. This also means that it will doubtless have to be yielded in favor of terms that do that political work more effectively.

But a term so unruly and so alive to its own provisionality and mortality, much less a term than a lawless, performative trope or motif, undecidalde as to its 'meaning' and irreducible to the lawful control of any governing taxonomy, economy or system, is perhaps paradoxically better equipped to survive than most. For, as Butler says elsewhere, 'normalizing the queer would be, after all, its sad finish' (1994, 21).

NOTES TOWARDS A READING OF *THE SWIMMING-POOL LIBRARY*

As a narrative concerned with matters of sexual identity, freedom and con-straint, repression and transgression, Alan Hollinghurst's *The Swimming-Pool Library* (1988) plays between conventionally understood, normative construc-tions of identity and a mobility focused through desire which crosses, and thereby calls into question, those very same identities and their limits.

Caught up in the double narrative of William Beckwith and Charles, Lord Nantwich, the novel moves between the various strata of class and between distinct, and significant, moments in time throughout the twentieth, or what Alan Sinfield terms, the 'Wilde' century. There is thus a series of multiple temporal allusions, from the birth of Charles, Lord Nantwich, in 1900, through 1958, the year in which Beckwith is born, to 1983, the year in which Beckwith recounts events and the two men meet while 'cottaging' (on the history of this term as an expression for cruising public conveniences, see Karen Sayer, 1996, 99–100), as instances of historicizing contextualization (see Kenneth Womack's discussion of the novel below) against which to place the question of gay or queer subjectivity. As Womack points out, the year of Beckwith's birth, 1958, is just one year after the publication of the Wolfenden Report into Homosexu-ality, which eventually led in 1967 to the Act repealing the 1885 Criminal Law Amendment Act on homosexuality. Thus, the principal characters' sexual identities are, in a particular fashion, circumscribed by various historical manifestations of legislation, discourse and policing (even though the role of these is, to a degree, only ever implicit in the text, inference and suggestiveness having greater potential than an expression of historiographical didacticism; on homosexuality and English culture in the post-Second World War period, see Sinfield, 1989, 60–85).

It might therefore be suggested that, while on the one hand, one can chart a history of 'homosexual' and, subsequently, 'gay' or 'queer' experience (keeping in mind all the while that the terms are not transhistorical), on the other hand, there is the temporally transgressive articulation of a persistence of same-sex desire which affirms itself through 'insubordination'. Resisting their placement in the marginalized, subordinate location to which normative, hegemonic Anglo-Saxon culture seeks to assign gay or queer cultures, such transgressive identities also refuse to be assigned to history in any simple fashion. It is sexuality itself which transgresses and exceeds history in this novel, and narrative makes it possible to bring back, in a particularly haunting fashion, moments of expression and repression. If we recall Eve Sedgwick's etymological exploration of the term 'queer' in the light of *The Swimming-Pool Library*'s temporal 'dislocations', we might suggest that Hollinghurst's text, in its play across times, subverts the very notion of history (as hegemonic, normative narrative), through a multiply transitive current or flux. The text is, itself, 'antiassimilationist', as Sedgwick has it. Or, to put this another way, this is a queer text.

Formally, therefore, the narratives play on the question of a historicization of sexuality, while simultaneously they resist being limited by a purely historical structure (which is one more imposition of a given identity). Moreover, the unreliability of the narrator further questions not necessarily the 'facts' of a given narrative but, rather, the uses to which historical detail is put to work in the name of the repressive power structures by which identity for social groups is asserted or erased. For example, consider the ambiguities and tensions surrounding the location of Lord Nantwich in the earlier part of his life when he serves the British Empire as a colonial administrator in Africa, in the service of the very power by which his sexuality is marginalized, a power which employs him in the control of its 'subaltern colonial subjects' (Chambers, 1999, 254). The uncomfortable matter of power relations involved here concerning self/other, hetero/homosexual, colonizer/colonized are all available through a consideration of the very structures and limits by which such binary oppositions operate, as Jonathan Dollimore's discussion above of such similar figures makes clear.

Concerning the ambivalence of the narrative on the matter of hedonism and the catastrophe of AIDs, there are the doubling effects of the text which expose and exceed the various limits of identity (including the very identity of narrative and narrator as, for example, realist or reliable) already mentioned, and through these there is traced by Hollinghurst what Kenneth Womack below describes as the 'simultaneously destructive and revelatory nature of cultural apocalypse'. This is most effectively marked in the double moment of Beckwith's narration: 1983. While desire and lawless sexuality may transgress historical containment, history has an all too violent way of leaving its mark. As Hugh David points out in his *On Queer Street: A Social History of British Homosexuality 1895–1995*, 1983 was perhaps the *annus mirabilis* 'of the British homosexual' (1997, 252), while it is described by Beckwith as his '*belle époque*' and 'the last summer of its kind there was ever to be' (*S-P L*, 6, 5–6). At the same time, however, it was also a turning point, marked by the narrative as 'a faint flicker of calamity, like flames around a photograph, something seen out of the corner of the eye' (*S-P L*, 6). This 'faint flicker of calamity' became in the next few years the then incalculable rise of the numbers of deaths through AIDS. Less devastating but also significant, 1983 saw Margaret Thatcher win a second General Election. (We might also note the historical irony of *The Swimming-*

Pool Library's year of publication, 1988, as another double instance, this being the year that Clause 28 of the Local Government Act was passed by the Conservative government.)

It is in the light of the intervening years, between the moment that Beckwith begins his narrative and the moment that Hollinghurst publishes the novel, that we have to contend with the fact, as Joseph Bristow points out, that '[n]owhere at all does AIDS surface' (Bristow, 1995, 172). At the heart of this novel which 'joyfully celebrates explicit eroticism between men' is what Bristow calls a 'terrifying absence' (172). This relative silence on Beckwith's part might lead the reader back to a question of Judith Butler's asked earlier: 'does a subject appear as author to the extent that the citational practice by which he/she is conditioned and mobilized remains unmarked?' (1993, 13). To what extent does William Beckwith produce himself as the conditioned locus of denials and silences, as so many 'citations' of a century of oppressive legislation and the policing of marginalization? To what extent does Hollinghurst open to our view through the figure of his narrator and that narrator's omissions, a figure 'whose sexual life and aesthetic tastes, if clearly running against the dominant ideology of the day, none the less remain committed to many of the determining patterns of patriarchal law' (Bristow, 1995, 178), whether that law be understood through the signatures of colonialism or Thatcherism?

QUESTIONS FOR FURTHER CONSIDERATION

1. Consider the nature of the term 'queer' as the central trope that represents an intellectual, social and political movement of remarkable proportions. How does it account (or fail to account) for queer theory's theoretical, ideological and cultural imperatives?

2. In what ways might queer theory's significance be understood as a particularly *postmodern* phenomenon. In short, why did queer theory emerge as a viable movement at such a remarkably late moment in the twentieth century, as well as in terms of the evolution of the contemporary theoretical project? What propitious political, social and historical conditions enabled queer theory's rapid development during the 1990s?

3. Consider contemporary queer theory's significant historical debt to the work of Oscar Wilde and Michel Foucault, respectively. How have their efforts influenced such theorists as Eve Kosofsky Sedgwick, Jonathan Dollimore and Judith Butler, among others?

4. Compare the narratives of Charles, Lord Nantwich, and William Beckwith, respectively. What do their historical, cultural and social differences say about the nature of gay subjectivity during ostensibly different historical eras of the twentieth century?

5. Drawing once again upon the divergent historical eras that produce the narratives of Charles, Lord Nantwich, and William Beckwith, respectively, consider the roles of politics and the English government in the

construction of each character's identity. How does each figure's respective ideological moment affect his freedom to make various lifestyle choices?

6. How does our understanding of the colonial dimensions of the novel have an impact on our analysis of the power relations in specific relation to sexuality that undergird *The Swimming-Pool Library*?

ANNOTATED BIBLIOGRAPHY

Bristow, Joseph, ed. *Sexual Sameness: Textual Differences in Lesbian and Gay Writing*. London, 1992.
An informative and useful collection of gay and lesbian readings examining the (textual) politics of representation of same-sex experience across a range of English and American literature by writers such as Shakespeare, Oscar Wilde, E. M. Forster, Virginia Woolf, Sylvia Townsend Warner, Joe Orton, H. D., Adrienne Rich, and Audre Lorde. Contributors include David Bergman, Diana Collecott, Terry Castle, Jonathan Dollimore, Sherron E. Knopp, Alan Sinfield and Liz Yorke.
Garber, Marjorie. *Vested Interests: Cross-Dressing and Cultural Anxiety*. London, 1992.
This incisively argued and beautifully illustrated book is a landmark study of the cultural significance of transvestism across a broad range of literature, art, film and television. Garber explores gay and lesbian theories and identities in relation to her much cited and debated central thesis that cross-dressing does not (as some theorists have argued) position the subject in one constructed gender identity or the other (masculine or feminine), but in fact constitutes a third category of identity – one which undoes or defies gender categorization altogether. Garber's controversial work has met with mixed reception from gay, lesbian and queer theorists.
Sedgwick, Eve Kosofsky, ed. *Novel Gazing: Queer Readings in Fiction*. Durham, NC, and London, 1997.
A lively collection of essays making diverse and imaginative use of queer theory to explore a range of British, French and American novels by both canonical and esoteric authors, including Willa Cather, Benjamin Constant, William Gibson, Henry James, Toni Morrison, Marcel Proust, T. H. White and Virginia Woolf. The contributors are: Stephen Barber, Renu Bora, Anne Chandler, James Creech, Jonathan Goldberg, Joseph Litvak, Michael Lucey, Jeff Nunokawa, Cindy Patton, Jacob Press, Robert F. ReidPharr, Eve Kosofsky Sedgwick, Melissa Solomon, Tyler Stevens, Kathryn Bond Stocktop John Vincent. Maurice Wallace, Barry Weller.
Warner, Michael, ed. *Fear of a Queer Planet: Queer Politics and Social Theory*. Minneapolis, MN, 1993.
An important collection of interdisciplinary essays by some of the leading names in queer theory. Warner's helpful introductory essay has been much cited, and stands as a useful introduction to the field. The book sets out to 'queer' social theory by offering queer perspectives on traditions in various disciplines including anthropology, marxism, psychoanalysis, psychology and law, and by inviting new engagements with the politics of identity, race, ethnicity, nationalism, gender and sexuality. The first part, 'Get Over It: Heterosexuality', includes Jonathan Goldberg on 'Sodomy in the New World', Diane Fuss on 'Freud's Fallen Women' and Eve Sedgwick on 'How to Bring Your Kids Up Gay'. The second part, 'Get Used to It: The New Queer Politics', includes Cathy Griggers on 'Lesbian Bodies in the Age of (Post)mechanical Reproduction', Henry Louis Gates on 'The Black Man's Burden' and Phillip Brian Harper on 'Black Nationalism and the Homophobic Impulse'. Other contributors are Laurent Berlant and Elizabeth Freeman, Douglas Crimp, Janet E. Halley, Andrew Parker, Cindy Patton, Steven Seidman and Robert Schwartzwarld.
Wittig, Monique. *The Straight Mind and Other Essays*. Hemel Hempstead, 1992.
The French writer, Monique Wittig, is a novelist and playwright as well as a theorist and

critic whose work is considered a radical engagement with the French feminist tradition established by Simone de Beauvoir. She has been a significant influence on many Anglo-American feminist, lesbian and queer theorists, including Judith Butler. The title essay in this entertainingly provocative and readable selection includes Wittig's most famous declaration: 'Lesbians are not women'.

SUPPLEMENTARY BIBLIOGRAPHY

Abelove, Henry, Michèle Aina Barale and David M. Halperin, eds. *The Lesbian and Gay Studies Reader*. New York, 1993.

Beemyn, Brett and Mickey Eliason, eds. *Queer Studies: A Lesbian, Gay, Bisexual, and Transgender Anthology*. New York, 1996.

Bredbeck, Gregory W. 'The new queer narrative: intervention and critique', *Textual Practice*, 9: 3, 1995.

Bristow, Joseph. *Effeminate England: Homoerotic Writing After 1885*. New York, 1995.

————. *Sexuality*. London, 1997.

Butler, Judith, *Gender Trouble: Feminism and the Subversion of Identity*. London, 1990.

————. 'Imitation and gender insubordination', in *Inside/Out: Lesbian Theories*, ed. Diana Fuss. New York, 1991.

————. *Bodies that Matter: On the Discursive Limits of 'Sex'*. New York, 1993.

————. 'Against Proper Objects', *differences: A Journal of Feminist and Cultural Studies*, 6, 1994.

Castle, Terry. *The Apparitional Lesbian: Female Homosexuality and Modern Culture*. New York, 1993.

Creekmur, Corey K. and Alexander Doty, eds. *Out in Culture: Gay, Lesbian, and Queer Essays on Popular Culture*. London, 1995.

de Lauretis, Teresa. 'Queer Theory: Lesbian and Gay Sexualities', *differences: A Journal of Feminist and Cultural Studies*, 3: 2, 1991.

Dollimore, Jonathan. *Sexual Dissidence: Augustine to Wilde, Freud to Foucaul*. Oxford, 1991.

————. 'Bisexuality, heterosexuality, and wishful theory', *Textual Practice*, 10: 3, 1996.

Dorenkamp, Monica and Richard Henke, eds. *Negotiating Lesbian and Gay Subjects*. New York, 1995.

Foucault, Michel. *The History of Sexuality. Vol. 1: An Introduction*, trans. Robert Hurley. Harmondsworth, 1979.

Fuss, Diana, *Essentially Speaking: Feminism, Nature and Difference*. New York, 1989.

————, ed. *Inside/Out: Lesbian Theories, Gay Theories*. New York, 1991.

Geltmaker, T. 'The Queer Nation Acts Up: Health Care, Politics, and Sexual Diversity in the County of Angels', *Society and Space*, 10, 1992.

Goldberg, Jonathan, *Sodometries: Renaissance Texts, Modern Sexualities*. Stanford, CA, 1992.

Hal, Donald E. and Maria Pramaggiore, eds. *RePresenting Bisexualities: Subjects and Cultures of Fluid Desire*. New York, 1996.

Harper, Phillip Brian, E. Francis White and Margaret Cerullo. 'Multi/Queer/Culture', *Radical America*, 24: 4, 1993.

Jagose, Annamarie. *Queer Theory: An Introduction*. New York, 1996.

Jeffreys, Sheila. 'The Queer Disappearance of Lesbians: Sexuality in the Academy', *Women's Studies International Forum*, 17, 1994.

Luckhurst, Roger. 'Queer Theory (and Oscar Wilde): Review Essay', *Journal of Gender Studies*, 4: 3, 1995.

Martin, Biddy. 'Sexualities without Gender and Other Queer Utopias', *Diacritics*, 24: 2/3, 1994.

Nordquist, Jean. *Queer Theory: A Bibliography*. Santa Cruz, CA, 1997.

O'Driscoll, Sally. 'Outlaw Readings: Beyond Queer Theory', *Signs: Journal of Women, Culture and Society*, 22: 1, 1996.

Parker, Andrew and Eve Kosofsky Sedgwick, eds. *Performativity and Performance*. New York, 1995.

Phelan, S. *Playing With Fire: Queer Politics, Queer Theories*. London, 1997.

Rich, Adrienne. 'Compulsory Heterosexuality and Lesbian Existence', in *Blood, Bread and Poetry: Selected Prose 1979–1985*. London, 1987.

Savoy, Eric. 'You Can't Go Homo Again: Queer Theory and the Foreclosure of Gay Studies', *English Studies in Canada*, 20: 2, 1994.

Sedgwick, Eve Kosofsky. *Between Men: English Literature and Male Homosocial Desire*. New York, 1985.

————. *Epistemology of the Closet*. Berkeley, CA, 1990.

————. *Tendencies*. Durham, NC, 1993.

————, ed. *Studies in the Novel*, 28: 3, 1996.

Segal, Lynne. *Straight Sex: The Politics of Pleasure*. London, 1994.

————. 'Diaspora and Hybridity: Queer Identities and the Ethnicity Model', *Textual Practice*, 10:2, 1996.

Sinfield, Alan. *Cultural Politics – Queer Reading*. London, 1994.

————. *The Wilde Century: Effeminacy, Oscar Wilde and the Queer Moment*. London, 1994.

Smith-Rosenberg, Carroll. 'The Female World of Love and Ritual: Relations Between Women in Nineteenth Century America', in *Disorderly Conduct: Visions of Gender in Victorian America*. New York, 1985.

Walters, Suzanne Danuta. 'From Here to Queer: Radical Feminism, Postmodernism, and the Lesbian Menace (Or, Why Can't a Woman Be More Like a Fag?)', *Signs: Journal of Women, Culture and Society*, 21: 4, 1996.

Weed, Elizabeth, and Naomi Schor, eds. *Feminism Meets Queer Theory*. Bloomington, IN, 1997.

OTHER WORKS CITED

Chambers, Ross. *Loiterature*. Lincoln, NE, 1999.

Dollimore, Jonathan. *Radical Tragedy: Religion, Ideology and Power in the Drama of Shakespeare and His Contemporaries*. Brighton, 1994.

Foucault, Michel. *Foucault Live*, trans. John Johnston, ed. Sylvere Lotringer. New York, 1989.

Sayer, Karen. 'A Cottage in the Country', *Imprimatur*, 2:1.2, Autumn, 1996.

Simons, Jon. *Foucault and the Political*. London, 1995.

Sinfield, Alan. *Literature, Politics, and Culture in Postwar Britain*. Berkeley, CA, 1989.

CHAPTER

13

THEORIZING CULTURE, READING OURSELVES: CULTURAL STUDIES

Kenneth Womack

Cultural studies, by encouraging readers to look outwardly at the social, artistic, political, economic and linguistic *mélange*, simultaneously challenges us to reflect inwardly upon the ethical norms and biases that constitute ourselves. As the twentieth century comes to a close, this wide-ranging field of study continues to dominate the contemporary direction of literary criticism and its examination of the politics of difference that define our senses of individual and cultural identity. Cultural studies manifests itself in a wide array of interpretative dimensions, including such intersecting fields of inquiry as gender studies, postcolonialism, race and ethnic studies, pedagogy, ecocriticism, the politics of nationalism, popular culture, postmodernism and historical criticism, among a variety of other topics. Concerned with the exploration of a given culture's artistic achievements, institutional structures, belief systems and linguistic practices, cultural studies highlights the interrelationships and tensions that exist between cultures and their effects upon not only the literary works that we consume, but also the authentic texts of our lives. A genuinely international and interdisciplinary phenomenon, the interpretative lens of cultural studies provides us with a means for exploring the cultural codes of a given work, as well as for investigating the institutional, linguistic, historical and sociological forces that inform that work's publication and critical reception. The reconstruction and analysis of the conditions of literary production afford us, then, with a venue in which to address the social and political contexts of literary works. This venue, fraught as it is with the ideology of difference inherent in an increasingly global society, comprises cultural studies.

The contemporary theoretical predominance of cultural studies finds its origins in the various processes that shaped the direction of our postwar global culture, including modernization, industrialization, urbanization and the unparalleled rise of technology and mass communication during the latter half of the twentieth century. Fuelled by the necessity of massive historical change, cultural studies emerged initially as a means for responding to the rapid shifts in the ways we live our lives, to the sudden transformation of the humanistic and historical norms that once governed – and, indeed, provided apparent constancy for – our social practices. Scholars often locate the rise of cultural studies to late-1950s Great Britain and the publication of seminal works by Richard Hoggart and Raymond Williams. Hoggart and Williams composed their early cultural studies manifestos in an era dominated by the monolithic critical ideology of F. R. Leavis and a renewed interest in 'cultural capital', or the dissemination of literary knowledge for the express purpose of enhancing the moral sensibilities of the nation's readers. In *The Great Tradition* (1948), Leavis argues for a restricted literary canon that shuns the experimental excesses of modernism in favour of the traditional humanism espoused by such writers as Jane Austen, Charles Dickens, Alexander Pope and George Eliot. Responding to the social didacticism of 'Leavisism', writers such as Hoggart and Williams recognized the inability of Leavis's aesthetic vision, with its express reliance upon an abbreviated cultural canon, to respond to the many facets of mass culture intrinsic to postwar life.

In *The Uses of Literacy* (1957), Hoggart explores postwar shifts in the lives of working-class Britons confronted with the changes inherent in modernization, as well as with the disintegration of traditional familial roles and social practices. Williams's *Culture and Society: 1780–1950* (1958) offers a critique of the radical consequences of making distinctions between conventional notions of 'culture' and 'society', and between 'high culture' and 'low culture'. Williams also discusses the demise of the 'knowable communities' that characterize prewar life, arguing that an increasingly politicized culture and the emergence of new forms of global imperialism will ultimately replace prewar conceptions of politics and society. In *Marxism and Literature* (1977), Williams explores the ideology of 'cultural materialism', or the concept that economic forces and modes of production inevitably impinge upon cultural products such as literary works. Proponents of cultural materialism contend that as a cultural artifact literature functions as a means for subverting social and political norms (see Chapter 10, above). 'At the very centre of a major area of modern thought and practice, which it is habitually used to describe, is a concept, "culture," which in itself, through variation and complication embodies not only the issues but the contradictions through which it has developed,' Williams writes in *Marxism and Literature*. 'The concept at once fuses and confuses the radically different experiences and tendencies of its formation' (1977, 11).

During the 1960s and 1970s, cultural studies continued to evolve as a viable interpretative paradigm. In 1964, for example, Hoggart and Stuart Hall founded Birmingham University's Centre for Contemporary Cultural Studies, an institution that soon became synonymous with the cultural studies movement of that era. The 1960s also saw the publication of E. P. Thompson's influential *The Making of the English Working Class* (1964), a volume that examines the political and economic components of the working-class identity and argues that conceptions of individuality have become fragmented in the postwar world and no longer restrict themselves to notions of shared cultural interests and value systems. During the 1970s, literary critics often discussed cultural criticism in terms of 'hegemony', the Italian marxist Antonio Gramsci's term denoting invisible relations of cultural or intellectual domination. The 1970s also witnessed the emergence of various structuralist modes of cultural criticism that intersected with the ideological theories of Louis Althusser and the psychoanalytic arguments of Jacques Lacan. While Althusser examines ideology as both a means of cultural identification and of social control, Lacan discusses the psychological anxieties of resolving individual and familial tensions in a modern world that lacks traditional and comforting social structures. The theoretical insights of writers such as Gramsci, Althusser and Lacan finally accorded cultural studies a terminology for exploring the emergence of literary art forms within a given culture and for addressing the social contexts within which a particular text is written, produced and ultimately read.

With the advent of poststructuralist interpretative modes and the arrival of the multicultural movement during the 1980s, cultural studies emerged as one of literary criticism's primary fields of critical inquiry. Cultural studies also owes its theoretical hegemony during the 1980s to the international rise of the 'new right', the political movement in the United States and the United Kingdom led by President Ronald Reagan and Prime Minister Margaret Thatcher respectively. As a political ideology, the new right advocated minimal governmental involvement in the lives of citizens in order to allow market forces to define the nature of social interrelations and economic exchange. At the same time, proponents of the new right promoted strong senses of nationalism in an effort to eschew any internal differences that might threaten national unity. Yet, as Simon During astutely recognizes in his introduction to *The Cultural Studies Reader*, the policies of the new right contain an 'internal contradiction' between its economic rationalism and its strident sense of nationalism: 'The more the market is freed from state intervention and trade and finance cross national boundaries,' During writes, 'the more the nation will be exposed to foreign influences and the greater the gap between rich and poor' (1993, 14). This internal contradiction subsequently threatened our individual senses of cultural identity by sublimating them via the nationalist rubrics of 'Americanness' and 'Englishness'. Suddenly, cultural studies – with its accent upon personal identity and the study of our rich diversity of cultural artifacts – provided readers and critics alike with an appealing form of intellectual cachet; it offered both a decentred view of culture in sharp contrast with the monocultural themes of nationalism, as well as an arena for investigating the politics of difference highlighted by the increasing social and economic globalization that resulted from the new right's conservative fiscal policies.

The new right's political pre-eminence during this era also served as the catalyst for the culture wars of the 1980s and early 1990s that tested the resiliency of cultural studies and multiculturalism while also challenging the intellectual dominion of the academy. Students of the culture wars typically attribute the inauguration of the intellectual crisis in Norther American higher education to Secretary of Education William J. Bennett's 1984 governmental report on the humanities, *To Reclaim a Legacy*, in which he fans the flames of nationalism and charges American academics with having lost their senses of moral and intellectual purpose when they enacted policies of canon expansion and multicultural study. While the power and publicity concomitant with Bennett's cabinet post provided him with the public voice necessary to strike a strident initial chord within the American public, Allan Bloom's *The Closing of the American Mind: How Higher Education Has Failed Democracy and Impoverished the Souls of Today's Students* imbued the culture wars with the intellectual cachet of a scholarly voice. Bloom, then a distinguished professor in the Committee on Social Thought and the College at the University of Chicago, derided the contemporary state of the humanities as an 'almost submerged old Atlantis' (1987, 371). In addition to arguing that higher education wallows in a state of chaos with little evidence of a scholarly or an ethical agenda, Bloom attacked the pluralistic motives of canon revisionists. As with the culture warriors who followed the ideological lead of *The Closing of the American Mind*, Bloom championed the literary touchstones of western civilization and the cultural capital that they would ostensibly impart to the minds of young readers. In *ProfScam: Professors and the Demise of Higher Education*, Charles J. Sykes similarly attacks what he perceives to be the professoriate's 'relentless drive for advancement [which] has turned American universities into vast factories of junkthink, the byproduct of academe's endless capacity to take even the richest elements of civilization and disfigure them into an image of itself' (1988, 7). In addition to calling for the broad abolition of tenure, Sykes refuses to address the policies of the multicultural project when he demands the unequivocal restoration of a Eurocentric canon and curriculum: 'Without apology', he writes, 'the undergraduate curriculum should be centred on the intellectual tradition of Western civilization. Quite simply,' he adds, 'there are certain books and certain authors that every college graduate should read if he is to be considered truly educated' (1988, 260).

As the culture wars advanced into the 1990s, proponents of the new right continued the culture warriors' onslaught against canon revision, while also increasingly objecting to the manner in which contemporary scholars resorted to the politicisation of literary and cultural studies. In *Tenured Radicals: How Politics Has Corrupted Higher Education*, Roger Kimball laments what he considers to be a concerted leftist effort to 'dismantle the traditional curriculum and institutionalize radical feminism, to ban politically unacceptable speech and propagate the tenets of deconstruction and similar exercises in cynical obscurantism' (1990, 167). In his divisive volume, *Illiberal Education: The Politics of*

Race and Sex on Campus, Dinesh D'Souza challenges the politicization of literary studies by contemporary scholars: 'The problem is that many of the younger generation of faculty in the universities express lack of interest, if not contempt, for the Western classics,' he writes. 'Either they regard the books as flawed for their failure to endorse the full emancipation of approved minorities,' he continues, 'or they reject their metaphysical questions as outdated and irrelevant' (1991, 255). Finally, in *Telling the Truth: Why Our Culture and Our Country Have Stopped Making Sense – and What We can Do about It*, Lynne V. Cheney, the former director of the National Endowment for the Humanities, continues Bennett and Bloom's attacks on canon revision and the politicisation of academic scholarship. In the conclusion to her study, Cheney remarks: 'The virtues that we have increasingly come to believe we must nurture if we are to be successful as a culture simply make no sense if we turn away from reason and reality' (1995, 206).

In each instance, the culture warriors argued in favour of the new right's nationalistic aims and its affirmation of a singular cultural identity. Yet their remarkably narrow approach to culture – particularly in light of the intense era of globalization that marked the 1980s and 1990s – only succeeded in underscoring the ideologies of difference that compose our divergent senses of identity. 'We face the outraged reactions of those custodians of Western culture who protest that the canon, that transparent decanter of Western values, may become – breathe the word – *politicized*,' Henry Louis Gates, Jr, observes (1992, 195). Gates's arguments underscore the manner in which ideology, despite the culture warriors' vehement claims to the contrary, invariably influences the selection and historical survival of cultural artifacts. Ironically, the culture wars not only resulted in a renewed interest in cultural studies, but also in the institutionalization of the aims of the multicultural project. 'Whether the topic is language; the construction of readers, writers, and texts; canon formation; curriculum; institutions; or the social positions of women, African Americans, and other marginalized groups,' Isaiah Smithson writes in his introduction to *English Studies/Culture Studies: Institutionalizing Dissent*, 'teachers and students are exploring the cultural relations of texts rather than settling for what are ultimately naturalist and essentialist explanations' (1994, 9). By responding to the explicit threats posed by the culture wars waged by the new right – the dominant ideology and the purveyors of the new nationalism – cultural studies strengthened its interpretative claims and clarified its position as an ideologically based form of critique.

As cultural studies continues to develop as an interpretative mode during the 1990s, its proponents celebrate the remarkable heterogeneity that characterises its contemporary nature. In dramatic contrast with its earliest manifestations in the late 1950s, cultural studies currently intersects a variety of disciplines and political forms of literary criticism, from deconstruction and postmodernism to gender studies and environmental criticism. In the wake of the globalization spurred on by the new right's economic policies and by unprecedented developments in technology and mass communications during the 1980s, cultural studies enjoys theoretical hegemony because of its capacity for addressing the issues that define the closing decades of the twentieth century. 'Whether we are discussing the multinational corporation, global agricultural development, the protection of endangered species, religious toleration, the well-being of women, or simply how to run a firm efficiently,' Martha C. Nussbaum remarks in *Cultivating Humanity: A Classical Defense of Reform in Liberal Education,* 'we increasingly find that we need comparative knowledge of many cultures to answer the questions we ask' (1997, 15). Cultural studies provides precisely such a mechanism, with its simultaneous interests in 'high' and 'low' culture, as well as in the nexus that it reveals between culture and society.

Cultural studies continues to evolve in a number of intriguing and significant directions. In addition to its ongoing academic institutionalization, cultural studies confronts contemporary scholars with a variety of pedagogical implications while continuing to engage other, ostensibly separate fields of inquiry in interdisciplinary forms of critique. North American universities and colleges actively support the aims of cultural studies as they create American Studies programmes and provide students with curricula that offer multicultural studies options. As Elizabeth Fox-Genovese notes, 'Scholars have succeeded in imaginatively reclaiming the voices, representations, productions, and values of the oppressed and excluded, and they have demonstrated the cultural strength and richness of those who have been ignored' (1990, 9). Cultural studies also provides the professoriate with an encouraging theoretical mode for exploring the politics of difference depicted by a variety of previously disenfranchised literary works. Simply put, cultural studies – rather than forcing instructors to engage literature in neutral, depoliticised terms – challenges teachers to investigate a given text's ideological properties in the classroom. Cultural studies, then, 'invokes the standard sense of the pedagogical contract,' Jeffrey Williams writes, 'that we can catalyze and generate social change via our relations with students. This possibility – to reach the minds of the young to effect social change – is perhaps the great hope of education and why it is cast as having significant stakes, from Socrates on' (1997, 301). By necessarily challenging literary critics to merge various interpretative modes, cultural criticism affords teachers and theorists alike with the opportunity to approach the act of reading in a multidisciplinary fashion. In this manner, cultural studies provides us with a valuable means for reinvigorating both our literary critiques and our classroom pedagogies.

While cultural criticism confronts the contemporary academy with a variety of interesting pedagogical implications, it nevertheless presents a number of ideological dilemmas regarding the ways in which we theorise literary study and the cultural discourses of the academy. The inevitable professionalization of culture studies, for instance, has resulted in a blurring and convolution of the movement's principal aims. As Gisela Ecker observes, 'All too often references to "gender, race, and class" have degenerated into a mere litany which has to turn up in academic work as a sign of belonging to a supposedly progressive group' (1994, 41). In short, the elevation of cultural studies has engendered a form of political correctness that requires theorists to address particular cultural issues in their critiques; this necessity invariably manifests itself in the iteration of requisite subjects, including 'gender, race and class'. While cultural studies clearly seeks to elevate these important social issues within the critical and social main, their repetition as an academic mantra only serves to mitigate their considerable intellectual import. Popular culture's apotheosis within the academy presents yet another dilemma. Although cultural studies certainly provides a forum for investigating the significant social and political meanings inherent in various forms of 'low' culture, the elevation of popular culture under cultural studies' rubric calls into question many of the movement's most important scholarly goals. 'What "cultural studies," as an academic profession [in North America], clearly lacks,' Paul Bové cautions, 'is "high intellectual" effort' (1997, 53). Clearly, the study of popular culture offers much insight into our contemporary approaches to art, politics and society; yet, as Bové warns, its overemphasis may ultimately dilute the attention afforded to other past and present cultural forms and their impact upon our cultural selves.

In three exemplary essays, J. Hillis Miller, Iain Chambers and Alan Sinfield demonstrate the interdisciplinary possibilities of cultural studies, as well as the theoretical elasticity of the paradigm as a means for interpreting our various senses of cultural identity. In 'Cultural Studies and Reading' (*LT*, 604–10), Miller continues his analysis of the cultural and ethical properties inherent in the act of reading that he began in such works as *The Ethics of Reading: Kant, de Man, Eliot, Trollope, James, and Benjamin* (1987) and *Versions of Pygmalion* (1990). Having achieved academic renown during the 1980s for his 'deconstructive' critiques of literature and culture, Miller has devoted much of his recent work to positing an 'ethics of reading' that seeks to explain the reflexive process that occurs between the text and the reader, in addition to offering testimony to the ethical possibilities of poststructuralism, particularly deconstruction. For Miller, such an activity allows readers – the *de facto* authors of the texts that they appraise – to offer relevant conclusions about the moral properties of literary works and the ethical sensibilities of their theoretical premises. In 'Cultural Studies and Reading', Miller underscores the cultural import of the act of reading, the process via which we consume contemporary culture even as technology continues to transform the textures of our lives. While Miller recognizes the many ways in which cultural studies has irrevocably altered the shape of the modern university and its curriculum, he argues that reading – indeed, the act of interpretation – still functions as the transaction that allows us to interact not only with 'literary or exclusively verbal texts but also works in visual or aural media like film, television, popular music, or advertising' (*LT*, 609).

Although he concedes that it provides a meaningful bridge between contemporary forms of 'high' and 'low' culture, Miller nevertheless sees cultural studies and its impact upon literary theory as potentially unsettling forces as we approach the new millennium. 'The universalizing idea of culture in cultural studies may be so all-inclusive as to be virtually empty,' Miller cautions. 'This process may occur even though all cultures and all persons may be seen as to some degree hybrid, not as univocal or essential'(607–8). In short, Miller argues, cultural studies possesses the capacity for undermining our notions of self and individuality because of its emphasis upon culture in its larger sense. Miller fears that 'individual works may be seen as unproblematically representative of the culture they reflect. A few carefully chosen examples can thus stand for a whole culture and offer a means of understanding it and taking it in,' he adds (608). Such an uncritical approach to our cultural artifacts would clearly undermine the political and institutional aims of cultural studies. Miller maintains that one solution for this 'disabling double gesture' may be the act of 'genuine' reading, a process in which readers consume a given text in its 'original language' and within the proper historical context. According to Miller, 'Only such a reading can hope to transmit or preserve some of the force that original work had or can still have as an event' (610). By insisting that cultural theorists address the artifacts of our civilisation in such a manner, cultural studies may yet succeed in achieving its democratic ends. As Miller argues in 'Is There an Ethics of Reading?', as the millennium approaches 'it would be beneficial to the health of our society to have an abundance of good readers' (1988, 100).

In 'Cities without Maps' (*LT*, 611–25), Iain Chambers constructs an elaborate reading of the city as a cultural metaphor. In addition to providing a useful analogy for an era of increasing globalization, the contemporary metropolis offers a virtual sea of interconnected histories, languages and cultures. While the city functions as a complex linguistic and social metaphor for the modern world, Chambers argues, maps of cities contradict the particularly human qualities of the urban landscapes that they reference, shape and outline. Although maps create contexts for our metropolitan adventures, they can never truly capture the reality inherent in a given city's historical memory and its convoluted array of cultures, stories, languages and experiences. Chambers writes:

> Beyond the edges of the map, we enter the localities of the vibrant, everyday world and the disturbance of complexity. Here we find ourselves in the gendered city, the city of ethnicities, the territories of different social groups, shifting centres and peripheries – the city that is a fixed object of design (architecture, commerce, urban planning, state administration) and yet simultaneously plastic and mutable: the site of transitory events, movements, memories. (*LT*, 612)

A genuinely living and fluid entity, the city – by virtue of its collective size and concentration of humanity – forces us to make cultural connections and to risk living our lives without maps. As Chambers notes, cities challenge us, like the larger cultures within which we live and work, to surrender portions of our identity in order to experience yet other, previously unrealized transcultural regions of our selves.

Chambers also offers a valuable defence of mass culture as the natural product of a historical era marked by globalization and cultural expansion. Rather than denigrating mass media and modern culture as an 'ideological façade' or as an 'infinity of commodity exchange', Chambers sees the contemporary metropolis as having its own aesthetics and its own complex, often ambiguous value systems and intercultural rhythms. Chambers illustrates the mutability of urban life through his description of Naples as a cultural metaphor. Nestled as it is below Mount Vesuvius, Naples must constantly confront its own potential destruction while simultaneously evolving as a human community. 'To live under the volcano, daily reminded of one's own mortality,' Chambers writes, 'is that the key to the city's schizophrenic energy, its languages of exultation and despair, its extremes of physical violence and mental resignation?'. Yet attempting to capture the essence of Naples – indeed, of any city – constitutes a cultural exercise in futility. As with any cultural phenomenon, cities consist of an infinitely complex series of signs and signifiers; these cities without maps, Chambers argues, 'can only be caught in fragments, in the economy of disorder, in the mythical half-light of an imagined decadence.' Always 'the sum of its collective histories, memories, and monuments', the city – in contrast with its various maps, which attempt to ascribe reality upon its cultural farrago – essentially functions as an 'imaginary place', in Chambers's words, that 'has a language that calls for a mode of interpretation' (621).

In 'Art as Cultural Production' (*LT*, 626–41), Sinfield offers a useful demonstration of cultural studies' intersections with marxist literary criticism and queer theory, while also elaborating upon the intellectual history of cultural criticism. Much of Sinfield's argument finds its origins in his postulation of an 'entrapment model', his theory about the interrelations of ideology and power. The entrapment model theorizes that attempts to challenge any prevailing ideological system only serve to maintain that system's locus of power, perhaps entrenching its power structures even deeper than before. Sinfield argues that the entrapment model functions as a barrier to dissidence, as a means for the ideology in power to sustain its oppressive constructions of class, race, gender and sexuality. Cultural materialism, according to Sinfield, provides readers and critics alike with a mechanism for understanding the power dynamics inherent in the entrapment model and for establishing the forms of cultural dissidence necessary for effecting genuine social change. Although cultural materialism reveals that 'there is no simple way through' the dominant's ideology's locus of power, Sinfield writes, it reminds us that there is 'every reason to go on trying' (*LT*, 631). Sinfield also offers several thoughtful conclusions about the degrees of value ascribed to art and literature by different cultures. Simply put, not all societies possess – or even attribute value to – cultural artifacts. According to Sinfield, the effective practice of cultural materialism recognizes this concept and understands that forceful cultural critiques investigate both modes of cultural production and the roles (or lack thereof) of art and literature in a given culture's social order.

As with Miller, Sinfield locates the genesis of contemporary cultural criticism to around 1980, when other political forms of critique, particularly feminism and gender studies, challenged the conventional norms of literary criticism and theory. 'Feminism created space for other kinds of question,' Sinfield writes. 'We saw that we didn't, after all, have to spend our psychic energy on ever more ingenious explanations of why Shakespeare on Shylock, or Joseph Conrad on Blacks, or D. H. Lawrence on women, or Alexander Pope on Sporus and effeminacy, is really expressing a profound universal truth' (634). In addition to discussing class variations regarding such concepts as masculinity and effeminacy, Sinfield considers what he perceives to be the misapplication of ideological critique by dissident cultural theorists. Cultural criticism falters, Sinfield argues, when it dismisses the cultural past as a useless means for addressing the 'world of material affairs' of the present in favour of texts grounded in the contemporary moment. Sinfield astutely undermines this contention, arguing that cultural critique demands the investigation of a given work's political context. 'Cultural materialists say that canonical texts have political projects,' he writes, 'and should not be allowed to circulate in the world today on the assumption that their representations of class, race, ethnicity, gender, and sexuality are simply authoritative.' Nevertheless, Sinfield reminds us, 'politics should be up for discussion' and 'textual analysis should address it' (640). Sinfield's remarks illustrate the decidedly *political* nature of cultural criticism. While literary critics – in our zeal for engendering democratic values and truths – often neglect this significant aspect of the interpretative act, cultural criticism, with its express interest in the circumstances of textual production, challenges us to contemplate a wider range of sociological, historical and ideological contexts.

As the essays by Miller, Chamber and Sinfield usefully demonstrate, cultural studies – with its capacity for illuminating our senses of self and their inextricable relations with the worlds in which we live – provides precisely such a venue for considering the various contexts of an increasingly diverse and heterogeneous global community. Although cultural studies emerged from the culture wars of the last decade with a renewed sense of purpose and with fully realized political and institutional aims, it must nevertheless continue to assert its interdisciplinarity in order to further its evolution as a viable and relevant interpretative paradigm. By highlighting the interpretative interconnections between the various subgenres of the theoretical project – and among such ostensibly divergent fields of inquiry as feminism, psychoanalysis, deconstruction and postmodernism – cultural studies offers a powerful means for comprehending the cultural realities that inform our perceptions of the world, as well as of the self. As Manthia Diawara observes, 'Cultural studies, in its attempts to draw attention to the material implications of the worldviews we assume, often delineates a literal and candid picture of ways of life that embarrass and baffle our previous theoretical understanding of those forms of life' (1995, 202). While this is urgently true, and offers a necessary justification for cultural studies, there is, however, a critical response to the rise of cultural studies, and the various forms of identity politics which are associated with this phenomenon and of which we should be aware.

Despite the obvious cultural differences between British and American academic models of cultural studies, we should perhaps note a certain wariness. Of course, J. Hillis Miller speaks on the difference culturally between cultural studies as academic *praxis* in the two countries in the essay on which we have drawn, while Stuart Hall has remarked that the rapid assimilation and in-stitutionalization of cultural studies in the US is 'extraordinarily' and 'pro-foundly' dangerous (Hall, 1996, 273), not least for the fact that, in the very name of politics, cultural studies, in undergoing institutionalization, has evinced a tendency to 'formalize out of existence the critical questions of power, history, and politics' (274). As a marxist, Hall blames this formalization in large part on the 'theorization' (by which he means the interpolation of 'poststructuralist' approaches to textuality with the political questions which cultural studies raises) of cultural studies in the North American academy today. There is, however, another way of considering the problem, as certain figures associated with 'high theory' have begun to pursue recently on both sides of the Atlantic.

Both Geoffrey Bennington and Tom Cohen have commented on a manifest problematic-in-common for cultural studies, which some of its practitioners share, whether one looks at the practice of cultural studies in universities of the British Isles or North America. The problem stems from a larger problem of, on the one hand, the institutionalization and subsequent excoriation of 'high theory' (in which certain practitioners of cultural studies and identity politics have had a hand) within the academy, and on the other, a return, whether inadvertent or deliberate, on the part of those very same practitioners to acts of reading and interpretation which owe more to pre-theoretical canonical modes of critical address grounded in humanism than even cultural studies would care to admit. And, at the same time, this has, in part, happened to come about as a result of a certain quietism and complacency among those who, apparently practitioners of 'high theory', have felt that all the battles for the establishment of theory institutionally have been won. (And, in a sense, they have, if theory has been so successfully institutionalized that it is taught everywhere as *just* a series of analytical schools and methodologies and not a fundamental epistemological and political questioning of the very grounds on which the idea of schools and methodologies come to institutional power in the first place.)

Bennington has commented on such quietism and cozy agreement in an essay, 'Inter', first published in 1999, and given at the 'Post-Theory' conference held at the University of Glasgow in 1998 (1999, 103–22). Turning his attention to the question of identity politics and cultural studies, and highly critical in passing of the legacy of Raymond Williams and Stuart Hall ('a sidestep from thinking into . . . "Late-Show" journalism' (Bennington, 1999, 105), he remarks on 'a thinly made-up return to pre-theoretical habits and a sort of intellectual journalism' (105), and identifying in this a 'more or less complacent historicism' (106).

While Bennington is addressing a broad-based leftist triumphalism in the name of a political urgency and horizon as an excuse for 'interring' theory, Tom Cohen identifies a similar tendency and turn specifically within cultural studies, describing a discernibly 'suspicious regression to precritical representationalism' (Cohen, 1998, 98) in critical practice which, unable adequately to theorize the past or otherwise to address matters of history, ideology and politics, finds itself in a stasis through being trapped analytically in commentary on the present. That for Cohen which goes by the name of cultural studies manifests in its critical mode a kind of 'mimetic humanism' (1998, 98) or a 'mimeto-humanist revanchism' (127) redolent of older more traditional critical methods, despite the ostensible politics expressed by practitioners of cultural studies. In this activity, it is argued, what goes by the name of cultural studies currently is engaged in a double 'archivism of the present' (121): on the one hand the texts of cultural studies are readable as projects which passively reinscribe and represent the present, thereby offering no political agency because the mimesis and representationality in which they are grounded offers no ideological distance from that which is being described. On the other hand, there takes place a critical process of substitution of 'new terms and conceptual types in a general (if still unreflected) reseeding of referential matrices' (127). What cultural studies must effect, argues Cohen, is a 'reconfiguration of the political' (which, after Walter Benjamin, he calls a politics of memory) that critically engages with the very question of culture (though never assuming this term 'culture' to be monolithic or static, which a representational politics pushes us towards), so as to 'disrupt the mimetic model of cultural historicism' (121). This is achieved through the post-Benjaminian location of the 'monad', whereby the text in question is read as that monadic figure: inscribed by the traces of memory which we call the past, it comes together as the crystallization of various relays and transmissions 'in a configuration pregnant with tensions' (122).

Iain Chambers's essay, in its comprehension of the role of cultural memory, and in its readings of the transmissions and relays between the differences of cultures which find themselves traced in the urban nexus both synchronically and diachronically, illuminates Cohen's theoretical argument. In a different fashion, and for different purposes, so too does Peter Greenaway's *Prospero's Books*, with its various heterogeneous concatenations between Baroque aesthetics and the teletechnology of the video age. However, as different as both texts are, what they, and what the work of Sinfield and Miller demonstrate amply, is that, in addition to affording us with a context for finally reading the texts of our own lives (and how those lives are, themselves, exemplary monads), cultural studies affords us a forum for reflecting upon the narrative spaces inhabited by the cultural others, both past and present, with whom we live.

NOTES TOWARDS READINGS OF
THE SWIMMING-POOL LIBRARY AND *PROSPERO'S BOOKS*

In *Marxism and Literature* (1977), Raymond Williams demonstrates the ways in which literature functions as a mechanism for the subversion of an array of social and political norms. As a form of 'cultural capital' in Williams's estimation, literature affords writers with the means for re-enacting the development and formation of culture, for revivifying the contradictions and complications inherent in social and cultural emergence. As an interpretive lens, cultural studies furnishes readers with a critical terminology and social philosophy for exploring the ways in which culture has an impact on our lives.

In *The Swimming-Pool Library* (1988), Alan Hollinghurst challenges the manner in which we understand England's 'subculture' of homosexuality and its often painful and tragic history of oppression. Hollinghurst's subtle juxtaposition of his educated narrator's contemporary tale of debauchery with an upper-class octogenarian's Edwardian memoirs destabilizes our beliefs about social progressiveness in the late twentieth century and underscores the enduring, historically specific power of brutality and hate. In the novel, Hollinghurst's pointedly unreliable narrator William Beckwith revels in the prodigious and exuberant pleasures available in a London health club, the Corinthian, in 1983. A gay nirvana of free love and sexual caprice, the club provides Will with access to the swimming pool that functions as a larger metaphor for the chance encounters that mark our convoluted lives despite our attempts at establishing order and making sense of our existence.

While cruising a public lavatory in a London park, Will revives an elderly man, Charles, Lord Nantwich. After his recovery, Charles entreats his young friend to write his biography, a task that will require Will to peruse Lord Nantwich's voluminous journals. The juxtaposition of Will and Charles's ages underscores one of Hollinghurst's most significant cultural aims in the novel: to demonstrate the often tragic iterability of the gay experience and the historicized comprehension of homosexuality's marginalized plight. Born in 1900, Charles's birth notably precedes the passage in 1915 of the Labouchere Amendment which criminalized homosexual behaviour. Likewise, Will was born in 1958, the year after the dissemination of the Wolfenden Report, a singular moment in the liberalization of English laws regarding homosexuality. Unlike Charles, Will can ostensibly lead an openly gay lifestyle, seemingly unfettered by the homophobia of another cultural era. While history forces Charles to live as a sexual pioneer, Will inherits a gay tradition for which his elders paid dearly via social ostracization and prison terms.

Yet Hollinghurst's novel finds its greatest strength in the ways in which it challenges us to look beyond what appears at first glance to be an emerging historical tolerance for homosexuality and difference. This aspect of *The Swimming-Pool Library* is revealed by the novelist's unsettling juxtaposition of two traumatic incidents involving Charles and Will in the 1950s and in 1983, respectively. In his journal, Charles recounts the horrors of his incarceration after being caught in a police sting operation in a London lavatory. Significantly, he spends his post-prison life as a leading philanthropist. Seemingly free to live an openly gay life after the suffering of Charles and multitudes of others during the first half of the century, Will finds his life and his senses of security and freedom transfixed after becoming the victim of a hate crime in modern London. After his brutalization at the hands of a group of skinheads, Will woefully remarks, 'It was actually happening. It was actually happening to me' (*S-P L*, 174). Will and Charles's parallel narratives of social derision, Catherine R. Stimpson writes, function as an 'ironic, meticulously designed history' of a cultural moment in which 'homosexuality changed from being a specific illegal act to a stigmatized illegal identity' (*S-P L*, 8).

As the novel comes to a close, Will returns to the Corinthian, where he begins to notice far more than the usual quarry of delectable young men: 'There were several old boys, one or two perhaps even of Charles's age, and doubtless all with their own story, strange and yet oddly comparable, to tell' (*S-P L*, 288). Understanding the rhythms of the past enables Will to recognize the vexing issues and violent potentiality of the present; with the spectre of the AIDS epidemic looming on the not-so-distant horizon, Will's chimerical vision of a gay paradise at the Corinthian will surely endure greater challenges in the very near future. Reading *The Swimming-Pool Library* in terms of cultural studies' interpretive machinery reveals the cultural interconnectedness that we all share with our precursors, as well as the manner in which our seemingly secure lives are always susceptible to social schism and change. As Richard Dellamora observes in *Apocalyptic Overtures: Sexual Politics and the Sense of an Ending* (1994), Hollinghurst's novel highlights the simultaneously destructive and revelatory nature of cultural apocalypse, particularly in terms of the 'motivated absences that mark the history of gay existence' (*S-P L*, 191).

Peter Greenaway's controversial film *Prospero's Books* (1991) performs a similar, culturally subversive role in the director's dramatic and experimental retelling of *The Tempest*. Known for its nudity, stunning visual imagery and opaque narrative design, Greenaway's film explodes our understanding of Shakespeare's play by narrating the story of *The Tempest* via the pages of Prospero's twenty-four cherished books – a collection of literature that ranges from the study of bestiaries and cosmographies to atlases and books of colours, love, pornography and architecture. Greenaway films the pages of the books themselves – their typography, calligraphy and illustrations – in luminous detail. A radical cultural and literary act in its own right, Greenaway's revision of Shakespeare's celebrated text directs our attention decidedly away from the characters' well-known interpersonal conflicts in *The Tempest* and toward the epistemology – and knowledge's ever-shifting nature – that undergirds the play's narrative. By telling his story from the literal point of view of the texts themselves, Greenaway reminds us, as Hollinghurst does in *The Swimming-Pool Library*, that culture (and our understanding of it in relation to ourselves) is inevitably contingent upon the knowledge and the whimsy of social perspective, notions of difference and historicity.

QUESTIONS FOR FURTHER CONSIDERATION

1. How do the notions of 'cultural capital' and 'cultural materialism' intersect with your understanding of literature and its political and cultural import? How does literature, in fact, effect meaningful social and ideological change?

2. Elizabeth Fox-Genovese writes that 'scholars have succeeded in imaginatively reclaiming the voices, representations, productions, and values of the oppressed and excluded, and they have demonstrated the cultural strength and richness of those who have been ignored.' In light of Fox-Genovese's remarks, consider the ways in which cultural studies as a theoretical and intellectual movement has impacted the literary canon.

3. Consider the nature of multiculturalism's theoretical, social, political and cultural agenda. How has this movement manifested itself in the United States, the United Kingdom and elsewhere? Has multiculturalism successfully achieved its institutional and ideological aims?

4. How does a reading of Alan Hollinghurst's *The Swimming-Pool Library* assist us in understanding the larger context of contemporary culture – British, American or otherwise?

5. Discuss the significance of 1983 as the temporal setting of Hollinghurst's novel. What issues regarding the early 1980s as a historical moment impinge upon (and perhaps help to shape) the lives of the characters in *The Swimming-Pool Library*?

6. Peter Greenaway's *Prospero's Books* met with considerable controversy when it was released in 1991. Critics and audiences alike were puzzled by the confusing array of texts and the nudity in the film. While potentially bewildering for audiences, how do these filmic effects help us to understand the cultural aspects of Shakespeare's *The Tempest*? What are the possible intersections, culturally, between nudity, sexuality, technology, aesthetics, and pornography?

ANNOTATED BIBLIOGRAPHY

Bourke, Joanna. *Working-Class Cultures in Britain, 1890–1960: Gender, Class, and Ethnicity.* London, 1994.
    Drawing upon a variety of historical approaches and methods, Bourke examines the construction of class within the intimate contexts of the body, the home, the marketplace and the nation in order to address the subjective identity of the working class in Britain through seven decades of intense social, cultural and economic change. In addition to arguing that class essentially functions as a social and cultural rather than an institutional or political phenomenon, Bourke explores the significant roles of gender and ethnicity and our conceptions of class. Bourke supplements her survey with discussion about the manner in which historians use evidence to understand change, as well as with several useful chronologies, statistics and tables of interest to cultural and literary critics alike.

Chambers, Iain. *Migrancy, Culture, Identity*. London, 1994.

Chambers explores the ways in which our senses of place and identity shift as we traverse myriad languages, worlds and histories. In addition to examining the uncharted impact of cultural diversity on contemporary society, Chambers discusses the 'realistic' eye of social commentary, the 'scientific' approach of the cultural anthropologist and the critical distance of the historian. Chambers analyses the disturbance and dislocation of history, culture and identity, while also investigating the manner in which migration, marginality and homelessness undermine our shared sense of cultural identity by disrupting our faith in linear progress and rational thinking.

During, Simon, ed. *The Cultural Studies Reader*. London, 1993.

The wide range of essays collected in During's volume provide a useful introduction to cultural studies. In addition to featuring selections by such influential voices as Roland Barthes, Theodor Adorno, Jean-François Lyotard, Cornel West, Eve Kosofsky Sedgwick, Michel Foucault, Raymond Williams and Meaghan Morris, among others, During's volume impinges upon a vast array of topics, from sports to postmodernism, from museums to supermarkets, and from gay and lesbian literature to popular music. During's introduction to cultural studies investigates the history and development of the discipline, as well as its intersections with such contemporary issues as postcolonialism, globalization and multiculturalism.

Easthope, Antony. *Literary into Cultural Studies*. London, 1991.

Easthope examines the necessary opposition in modern literary studies between 'high' and 'low' forms of culture, between canonical literary texts and popular culture. In addition to discussing the theory and culture wars of the 1970s and the 1980s, and particularly the advent of structuralist and poststructuralist theory, Easthope investigates the ways which literary critics attempt to transform the oppositional nature of this relationship. Easthope argues that cultural studies must delineate an interpretative methodology for its analysis of canonical and popular texts. Drawing upon a host of competing theories – including cultural studies, new historicism and cultural materialism – Easthope offers a wide range of cultural materialist readings, from analyses of Conrad's *Heart of Darkness* to Edgar Rice Burroughs's *Tarzan of the Apes*, among other works.

Smithson, Isaiah and Nancy Ruff, eds. *English Studies/Culture Studies: Institutionalizing Dissent*. Urbana, IL, 1994.

The essays in Smithson and Ruff's collection investigate cultural studies' role as a mechanism for registering dissent and for effecting social change. In addition to addressing a wide range of topics from Native-American cultural studies and autobiography to curricular reform and the institutionalization of English literature, the selections in Smithson and Ruff's volume provide valuable insights into the future of cultural studies and the political hurdles that confront the discipline as the millennium approaches. Smithson's introduction offers a useful overview of the contemporary state of cultural studies and affords attention to such issues as multicultural pedagogy and literary theory's approach to ethnicity and gender studies.

SUPPLEMENTARY BIBLIOGRAPHY

Bloom, Allan. *The Closing of the American Mind: How Higher Education Has Failed Democracy and Impoverished the Souls of Today's Students*. New York, 1987.

Bové, Paul. 'Should Cultural Studies Take Literature Seriously?', *Critical Quarterly*, 39, 1997.

Boyd, Todd. *Am I Black Enough for You?: Popular Culture from the 'Hood and Beyond*. Bloomington, IN, 1997.

Cheney, Lynne V. *Telling the Truth: Why Our Culture and Our Country Have Stopped Making Sense – and What We Can Do about It*. New York, 1995.

Cohen, Tom. *Ideology and Inscription: 'Cultural Studies' after Benjamin, de Man and Bakhtin*. Cambridge, 1998.

Diawara, Manthia. 'Cultural Studies/Black Studies', in *Borders, Boundaries, and Frames: Essays in Cultural Criticism and Cultural Studies*, ed. Mae G. Henderson. New York, 1995.

D'Souza, Dinesh. *Illiberal Education: The Politics of Race and Sex on Campus*. New York, 1991.

Ecker, Gisela. 'Cultural Studies and Feminism', *Journal for the Study of British Culture*, 1, 1994.

Fox-Genovese, Elizabeth. 'Between Individualism and Fragmentation: American Culture and the New Literary Studies of Race and Gender', *American Quarterly*, 42, 1990.

Fuss, Diana, ed. *Human All Too Human*. New York, 1996.

Gates, Henry Louis, Jr. 'Whose Canon Is It, Anyway?', in *Debating P.C.: The Controversy over Political Correctness on College Campuses*, ed. Paul Berman. New York, 1992.

Gordon, Avery F. *Ghostly Matters: Haunting and the Sociological Imagination*. Minneapolis, MN, 1997.

Halberstam, Judith, and Ira Livingston, eds. *Posthuman Bodies*. Bloomington, IN, 1995.

Hall, Stuart. *Critical Dialogues in Cultural Studies*, eds David Morley and Kuan-Hsing Chen. London, 1996.

Hirsch, Marianne. *Family Frames: Photography, Narrative, and Postmemory*. Cambridge, MA, 1997.

Hoggart, Richard. *The Uses of Literacy: Aspects of Working-Class Life, with Special Reference to Publications and Entertainments*. London, 1957.

Kellner, Douglas. *Media Culture: Cultural Studies, Identity, and Politics between the Modern and the Postmodern*. London, 1995.

Kimball, Roger. *Tenured Radicals: How Politics Has Corrupted Higher Education*. New York, 1990.

Kincaid, James R. *Erotic Innocence: The Culture of Child Molesting*. Durham, NC, 1998.

Miller, J. Hillis. *The Ethics of Reading: Kant, de Man, Eliot, Trollope, James, and Benjamin*. New York, 1987.

————. 'Is There an Ethics of Reading?', in *Reading Narrative: Form, Ethics, Ideology*, ed. James Phelan. Columbus, OH, 1988.

————. *Versions of Pygmalion*. Cambridge, MA, 1990.

Modleski, Tania. *Feminism without Women: Culture and Criticism in a 'Postfeminist' Age*. London, 1991.

Nussbaum, Martha C. *Cultivating Humanity: A Classical Defense of Reform in Liberal Education*. Cambridge, 1997.

Regan, Stephen, ed. *The Politics of Pleasure: Aesthetics and Cultural Theory*. Bristol, PA, 1992.

Sinfield, Alan. *Literature, Culture, and Politics in Postwar Britain*. Berkeley, CA, 1989.

Smith, Anna Marie. *New Right Discourse on Race and Sexuality: Britain, 1968–1980*. Cambridge, 1994.

Sykes, Charles J. *ProfScam: Professors and the Demise of Higher Education*. Washington, DC, 1988.

Thompson, E. P. *The Making of the English Working Class*. New York, 1964.

Williams, Jeffrey. 'Renegotiating the Pedagogical Contract', in *Class Issues: Pedagogy, Cultural Studies, and the Public Sphere*, ed. Amitava Kumar. New York, 1997.

Williams, Raymond. *Marxism and Literature*. Oxford, 1977.

————. *Culture and Society: 1780–1950*. New York, 1983.

OTHER WORKS CITED

Bennington, Geoffrey. 'Inter', in *Post-Theory: New Directions in Criticism*, eds. Martin McQuillan, Graeme MacDonald, Robin Purves and Stephen Thompson. Edinburgh, 1999.

Dellamora, Richard. *Apocalyptic Overtures: Sexual Politics and the Sense of an Ending.* New Brunswick, NJ, 1994.

Greenaway, Peter, dir. *Prospero's Books.* Miramax, 1991.

Leavis, F. R. *The Great Tradition.* Harmondsworth, 1948.

Stimpson, Catherine R. 'Not Every Age Has Its Pleasures', *New York Times Book Review*, 9 October 1988.

14

POSTMODERNISM AND POSTMODERNITY: LITERATURE, CRITICISM, PHILOSOPHY, CULTURE

Arkady Plotnitsky

THE POSTMODERNIST AND THE POSTMODERN: THE CONCEPTS

The critical denominations 'postmodernist' and 'postmodern' appear to be even more persistently (self-)diverging in their meaning and reference than other key denominations, such as deconstructive or poststructuralist, defining the contemporary – 'postmodern' – theoretical and cultural scene. Both taking advantage of and, for the moment (it will re-emerge immediately), suppressing this divergence, I shall use the term 'postmodern*ist*' to designate a certain view or spectrum of views of such divergence, which pertains to other terms or concepts and, with regard to some of these views, to all conceivable terms and concepts. *At stake* in such views is the potentially radical character of this divergence: which is, that it is uncontainable by any means that either is or ever can be available to us – at least as a question, since, even among 'postmodernist' theories, not all subscribe to the most radical version of this understanding. This understanding thus concerns the very nature of our theoretical knowledge (and, to some degree, all our knowledge) and, hence, may be seen as epistemological. I shall also refer by 'postmodernist' to cultural (theoretical, artistic, literary and other) practices defined by or closely linked to such views. By contrast, I shall use the terms 'postmodern' and 'postmodernity' as designating the culture in which such views emerge and which they describe and sometimes shape, in particular the culture of the last three decades or so of the twentieth century. Thus, 'postmodernist' and 'postmodernism' will be used here primarily as (meta)theoretical, (meta)critical or (meta)aesthetic categories (one can also speak of postmodernist science or politics), largely defined by epistemological considerations, including those pertaining to our understanding of postmodernism and postmodernity themselves. 'Postmodern' or 'postmodernity' will be used as a broad cultural-historical category designating the culture or the world that we inhabit, which is responsible for postmodernism and, reciprocally, shaped by it.

The view of postmodernism and postmodernity here adopted may, then, itself be seen as *a* postmodernist view, but, according to this view and by definition, not as *the* postmodernist view. First, from this perspective, the general denominative and conceptual divergence invoked above makes an assignment of *the* postmodernist or *the* postmodern ultimately impossible. One can easily see how both terms fluctuate and mix in our culture so as to designate various aspects of postmodern culture, some of which are quite different from what is designated as postmodern and postmodernist here; the present understanding aims take into account, and account for, this multiplicity. Secondly, there are, as mentioned, different conceptions of the *character* of such denominative multiplicities operative on the current theoretical scene and different terms that designate them, and one should exercise some caution in grouping them all as postmodern(ist). Among the better-known examples are *heterogeneity* or *heterology* (Georges Bataille), *incommensurability* (Thomas Kuhn, Paul Feyerabend, Jean-François Lyotard), *difference* (Gilles Deleuze), and *différance* or/as *dissemination* (Jacques Derrida). According to the more radical among these, which this essay follows, no term or concept can define or govern uniquely the multiplicity/ies such as the one in question here. They exceed, overflow, any given denomination, conception and so forth. Hence, aspects (other than epistemological) – cultural, historical or political – of postmodernism and postmodernity become necessary for an adequate understanding of both. These denominations and, in turn, their various meanings and referents become part of the overall architecture of the concept of the postmodern(ist) or (and as a consequence of) the general concept of the multiple in question. Still other conceptions of the postmodern and the postmodernist can enter one's analysis and become locally indispensable. The epistemology here in question remains crucial, however, in particular as it concerns the radical nature of the multiple and the heterogeneous, as against other concepts operative on the postmodern scene (which may seem similar or even equivalent, but which are different). At the same time, this multiplicity is defined by the interactive or interactively heterogeneous, and heterogeneously interactive, dynamics of the relationships between different elements or attributes comprising it (such as 'theoretical', 'cultural', 'political', 'aesthetic' and so forth), rather than by the absolute heterogeneity of such elements and attributes.

It does not follow that, in view of this multiplicity, the terms 'postmodern' or 'postmodernist' become merely convenient clichés or designate just about everything in our culture and lose their meaning altogether, as some suggest (often meaning 'everything bad' in it). While caution is justified, the last claim is not or need not be the case, and I do not think is the case. To mean many things need not mean to mean everything. Darwin's evolutionary theory and theories of relativity and quantum physics have changed mostly everything in our understanding of life and nature (at least for some of us); everything became 'evolutionary' and 'quantum', but that does not mean that the terms 'evolution' and 'quantum' are meaningless. Indeed there is a great deal more specificity to 'postmodern' and related denominations than is often argued. The resistance to specificity is mobilized sometimes in order to avoid confronting the postmo-dern(ist) features of contemporary culture or, indeed, the world and thought. In other words, the idea of the 'postmodern' designates a different way of living in, perceiving and understanding the world, or different *ways* of doing so. To be sure (this is hardly surprising), some of the deployments of the term, are superficial and, sometimes, unfortunate as with (and sometimes *together with*) the terms 'evolutionary' and 'quantum'. Others, however, are not only viable, but also effective and productive, especially once properly analytically defined.

However, and to reiterate, the terms in question may not be absolutely indispensable for our understanding of culture or 'postmodernist' theory; for, as I have indicated and as I will explain below, one of the key implications (primarily due to Nietzsche and Derrida) of the epistemology to be presented here is that there are no absolutely indispensable terms. There are no final or unique concepts or names, by and on which we like to capitalize, whether old (Being, for example) or new, such as 'Postmodern'. Such master words or concepts cannot, in practice and in principle, contain the multiplicities which they aim to contain, beginning with their own meaning and definition. This understanding will inflect the present discussion of the postmodernist/postmo-dern throughout. So, Deleuze or Derrida may be better characterized as 'postmodernist' than they realize, while the more overtly 'postmodernist' Lyotard or Fredric Jameson may not always be seen effectively as the post-modernists they appear to some of us, or, indeed, to themselves. It is true, however, that, while these thinkers are significant for postmodernism, some of the figures here mentioned, including those who pursue the radical epistemology with regard to its limits, may not be easily associated with it and sometimes resist this association. Arguably the main reason for this resistance is that these thinkers appear to associate the term with much that is different and sometimes in conflict with their ideas, including those (according to this view) misappro-priated by (some versions of) postmodernism itself, and, I should add, for reasons that are sometimes different from the epistemological ones in question here. There are good reasons for this view and for the sometimes sharp criticism of (some) postmodernism on the part of those in question. Accordingly, the application of the term 'postmodernist' to the ideas of the thinkers in question requires considerable caution, which is not always exercised by commentators. Such caution is not out of place. I would also argue that some of these thinkers do not always sufficiently grasp certain aspects of postmodernist thought and culture, including the postmodernist deployment or implications of their own ideas, especially when this deployment works against the grain of their thought. The situation is hardly surprising and is not a matter of fallacy or incoherence of thought on the part of these thinkers. Instead it appears to be a de-coherence – a structural split from a single or totalizing wholeness – proper to the radical, irreducible heterogeneity of the landscape of postmodernism and postmodernity, as here considered. Thus, while complex and ambivalent (indeed differences and proximities are always determinable), the connections between these figures and postmodernism are more logical or even inevitable than arbitrary.

Now, in general, there are always provisionally containable denominations and determinations: we would not be able to work with any theory or, indeed, to think and live without such key terms. Ultimately, however, all denominative, determinative or conceptual pluralities are and have always been uncontainable. Moreover, no given term or concept is uniquely determinable or determining with respect to that to which it applies. Most significant intellectual projects either before or after Plato recognize and take into account the question of plurality (heterogeneity, difference and so forth) in the practice of knowledge and culture. The question whether this plurality is containable or, as in the (radical) postmodernist view, uncontainable in principle by any means that either is or will ever be available to us, is what confronts us. Part of the postmodernist (in the present definition) critical project is to offer a critique or, in the wake of Derrida's work, specifically a deconstruction of such projects, from Plato to Hegel to Heidegger (in certain projects at least, since these texts can be read as being closer, say, to Derrida's own work). The difference defining the postmodernist view, from other critical or philosophical practices, is in the recognition or, at least, a much greater awareness of the uncontainability or instability of conceptual denominations, and the subsequent theoretical engagement with this knowledge and putting it into practice in the postmodern world and culture. Between the juxtaposition of the 'modern' and 'postmodern' identified by Lyotard there is also an accompanying difference of attitude toward this 'loss' of containability of knowledge and culture, recognized in particular in the modern(ist) 'nostalgia' for the lost realm or, at least, in the possibility of locating the unity or harmony of knowledge and culture. Arguably this modern(ist) 'nostalgia is also seen in the desire for the proper word and the unique name, evidenced in terms such as Being or Modern and Postmodern, as opposed to the postmodern(ist) affirmation or even celebration of this loss, often correctly linked to Nietzsche.

It does not follow, however, as some commentators have argued, that the difference here (especially between the modern and the postmodern, the modernist and postmodernist) is defined only as, or perhaps even primarily by, this (self-) awareness or attitude, often in conjunction with the lack of nostalgia, as just indicated. (A prominent example of this argument is found in Linda Hutcheon's works (1988, 1993), both of which are indebted on this point to Jean-François Lyotard's original and rather more subtle argument in *The Postmodern Condition* (1984), which I shall consider extensively below.)

The nature of knowledge and epistemological concerns are often different as well, from Nietzsche on, especially, as will be seen, insofar as the irreducible multiplicity in question in postmodernist epistemology relates to a certain equally irreducible unknowable, ultimately unknowable *even as (absolutely) unknowable*, and to several correlative concepts. Two of these are of particular and immediate significance both for this epistemology and for the contemporary debates concerning it. The first is that of *reality* or rather the lack thereof in any sense hitherto available or perhaps even conceivable. The second is the radical concept of *chance*. In speaking of these concepts in the context of addressing the postmodern and postmodernism, one should stress again not postmodernism in the singular, but rather *some* (I would argue, more radical) versions of postmodernist epistemology, with regard to the point that, in all historical rigour, we may not quite speak of this epistemology as postmodernist if we carefully consider who in fact adheres to and deploys it and how it is deployed.

For example, as I shall suggest here, such key theorists of postmodernism as Jameson or even Lyotard (a more radical thinker), or even most of their followers, do not engage with this epistemology, even though they do offer critiques of causality and reality, and deploy certain concepts of the unknowable, the unrepresentable, the inaccessible and so forth. The difference is, again, in the nature or structure, the architecture, of these concepts, which, as I have argued, defines the work of such thinkers as Nietzsche, Bataille, Blanchot, Derrida and de Man. Their thought may be as much juxtaposed to some forms of postmodernism as it is linked to others epistemologically, which I argue are more radical and effective. For that reason, I shall give this epistemology yet another name, 'nonclassical', which I shall explain below. By contrast, by these criteria, the irreducibility of the multiple, as here considered, may be seen as more radically postmodernist. This may be argued, even though, as I have suggested, the postmodern/postmodernist multiplicity is an effect of a certain dynamics which, in order to be treated adequately (it may not be ultimately possible to describe it), requires the radical epistemology of the unknowable, as just explained, which the avowed theorists of the postmodern sense (Lyotard, Jameson) sometimes invoke but do not quite explore to the radical limit of such a concept. Indeed, if one is willing to retain, as I shall do here, the term 'postmodernist' in this context, it is this enigmatic link between the irreducible loss and the irreducible and ever multiplying (with ever great acceleration in the postmodern world) plurality of knowledge that defines postmodernist epistemology in its arguably most radical, but also most effective form. At the very least, I would argue that this epistemology enables a more effective understanding of both the postmodern world and postmodernist endeavours, including those directed toward understanding this world, the world which, for better or worse, we inhabit or, at least (for some of us live elsewhere), that we (or, again, some of us) want to understand.

POSTMODERNIST EPISTEMOLOGY AND POSTMODERN CULTURE

With these considerations in mind, I shall here address five analytically indispensable aspects of postmodernism and postmodernity – the epistemological, the cultural, the political, the historical-periodical and the aesthetic – and/in their postmodern, interactively heterogeneous and heterogeneously interactive relationships. Building upon the preceding discussion, I shall centre my argument around epistemological postmodernism, or postmodernist epistemology, even though, as I have said, other dimensions of postmodernism and postmodernity, such as those just mentioned, unavoidably enter the discussion throughout and, equally unavoidably, sometimes take centre stage. My point of departure and my main focus is the work of Jean-François Lyotard, arguably the most significant philosopher of postmodernism and postmodernity, in his *The Postmodern Condition: A Report on Knowledge* (originally published in French in 1979 and in English in 1984), with reference to related writings. Lyotard's book, along with his debate with Jürgen Habermas, initiated the discussion concerning postmodernism during the last two decades and has served as a key reference in most discussions of the subject. It is true that Fredric Jameson's subsequent (and more politico-economically oriented) *Postmodernism, or the Cultural Logic of Late Capitalism*, first as an essay (1985) and then as a book (1991), has become nearly as prominent in recent years. This work, however, is itself crucially indebted to Lyotard, and may indeed be seen as extending primarily from Jameson's 'Foreword' to the English translation of *The Postmodern Condition* (Lyotard, 1984: vii–xxii).[1]

As Lyotard's title, '*the* postmodern condition', and subtitle, 'a report on *knowledge*', jointly indicate, and in accordance with the analysis given above, our understanding of postmodernism and postmodernity appears to be indissociable from epistemological considerations and a particular (postmodernist) concept – or cluster of concepts – of knowledge and cognition, the terms to which Lyotard appeals throughout the book. However, as this title equally points out, these concepts or, one might say, postmodern(ist) ideologies of knowledge reciprocally shape and are shaped by postmodern cultural practices. This reciprocity is itself postmodern and, accordingly, this view of knowledge postmodernist, especially once they are given other postmodernist features, as they are in Lyotard and elsewhere in postmodernist writings. Arguably, the most significantly postmodern(ist) feature among them is the multiple – heterogeneously interactive and interactively heterogeneous – character of the relationships between knowledge and culture, and the irreducible – heterogeneously interactive and interactively heterogeneous – multiplicity of elements constituting each, assuming that we can so separate them in the first place. The very grammar of Lyotard's title is worth paying attention to. The book is 'a report on knowledge' (hence, again, the epistemological nature of it) and a particular – the postmodern – condition of it and the culture that conditions it (keeping in mind the reciprocity of knowledge and culture, just indicated) at a particular point or rather interval of history, say from the 1960s to the present and, perhaps, beyond. (This dating requires qualification, to be offered below, but is pertinent and significant.) This condition has especially to do with the revolution, ultimately the digital revolution, in the processing and dissemination of information, seen as analogous to and, to some degree, an extension of the industrial revolution, which, linked to capitalism, in large measure defined the condition of 'modernity'. However, the field of forces responsible for the condition of postmodernity is much richer and far more complex. The key elements responsible for this condition include the following factors, which are interrelated and mutually conditioning in a postmodern fashion. Accordingly, this list must be seen as 'postmodernly' horizontal, network-like, rather than vertical, hierarchical:

1. A different manifestation (from that of 'modernity') of the legitimation and delegitimation of knowledge, including mathematical and scientific knowledge, seen by modernity as paradigmatic, in particular in terms of paralogy (a form of strategic legitimation), rather than merely by a correspondence to truth (of logic or of experiment) and by performance.

2. The emergence and development of new areas of mathematics and science (mathematical logic, topology, quantum physics, chaos theory and catastrophe theory, and post-Darwinian biology and genetics, among them), which are different – more postmodernist – both in the character of their practice and in what they tell us about physical nature or the human mind.

3. New technologies, especially those such as digital technology, enabling new forms of information processing and communication, in particular the role of television and the Internet, or the (all-pervasive) media culture in general.

4. The (related) globalization and geopoliticization of political, economic and cultural connections, and of the distribution of (global) capital.

5. A radical restructuring of spatio-temporal continua, or discontinuities of culture and human life, in part by shifting the (modern) centring on time to the (postmodern) emphasis on space.

6. A reorganization of the physical and cultural space of the postmodern urban environment, from single buildings to cities as a whole.

7. The accelerating proliferation of cultural practices initiated and defined by what was previously seen as marginal groups, and accompanying reconsiderations of such categories as ethnicity, gender, sexuality and so forth.

8. The dismantling of colonialism and, during the postmodern period, even of certain forms of postcolonialism, and a more general economic, cultural and political multi-centring of the global geopolitical space.

9. A radical reorganization of the European political landscape and the impact of this reorganization in the areas described above.

10. The development in Europe, Japan and the US of the post-industrial society, in which national economies have shifted from manufacturing to information and services bases, alongside the rise of transnational corporations and the interconnected global economy.

11. The emergence of new forms of cultural production in literature, film, art, music, dance, architecture and television, in part correlative to politico-economic transformations ('the cultural logic of late capitalism'), and in part relatively independent of them, and arising in view of other forces operative in the postmodern environment.

12. A different political configuration of justice – the ultimate agenda of Lyotard's book and his key subsequent works, such as *Just Gaming* [*Au Juste*] (with Jean-Loup Thébaud) and *The Differend*, in which he argues that, far from becoming an outmoded category under postmodernism, justice may be more conducive to the postmodern condition than under modernity (Lyotard, 1984, 66–67).

This list indicates a number of positive or neutral (if any neutrality is possible here) postmodern developments, and some new hope, such as that for greater justice. One can, however, also think of problems accompanying these developments, such as new forms of exploitation and conflict arising in this postmodern geopolitical world (the former Yugoslavia or Rwanda offer perhaps the most tragic examples), or such problems as the destruction of the environment, the intolerable medical conditions in much of the world, world hunger and the international drug traffic. (On these issues, see Jacques Derrida, 1994.) The question marks accompanying hopes loom large as well. Some of the developments listed have reached their truly postmodern measure, or even emerged, since the appearance of Lyotard's book about two decades ago, and Lyotard deserves credit for envisioning these developments and their significance.

The key new attitude of this culture, determined by and, again, reciprocally determining these conditions is, for Lyotard, its incredulity toward (culturally uniquely defining) 'grand narratives' and (narratively all-comprehending) 'meta-narratives'. Such narratives have sought to explain the world through particular legitimating historical or political teleologies and, as such, have defined (European) modernity, roughly, from the Enlightenment or early Renaissance (or, at least, what modernity saw as such). Lyotard thus sees modernity as the Enlightenment (both in its historical and in its broader conceptual sense) and, also, as the culmination of Enlightenment thought. This genealogy entails other key determinations of modernity, specifically politico-economic ones (such as those defined by the scientific and industrial revolutions), since the grand narratives involved have much earlier genealogies. Indeed they are epic, and hence Homeric, narratives, a point made by Theodor Adorno and Max Horkheimer in their *Dialectic of Enlightenment* by linking the epistemology and cultural practice of the Enlightenment to *The Odyssey* (Adorno and Horkheimer, 1990).

It is through the question of narrative that Lyotard initially defines the postmodern in the book (the emphasis shifts in his later works, or even in the book itself as it proceeds). This incredulity or, more accurately, the conditions of its possibility, may be shown to be correlative to or derivative from the more general postmodernist epistemology of the multiple, as outlined above. Proceeding via Wittgenstein, Lyotard pursues this epistemology through the concept of 'heterogeneous language games' and its extensions, most especially his concept of 'differend', which are crucial to his subsequent ethico-political works extending *The Postmodern Condition*, such as *Just Gaming* and *The Differend*. Proceeding from this concept, Lyotard's critique of consensus, specifically in the context of justice, which Lyotard argues (against Habermas) need not depend on consensus, is one of the most striking features of *The Postmodern Condition* (Lyotard, 1984, 66–7) and of all these works. I think Lyotard is quite right on consensus as concerns its role in securing justice (the historical record is hardly impressive). His argument or hope for justice under the postmodern condition may be less compelling. Grand and meta-narratives may no longer govern (and in truth have never governed, only claimed to govern) the plurality of narratives deployed by culture, and must at best be rescaled to local narratives within this plurality. Under the postmodern condition(s) narrative itself becomes a limited category, even though postmodernist theories have shown that it has played a much greater role in both historical or theoretical (including mathematical and scientific) knowledge than has been previously recognized or acknowledged.

More generally, from the postmodernist perspective, the cultural determination of knowledge is irreducible. By the same token, we must acknowledge that knowledge cannot be subsumed absolutely even in the name of postmodernism, as is sometimes (wrongly) argued. In other words, there is no such a thing as knowledge *qua* knowledge, knowledge as such, as Plato was perhaps first to intimate in *Theaetetus*. There is an irreducible and irreducibly entangled reciprocity between epistemology and culture, and this reciprocity is part of postmodern epistemology, even though, as the reference to Plato would suggest, it has a much earlier (and multiple) genealogy. Culture both defines epistemology and is defined by epistemology, by the particular conditions of knowledge – its character, forms and methods, ways of acquiring and processing, or possessing, and so forth. This argument applies to every aspect of postmodern culture listed above. In particular, while they emerge from and through particular instances of modern and postmodern culture, postmodernist epistemology and the radical critique of previous forms of knowledge have fundamentally transformed our culture. (For a perspective proceeding from the scientific revolution, see Latour, 1993.) Lyotard sees 'postmodern' as 'the state of our culture following the transformations which, since the end of the nineteenth century, have altered the game rules for science, literature, and the arts', and 'postmodern knowledge . . . [as] . . . refin[ing] our sensitivity to differences and reinforc[ing] our ability to tolerate the incommensurable'; that is, as reciprocally transforming our culture (Lyotard, 1984, xxiii, xxv; Lyotard's reference to 'game rules' proceeds via Wittgenstein's definition: 'each of the varieties of utterance can be defined in terms of rules specifying their properties and the uses to which they can be put': Lyotard, 1984, 10).

This reciprocity is sometimes linked to the so-called constructivist (social, cultural or other) understanding of knowledge prominent in a variety of fields, in particular in certain theories of scientific knowledge, in the wake of Thomas Kuhn's and Paul Feyerabend's work (both are important references for Lyotard). This link is justified beyond the areas just indicated, for example in the case of certain postmodernist artistic practices of the 1980–90s, shaped by their constructivist cultural-political concerns. Postmodernism is constructivism or, more accurately (a crucial qualification), has an irreducible constructivist component. Constructivist theories or artistic practices just mentioned often see the situation in question in terms of the culture (social, political and so forth) determination of knowledge, rather than in terms of interactive reciprocity (cf. Latour's critique of social constructivism in *We Have Never Been Modern*). The latter is ultimately a more radical view, especially if coupled to the postmodernist epistemology as understood here, which entails and enacts a more radical critique and dislocation (which is not to say abandonment) of traditional views of knowledge, truth, meaning, representation, interpretation, communication and so on. Thus understood, postmodernism is philosophically closer to much of poststructuralism. There is a degree of (interactive) heterogeneity here as well, for example among the views of different figures associated (which, again, is not the same as being) or associating themselves with postmodernist thought, such as Lyotard, Deleuze, Foucault and Derrida, or, earlier, Bataille and Nietzsche. While centring my discussion around Lyotard, I shall now further delineate radical postmodernist epistemology, by considering and, sometimes, combining the views of these and several other figures. For, as I said earlier, the most radical form of this epistemology appears to exceed the limits of Lyotard's theories and others which are avowedly postmodernist, most particularly as concerns the radical character of the unknowable and the unrepresentable, or indeed that which is inaccessible by any means. And yet (there is, as will be seen, no paradox here), at the same time the unknowable, the unrepresentable, the inaccessible accompany and condition all possible knowledge, representation, access, including – and in particular – their ultimately equally irreducible heterogeneity and interaction, which may be seen as more properly postmodern(ist). Accordingly, it may not be coincidental that while Lyotard offers what is arguably his most crucial epistemological characterization of the postmodern in terms of loss in representation in his (1983) essay 'Answering the Question: What is Postmodernism?' (Lyotard, 1984, 71–82), the set-up is that of postmodern(ist) epistemological and/as cultural multiplicity, and the critique of the Enlightenment, via his confrontation with Habermas. It may be worth commenting upon this set-up here, before considering Lyotard's epistemology of the loss in representation. Lyotard writes:

> Jürgen Habermas . . . thinks that if modernity has failed, it is in allowing the totality of life to be splintered into independent specialties which are left to the narrow competence of experts, while the concrete individual experiences 'desublimated meaning' and 'destructured form', not as a liberation but in the mode of the immense *ennui* which Baudelaire described over a century ago.
>
> . . . What Habermas requires from the arts and the experiences they provide is, in short, to bridge the gap between cognitive, ethical, and political discourses, thus opening the way to a unity of experience.
>
> My question is to determine what sort of unity Habermas has in mind. Is the aim of the project of modernity the constitution of socio-cultural unity within which all the elements of daily life and of thought would take their places as in an organic whole? Or does the passage that has to be charted between heterogeneous language games – those of cognition, of ethics, of politics – belong to a different order from that? And if so, would it be capable of effecting a real synthesis between them?
>
> The first hypothesis, of a Hegelian inspiration, does not challenge the notion of a dialectically totalizing *experience*, the second is closer to the spirit of Kant's *Critique of Judgement*; but must be submitted, like the *Critique*, to that severe re-examination which postmodernity imposes on the thought of the Enlightenment, on the idea of the unitary end of history and of a subject. (Lyotard, 1984, 72–3)

Indeed, as we have seen, the postmodern, or modern, heterogeneity here in question invades equally each area invoked by Lyotard (cognition, politics, ethics), as it does other fields of human knowledge and practice, and the relationships between them. It is thus in Kant and 'that aesthetic of the sublime', in which '*modern* art (including literature) and the logic of *avant-garde* finds its axioms' (Lyotard, 1984, 77). The displacement of categories is of some interest here, and, historically speaking, it is not unjustified on Lyotard's part, but would require a separate discussion. It is of more interest and significance that Lyotard's definition of the postmodern in terms of the unrepresentable is offered primarily in the aesthetic context and specifically to the postmodern(ist) in art, which art itself is, as I shall discuss later, the art of modernism and, in some cases, locatable much earlier by most standard definitions (Cézanne, Duchamp, Picasso, Malevitch, Mallarmé and Joyce, but also Montaigne, are among the key examples). For the moment however, let me make two points: first, the Kantian sublime and modernist/avant-garde art offer both examples and models for the postmodernist epistemology (on both scores, heterogeneity and the relation to the unrepresentable), and these are for Lyotard arguably uniquely significant and conjoined models. Secondly, following Kant's analytics of the sublime (where the same conjunction is found and is equally crucial), the epistemological, the aesthetic and the political are fundamentally linked in all of Lyotard's work on postmodern. His epistemological definition of the post-modern in the essay in question follows and depends on this programme. He writes:

> The postmodern would be that which, *in the modern*, puts forward the unrepresentable in presentation itself; that which denies itself the solace of good forms, the consensus of taste which would make it possible to share collectively the nostalgia for the unattainable; that which searches for new presentation, not in order to enjoy them but in order to impart a stronger sense of the unrepresentable. (Lyotard, 1984, 81)

My own main question here concerns the nature of this unrepresentability, the degree of this loss and this unattainability, where Lyotard and, perhaps, postmodernism by most definitions hitherto offered appear to stop short, in contrast to his view of the postmodern multiplicity and nostalgia, which are well justified. The concept and the positioning of the modern crucially depend on this point as well. It is clear, however, that in question and at stake here are complex and, ultimately, irreducible relationships (epistemological, cultural and histor-ical) between the modern and the postmodern, or the modernist and post-modernist in my terminology, to which Lyotard's (terminologically less stable) argument does not conform. Neither the modern nor the postmodern (neither the modernist nor the postmodernist) is possible without each other. On the one hand, the view transpiring here allows for and depends on the emergence of the postmodern (from) within the modern, and for the persistence or, indeed, indispensability of the modern in the postmodern. On the other hand, Lyotard famously argues that the modern is ultimately preceded by the postmodern, and indeed needs, first, to be postmodern in order to be modern: 'a work [of art] can become modern only if it is first postmodern' (Lyotard, 1984, 79). There is no contradiction between these two arguments, if we see – and, as I would argue, we must – the second contention more in its pre-logical than ontological or historical terms. For Lyotard adds: 'Postmodernism thus understood is not modernism as its end but in the nascent state, and this state is constant' (Lyotard, 1984, 79). It may be more accurate to say that a certain richer and more complex – 'richer' and 'stranger' – efficacious dynamics that (perhaps) manifests itself more radically in the postmodern produces both the modern and the postmodern, than to identify this dynamics with the postmodern, as Lyotard appears to do. (I am not sure that one can speak of a constant state here without further qualifications.) In this view, this dynamic itself is neither modern nor postmodern and ultimately not subject to any denomination, in accordance with the radical epistemology of the unrepresentable and the unknowable, which I shall discuss presently. As will be seen, Shakespeare's *The Tempest* (see I.ii, 402–4) may be read as an allegory of this situation in its most radical aspects. The situation itself would complicate all genealogies involved, since, on this view, the emergence of at least some postmodern(ist) elements can be pushed to the origin of modernism (an aesthetic category in need of further discussion, but usefully dated by Lyotard as extending from Baudelaire on, roughly) or modernity (the genealogy suggested by Lyotard as well), if not, however approximately, to the earliest conceivable moments of human history. This argument would not make such genealogies irrelevant, especially once they are properly qualified. For the particular postmodern(ist) or 'postmodern(ist) postmodern(ist)' manifestations or effects of these more complex and (epistemologically) more remote dynamics emerge under the postmodern conditions of a specific culture, such as, and in particular, the concern with the unrepresentable, the unknowable, the inaccessible and so forth, which is both modern(ist), say, from the Enlightenment on, and postmodern(ist).

As I mentioned earlier, one might argue – and many have – that modernism and postmodernism (at least in philosophy and the arts) do in fact share the same epistemology. The difference between them would then be seen in their attitude towards the loss in reality and representation – 'modern(ist) nostalgia' vs. 'postmodern(ist) enjoyment' – assuming for the moment that epistemology can ever remain quite the same once this or any attitude is changed. Lyotard appears to think so (the case is not altogether clear cut), in part, again, by arguing that both are linked to the view that 'the unrepresentable exists' and there occurs 'the withdrawal of the real', and linking both (the link well taken) to the aesthetics of the Kantian sublime (Lyotard, 1984, 78, 79, 81). In a proposition put forward in the essay 'Différance' (1968), which was well known to Lyotard and perhaps influenced his view, Derrida (rightly) gives a Nietzschean twist to an analogous, although not identical, view. Derrida does not speak in terms of postmodernism, which, as I've said, he shuns in general. Nor does he appear to see the resulting epistemology as unchanged (although some ascribe such a view to him). Finally, his argument is more philosophically comprehensive in extending the problematic to a more encompassing epistemological problematic. He writes: 'There will be no unique name, even if it were the name of Being [as in early Heidegger]', or any form of ontotheological determination, that is, that which is ultimately modelled on theology, positive or negative, as are many philosophies or ideologies of modernity, or even postmodernity, often in the name of these names. He also makes clear that this applies to his own terms, such as différance, even though these are not names in any sense hitherto available or, indeed, in any conceivable sense, but instead 'name' this impossibility of all unique and final names, which makes them irreducibly nontheological and nonontotheological. Derrida adds:

> And we must think this without *nostalgia*, that is, outside of the myth of a purely maternal or paternal language, a lost native country of thought. On the contrary, we must *affirm* this, in the sense in which Nietzsche puts affirmation into play [*jeu*], in a certain laughter and a certain step of a dance . . . [the] affirmation foreign to all dialectic, the other side of nostalgia. (Derrida, 1982, 27)

Is there, then, more to the difference between modern and postmodern knowledge and this view of knowledge than the affirmation of this loss and (they, once again, accompany each other) irreducible multiplicity – interactive heterogeneity and heterogeneous interactiveness – of postmodern(ist) knowledge? And beyond a more general knowledge/culture reciprocity described above, what would make one abandon nostalgia? There is no simple or single answer to these questions. I would argue, however, that, at least if we consider modernity within its more standard historical limits, say, from the Renaissance or even the eighteenth century to, say, the late nineteenth century, then one can think of a more radical conception of the unrepresentable (or the unknowable, the unattainable, the inaccessible and so forth). Naturally, such concepts have developed throughout the history of modernity, or even throughout much earlier moments in history. The concept reached its radical limit in and in the wake of Nietzsche's thought (still unsurpassed on this score) and is readable in the work of such figures as Heidegger, Levinas, Lacan, Bataille, Blanchot and Derrida, as well as certain scientific thinkers, in particular Niels Bohr. As I have argued, postmodern culture may be more effectively dated to a more recent period, roughly of the last two or three decades, on which point I shall comment below. There are also differences between the thought of these figures, as these concern the degree in which they approach the radical limits here in question.

I shall now outline this concept and then revisit the question of the modern and nostalgia. I shall do so via a juxtaposition different from that of 'modern' and 'postmodern'. I will first define, as I shall call them, classical theories. Then I shall define nonclassical theories, which conform to the radical epistemology in question, and consider the question of, respectively, classical and nonclassical chance from this perspective. Then I shall position the modern and the postmodern (specifically in Lyotard's sense) in relation to classical and nonclassical knowledge. The latter will be seen as indicative of the epistemological limits of both modern and, especially, postmodern knowledge. This scheme can be given a historical periodization (in part via Foucault's concepts of classical and modern knowledge), linked to Lyotard's historical scheme, since classical theories as here defined are, by and large, well correlated with what Foucault calls classical knowledge. As must be clear from the above remarks, while it may seen as succeeding classical thought and knowledge, modern thought, roughly from Galileo, Descartes and Newton on, is a more complex question (see, in particular, Foucault, 1994). The subject requires a separate consideration and will not be addressed here beyond necessary indications and certain key examples of such theories – classical, nonclassical, modern and postmodern – with reference in particular to certain scientific theories, to which Lyotard refers throughout his work on postmodernism as well.

I define classical theories as allowing, at least in principle, for the representation of all the objects with which such theories are concerned, and of the properties of these objects. Thus, classical physics is, or at least may be interpreted as, such a theory, and may be seen, as it is by Lyotard, as a primary, perhaps even *the* primary, model for most subsequent classical theories throughout modernity, Marx's political economy among them. Classical physics fully accounts, at least in principle, for its objects, such as, suitably idealized, material bodies (for example, planets or, up to a point, molecules) and their behaviour. The equations of classical mechanics allow us to know the past state or to predict the future state of the system under investigation at any point once we know it at a given point. Hence it is both causal (in terms of the nature of the processes it describes) and deterministic (as concerns our ability to make predictions concerning the behaviour of the systems it considers). Not all of the causal theories are deterministic in this sense. Classical statistical physics or (differently) chaos theory (which, a postmodern[ist] icon though it has become, is classical as a physical theory) are causal. They are, however, not deterministic even in ideal cases in view of the great structural complexity of the systems they consider. This complexity blocks our ability to predict the behaviour of such systems, either exactly or at all, even though, in the case of chaos theory, we can write equations that describe them, which makes it a realist theory, and assume their behaviour to be causal.

In contrast to chaos theory, whose equations are assumed to describe the actual (causal) behaviour of physical objects – even though, again, without us being able to predict this behaviour – classical statistical physics is, also, not realist insofar as its equations do not describe the behaviour of its ultimate objects, such as molecules of a gas. It is, however, based on the realist assumption of an underlying non-statistical multiplicity, whose individual members conform to the strictly causal laws of Newtonian physics. We may expand the denomination 'realist' to theories that are approximate in this sense or, further, to theories that presuppose an independent reality that cannot be mapped or even approximated, but which possesses structure and attributes, or properties, in the usual sense. Indeed, realist theories may be described most generally be the presupposition that their objects in principle possess independently existing attributes (such as those conceived by analogy with classical physics) whether we can, in practice or in principle, ever describe or approximate them or not. Some (Einstein among them) see this latter presupposition as a hallmark of realism. As will be seen, this point bears crucially on the modernist/postmodernist problematic of reality or lack thereof, in Lyotard and in general, since even though lost to any conceivable representation a certain form and even structure of reality would still be presupposed – the presupposition rigorously suspended by nonclassical theories. This suspension is, naturally, not the same as a denial of the existence of that to which no concept of reality or any other concept can apply. It does follow – which is indeed the point here – that this view entails a radically different form of epistemology, in which, as will be seen, one can only know certain effects but never the ultimate efficacity of these effects.

More generally, nonclassical theories are defined by the act that the *ultimate* 'objects' with which they are concerned are irreducibly unrepresentable and inconceivable – unrepresentable even as (absolutely) unrepresentable, inconceivable even as (absolutely) inconceivable – by any means that are, or will ever be, available to us. Thus, in quantum theory (again, a key reference for Lyotard), which is nonclassical in certain interpretations such as Niels Bohr's, we cannot, as in classical physics, ascribe conventional properties (such as 'position' and 'momentum') or indeed, ultimately, *any* physical properties to quantum objects (say, elementary particles, such as electrons or photons), which we now see as the ultimate constituents of matter. Quantum theory can predict, statistically, the outcome of the experiments involved as well as classical physics (which may be statistical), which enables its extraordinarily successful functioning as a physical theory. In Bohr's interpretation, this possibility is enabled by the interactions between quantum object and measuring instruments, technology, in quantum physics. We have no access to quantum objects themselves but we can work with the effects of their interactions within measuring instruments upon the latter, which are available to us, indeed classically available to us. In this interpretation quantum mechanics does not describe, even in principle and as an idealization, the actual behaviour of its objects in the way classical mechanics describes the behaviour of its objects. Hence it is not realist in any sense hitherto available. Nor, by the same token, is it causal, let alone deterministic: for, if one cannot ascribe properties or states to quantum systems, one can hardly speak of them as evolving causally. Thus, the role of technology becomes irreducible and constitutive in quantum mechanics and in nonclassical theories elsewhere, especially if we give the term 'technology' its broader meaning of *tekhne*, specifically in Derrida's sense of writing. By contrast, it may be seen as merely auxiliary and ultimately dispensable within classical physics. Indeed, one can define nonclassical theories through the irreducible role of technology in them and, conversely, classical theories by the auxiliary and ultimately dispensable functioning of technology there. It is, accordingly, not surprising that in these theories, including the postmodernist model, and in postmodernism itself, the concept of technology (at all levels, from the materiality of writing in Derrida or de Man's sense to digitalization) plays such a crucial role.

Obviously, classical theories, too, involve things that are, at least at certain moments, unknowable and inconceivable to them, while nonclassical theories enable new knowledge which is otherwise impossible. These are of the nature of the unrepresentable, the unknowable and the inconceivable, and the relationships between them; also involved are matters of what we can know and conceive, and hence the very nature of knowledge or representation (or the lack thereof), which are different in nonclassical theories. The ultimate knowledge concerning the objects of nonclassical theories becomes no longer possible, while their existence and impact upon what we can know is indispensable. In other words, classically the unknowable is reducible, at least in principle if not in practice, to something that could in principle be known, or at least to something that is analogous in nature or structure to what can be known. It is the latter that appears to define modern knowledge in Lyotard's sense. By contrast, the nonclassical unknowable is not only unknowable in practice and in principle, but is also in principle irreducible to anything that can or could ever be known or conceived, say, as analogous to anything we know or can possibly know, or what we can conceptualize based on the models of what we know.

At the same time, however, indeed as a corollary, nonclassical theories do not dispense with classical theories, since (beyond the fact that they are indispensable elsewhere) they serve as a pathway, indeed the *only* pathway, to establishing the existence of and the connections to the unknowable. Or, more accurately, classical theories allow us to handle the classically manifest *effects* of the unknowable in question in nonclassical theories, which cannot be inferred or treated otherwise. Certain configurations of such effects cannot, however, be treated by means of classical theories and require nonclassical theories which are able to account for them, while leaving the ultimate nature of the efficacy of these effects unknowable and inconceivable. I use the term 'efficacy' here in its dictionary sense of power and agency producing effects but, in this case, without the possibility of ascribing this agency causality. The ultimate nature and character of this efficacy must, thus, be seen in turn as disallowing any unambiguous reference to it. Indeed it is now seen not only as inaccessible, but also as inconceivable by any means that are or perhaps may be ever available to us, naturally, including the very term or any given conception (itself, accordingly, provisional) of 'efficacy', especially as a single agency behind all the effects involved.

This conception of the unrepresentable or the unknowable in general thus entails a new form of epistemology. This epistemology is that of knowledge and conceptualization (only) in terms of material or technological (again in the broadest sense) effects. It leaves the nature and character of the ultimate efficacy, which involves the ultimate objects of the theories involved (such as the ultimate constitution of matter in quantum physics) behind these effects outside the limit of all the available or even conceivable knowledge and conceptualization. That is, we cannot assign to this efficacy any given or conceivable general character, say, in quantum physics (or even elsewhere) by analogy with classical physics, while assuming that some specific elements involved, or even all of them, are partially or even altogether unknown. It is crucial that the radical loss in representation and knowledge at the level of the efficacy is accompanied by the (postmodern) irreducible multiplicity at the level of the effects and representation, or knowledge. Why both accompany each other or, one might say, 'conspire' together is, by definition (this 'conspiracy' is part of the unknowable efficacy in question), enigmatic or even mysterious, which my appeal to 'conspiracy' is aimed to indicate. However, these workings are, also by definition, not mystical, in the sense of the presence of a single unknown, especially divine, agency behind this or all other effects involved. In quantum mechanics, this multiplicity especially manifests itself in what Bohr calls complementarity – the necessity of mutually incompatible (and hence never simultaneously applicable) modes of describing such effects, most famously, as the wave and the particle descriptions. Quantum theory, however, involves many other complementarities (dual or more multiple) and other multiplicities, as do nonclassical theories elsewhere (on these issues in the present context, see Plotnitsky, 1994).

By the same token, the efficacy of these effects cannot be thought of in terms of an underlying (hidden) governing wholeness, either indivisible or 'atomic', so as to be correlated with manifest (lawless) effects, while remaining subject to an underlying coherent architecture that is not manifest itself. Either type of understanding would (classically) reduce the (nonclassical) multiplicity. This efficacy is neither single in governing all of its effects (individual and collective), nor multiple so as to allow one to assign an unambiguously separate efficacy to each effect. This understanding would, accordingly, affect the difference between 'classical-like' and 'nonclassical-like' conceptions of multiplicity or plurality (controlled vs. uncontrolled), including those operative in or related to the postmodernist theories. Thus, Nietzsche's 'perspectival' plurality, Bohr's complementarity, Boatel's 'heterological' plurality and Derrida's 'dissemination' would offer nonclassical examples, while, especially (in part by virtue of its marxist appurtenance), Jameson's or (these cases are more ambivalent) Lyotard's and Deleuze's conceptions of multiplicity may be seen as ultimately more 'classical-like'.

It follows, however, that nonclassical theories are defined by the interaction between what is representable (it follows by classical means) and what is unrepresentable, inconceivable, unknowable or otherwise inaccessible by any means, classical or nonclassical. The (irreducibly) unknowable itself in question is no more available to nonclassical theories than to classical theories. Nonclassical theories, however, allow us rigorously to infer the existence of this unknowable (rather than merely imagine its existence) and its significance for what we can know, and account for the (manifest) effects of this interaction, while this cannot be done by means of classical theories.

Before considering the question of the modern and its epistemology, and in order to do so more effectively, I would like to recast the preceding argument in terms of chance, the concept that plays a major role in discussions around postmodernism, specifically in Lyotard – there is no postmodernism without the play of chance. In commenting on Einstein's famous 'God does not play dice', Lyotard offers an image of God playing bridge, which offers, he argues, a more radical idea of 'primary chance' (Lyotard, 1984, 57). Chance, too, however, may be conceived classically and nonclassically (which may be more radical than either Einstein's or Lyotard's sense of it), thus leading to two fundamentally different concepts of chance.

Classically, chance or, more accurately, the appearance of chance is seen as arising from our insufficient (and perhaps, in practice, unavailable) knowledge of the total configuration of forces involved and, hence, of the lawful necessity that is always postulated behind a lawless chance event. If this configuration becomes available, or if it could be made available in principle (it may, again, not ever be available in practice), the chance character of the event would disappear. Chance would reveal itself to be a product of the play of forces that is, in principle, calculable by man, or at least by God. Most classical mathematical or scientific theories and the classical philosophical view of probability are based on this idea: in practice, we have only partially available, incomplete information about chance events, which are nonetheless determined by, in principle, a complete architecture of necessity behind them. This architecture itself may or may not be seen as ever accessible in full (or even partial) measure. The *presupposition* of its existence is, however, essential for, and defines, the classical view as causal and, by the definition given earlier, realist. On this point, classical reality and classical causality come together. Subtle and complex as they may be, all scientific theories of chance and probability prior to quantum theory and many beyond it (such as, as indicated earlier, chaos theory and most philosophical theories of chance from the earliest to the latest) are of the type just described. They are *classical*. Most of them are also, and interactively, realist. Thus, due to the complexity in the behaviour of the systems involved, chaos theory prevents us from making deterministic predictions of this behaviour. In other words, it is not a deterministic theory, as standard Newtonian (rather than statistical) classical physics is. That does not mean, however, that there is no underlying causal dynamics defining the behaviour. On the contrary, it depends on the latter. This is why I call such theories causal. Causality and order underlie randomness and chaos. (In quantum physics and nonclassical theories elsewhere these relationships are reversed and enriched: randomness and chaos underlie and constitute the efficacy of both manifest order and manifest chance.) Certain (complex) patterns of order, which we can sometimes partially access, as in the case of fractal entities such as the Mandelbrot set, are manifestations of this underlying causality and order. Indeed a better name for it would be the order theory if we comprehend it as the theory of certain complex and unpredictable forms of order.

Combined, two of Alexander Pope's famous utterances – the closing of Epistle 1 of *An Essay on Man* and his 'Proposed Epitaph for Isaac Newton' – admirably encapsulate the classical view of chance and law, even though they are not without a few ironies. Indeed, as will be seen, they may even represent a modern view, since there is here a loss, at least, in (all?) knowledge or representation of reality for us as well. Pope writes:

> All Nature is but art, unknown to thee;
> All chance, direction, which thou canst not see;
> All discord, harmony not understood;
> All partial evil, universal good:
> And, spite of pride, in erring reason's spite,
> One truth is clear: Whatever IS, is RIGHT.
>
> (*An Essay on Man*, 289–94)

> Nature and Nature's laws lay hid in night;
> God said, let Newton be! and all was light.
> ('Proposed Epitaph for
> Isaac Newton, who died in 1727')

The *nonclassical* understanding of chance and, again, reality (or the lack thereof), which defines quantum theory in particular, is fundamentally different. Nonclassically, chance is irreducible not only in practice (which, as I have explained, may be the case classically as well) but also, and most fundamentally, in principle. There is no knowledge, in practice or in principle, that is or will ever be, or could in principle be, available to us that would allow us to eliminate chance and replace it with the picture or assumption of necessity behind it. Nor, accordingly, can one postulate such a (causal/lawful) architecture of necessity as unknowable (to any being, individual or collective, human or even divine), but existing, in and by itself, outside our engagement with it. This qualification is crucial. For, as I explained above, some forms of the classical understanding of chance allow for and are indeed defined by this type of (realist) assumption. In other words, in contrast to the classical view, there is not nor will ever be, nor could in principle be, any possibility that would allow us to assign any properties or even in any way to conceive of 'efficacity' in terms of knowable effects; or, especially, postulate a single efficacity of that type, human or divine, material or cultural, or whatever, even if it remains unknowable to any being, individual or collective. Nor, accordingly, can we assign to this efficacity an unknown or even unknowable but conceivable architecture, for example, in physics, analogous to that of classical physics. Thus, nonclassical chance, such as that which we encounter in quantum physics, is not only inexplicable in practice and in principle but is also irreducible in practice and in principle. It is irreducible to any necessity, knowable or unknowable. It is, in David Bohm's words, *irreducibly* lawless (1995, 73). Anything – well *almost* anything – can happen in a given individual event, in which respect quantum mechanics is indeed very much like life.

Milton's conception of chaos in *Paradise Lost* comes arguably closest to this concept, even if only up to a point, before Milton gives it back to a more classical-like or at least epistemologically modernist (rather than postmodernist) view. Milton writes in one of the most extraordinary passages in literature (or indeed philosophy):

> Before thir [Satan's, Sin's and Death's] eyes in sudden view appear
> The secrets of the hoary deep, a dark
> Illimitable Ocean without bound,
> Without dimension, where lengths, breadth, and highth,
> And time and place are lost; where eldest *Night*
> And *Chaos*, ancestors of Nature, hold
> Eternal Anarchy, amidst the noise
> Of endless worth, and by confusion stand.

For hot, cold, moist, and dry, for Champions fierce
Strive here for Maistry, and to Battle bring
The embryon Atoms; they around the flag
Of each his Faction, in thir several Clans,
Light-arm's or heavy, sharp, smooth, swift or slow,
Swarm populous, unnumber'd as the Sands
Of *Barca* and *Cerene's* torrid soil,
Levied to side with warring Winds, and poise
Thir lighter wings. To whom these most adhere,
He rules the moment; *Chaos* Umpire sits,
And by decision more imbroils the fray
By which he Reigns: next his high Arbiter
Chance governs all. Into this wild Abyss,
The Womb of Nature, and perhaps her Grave,
Of neither Sea, nor Shore, not Air, nor Fire,
But all of these in thir pregnant causes mixed
Confus'dly, and which this must ever fight,
Unless th' Almighty Maker them ordain
His dark materials to create more Worlds,
Into this wild Abyss the wary fiend
Stood on the brink of Hell and look'd a while
Pondering his Voyage: for no narrow firth
He had to cross

(*PL*, Book II, 890–920)

This extraordinary vision is, I would argue, closer to the quantum-mechanical than the chaos-theoretical and, hence, epistemologically a more radical conception of material (it is actually more than merely material given God's role in it) nature or reality, or lack thereof, and representation, or the lack thereof. (It is true that Milton's conception has a long history, extending at least from Democritus and Lucretius on, but introduces highly original and nontrivial elements, in particular in its suspension of denominations defining the ultimate constituent elements of chaos.) It is a little more difficult to ascertain which one – the quantum-mechanical or the chaos-theoretical – is more postmodern(ist), but that is primarily due to the complexities of the latter determination, or, again, that of modern(ist) rather than Milton's. That is, it would be quantum-mechanical were one to suspend its theological or, in Heidegger's and Derrida's terms, ontotheological aspects. Even if he had such a radical conception (i.e. that of nonclassical epistemology), Milton, as I have said, returns it to, in present terms, classical epistemology. Chaos, however, remains the primordial material out of which order – 'new worlds' – are created, and in a sense, the ultimate beneficiary, as it were (I do not think Milton would like to see God in this role) of the events in the poem. At least, chaos never loses in the poem. Satan and the humans (the latter with some future promise) do. From this perspective, beyond its extraordinary literary and philosophical significance in its own right and its role in the poem, the passage becomes an allegory of Milton's overall vision and of the poem as a whole. Milton's 'justify[cation of] the *ways* of God to men' (*PL*, Book I, 26, emphasis added), to cite what is perhaps his most famous line, proceeds (in either sense) through Chaos and a vision of chaos. What reinstates the classical-like epistemology and metaphysics or/as ideology, as ontotheology, is an assignment of a *single* efficacious power or agency to creation, which is never possible in nonclassical epistemology, which by the same token is materialist, unless, of course, one conversely inscribes matter as a classical and especially ontotheological term. This has of course often been done, including in certain versions of postmodernism, theoretical, literary and artistic, specifically proceeding along marxist lines. There are ontotheologies, or even outright theologies, and, as it were, idealist, classical-like (in the present sense) idealizations of matter as much as of spirit.

Would these aspects of Milton's vision also make it modern, especially given the historical conditions of Milton's work and corresponding appurtenances of the poem, defined by the reciprocities between Milton's epistemology and its culture, and much commented upon in recent years? It would depend on how one defines the modern, culturally and here, specifically, epistemologically. I am specifically concerned here with Lyotard's definition of modernity (which is close enough to Milton) and modernism, which he locates much later.

Now, is modern or modernist epistemology classical or nonclassical? Or indeed, is all this a question of thinking a postmodernist epistemology, specifically Lyotard's, which, whether classical or nonclassical, will establish a more complex relationship between postmodernism as such and certain of the key figures, such as the nonclassical thinkers mentioned above, whose ideas postmodernism has employed so extensively? There are, as already suggested, no single or simple answers to such questions and perhaps cannot be. Any rigorous answer will always depend on reading postmodernist figures, or of course attempting to define the terms involved. The preceding analysis offers a certain array of possibilities in this respect, which is perhaps quite enough, and I shall indeed refrain from strong or at least definitive claims. I would, however, like to add some further remarks.

The above questions and answers to them would be defined, first, by how one inscribes – more or less classically or, more or less, nonclassically – the modernist/postmodernist loss in reality and in representation (at least some more-or-lessness is irreducible); and, again – on the question of attitude – the issue of modernist nostalgia vs. postmodernist affirmation of this loss. The postmodernist multiplicity would remain in place in any event, although the concept of multiplicity may be more radical if defined nonclassically as well. It is the nature of the unrepresentable that is in question – the nonclassical vs. classical. Both deal with the unrepresentable or the unknowable and the inaccessible. In the nonclassical case, however, there is not nor ever will be, nor could be in principle, any possibility that would allow us to assign any structure or attributes to or, crucially, claim any possible conception (again, 'efficacity' itself included) of the efficacity of knowable, representable (and in this sense classical) effects. For example and in particular, one cannot postulate a single efficacity of that type, even as unknowable to any being, individual or collective. The classical epistemology, however postmodern(ist) (a postmodernist marxism, or marxist postmodernism, such as Jameson's, offers a good example), would allow for the latter possibility at least, of what we might refer to as 'quasi-classical' for the moment. Or, more often, it would assign to this efficacity an unknown, hidden or unknowable but conceivable architecture, which is a more determinately classical move. The basic possibilities would, then, be as follows:

1. both the modern(ist) and the postmodern(ist) unrepresentable are classical, or at least quasi-classical;
2. both are nonclassical;
3. the modern(ist) unrepresentable is classical or quasi-classical, while the postmodern(ist) is nonclassical.

In the first two cases, the difference between the modern(ist) and the postmodern(ist) would be defined in terms of the modern(ist) nostalgia for the unattainable. The picture could be further refined by distinguishing between the modern, which could be defined in terms of a more Hegelian (in Lyotard's reading) classical-like or quasi-classical inspiration, and the modernist, referring to the modernist or even postmodern(ist) art (we recall that it may include earlier figures of modernity, say, Shakespeare or Montaigne) considered by Lyotard. Such works may be more likely to be epistemologically nonclassical, but they also present even greater interpretative complexities and ambiguities than theoretical texts (although some, such as Montaigne belong to both genres). I do think, however, that a certain space of theories and interpretations of the key authors involved is sufficiently outlined here.

While, again, refraining from definitive or even strong, claims, it appears to me that Lyotard's epistemology remains ultimately quasi-classical, if not classical, and to conform to definition 1, above. Jameson's postmodernist epistemology appears to be classical-like, on the present definition, and perhaps aims to be, for the reasons of politico-economic determination in, and as a 'cultural logic' of, 'late *capitalism*'. It is worth observing, in general, that such distinctions may be the subjects of different evaluation as well, rather than (only) of theoretical work, perhaps ultimately more difficult and complex in the nonclassical case. It is true that Lyotard argues that 'modernity, in whatever age it appears, cannot exist without a shattering of belief and without discovery of the "lack of reality" of reality, together with the invention of other realities' and that 'modern art [in Lyotard's definition] . . . presents the fact that the unrepresentable exists' (Lyotard, 1984, 77, 78). These statements and accompanying commentaries may be sufficiently ambivalent to warrant a nonclassical reading, although I have not encountered one, either by advocates or by critics of Lyotard. It does not appear to me, however, that Lyotard ever reaches or even quite approaches the nonclassical in the present sense given in this essay or elsewhere, with a possible exception of *The Differend*. I am not sure that he aims or wants to do so either. One certainly does not find the same type of articulation, either directly or by way of reference, or through a reading of the nonclassical as in the work of key nonclassical figures here invoked – Nietzsche, Bohr, Bataille, Blanchot, de Man and Derrida, in (sometimes ambivalent) contrast to, in addition to Lyotard, Deleuze and more recently Bruno Latour (Latour, 1993). This appears, for example, to apply to Lyotard's reading of the Kantian sublime. His commentary on mathematics and science is not always helpful here either, since one does not quite find sufficient episte-mological discrimination of the type indicated above, between classical or classical-like models (such as chaos theory) and, say, quantum theory, which in fact appear to be read quasi-classically. The same appears to be the case as concerns chance. However, Lyotard's commentary on these questions remains important insofar as it tells us that, if want to use mathematics and science and what they tell us about mind and nature as our model (in the way the Enlightenment does), we might as well look carefully at what they in fact reveal. And they do tell us things, at least some things, which are closer to postmodernism (or nonclassical thought) than to some of the claims of the Enlightenment. It is not a question of dispensing with the latter, even assuming that we could, but of the theoretical, the Enlightenment-like, rigour.

Once again, however, some might read Lyotard or others here mentioned, otherwise – in either direction, towards or away from the nonclassical or postmodern, however conceived. It is perhaps the new spaces of interpretation that postmodernism, along with other developments here considered, has brought us above all, perhaps especially in the case of literature.

THE POSTMODERN, LITERATURE AND CRITICISM

As we have seen, most literature considered by Lyotard, both *in* a postmodernist context and *as* postmodern, is the literature of modernism or as it is sometimes called high modernism, from roughly the late-nineteenth to the mid-twentieth century. This historical range accords with his overall scheme, in which the postmodern is *in* the modern, which argument is pertinent enough given the immense impact of this art throughout this century in general and on post-modern culture in particular, including specifically its influence on the art of the last two decades. To name just a few among the more well-known artists of the last twenty years, one might think specifically of Jennie Holzer, Barbara Kruger, Jeff Koons, Bruce Nauman, Julian Schnabel, Cindy Sherman and Kiki Smith or, in literature, the language poets and hypertext authors, the novels of Kathy Acker or the films of Peter Greenaway, along with other postmodern cinema. The boundaries are uncertain, even leaving aside the influence of earlier (modernist) figures upon those just mentioned. One can certainly see what is recognizable as the postmodernist period in art dating from the 1960s on, especially pop-art and the work of such authors as Thomas Pynchon (see, for example, Paula Geyh et al., 1998). There are of course earlier, and some *much* earlier, examples in Lyotard, but this is next to nothing in contrast with his analysis of the postmodern culture of the last two decades, or in contrast to Jameson, who, in his analysis of postmodernism, is primarily concerned with contemporary literature and art as part of the superstructure of 'late capitalism'. I shall bypass the subject of modernist art and its various aspects or definitions as such (a massive and exhaustively discussed subject, well beyond my scope here), even though some of Lyotard's analysis depends on questions involving modernist art and aesthetics. I shall also bypass the discussion of postmodern art mentioned above, defined largely by its postmodern cultural and political concerns, although certain key 'aesthetic' features are of much interest as well. It is the subject of much recent analysis, in which one finds a variety of arguments as to the relationships between postmodernist (in this sense) art and postmodernist (in my sense) theory or postmodern culture, particularly for example as to whether this art challenges such theories or, conversely, fails to rise to their level. I shall remain primarily within the scheme of Lyotard's epistemological definition of putting forward, without nostalgia, the unrepresentable in (re-)presentation itself, which is cogent enough and sufficient for my purposes here, which is the consideration of postmodernist literary criticism or literary studies more generally.

One may broadly, but accurately, define postmodernist literary studies (criticism, history, theory and so forth) by their concerns with the relationships between literature and postmodernist theory (specifically, epistemology) and culture. Of course, postmodern culture has been a subject of much debate in, as it has become known, the field of cultural studies, which is a prominent and important part of the current – postmodern – academic culture. This is a separate, even if related, topic, however. As such, postmodernist literary studies may be, and has been, concerned with any literature, even though literary modernism and postmodernism may be and have been the main preoccupation of postmodern literary studies at least in its earlier stages, following Lyotard and related postmodernist and poststructuralist figures such as Derrida and de Man. Their readings of literary figures have contributed decisively to the development and dissemination (in either sense) of their philosophical ideas, such as those considered here in relation to the question of the postmodern. Literary works of, among other modernists, Joyce, Faulkner and Blanchot (or earlier Dostoyevsky) offer particularly effective dramatization of the postmodern critique of narrative, as discussed above (Plotnitsky, 1993, 113–48). Clearly, however, a much broader set of postmodernist (or nonclassical) concerns emerges virtually at any point of such engagement, which is not merely or even primarily a matter of proleptic anticipation on the part of literature. The latter make take place and has guided most theoretical authors here mentioned, certainly both Lyotard and Derrida, who followed Freud's famous and oft repeated or reinvented maxim 'Poets were there before me'. This is true enough, but it is also untrue enough. At the very least, the space of the 'there' involved has all the postmodernist or nonclassical complexity we can master to understand it.

This is not only a matter of engagement defined by the academic canon (ever expanding in all directions during the postmodern epoch), but is also – or can be – a rigorous conceptual pursuit. For, as we have seen, at least the epistemological boundaries of the postmodernist or the nonclassical can be pushed very far back in history, especially as (our reading of) literary works is concerned. We have also seen already how such relationships emerge in the case of Milton's *Paradise Lost*, with regard to the defining works of modernity. For, even if, as was indicated earlier, Milton wants 'to justify the ways of God to men', this justification must take place in the modern world. It is the world of new, post-Cartesian philosophy, post-Galilean mathematics and science, emerging industrialization and capitalism, geopolitics and so forth, all of which find their way into Milton's 'Garden of Eden' and our exile from it. Epistemologically, *Paradise Lost* is or may be effectively read as a paradigmatically modern work according to Lyotard's criteria and (in my argument here, correlatively) as a quasi-classical work by the present criteria. I would now like, by way of conclusion, to suggest an example of a work that may be and, perhaps, *must* be read as both a nonclassical and postmodernist text: Shakespeare's *The Tempest*. It has also been the subject of much prominence and reinterpretation in recent (and to some degree, more postmodern) discussions in new areas of literary studies, especially in the so-called new historicism and cultural studies.

NOTES TOWARDS A READING OF *THE TEMPEST*

I shall start with *Henry V*, however, where a few opening lines of the 'Prologue' to Act V contain virtually the whole nonclassical/postmodernist problematic here discussed or, at least, offer the possibility of making the problematic available to us:

> Vouchsafe to those that have not read the story,
> That I may prompt them – and of such as have,
> I humbly pray them to admit th'excuse
> Of time, of numbers, and due course of things,
> Which cannot in their huge and proper life
> Be here presented.
>
> (*Henry V*, v.i., 1–6)

The '*huge*' (an extraordinary, *huge*, word here) 'life of things' can indeed never be presented by a single narrative, however 'grand'. Shakespeare's hugeness defeats all possible grandeur, even his own. It is Milton's Chaos without, as Shakespeare or, later, Darwin and Nietzsche grasped so well, 'the almighty maker'. Things are ordained and dis-ordained all the time, but there is no almighty maker to direct the process uniquely. Life cannot be presented in and by anything, neither narrative, nor even a play – Shakespeare's, for example – but not even Nietzsche's concept of play, which takes off from the Heraclitean play of becoming and the Democritean play of chance and necessity and takes them to his nonclassical quantum-theory-like epistemology. Derrida, following Nietzsche, describes 'the history of *life* . . . as the history of *gramme*', that is of nonclassical writing in his sense, the concept that he ultimately brings into (derived from) his readings of Shakespeare as well, as does Nietzsche earlier (Derrida, 1974, 84, emphasis added). But then – Was that what Shakespeare had in mind? Not impossible! – was this 'life', which can never be 'proper' and about which there can be no unique due sequence of 'time', 'numbers' or 'things' to direct it be read in this way; or rather, is it that which gives rise to the effects which we call life, or at some points death, but which may not be either life or death, life and not life, death and not death, life/death, neither one nor the other? Instead, in these transformations, which brings us (in)to *The Tempest*, 'nothing [of life or life/death] that does fade,/ But doth suffer a sea change / Into something rich and strange' (I.ii, 402–4).

Now one can think here of Alfred Hitchcock's movie, by the same title, *Rich and Strange*, his own favourite of all his movies. A great master of narrative, Hitchcock is, almost like Shakespeare, a master, on the one hand, of what cannot be narrated, and what upsets narrative radically, and yet, on the other hand and at the same time, also that which makes all specific narratives (there are no others) possible. One can also think of Peter Greenaway's more postmodern(ist) and post-deconstructive, version of *The Tempest, Prospero's Books* (1996). A cruder and more crudely postmodern version of Shakespeare is the still more recent *Titus* (2000). Shakespeare can be, or can be made to be, postmodern enough in any given sense, even as he can resist or be made to resist any postmodernism, crude or refined. I want, however, to make a somewhat different point.

I would argue that, somewhat similarly to Milton's passage on chaos, which may even allude to Shakespeare's lines just cited, these lines themselves can be read as an allegory of the whole play, while the play itself can be read as an allegory of a nonclassical vision of the huge life of things. It offers an allegory of their constant life/death transformation of all things into something rich and strange under the optics of nonclassical vision, but also of the nonclassically invisible and the unknowable. I can only suggest such a reading here, rather than offer it, which would be difficult to do because most of the key elements involved are found in the subtle textual details, such as those (more obviously) of the lines in question. Nor can I quite consider the key allegorical figures involved, in particular Prospero's book or the act of drowning it, 'deeper than did ever plummet sound' (*T*, V.i, 56–7). Both may well allegorize something like 'the end of the book and the beginning of writing', that is the book, both Prospero's and Derrida's, suffering a sea change into something 'rich and strange', of which Derrida speaks at the outset of *Of Grammatology* and of the postmodern era in 1967, of seeing life as that differance which is the history of gramme/writing. Shakespeare may well have seen his genre – theatre – rather than the book somewhat along this line, as writing instead of the book.

The Tempest is a romance and, as such, carries more conventional and often more luminous allegorical dimensions. My point, however, is that it ultimately allegorizes life or, again, life/death as it would appear in a nonclassical vision, such as Nietzsche's, which finds its more direct or rather more dramatic or tragic representation (or the unrepresentable) in Shakespeare's greatest and darkest tragedies, *King Lear, Othello, Hamlet* and *Troilus and Cressida* among them, or in his greatest comedies. Shakespeare's or Nietzsche's are always affirmations of life even under the conditions of the greatest tragedy, but, by the same token, the tragedy is never far away. Are they postmodern? Not altogether. The postmodern perhaps ultimately lacks tragedy. They may be more postmodernist or, especially, nonclassical, specifically in the sense that the radically unknowable and the ultimate efficacity of things, of the huge life of things, is irreducibly enigmatic, always beyond reach. In this sense, in referring to this unknowable, all Shakespeare's allegories, say, in *The Tempest* are allegories in de Man's radical, nonclassical sense, whereby 'the difficulty of allegory is rather that this emphatic clarity of representation does not stand in the service of something that can be represented', as de Man writes on Pascal (not that far from Shakespeare: de Man, 1996, 51). The play overall, accordingly, would in this reading be an allegory of allegorical vision, an allegory of allegory in its nonclassical sense. As such, it is something more than postmodern or even postmodernist, unless taken in its most radical, and therefore its richest and strangest, sense. It is a (nonclassical) allegory of the rich and strange, and yet also ultimately unreachable, process that makes both the postmodern and the postmodernist possible, among many other things, amid the huge life of things, where everything always suffers a sea change into something rich and strange, amid the tempest of life.

QUESTIONS FOR FURTHER CONSIDERATION

1. Consider the relationships between narrative and realism, on the one hand, and narrative and knowledge, on the other, from a Lyotardian perspective. Apply your analysis to various narratives told in *Paradise Lost* and the (grand?) narrative of Wordsworth's *The Prelude*.

2. Do you see the Enlightenment agenda of modernity (as defined by Lyotard) at work in *Paradise Lost*? Does it sometimes work against its own grain, suggesting to us that, once rigorously pursued, the Enlightenment, just as modern art, is bound to bring the postmodern(ist) in it, or even emerge from the postmodern(ist), as Lyotard suggests? Discuss from this point of view Rafael's narratives and educational strategies in Book V. Compare them to those found in *The Tempest*, which deals with questions of education and enlightenment (broadly conceived).

3. Can you find some elements of Lyotard's 'postmodern condition' of justice in terms of 'heterogeneous language games' (Lyotard, 1984, 66–7) in *Paradise Lost* and *The Tempest*, as books fundamentally, if differently, dealing with the question of justice? Discuss their difference

from the postmodernist perspective of heterogeneity and the difficulty, or impossibility, of forming the Enlightenment consensus, specifically in the way Habermas conceives of it. Consider the characters of Satan and Caliban from this perspective.

4. This essay lists twelve key aspects of postmodernity. Can *Paradise Lost* or *The Tempest* help us to understand some of them and teach us how to confront them, either by specific episodes, narrative situations or storytelling, and so forth, or in more general terms, for example as epistemological allegories of the type discussed in this essay?

5. The sense of nostalgia for the unattainable, for the loss of a 'native country' of thought and knowledge, a kind of paradise, that defines modernity, according to Lyotard, has obvious resonances with *Paradise Lost, The Tempest* and *The Prelude*. Consider these resonances, keeping in mind that the first two works belong to the rise of scientific and economic modernity (the Copernican scientific revolution and the birth of capitalism, including as a geopolitical power), while *The Prelude* was written in the wake, and to some degree against, the Enlightenment. In other words, bring a Lyotardian view to bear on and understand these works, rather than think in terms of a more obvious sense of the lost paradise of knowledge, justice and so forth in Lyotard's view of it.

6. Consider the question of knowledge in *The Prelude* from the epistemological perspective suggested by this essay. You can also relate this question to the question of the sublime in Kant, Wordsworth and Lyotard.

NOTE

1. I shall, by and large, bypass Jameson given my limit here. I think that ultimately Lyotard's remains the most effective treatment of the subject. I have considered postmodernism, the Habermas–Lyotard debate and Jameson's work from a perspective of the Nietzsche–Bataille–Derrida interface in My *Reconfigurations: Critical Theory and General Economy* (1993), which also contains further references. I shall also bypass Jean Baudrillard's work, significant as it has been for the recent approaches, primarily, to postmodern culture. The literature on postmodernism is, by now, nothing short of immense and it would not be possible even to begin to address it here. Among the more prominent works are David Harvey, *The Condition of Postmodernity: An Inquiry into the Origin of Cultural Change* (1988) and Brian McHale, *Postmodernist Fiction* (1997).

ANNOTATED BIBLIOGRAPHY

Amiram, Eyal and John Unsworth, eds. *Essays in Postmodern Culture*. New York, 1993. Interdisciplinary in nature and drawing on a range of theoretical models, the essays in this collection are drawn from the journal *Postmodern Culture*, which first existed as an on-line journal, one of the first of its kind. The essays address the politics of postmodernism, through various manifestations of postmodern culture in art, disease, literature, cyborgs, hypertexts, cities and the body, while also discussing issues of representation and history in postmodern culture.

Appignanesi, Lisa, ed. *Postmodernism: ICA Documents*. London, 1989.
A collection of essays, documents and interviews drawn from events held at the Institute of Contemporary Arts, London. The various documents discuss the postmodern condition to epistemology, the arts and architecture, television, the sublime and popular culture. Contributors include Jean-François Lyotard, Philippe Lacoue-Labarthe and Jacques Derrida.

Baudrillard, Jean. *Jean Baudrillard: Selected Writings*, ed. Mark Poster. Stanford, CA, 1988.
A thought-provoking collection of essays drawn from the range of Baudrillard's publications. Essay topics include advertising and commodity culture, as well as simulation and desire. Baudrillard's writing presents a sustained critique of cultural production in western society through an understanding of the ways in which human subjectivity has come to be defined by the flow of commodified images as part of a larger 'hyperreality'.

Jameson, Fredric. *Postmodernism, or, the Cultural Logic of Late Capitalism*. Durham, NC, 1991.
From the Hegelian high-ground of his politicized discourse, Jameson pursues the concept of the postmodern and its various definitions through a variety of discourses and disciplines, such as architecture, film studies, literature, literary theory, cultural studies and economics. His discussions include considerations of video as the 'dominant form' of postmodern art, and the disappearance of the subject, space and nostalgia as these inform and are transformed by the narratives of the postmodern. The volume turns, as Jameson puts it, on four themes: interpretation, Utopia, survivals of the modern, and 'returns of the repressed' of historicity.

Lyotard, Jean-François. *The Postmodern Condition: A Report on Knowledge*, trans. Geoff Bennington and Brian Massumi. Minneapolis, MN, 1984.
Lyotard defines the object of his study as 'the condition of knowledge in the most highly developed societies', and gives the name *postmodern* to that condition. He examines how the grand narratives of modernism have collapsed and given way to flows of information and knowledge controlled by science and technology, and by their self-legitimating discourses in the contemporary moment of advanced industrial societies. Lyotard proposes a 'technocracy', which determines the social form of knowledge, and questions this through the consideration of narrative and scientific knowledge, the nature of research and education, and issues of legitimation and delegitimation.

SUPPLEMENTARY BIBLIOGRAPHY

Baudrillard, Jean. *The Mirror of Production*, trans. Mark Poster. New York, 1975.
————. *Simulations*, trans. Paul Foss et al. New York, 1983.
Bauman, Zygmunt. *Postmodern Ethics*. Oxford, 1993.
Benhabib, Seyla. *Situating the Self: Gender, Community and Postmodernism in Contemporary Ethics*. Cambridge, 1992.
Bertens, Hans. *The Idea of the Postmodern: A History*. London, 1995.
———— and Douwe Fokkema, eds. *International Post-modernism: Theory and Literary Practice*. Amsterdam, 1996.
Best, Steven, and Douglas Kellner. *Postmodern Theory: Critical Interrogations*. New York, 1991.
Bewes, Timothy. *Cynicism and Postmodernity*. London, 1997.
Calinescu, Matei. *Five Faces of Modernity: Modernism, Avant-Garde, Decadence, Kitsch, Postmodernism*. Durham, NC, 1987.
Callinicos, Alex. *Against Postmodernism: A Marxist Critique*. New York, 1989.
Connor, Steven. *Postmodern Culture: An Introduction to the Theories of the Contemporary*. Oxford, 1989.
Currie, Mark. *Postmodern Narrative Theory*. Basingstoke, 1998.

Dellamora, Richard, ed. *Postmodern Apocalypse: Theory and Cultural Practice at the End*. Philadelphia, 1996.

D'haen, Theo, and Hans Bertens, eds. *'Closing the Gap': American Postmodern Fiction in Germany, Italy, Spain, and the Netherlands*. Amsterdam, 1997.

Durham, Scott. *Phantom Communities: The Simulacrum and the Limits of Postmodernism*. Stanford, CA, 1998.

Ebert, Teresa L. *Ludic Feminism and After: Postmodernism, Desire, and Labor in Late Capitalism*. Ann Arbor, MI, 1996.

Elam, Diane. *Romancing the Postmodern*. New York, 1992.

Elliott, Anthony. *Subject to Ourselves: Social Theory, Psychoanalysis and Postmodernism*. Cambridge, 1996.

Federman, Raymond. *Critification: Postmodern Essays*. Albany, NY, 1993.

Foster, Hal, ed. *The Anti-Aesthetic: Essays in Postmodern Culture*. Port Townsend, WA, 1983.

——, ed. *Postmodern Culture*. London, 1985.

Geyh, Paula et al., eds. *Postmodern American Fiction: A Norton Anthology*. New York, 1998.

Gregson, Ian. *Contemporary Poetry and Postmodernism: Dialogue and Estrangement*. Basingstoke, 1996.

Halberstam, Judith, and Ira Livingston, eds. *Posthuman Bodies*. Bloomington, IN, 1995.

Harvey, David. *The Condition of Postmodernity An Inquiry into the Origin of Cultural Change*. London, 1993.

Hogue, Lawrence W. *Race, Modernity, Postmodernity: A Look at the History and Literatures of People of Color Since the 1960s*. Albany, NY, 1996.

Hutcheon, Linda. *A Poetics of Postmodernism: History, Theory, Fiction*. New York, 1988.

——. *The Politics of Postmodernism*. New York, 1993.

Klinkowitz, Jerry. *Literary Disruptions: The Making of Post-Contemporary American Fiction*, 2nd edn. Urbana, IL, 1980.

Leitch, Vincent B. *Postmodernism: Local Effects, Global Flows*. Albany, NY, 1996.

Lucy, Niall. *Postmodern Literary Theory: An Introduction*. Oxford, 1997.

Lyotard, Jean-François. *The Differend: Phrases in Dispute*, trans. George Van Den Abbeele. Minneapolis, MN, 1988.

——. *The Postmodern Explained*, trans. Don Barry et al., eds Julian Pefanis and Morgan Thomas, afterword, Wlad Godzich. Minneapolis, MN, 1992.

—— and Jean-Loup Thébaud. *Just Gaming*, trans. Wlad Godzich. Minneapolis, MN, 1985.

McHale, Brian. *Postmodern Fiction*. New York, 1987.

McHale, Brian. *Constructing Postmodernism*. New York, 1992.

Maltby, Paul. *Dissident Postmodernists: Barthelme, Coover, Pynchon*. Philadelphia, 1991.

Marshall, Brenda K. *Teaching the Postmodern: Fiction and Theory*. New York, 1992.

Newman, Charles. *The Post-Modern Aura: The Act of Fiction in an Age of Inflation*. Evanston, IL, 1985.

Nicholson, Linda, ed. *Feminism/Postmodernism*. New York, 1990.

Plotnitsky, Arkady. *Reconfigurations: Critical Theory and General Economy*. Gainesville, FL, 1993.

Sarup, Madan. *Identity, Culture, and the Postmodern World*. Athens, OH, 1996.

Shildrick, Margerit. *Leaky Bodies and Boundaries: Feminism, Postmodernism and (Bio)ethics*. London, 1997.

Smith, Bruce Gregory. *Nietzsche, Heidegger, and the Transition to Postmodernity*. Chicago, 1996.

Soja, Edward. *Postmodern Geographies*. London, 1989.

OTHER WORKS CITED

Adorno, Theodor, and Max Horkheimer. *Dialectic of Enlightenment*, trans. J. Cumming. New York, 1990.

Bohm, David. *Wholeness and the Implicate Order*. London, 1995.

De Man, Paul. *Aesthetic Ideology*, ed. and intro. Andrzej Warminski. Minneapolis, MN, 1996.

Derrida, Jacques. *Of Grammatology*, trans. Gayatri Chakravorty Spivak. Baltimore, MD, 1974.

———. *Margins of Philosophy*, trans. Alan Bass. Chicago, 1982.

Derrida, Jacques. *Specters of Marx: The State of Debt, the Work of Mourning, and the New International*, trans. Peggy Kamuf, intro. Bernd Magnus and Stephen Cullenberg. London, 1994.

Foucault, Michel. *The Order of Things: An Archeology of Human Sciences*, n.t. New York, 1994.

Latour, Bruno. *We Have Never Been Modern*, trans. C. Porter. Cambridge, MA, 1993.

Plotnitsky, Arkady. *Complementarity: Anti-Epistemology after Bohr and Derrida*. Durham, NC, 1994.

GLOSSARY

Abject/Abjection – Term used by Julia Kristeva in *Powers of Horror: an Essay in Abjection* as an attempt to undo the binary logic of much psychoanalytic thought, where the concepts of (desiring) subject and object (of desire) often represent a co-dependent opposition. The abject, says Kristeva, is 'neither subject nor object'; instead it opposes the ego by 'draw[ing] me to the place where meaning collapses'. The point here is that the structure of subject/object makes logical meaning possible, but the abject is an uncanny effect of horror, threatening the logical certainty of subject/object binary. The abject is, however, absolutely essential to all cultures; it is, among other things, the forbidden desires and ideas whose radical exclusion is the basis of cultural development.

Absence/Presence – Example of binary opposition, whereby, according to structuralist linguistics and, subsequently, structuralist critical analysis, neither term or, in fact, the concept articulated by such a term, generates its meaning without implicit acknowledgement of its opposite term and the necessary implication of one in the other. Jacques Lacan draws on the linguistic work of Roman Jakobson to explore the dynamic of absence/presence in the symbolic order.

Aesthetic – From Greek *aistetikos*, meaning perceptible to the senses, aesthetic approaches to literature are ones which concern themselves primarily with the work's beauty and form, rather than with extra-textual issues such as politics or context.

Aetiology – From Greek words *aitita* meaning cause, and *logos*, meaning rational discourse, aetiology is the philosophical or scientific pursuit of laws of cause and effect.

Agency – Literally 'activeness'; more usually used to suggest one's ability to act on the world on one's own behalf or the extent to which one is empowered to act by the various ideological frameworks within which one operates.

Alienation – In marxist theories, alienation is the experience of being distanced or estranged from the products of one's labour, and by extension from one's own sense of self, because of the effects of capitalism.

Alterity – Condition of otherness or difference in critical and philosophical discourse to signal a state of being apprehended as absolutely, radically other. Philosopher Emmanuel Levinas in *Time and the Other* addresses the absolute exteriority of alterity, as opposed to the binary, dialectic or reciprocal structure implied in the idea of the other.

Ambivalence – Employed in particular strands of postcolonial critical discourse, and developed specifically from the work of Homi Bhabha, ambivalence in this context signifies the condition produced through the discourse of mimicry, whereby in the process of imposing on the colonial subject the desire to render that subject the same as the colonizer (for example, through the colonizer's language), there is produced, says Bhabha, a difference, slippage or excess. Thus, the colonial other is produced as almost, but not quite, the same, thereby producing disquiet in the colonialist, and thus a renewal of the fear of the other.

Analogy – From the Greek, *ana*, according to, and *logos*, rational discourse: an analogy is a comparison made between one word, object, story or concept and another for purposes of comparison and explanation.

Anthropologism – From the Greek *anthropos*, human, and *logos*, rational discourse: anthropology is the science of humanity; by extension, anthropologism is the application of anthropological insights, methods and practices to other fields of intellectual engagement.

Anthropomorphism – The transformation of a non-human subject through an analysis which imbues with qualities peculiar to human beings and thereby makes familiar or 'quasihuman' the subject in question.

Anti-intentionalism – A critical position in which the intentions of the author are regarded as immaterial to the interpretation of the work.

Antimaterialist – Any critical or theoretical stance which opposes a materialist viewpoint; that is, any stance that refuses the conditions of material life as the basis of its interpretation. Antimaterialism can be mystical or religious, or it can be simply a depoliticized position.

Aporia/Aporetic – Deriving from the Greek for 'unpassable path' or 'impasse', aporia has been used by Jacques Derrida to describe the effects of *différance*: aporia is figured in those multiple (perhaps infinite numbers of) moments when meaning cannot be decided satisfactorily, when language, subjected to severe analysis, collapses into a radical undecideability.

Archaeology – Term used by Michel Foucault which indicates a mode of analysis of discursive formations and statements without assigning or seeking origins in the human sciences (e.g. psychiatry, political economy). For Foucault, such discursive strata distinguish the human sciences from any 'pure' scientificity.

Architectonic – Referring to construction or structure, and, as Aristotle employs it, having control over structure, the term is used critically as addressing the systematization of knowledge.

Aristotelian – Ideas deriving from the writings of Aristotle, whose *Poetics* in particular is an early example of literary criticism. The *Poetics* is an analysis of the elements of tragedy that make one example of the genre more or less successful than another example. His focus is on the structure of the plot, especially as it connects to the moral lesson of the play. He isolated the features that have since come to be known as the unities: the unities of time (the action takes place in one day), place (it takes place in one location) and action (it is concerned with one significant action). The highest shape of the tragic plot in Aristotle's terms was one which focused on elements of reversal in the fortunes of the protagonists, recognitions of moral lessons and catharsis in the audience, whereby the viewer is purged by his or her experience of seeing the action played out. The emphasis is thereby on structure and the audience's moral response to structure.

Aura – The 'aura' of a work of art is what Walter Benjamin calls the 'unique phenomenon of distance' that is to be found in high cultural forms. The work's aura appears to be threatened by 'mechanical reproduction' which theoretically dissipates the work's uniqueness and brings it into the grasp of everyone. The unique artifact is distanced by its uniqueness – its unattainability. Benjamin argues, however, that though dissipated by modern technologies of reproduction, a work's 'aura' continues to give it authority and mystery.

Authority – The power that comes from being the originator or author (from which the word derives) of a given work. Thus, the limits placed on meaning when interpreters turn to the biographies or the known intentions of the author.

Autonomy of Art – The view that art/literature is autonomous – that is, that it has no function beyond itself, that it is politically, socially, economically and personally disengaged.

Avant-garde – From the French for 'vanguard', avant-garde in art or literature means artistic practices that deviate daringly from conventional practice: the art of the new.

Base/Superstructure – Concepts derived from Marx's Preface to *A Contribution to the Critique of Political Economy*. Marx argued that the economic organization of any given society (what he called the relations of production or Base) was the foundation of all other social relations and cultural production: that is, the economic Base makes possible or determines the kinds of legal, political, religious and general cultural life of the world – what Marx termed the Superstructure. The relationship between Base and Superstructure has variously been understood as absolutely determining (the Base is like the foundations for a Superstructure like a house), or as mutually dependent (with the Base acting like railway tracks and the Superstructure as rolling stock).

Becoming – Mikhail Bakhtin conceives Being as a constant process of becoming.

Bourgeois – Literally, bourgeois is the French for middle class. By extension, it has come to mean a set of conventionalized attitudes which tend to support a conservative status quo.

Bourgeois Individualism – A key term in Ian Watt's proto-marxist study *The Rise of the Novel*, used to define one of the conditions for the novel's appearance. The bourgeois individual exhibited a new kind of (middle-class) consciousness, and new sensibility in relation to his or her relations with God, other people generally and servants in particular, and the market, consisting primarily in a view that the individual is significant in his or her own right, rather than having his or her significance subsumed by the general needs of society.

Canon/canonical/canonicity – Originally, the term canon referred to those books of the Bible that had been accepted by church authorities as containing the word of God. More recently, in literary studies, it has come to mean the 'great books', or 'great tradition' of texts that everyone should study or know in order to be considered educated in literature – that is, works called 'canonical'. The means by which the canon has been constructed, however, have been radically exclusionary – leaving out, for example, works written by those in marginal or excluded groups. Contemporary focus on canonicity, therefore, has tended to move to broadening the category of what 'counts' as literature.

Capitalism – Any system of economic relations which is driven by the profit motive; capitalism depends on the investment by private individuals and companies of their own funds to provide the economic means of production, distribution and exchange in return for profits from their investment while exploiting the workers who provide the labour but neither own nor control the means of production.

Chora – Originally deriving from Plato's *Timaeus*, where the word is a figure of multiple ambiguity meaning 'the receptacle of meaning, invisible and formless, which contains intelligibility but cannot itself be understood'. Julia Kristeva has adapted the term to describe a pre-linguistic realm which underpins language and meaning, but which cannot itself be pinned down. In the process of language development the chora is split to enable words (defined by limitation – by what they leave out) to come into meaning. The chora represents endless possibility but no single significance – single significance being what defines language itself.

Chronotope – Concept developed by Mikhail Bakhtin, which refers to the aesthetic envisioning of the human subject as situated materially within a specific geo-temporal location or spatial/temporal structure which determines the shape of a narrative; thus, protagonists of epic narratives can be described as defined by, as well as inhabiting, a particular chronotopic space.

Code – The signification system that allows for the comprehension of a text or event.

Codification – The process of establishing rules and procedures that are apparently consistent and coherent for any intellectual practice. In structuralist literary theory, the process of unravelling and interpreting codes of signification – for example, the codes that tell you that this is a detective novel, and that that is an advert for pizza.

Commodification – The process by which an object or a person becomes viewed primarily as an article for economic exchange – or a commodity. Also the translation of the aesthetic and cultural objects into principally economic terms. The term is used in feminist theory to describe the objectification of women by patriarchal cultures. Through the processes of commodification, the work of art lacks any significance unless it can be transformed by economic value.

Commodity fetishism – Term used by marxist critics after Marx's discussion in Volume One of *Capital* to describe the ways in which products within capitalist economies become objects of veneration in their own right, and are valued beyond what Marx called their 'use-value'. Commodity fetishism is understood as an example of the ways in which social relations are hidden within economic forms of capitalism.

Condensation – A psychoanalytic, specifically Freudian, term referring to the psychic process whereby phantasmatic images assumed to have a common affect are condensed into a single image. Drawing on the linguistic work of Roman Jakobson, Jacques Lacan compares the Freudian notion of condensation to the work of metaphor.

Connotation/Denotation – A word's connotations are those feelings, undertones, associations, etc. that are not precisely what the word means, but are conventionally related to it, especially in poetic language such as metaphor. The word gained popular currency in relation to structuralist theories of language and literature, where connotation is opposed to denotation – the precise meaning of a word, what it means exactly as opposed to what it might mean by association.

Consciousness – In Freudian discourse, one of the principal manifestations of the psychic apparatus, the others being the unconscious and the preconscious.

Constellation – The idea of the constellation names for Walter Benjamin the critical observation of heterogeneous, yet not absolutely dissimilar, images and figures of thought gathered from both present experience and other historical moments. Benjamin seeks to maintain the difference of the historical condition of thought, rather than troping figures, concepts and ideas from the past in terms of present conceptualization by some transhistorical critical gesture.

Consumer culture – A description of postwar western-type economies in which the consumption of commodities – and of cultural artifacts as commodities – is a principal determining feature of a specific society.

Context – Usually used simply to describe all the extra-textual features (conditions of production and reception, historical events, general cultural milieu, biography, etc.) which may have a bearing on the interpretation of a literary text. The term has also been co-opted and adapted by Luce Irigaray to describe a kind *écriture féminine* in which the analogy between pen and penis derived from Freudian thought is rewritten to an analogy between cunt (in French *con*) and writing, hence *con-texte*.

Co-optation – The process of borrowing from one discourse the methods and theoretical models of another, often with radical effects. Politically, the appropriation of an individual or group, or the ideas of an opposition, and put to work willingly or otherwise in the service of those who effect the appropriation.

Countertransference – Psychoanalytic term, coined by Freud but employed to a far greater extent after his death by other analysts, to indicate the analyst's unconscious emotions towards the analysand. Lacan reformulates the idea of countertransference in terms of resistance, a structural dynamic typical of the analytic experience, and grounded in a fundamental incommensurability between desire and speech.

Cultural Capital – A phrase used by Pierre Bourdieu to describe the hidden value attached to learning and education in otherwise apparently ruthlessly capitalist western societies; also, the dissemination of literary knowledge for the express purpose of enhancing the moral sensibilities of a given nation or culture's readership.

Cultural Materialism – A term first associated with marxist critic Raymond Williams that refers to the manner in which economic forces and modes of production inevitably impinge upon cultural products such as literary works.

Cyborg – Term which has been used by feminist theorist Donna Haraway to posit an alternative mode of being which, in being a hybrid of human and mechanical elements, would be beyond the constraints of biological sex and culturally stereotyped gender.

Death of the Author – From Roland Barthes's essay of the same title, the phrase has come to mean the resistance to using information derived from the writer's life or known intentions as part of the process of interpretation since this presumes that the author imposes the final limit on meaning and attributes to him (or her) a godlike status.

Deconstruction – Commonly, though mistakenly, assumed to be a school of criticism, critical methodology or mode of analysis, deconstruction is an old term in both French and English with legal connotations, which has been reintroduced to critical language through the work of Jacques Derrida. Derrida employed the term initially as a French translation for the terms 'Destruktion' and 'Abbau' in the text of Martin Heidegger. Derrida's choice was governed by the need for a word which could operate in French in a manner similar to Heidegger's terms in the German philosopher's critique of metaphysics, but without the negative implications of the German. Deconstruction, if it can be defined at all, is that within any system or structure, whether one is speaking of linguistic, grammatical, conceptual, institutional or political structures, which makes possible the articulation of the structure, and yet which escapes or is in excess of the systematic logic or economy of the structure in question. In Derrida's words, it is an 'economic concept designating the production of differing/deferring'.

Defamiliarization – A concept employed by Russian formalists, defamiliarization signifies the attribute of some kinds of writing or other works of art which communicates in non-transparent ways that make the world seem strange. The point of defamiliarization is that it shakes up reading and writing habits, undercuts conventional propriety in language and literature, and thus prevents the reader from making merely habitual or conventional responses.

Demystification – Term often associated with philosophies of cultural materialism which maintain that only social contradictions and economic conditions, rather than literary criticism and theory, possess the capacity for altering the course of reality; hence, materialist philosophy attempts to 'demystify' bourgeois pretensions toward totality and completeness.

Desire – An ineluctable force in the human psyche distinguished from need, desire holds a crucially central position in Lacanian psychoanalysis and, subsequently, in psychoanalytically inflected critical discourses. Desire for Lacan is always an unconscious drive, conscious articulations of desire being merely symptomatic of this unstoppable force. Need is seen as a purely biological instinct, while desire, a purely psychic phenomenon, is a surplus or excess beyond all articulation of demand. Desire, writes Lacan, comes always from the unconscious, and is thus unlocatable as such, while being, equally, 'desire for something else' (as it is expressed in *Écrits*), by which formula Lacan indicates that one cannot desire what one has, while what is desired is always displaced, deferred.

Determinism – Doctrine maintaining that acts of will, natural occurrences or social phenomena find their origins in preceding events or the laws of nature.

Diachronic/Synchronic – Terms often associated with Ferdinand de Saussure that account for the relationships that exist between phonemes, which he explained in terms of their synchronic and diachronic structures. A phoneme exists in a diachronic, or horizontal, relationship with other phonemes that precede and follow it. Synchronic relationships refer to a phoneme's vertical associations with the entire system of language from which individual utterances derive their meaning.

Dialectic – Broadly speaking, argument or debate; systematic analysis. A term associated with marxism, derived from the work of G. W. F. Hegel, indicating both a scientific method and the rules of antagonism governing the historical transformations of reality. The Hegelian dialectic is defined, at its simplest, as *thesis – antithesis – synthesis*.

Dialectical Materialism – Marxist theory that postulates that material reality exists in a constant state of struggle and transformation, prioritizing matter over mind. The three laws of dialectical materialism stress: (a) the transformation from quantity to quality making possible revolutionary change; (b) the constitution of material reality as a unity composed of opposites; (c) the negation of the two oppositions in the condition of material reality, as a result of their antagonism, out of which historical development takes place which, however, still retains traces of the negated elements.

Dialogism – Term derived from the work of Mikhail Bakhtin, indicating the polyphonic play of different voices or discourses in a text, without the assumption of a dominant, monolithic authorial position or voice.

Diaspora – Dispersal of various peoples away from their homelands; often associated with the notion of the Jewish diaspora in modern Israel, but extended in cultural studies, postcolonial studies and race theory to consider the displacement of peoples by means of force, such as slavery.

Diegesis – Term used by Roland Barthes and Gérard Genette, amongst others, denoting narration or description presented without judgement or analysis.

Différance – Neologism coined by Jacques Derrida. Derrida makes the term differ from the more conventional 'difference' by spelling it with an 'a'. The purpose is to point out that there is that in writing which escapes aural comprehension ('a' in the French pronunciation of 'difference' sounding the same as 'e' in 'différence'). Thus, the difference in 'différance' is purely graphic. In this manner, Derrida signifies the graphic element in the production of meaning, whereby writing silently inscribes the spacing, the deferral and differentiation (both terms implied in 'différance'), spatial and temporal, without which no writing or reading is possible.

Difference – A concept deriving from the political necessity to recognize that different groupings (female people, black people, gay and lesbian people) differ not only from the white heterosexual norm favoured by Enlightenment thought, but also differ among themselves: women, for example, may be middle-class or working class, black or chicana, straight or gay or bi, and/or any combination of any set of attributes.

Discourse – Defined by Michel Foucault as language practice: that is, language as it is used by various constituencies (the law, medicine, the church, for example) for purposes to do with power relationships between people.

Displacement – Freudian term for psychic process whereby one psychic figure is relocated in another manifestation or image. Lacan likens the work of metonymy to displacement.

Dominant/Residual/Emergent – Marxist terms derived from the writings of Raymond Williams to describe the ways in which there are competing discourses, beliefs and practices in any given culture. Roughly speaking, the dominant discourses are those to which the majority subscribe at a particular historical moment; the residual are those to which an older generation continues to subscribe or which have left their traces in present ideological formations; and the emergent are those discourses which are emerging in a culture, but which have yet to achieve consensus across the majority of the population.

Ecriture/écrivance – In Roland Barthes' conception, the former is the term for literary writing, that is language which draws attention to its artificiality; the latter term, Barthes contends, signifies that kind of writing, as in realist narrative, which strives for transparency, thereby being complicit with the prevailing dominant ideology.

Ecriture Féminine – 'Feminine/female writing' (French). Term derived from the writings of Hélène Cixous to describe a mode of textual production that resists dominant phallic models of communication. It is not necessarily written by women, but is produced instead by those who occupy what might be called a 'feminine' space in culture – which will often be women, but might also include certain kinds of excluded men.

Embodiment – The state of giving body to or becoming incarnate.

Empiricism – Philosophical approach to knowledge which puts forward the idea that all knowledge is derived from experience and not derived from reason or logic.

Epic Theatre – A style of dramaturgy developed primarily in both practice and theory by Bertolt Brecht from the 1920s onwards. Epic theatre is episodic rather than dramatically unified; it intersperses action with songs, poetry and dance; and it focuses the audience's attention on the fictionality of what they are observing.

Epistemology – Branch of philosophy which addresses the grounds and forms of knowledge. Michel Foucault employs the idea of the episteme to indicate a particular group of knowledges and discourses which operate in concert as the dominant discourses in any given historical period. He also identifies epistemic breaks, radical shifts in the varieties and deployments of knowledge for ideological purposes, which take place from period to period.

Essentialism/Essentialist – An essentialist belief is one that mistakenly confuses the effects of biology with the effects of culture; in particular it refers to the belief that biology is more significant than culture in subject formation. It is used as a term of disapproval by critics whose interests are in race and gender.

Estrangement – Like defamiliarization, estrangement is a process of making one's experience of text or artwork strange or, more particularly, distant. Its aim is usually to subvert the reading experience (or viewing experience in the visual arts, theatre and film) away from conventions and habits. Sometimes given as a translation for the Brechtian term *Verfremdung*, which is more commonly translated as *Alienation*. In the context of Brechtian theatre, estrangement names the theatrical practices by which the audience are encouraged to engage intellectually and ideological with the political and philosophical issues of a play by the deliberate foregrounding of theatrical artifice, thereby seeking to prohibit the audience's engaging empathetically with the subject material or the characters.

Ethnography – Systematic and organized recording and classification of human cultures.

False Consciousness – Illusory or mistaken beliefs, usually used in marxist theories to designate the beliefs of groups with whom one disagrees or who are in need of liberation and enlightenment.

Fantasy – In everyday language, fantasy refers simply to the workings of the imagination, but in different theoretical models it has more force. In psychoanalysis, for example, fantasies are often compensatory dreams of wish-fulfilment that allow the dreamer to cope with disappointment – and the dreamer may even convince him or herself that the fantasy is real. In structuralist writings, fantasy in literature (or the Fantastic) as defined by Todorov refers to stories or events within them whose status is left unclear to the reader: is it real or not? The term has also been used to describe any narrative mode that is set in an imagined world that echoes an imagined past – especially one of dwarves and fairies (as opposed to science fiction/cyberpunk which look to the future and to technology for fantastic effects).

Fetish/ism – Sexual excitement, in Freudian discourse, brought about by the subject's focus on a specific object or body part. Further employed in postcolonial discourse by Homi Bhabha in relation to the processes of racial stereotyping.

Formalism – Refers to the critical tendency that emerged during the first half of the twentieth century and devoted its attention to concentrating on literature's formal structures in an objective manner.

Gaze – Psychoanalytic concept, developed by Lacan following Jean-Paul Sartre's analysis of 'the look' and subsequently adopted in feminist film studies, which theorizes the ways in which one sees another subject and also comprehends how one is seen. In understanding how one is looked at, the human subject comprehends that the other is also a subject. Lacan develops a theory of the gaze distinct from Sartrean conceptualization along with the concept of *objet petit a*. In this theorization, the gaze names the object of a scopic drive, impersonal and irreducible to the sight of the subject.

Genealogy – Modelled on Friedrich Nietzsche's genealogies, Michel Foucault conceives of genealogy as a method for searching for hidden structures of regulation and association, of tracing etymological, psychological and ideological ancestors of modern social, cultural or political practices. Genealogical methodology is interested in ruptures as well as continuities, contradiction as well as coherence. The genealogist, moreover, is aware of the provisional nature of her or his own subject position in relation to interpretations of the past, in contrast to the historian's pretence of neutrality.

Genotext/Phenotext – Corresponding terms often associated with Julia Kristeva that refer to a set of horizontal and vertical axes establishing an organizing principle structured on the repetition and displacement of language.

Globalization – the transnational and multinational tendency toward a new world order in which economic, cultural, social and political issues become increasingly driven on a global, as opposed to localized, basis.

Grand Narrative – Discourses of science, religion, politics and philosophy which are supposed to explain the world in its totality, and to produce histories of the world as narratives of progress. Jean-François Lyotard has, however, in part, defined post-modernism as the collapse of such totalizing explanatory frameworks.

Gynocentrism – Literally, woman-centred. In critical practice, it refers to the presumption that the reader and the writer of a literary work are both female, and that the critical act is also aimed towards the woman reader.

Gynocritics – Literally, criticism of women. The term was coined in English by Elaine Showalter to describe a literary-critical presumption that feminist criticism would focus its attention on the works of women writers.

Hegemony – Term associated with Italian marxist Antonio Gramsci that refers to the cultural or intellectual domination of one school of thought or ideology over another (or others).

Hermeneutic Circle – The phrase used to describe the impossibility of knowing anything except through what is already known.

Hermeneutics – Originally a term associated with biblical exegesis and the interpretation of religious texts, now a term describing the process or method of interpretation which assumes the absolute interpretability of the object of study.

Heterogeneity – Those elements or aspects of texts or other subjects of analysis which are dissimilar and incongruous, or which cannot be incorporated by analysis into an organic whole.

Heteroglossia – Term often associated with Mikhail Bakhtin that refers to the many discourses that occur within a given language on a microlinguistic scale; 'raznorechie' in Russian, heteroglossia literally signifies as 'different-speech-ness'. Bakhtin employed the term as a means for explaining the hybrid nature of the modern novel and its many competing utterances.

Heuristic – A heuristic argument is one that depends on assumptions garnered from past experience, or from trial and error.

Homophobia – Fear and hatred of homosexuals.

Homosocial – Term coined by Eve Kosofsky Sedgwick to describe the networks of male – male relationships in literature and in culture at large. Homosociality covers a spectrum of male relationships from father and son, buddies, love rivals, sports opponents and teammates, club members and so on, which might all be undertaken by strictly 'straight men' – through to entirely homosexual relationships at the other end of the spectrum.

Humanism/Humanist – Western European philosophical discourse, the first signs of which emerged in the Early Modern Period, and, subsequently, a critical mode that argues for the centrality of man (or more broadly, humanity) as a critical category; often, though not always, implicitly or explicitly secular.

Hybridity – Originally naming something or someone of mixed ancestry or derived from heterogeneous sources, the term has been employed in postcolonialism, particularly in the work of Homi Bhabha, to signify a reading of identities which foregrounds the work of difference in identity resistant to the imposition of fixed, unitary identification which is, in turn, a hierarchical location of the colonial or subaltern subject.

Idealism – Belief in a transcendent or metaphysical truth beyond reality.

Identity Politics – Refers to the ideologies of difference that characterize politically motivated movements and schools of literary criticism such as multiculturalism, in which diversity or ethnicity functions as the principal issue of political debate.

Ideological State Apparatus – Term coined by Louis Althusser, in his essay, 'Ideology and Ideological State Apparatuses'. Althusser argues that ideology is not only a matter of ideas or mechanisms of representation but of material practices which exist in the form of apparatuses and institutions, such as schools, the church and so on. Literature is not simply a text but a production of legal, educational and cultural institutions.

Ideology – Systems of cultural assumptions, or the discursive concatenation of beliefs or values which uphold or oppose social order, or which otherwise provide a coherent structure of thought that hides or silences the contradictory elements in social and economic formations.

Imaginary/Symbolic/Real – Jacques Lacan's version of psychoanalytic thought posits three psychic realms. The aim of the 'healthy' adult is to achieve a certain mastery within the Symbolic realm: that is, the realm of ordered, structured paraphrasable language, the realm of Law. However, the Symbolic realm is not ideal because language itself is, following Saussure, conventional and only arbitrarily connected to the objects its describes. Indeed, language in Lacan's definition describes what is not there. He argues that a child learns to speak in response to the absence of his object of desire (the mother, or her breast); he learns to say 'I want' and thus becomes initiated into the beginnings of his necessary if painful accommodation with the Symbolic. This process of 'joining' the Symbolic order begins with the mirror phase which initiates the child into the beginnings of language after he catches sight of himself – or rather of a reflection of himself – in a mirror, and recognizes himself for the first time as a separate and distinct being, not one with either the world or with his mother. Lacan call this very early beginning of acculturation 'Imaginary' because the mirror image that the child understands as himself is, in fact, merely an image – or a signifier. His recognition of himself is therefore a misrecognition of an image, not a fact. No one, Lacan argues, no matter how well adjusted, ever leaves the Imaginary realm completely; there are always Imaginary residues (misrecognitions) even in the most powerful Symbolic forms. The Real, Lacan's third realm, is by far the least important. He uses the term to refer to the merely contingent accidents of everyday life that impinge on our subjectivity, but which have no fundamental psychic causes or meanings: trapping your hand in the car door might hurt, but it doesn't signify, and it belongs to the realm of the Real.

Intentional Fallacy – Term coined by W. K. Wimsatt and Monroe C. Beardsley to describe critical methods that seek to interpret a literary work by reference to the author's intentions. Wimsatt and Beardsley argued that this position was necessarily untenable since: (a) the author's intentions could never be satisfactorily recovered; and (b) the work could only be read and judged in its own terms, without reference to extra-textual information.

Intertextuality – Term coined originally by Julia Kristeva, intertextuality refers to the ways in which all utterances (whether written or spoken) necessarily refer to other utterances, since words and linguistic/grammatical structures pre-exist the individual speaker and the individual speech. Intertextuality can take place consciously, as when a writer sets out to quote from or allude to the works of another. But it always, in some sense, takes place in all utterance.

Intervention – Term often associated with theorist Gayatri Chakravorty Spivak that refers to the political act or strategy of entering into, or 'intervening' in, a given debate or historical moment so as to have a voice on a particular subject.

Isotopy – A semantic strategy that allows for a uniform reading of a story.

Iterability/Iteration – Idea, formalized in the work of Jacques Derrida, specifically in *Limited Inc*, which, as a quasi-concept, challenges the very idea of the stability of concepts and conceptuality in general. Iterability does not signify repetition simply; it signifies an alterability within the repetition of the same: a novel is a novel, generically, but every novel will inevitably differ from every other. Thus the concept of the novel is destabilized by our experience of every novel we read and, argues Derrida, we have to deal with the paradox of the simultaneity of sameness *and* difference.

Jouissance – Literally, in French, 'pleasure, enjoyment' but with legal connotations relating to property and rights, lost in translation, referring to the right to enjoy. The word has come to be used in psychoanalytic and feminist theories to mean more especially pleasures associated with sensuous and sexual gratification, or orgasm. As such, it refers to a fulfilment that is necessarily merely temporary, and that must therefore always be sought anew.

Labour Theory of Value – Tendency of the value (or price) of goods produced and sold under competitive conditions to be in proportion to the labour costs incurred during production.

Langue/Parole – In Saussurean linguistics, *Langue* refers to the whole system of a given language (its grammar, vocabulary and syntax); *Parole* refers to the individual instance of utterance that takes place within the framework of the *Langue*. Saussure's interest was primarily in the study of the system or *Langue*.

Law of the Father (*Le nom du pére*) – Phrase used by Jacques Lacan in relation to the Oedipus complex, which signals the subject's comprehension of paternal or author-itative prohibition, a prohibition constitutive of authority. Lacan plays on the homo-phonic quality of the French for name (*nom*), which sounds like the French for 'no' (*non*).

Liberal Humanism – Often used as a pejorative term, the values of liberal humanism have to do with democracy, decency, tolerance, rationality, the belief in human progress and a wholehearted support of the individual against the machinations of 'inhuman' political systems. The problem of liberal humanism is that it frequently lapses into universalism or idealism, and has no proper responses to totalitarianism where the individual is frankly powerless. It is a belief system that also disguises the very profound inequities and horrors of even western democratic societies. It is a rejection of systematized thought in return for a generalized belief in the essential goodness of most people most of the time.

Libidinal Economy – By positing the libidinal as an 'economy', Jean-François Lyotard reads desire as a material, rather than simply psychic, process. He is less concerned with what desire 'is' than it is how it functions. He sees desire as the energy of society, but it is an unstable energy, unpredictably connecting the psychological to the economical in a type of feeling and desire Lyotard calls an 'intensity'. Narrative binds these moments of intensities into an apparently coherent pattern in order to exploit the power residing there.

Lisible/Scriptible – Used by Roland Barthes in the definition of types of text, the terms are translatable as 'readable' and 'writerly' respectively. The readerly text does all the work for the reader, leaving the reader in the role of passive consumer. The writerly text makes the reader work and resists the conventions of readerly or realist textuality, principally the assumptions of linguistic transparency and the self-evidence of mean-ing.

Logocentrism – Term ascribed to French philosopher Jacques Derrida that refers to the nature of western thought, language and culture since Plato's era. The Greek signifier for 'word', 'speech' and 'reason', logos possesses connotations in western culture for law and truth. Hence, logocentrism refers to a culture that revolves around a central set of supposedly universal principles or beliefs.

Manicheanism – Belief in a kind of philosophical or religious dualism.

Masquerade – In contemporary gender theory, the concept of masquerade, derived from the writings of Joan Rivière, is central. It argues that gender is a performance rather than a natural phenomenon with which one is born; it has to be acquired, learned and polished and is in no sense natural.

Mass Culture – Term often associated with British cultural theorist Richard Hoggart that refers to a new commercialized social order that finds its roots in the mass dissemina-tion of television, radio, magazines and a variety of other media; in Hoggart's view, mass culture shapes and reconstructs cultural, social and intellectual life in its image and via its mediated depiction of artificial levels of reality.

Master/Slave Dialectic – Hegel's model for understanding the interaction between two self-consciousnesses and the manner in which each entity considers the other in terms of the self. Hegel argues that this admittedly 'primitive' model reveals the ways in which each figure functions as a 'mirror' for the other and ultimately eschews cooperation because of their inherently subordinate relationship.

Materialism – Doctrine or system of beliefs that maintains that economic or social change occurs via material well-being rather than intellectual or spiritual phenomena.

Materialist Feminism – Any mode of feminism that is interested in the material conditions of women – in equal rights before the law, in questions of pay and employment, in access to education for women, in non-discriminatory practices generally – can be described as a materialist feminism.

Mediation – The manner in which various conflicting parties either intervene or promote reconciliation or settlement on behalf of others. Concept of textual transformation, often employed in marxist and other materialist criticisms, which supercedes reductive or crude models of reflection which assume that any given text simply reflects the world, instead of mediating that image and thereby shaping or influencing the reader's comprehension in a particular way. Also, the notion of mediation is employed to suggest that the text is itself not a simple recording or representation but is influenced in its shaping by a number of factors including matters of historical, cultural and ideological relation.

Metafiction – A fictional mode that takes fictionality – the conventions of writing fiction – as part of its own subject matter.

Metalanguage – Roman Jakobson defines metalanguage as any form of language which defines linguistic properties. Following the work of Alfred Tarski, Colin MacCabe describes metalanguage as that which announces its object languages as material, and signals them so through the conventions of the imposition of quotation marks and other diacritical markers, while assuming an implicit transparency for itself. Thus, for MacCabe, the 'narrator' or 'narrative voice' in a realist novel assumes the role of a metalanguage, in that it appears to 'observe' rather than to interpret or analyze.

Metaphysics – A division of philosophy that explores the fundamental nature of reality or being; includes such disciplines as ontology, cosmology and epistemology, among others. Originally derived from the order of Aristotle's works, where all writings that did not fit within the various disciplines were put together in a volume 'next to the physics', metaphysics has come to mean the total structure of a philosophical system trying to determine being as such and in general. Accordingly metaphysical systems differ according to the relation they posit between ontology (the science of being), epistemology (the science of knowledge), ethics and politics. At the same time metaphysics characterizes a thinking that determines the physical by means of a principle that resides outside of this world, such as God for example. One distinguishes between a *metaphysica specialis*, concerning questions for the divine being, immortality and freedom, and a *metaphysica generalis*, determining the meaning of being as such and in general.

Mimesis – Can be used in two distinct ways. Firstly, mimesis (from the Greek *mimos*, a mime) refers to the imitation or representation of reality in art. Mimesis can also be used to describe the process by which one writing mimics another kind: for example, a fiction might pretend to be a historical document in order to gain authority for its account.

Mimicry – Generally, the practice, act or art of imitation, often for the purpose of ridicule. Homi Bhabha uses the term to identify a form of colonial control of its subjects. The colonizer seeks to impose on the colonial subject the forms and values of the colonial master, hence the Anglicization of Indians and Africans during British colonial rule. However, as Bhabha identifies, there remains a gap between the desire to erase difference and the identity which is constructed, indicated by Bhabha in the phrase 'not white/not quite', from which emerges ambivalence.

Mirror Phase – Jacques Lacan posited that a baby, at first an oceanic bundle of undifferentiated desire who believes himself to be continuous with the larger world and his mother, first comes to a realization of himself as a unitary and separate being when, at age 6–18 months, he first sees his own reflection in a mirror. For Lacan, this is the beginning of the ego's development, but it is significantly founded on a mis-apprehension, since the image in the mirror is a signified – a substitute image of the self, not the self itself. Hence, the mirror phase implies that the ego is founded on highly unstable grounds rather than in any essential personality.

Mise en abime – From the French for 'placed into the abyss' *mise en abime* has come to mean narrative or philosophical moments of infinite regression. Although Chinese boxes or other infinite regressive features are often used for comic effect, the French term emphasizes the terror of emptiness that is also part of the play of language where language has only the most tangential, arbitrary and conventional relationships with reality.

Monist – A person who reduces all phenomena to a single viewpoint or principle; also, a given individual who views reality as the product of a singular, unified vision, rather than as the sum of a series of component parts. Monist analysis is that which focuses solely or primarily on one form of domination (for example, gender or race or class).

Monologism – Term coined by Mikhail Bakhtin to describe characters representing multiple points of view while being clearly dominated by a single voice or ideology.

Morpheme – The smallest linguistic or structural unit of language.

Multiculturalism – Refers to the social and political movement and/or position that views differences between individuals and groups to be a potential venue of cultural strength and renewal; multiculturalism celebrates and explores different varieties of experience stemming from racial, ethnic, gender, sexual and/or class differences.

Multiplicative Analysis – Analysis developed by feminists of colour. It seeks to account for the experiences of people who have been subordinated to several forms of domination. Whereas an additive approach would see (for example) race, class and gender as three discrete systems that accumulate oppressions on poor women of colour, a multiplicative approach analyzes how race and class change the meanings of gender, how race and gender change the meanings of class, and how class and gender change the meanings of race. A multiplicative approach highlights the differential experiences of women of colour rather than their 'double' or 'triple' oppression. Finally, a multiplicative approach is contextual and historically informed. It recognizes that in certain cases, one of the features (race, gender, class, sexuality, etc.) may be more salient than the others. Also called multiaxial analysis or intersectionality.

Narratology – Theories and systematic study of narrative.

Nominalism – A theory that argues against the notion of universal essences in reality and maintains that only individual perspectives, rather than abstract generalities, exist.

Normativity – The postulation of hegemonic, culturally prescribed norms or standards such as heterosexuality.

Objectification – The manner in which various individuals or social groups treat others as objects and expressions of their own senses of reality; reducing an other's sense of being into a form that can be experienced universally by other individuals and social groups.

Objet petit a – A complex term from Lacanian psychoanalysis. Lacan suggested that objects of desire are always changing because the desiring subject is always changing too. He wanted to find a term to describe the mutability and mortality of the desired object, and to describe it in a way that disrupted what he saw as the stability of the binary desiring subject/desired object in Freudian thought. The term he came up with is 'object petit a', where 'a' stands for 'autre' (French for other), distinguished from the Other elsewhere in his writing by the lower case initial letter. *Objet petit a* can be anything at all that is touched by desire. Desire is fleeting and mutable hence the object of desire is always in flux and is always just out of reach.

Oedipus Complex – In Freudian psychoanalysis the Oedipus Complex refers to the whole complex of both loving and hostile feeling experienced by a child towards its parents in the process of achieving acculturated maturity. The Oedipus Complex manifests itself as an intense rivalry with the parent of the same sex for the love of the parent of the opposite sex (which is to be understood as a libidinal or sexualized desire). Negotiation of this complex, the relinquishing of forbidden (incestuous) desire and its displacement onto suitable substitute objects (a boy must love not his mother, but a woman *like* his mother; a girl must love not her father, but a baby given to her by a man *like* her father) is required to achieve healthy adulthood. The complex is never completely successfully negotiated, however, and there are always residual Oedipal problems in even the healthiest of adults.

Ontology – Branch of philosophy addressing the meaning or essence of being.

Orientalism – Term coined by Edward Said naming the ensemble of western, usually though not exclusively European discourses and other forms of representation of non-western cultures. Said traces the history of Orientalist discourses in literature, the arts and other documents from the eighteenth century onwards.

Other/otherness – Term employed throughout critical discourse in differing ways, otherness names the quality or state of existence of being other or different from established norms and social groups; the distinction that one makes between one's self and others, particularly in terms of sexual, ethnic and relational senses of difference; in Lacanian psychoanalysis, there is the other and the Other: the former signifies that which is not really other but is a reflection and projection of the ego; the latter signifies a radical alterity irreducible to any imaginary or subjective identification.

Overdetermination – The act or practice of over-emphasizing, or resolving in an excessive fashion, a given conclusion or psychological factor. Alternatively, a text which is said to be overdetermined is available for multiple readings from various heterogeneous, if not theoretically or polemically incompatible, positions.

Patriarchy – Literally 'the rule of the father'. Patriarchy is the name given to the whole complex systems of male dominance by which most societies are organized. Patriarchy includes the systematic exclusion of women from rights of inheritance, education, the vote, equal pay, equality before the law; it also includes the ways in which even more liberal regimes tend to leave women out of structures of power despite claiming to be based on equality.

Performance/Performative – The act of public exhibition that results in a transaction between performer and audience; an utterance that, via its public display, causes a linguistic interaction with the exhibition's object. In textual terms, the performative is that statement which enacts the condition of which it speaks, thereby collapsing the distinction between connotative and denotative speech utterances. The condition of performative articulation is given particular consideration by Jacques Derrida in the context of the instability of speech acts and, after him, with specific regard to the discursive formation of gender and transgender, by Judith Butler.

Phallic – Relating to or resembling the phallus, a symbol of generative power; refers to an interest in the phallus or a masculinist point of view; in psychoanalysis, a reference to a particular stage in male development when the subject is preoccupied with the genitals.

Phallic Primacy – Concept often associated with Freud's castration complex, phallic primacy refers to the presence of male genitalia and its impact upon psychosocial relations.

Phallocentrism – Privileging of a masculinist, specifically unitary, singular, point of view in terms of individuals, institutions or cultures.

Phallocratism – The institutionalization and hegemony of a masculinist perspective; in the parlance of French feminist Luce Irigaray, phallocratism refers to the often masculinized division of labour that exists between the sexes.

Phallogocentric – Term coined by Jacques Derrida to describe the privileging of origins, centres, or unities in western culture, language and thought. Derrida's neologism combines the ideas of phallocentrism and logocentrism (the idea that all ideas are centred on certain key concepts, such as truth, beauty, reason, goodness, God).

Phantasm – The product of fantasy, the imagination or delusion; imaginary projection.

Phenomenology – School of thought founded by German philosopher Edmund Husserl that maintains that objects attain meaning through their perception in a given person's consciousness.

Phoneme – The basic sound unit of pronunciation in language; English, for example, includes 45 phonemes.

Pluralism – Variety of approach and assumption. A pluralist approach to criticism is one that has many different methods and assumptions at its disposal, rather than an approach that imposes a single model on all texts, no matter what the circumstances.

Point de capiton – Phrase employed by Jacques Lacan, usually translated as 'quilting', 'anchoring' or 'suturing' point. Taken from embroidery, the phrase indicates for Lacan moments in the psyche where signifier and signified are gathered or stitched together, thereby momentarily bringing to a halt the slippage of signification by which subjectivity is constituted.

Polysemy – Relating to the possibility of a simultaneous multiplicity of meaning encoded within a single phrase or text.

Positivism – Philosophical theory, formulated by Auguste Comte, which privileges observable facts and phenomena over modes of knowledge such as theology and metaphysics.

Power – In the work of Michel Foucault, power constitutes one of the three axes constitutive of subjectification, the other two being ethics and truth. For Foucault, power implies knowledge, and vice versa. However, power is causal, it is constitutive of knowledge, even while knowledge is, concomitantly, constitutive of power: knowledge gives one power, but one has the power in given circumstances to constitute bodies of knowledge, discourses and so on as valid or invalid, truthful or untruthful. Power serves in making the world both knowable and controllable. Yet, the nature of power, as Foucault suggests in the first volume of his *History of Sexuality*, is essentially proscriptive, concerned more with imposing limits on its subjects.

Presentism – Refers to a radical overemphasis or privileging of the present over what is perceived to be a less culturally and technologically effectual past.

Primal/Horde/Scene – That which is primal refers in Freudian psychoanalysis to the desires, fears, needs and anxieties constitutive of the origins of the subject's psyche. The idea of the primal horde signifies an originary human social collective. The primal scene is that moment when the infant subject becomes aware of sexual relations between its parents.

Projection – In psychoanalytic discourse, the transference of desire or fantasy onto another person, object or situation in order to avoid the recognition of the subject's responsibility for his or her behaviour or actions.

Rationalism – Refers to the reliance upon reason as the basis for establishing religious or philosophical truth. In addition, philosophical notion, deriving from the work of Descartes, which emphasizes the constitution of knowledge based on reason rather than observation or sense perception.

Realism/Realist – Realism has many meanings and is potentially an unusable word since people differ over what they mean by reality. In literature and the arts, however, it describes a common tendency from the early nineteenth century onwards to represent real life in fiction and painting, and to do so using common conventions of representation. One of the key problems with the term, though, is that nineteenth-century realist writers were generally ruthlessly selective in their materials, presenting not so much real life in the raw, but reality filtered and purged. Realism is often associated with representing average experience – the lives of middle-class characters who do little that is unusual or exciting; it prefers an objective standpoint, and is illusionist in that it asks its readers to forget that they are reading fiction. Readers are meant to 'identify' with characters as if they were real people. Events should be probable (or at the very least, possible); narrators should on the whole maintain a third-person distance and perspective; judgement should be easy for the reader. These conventions have become naturalized in many people's reading habits so that it is often difficult to disentangle reality from its representation. Nonetheless, many critics have attacked bourgeois realism for its narrow focus, moral certainties and social exclusivity.

Reality effect – Term often associated with French theorist Jean Baudrillard that relates to the ways in which reality is often established and becomes represented for some individuals and cultures through hyperreal media such as photography, film and other media.

Referent – In Saussurean linguistics, the referent is that to which the word or sign refers: the real object in the real world for which the word or sign is an arbitrary and conventional signal.

Referential – A text that is referential is one that disguises its status as a work or text by making extended reference to the conditions of real life. The reader, that is, is encouraged to forget that what he or she is reading is *merely* a text.

Reification – The process or result of rendering some idea or philosophy into a material or concrete entity. The process by which philosophical or ideological concepts disappear to the extent that they become incorporated into the everyday. Concept employed in marxist discourse, which emphasizes the depersonalization of the subject as a result of capitalist modes of production and the alienation of labour.

Repetition compulsion – The neurotic and often harmful psychological condition in which the afflicted continue to engage in patterns of self-destructive and dangerous behaviour.

Repression – In psychoanalytic thought, repression is the process by which subjects try to get rid of desires, linked to instincts and imaged in thoughts and memory, that are somehow known to be forbidden by the wider culture. The forbidden thoughts are consigned to the Unconscious; but they do not disappear, and may manifest themselves in symptomatic behaviours, in dreams, slips of the tongue and physical tics. Such symptoms are examples of what Freud called 'the return of the repressed'.

Saussurian Linguistics – A linguistic model deriving from the lectures of Ferdinand de Saussure. Saussure argued that the meanings that we give to words are not intrinsic but arbitrary; there is no connection between a word and its meaning except the one that we choose to give it. He further suggested that meanings are also relational. If a word has no inherent connection with its meaning, then its meaning derives from relations to do with context and syntax. Thirdly, Saussure also argued that language constitutes our reality: since our only access to meaning is through language, language itself must form us and our thoughts, not the other way around. However, if language is only ever arbitrary and relational, then reality is also contingent. His interest in language was to study the linguistic system (or langue) rather than the individual utterance (or parole) in order to understand the complete picture of human language, an approach taken up by structuralist theory which concentrates on larger structures.

Scopophilia – The (often sexualized) pleasure in looking. Feminist critics in particular have criticized Freud's theories of infantile sexuality for their scopophilic emphasis on 'looking' and seeing the (absence or presence of the) sexual organs of the other sex. Feminist film theory, following the work of Laura Mulvey and influenced by Lacanian psychoanalysis, has theorized the gaze – that of both the camera and the audience – in terms of a scopophilic drive.

Selective Tradition – Term coined by Raymond Williams to denote how a cultural heritage, apparently bequeathed to the present by the past, is in fact constructed in the present through processes of active selection.

Self-referentiality – A self-referential text is one that refers to its own processes of production – a text that talks about its textuality. Unlike the referential text, it encourages its readers continually to recall that what is being read is fictive or illusory, not real at all.

Semiology – Analysis of linguistic signs; coined by Swiss linguist Ferdinand de Saussure in the early twentieth century as the linguistic study of socially and culturally inscribed codes of human interaction.

Semiotic/s – In the plural, semiotics refers to the 'science of signs' – systematic codes of representation. Julia Kristeva, however, has coined the term 'the Semiotic' to refer to a mode in language. Language, she says, consists of the Symbolic (derived from Lacan), the linguistic realm of transparency, paraphrasability, conformity and power. The Semiotic is the pre-linguistic residue of language, made up of sounds, rhythms, the babbling incoherence of the child, the language of poetry and the language of psychosis. It is not precisely meaningless, but it cannot be subsumed in the Symbolic. The Semiotic pulses against Symbolic language, making it mean both more and less than it intends.

Sexuate – Term associated with French feminist Luce Irigaray's notion of suppressed maternal womanhood.

Sign – According to C. S. Peirce, a sign, or *representamen*, is 'something that stands to somebody for something in some respect or capacity'. According to Saussure, a sign comprises a sound image, or signifier, and a concept, or signified.

Signifier/Signified – Saussure argues that a word or image (the sign) comes in two parts. There is the sound it makes (or its graphic equivalent) which he terms the 'signifier'; and there is the mental image that the sound or graphic equivalent produces in the reader/viewer – the signified. The relationship between signifier and signified is entirely arbitrary and conventional; it is also impossible to separate the two. Furthermore the relationship between the sign in its constituent parts of signifier/signified and its referent (the real object to which it refers) is also arbitrary. In other words, signified and referent are not interchangeable terms for Saussure.

Simulacra/Simulacrum – Term often associated with Jean Baudrillard's notion of the reality effect, which relates to the ways in which reality is often established and becomes represented for some individuals and cultures through hyperreal media such as photography, film and other media; hence, simulacrum refers to the image, representation or reproduction of a concrete other.

Singularity – Jacques Derrida postulates that our understanding of every sign involves an assumption of the absolute singularity, the uniqueness of that sign or mark. However, for it to be possible for the sign to communicate or have meaning, it has to be transmissible, reiterable. It therefore cannot be absolutely singular. Yet, paradoxically, the possibility of inscription outside of any finite or determinable context – in order to function properly as my name, my proper name must be able to be transmissible outside my presence – while denying absolute singularity, also suggests the singularity which apparently gives the sign its authority. The term is employed by Jean-Luc Nancy to describe a given individual's particularity, or the essence that establishes and maintains their irreducible sense of self, with the proviso that any sense of self, subjectivity or being is also, always, a being-with, or being-common.

Sinthome – Lacanian term, meaning symptom, the spelling of the word is archaic. For Lacan, the symptom is a radical signifier of the unconscious irreducible to any interpretation or meaning.

Social construction – Concept that explains the ways in which ideas, identities and texts result from the interaction among socialized norms of existence, cultural politics and individualized senses of identity.

Solipsism – The belief that one can only ever have proper evidence of one's own existence; an absolute egotism which depends on refusing to admit the existence, demands and needs of others.

Structure of Feeling – Term coined by Raymond Williams as a mediating concept between 'art' and 'culture' to denote the 'deep community' that makes communication possible. A structure of feeling is neither universal nor class specific, but 'a very deep and wide possession'. The term was meant to embrace both the immediately experiential and the generationally-specific aspects of artistic process.

Subaltern – Term, taken from the work of Antonio Gramsci and used initially to define proletarian and other working-class groups, *subaltern* is employed in postcolonial studies after Gayatri Spivak to address dominated and marginalized groups.

Subject Position – The location in a text identified as that belonging to the human subject, or the assumed position within a text that is identified as its 'voice'.

Subject/Subjectivity – The concept of selfhood that is developed in and articulated through the acquisition of language. A subject is a self in language; subjectivity is the process of attaining and expressing selfhood in and through language or the location of the self situated and subjectified by cultural, epistemological, ideological and other social discourses and institutions.

Supplement/Supplementarity – Quasi-concept which, as Jacques Derrida points out, means both an addition and a replacement, developed in response to Rousseau's understanding of writing as a supplement to speech. The idea of supplementarity puts into play the disruption of the full presence of a sign in making possible signification, indicating the work of difference within the self-same. The supplement is supposed to act as an addition or complement which completes. In so doing, the supplement is meant to cover up a lack, but, in being a supplement, in producing the meaning of the 'original', it disrupts the very idea of the original as self-sufficient.

Suture – Term in Lacanian psychoanalysis describing the moment that a given subject enters into language; hence, the suture denotes the linguistic gap that the subject subsumes within a given language.

Symptomatic Reading – Refers to a kind of reading practice that accounts for the power/ knowledge relations that exist when the notion of meaning is in intellectual or ideological conflict; symptomatic readers reconstruct a given text's discursive conditions in order to treat the text as a symptom, understand its internal relations and comprehend – by challenging the text's intellectual properties – the ways in which it ultimately produces (or fails to produce) meaning.

Syntagm – Term often associated with Roman Jakobson that refers to an orderly combination of interacting signifiers that establish a meaningful whole; in language, for example, a sentence functions as a syntagm of words.

Telos/Teleology – Telos refers to any form of ultimate end or conclusion; teleology denotes the study of the role of design in nature and an attempt to explain the existence of natural phenomena.

Text/Textuality – Since the work of Roland Barthes and other critics who are associated with the terms structuralism and poststructuralism, the term *text* has taken on the sense of a process rather than a finished product, of which books and other literary forms are examples. A novel may be a text, but textuality is not confined by the idea of the book. Textuality thus names the interwoven discourses, phenomena or other grouping of signs, images and so forth by which we perceive the world and by which we, as subjects, are situated.

Trace – Jacques Derrida formulates the idea of the trace as what remains when an instance of singularity, such as a signature, has erased the possibility of its absolute singularity in having been inscribed. The trace is the mark of that which has never been presentable as such. The trace makes meaning possible by being, for Derrida, the *différance* which disrupts any notion of absolute origin. Jean Baudrillard's use of the term refers to the trace of meaning that the reality effect fosters; arguing that postmodernity has resulted in an artificial era of hyperreality, Baudrillard explains the notion of trace as a kind of nostalgia via which we establish meaning in our lives.

Transference – Psychoanalytic term indicating the process by which the analysand transfers and thereby repeats the psychic dynamic developed in early childhood pertaining to desire of the other onto the analyst.

Transparency – The idea that the narrative voice in realist fiction does not mediate or interpret the world it presents but that it allows direct access to that world in neutral terms.

Typology – A system or scheme of classification based upon a set of principles, concepts or types.

Unconscious – In psychoanalysis, the unconscious is the mental realm into which those aspects of mental life that are related to forbidden desires and instincts are consigned through the process of repression. The unconscious is absolutely unknown to the subject except where it exerts pressures on conscious life, as when repressed objects refuse to remain repressed. The instincts and desires it contains are usually disguised through a repressive censorship that turns forbidden ideas into different images by the processes of condensation and displacement (Freud's terms), where they become metonymies and metaphors (Lacan's terms). These censored images seek to re-enter consciousness through dreams, symptoms, verbal and physical tics. The subject is unable to interpret the new images him or herself and must submit to analysis to 'read' the pulsions of his or her own unconscious realm.

Universalism – Refers to the practice of perceiving generalization in all aspects of human life or intellectual discourse; the ideology of making universal assumptions (e.g. concerning 'humanity') which ignores culturally or historically specific or determined aspects of societies, cultures and individuals.

NOTES ON CONTRIBUTORS

Jill Barker is Senior Lecturer in Literary Studies at the University of Luton. She has published on psychoanalytic literary theory and on editions of Shakespeare. Her academic interests range from postmodern critical theories (in particular psychoanalysis and feminism) through feminist readings of Shakespeare to the rhetorical strategies of sixteenth-century popular theatre. She researches attitudes to language, to the nature of humanity, to women and to class and racial outsiders.

John Brannigan is Research Fellow at the Institute of Irish Studies at the Queen's University of Belfast. He is the author of *New Historicism and Cultural Materialism* (1998) and *Beyond the Angry Young Men: Literature and Culture in England, 1945–1965* (forthcoming 2001). He has also published essays on literary theories and twentieth-century British and Irish writings. He is currently working on a book-length study of the writings of Brendan Behan.

Mark Currie is Professor of English at Anglia Polytechnic University in Cambridge. He studied at the Universities of Aberdeen and Cambridge, was a lecturer in the English Department of the University of Dundee until 1999, and was Head of English Literary and Cultural Studies at the University of Westminster from 1999 to 2000. His research has mainly been in the field of literary theory, narrative theory and twentieth-century fiction. He is the editor of *Metafiction* (1995), author of *Postmodern Narrative Theory* (1998), and *Difference* (2001) and has published widely on literary theory, modernism and postmodernism.

Jane Goldman is Senior Lecturer in English at the University of Dundee. She is the author of *The Feminist Aesthetics of Virginia Woolf: Modernism, Post-Impressionism and the Politics of the Visual*, and co-editor of *Modernism: An Anthology of Sources and Documents*.

Moyra Haslett is lecturer in English at Queen's University, Belfast. She is the author of *Byron's* Don Juan *and the Don Juan Legend* (1997) and of *Marxist Literary and Cultural Theories* (1999). She is currently preparing a book on eighteenth-century literature for the *Transitions* series.

R. Brandon Kershner is Alumni Professor of English at the University of Florida. He is the author of three books: *Dylan Thomas: The Poet and His Critics* (1977), *Joyce, Bakhtin, and Popular Literature* (1989) *and The Twen-*

tieth-Century Novel: An Introduction (1997). He is also the editor of the Bedford Books edition of Joyce's *A Portrait of the Artist as a Young Man* (1992) and of *Joyce and Popular Culture* (1996). He has published some thirty-five articles and book chapters on various aspects of modern literature and culture, and a similar number of reviews and poems. *Joyce, Bakhtin, and Popular Literature* won the 1990 award from the American Conference for Irish Studies as the best work of literary criticism in the field. Kershner is a member of the Board of Advisory Editors of the *James Joyce Quarterly*, and was recently elected to the Board of Trustees of the International Joyce Foundation.

Gail Ching-Liang Low has taught at the University of Southampton, the University of East Anglia, the Open University, Staffordshire University and the University of Dundee. She is the author of *White Skins/Black Masks: Representation and Colonialism* (1996) and is currently working on pedagogy and canon formation in the institutional transformation of 'Commonwealth' to 'Postcolonial' in Britain.

Martin McQuillan is Lecturer in Cultural Theory and Analysis at the University of Leeds. He is co-editor of *Post-Theory: New Directions in Criticism* (1999) and co-author of *Deconstructing Disney* (1999). He is currently preparing *Deconstruction: A Reader* and *The Narrative Reader*.

K. M. Newton is Professor of English at the University of Dundee. Among his publications are *George Eliot: Romantic Humanist* (1981), *In Defence of Literary Interpretation* (1986), *Interpreting the Text* (1990) and *Twentieth-Century Literary Theory: A Reader* (1997).

Arkady Plotnitsky is Professor of English and Director of Theory and Cultural Studies Program at Purdue University. His books include *Reconfigurations: Critical Theory and General Economy*, *In the Shadow of Hegel* and *Complementarity: Anti-Epistemology After Bohr and Derrida*. He has also coedited (with B. H. Smith) a volume titled *Mathematics, Science, and Postclassical Theory*, published in 1997. His new book, *The Knowable and the Unknowable: Modern Science and Nonclassical Thought*, is in press and is expected to appear in 2001. He is currently at work on two books: *Minute Particulars: Romanticism and Epistemology* and *Niels Bohr: Physics, Philosophy, and the Practice of Reading*.

Ruth Robbins is Senior Lecturer in English at University College Northampton. She is author of *Literary Feminisms* (2000) and of many articles on feminist theory and late-nineteenth-century literature. With Julian Wolfreys, she is editor of *Victorian Gothic*. She is currently working on a period study of English Literature from 1873 to 1924 entitled *Pater to Forster*.

Julian Wolfreys is Associate Professor of English at the University of Florida. In addition to editing and co-editing numerous collections of essays on Victorian literature and culture, literary theory and Jacques Derrida, he is the author of *Spectrality, the Gothic and the Uncanny in Literature, Film and Theory* (2001), *Readings: Acts of Close Reading in Literary Theory* (2000), with Jeremy Gibson, *Peter Ackroyd: The Ludic and Labyrinthine Text* (2000), *Writing London: The Trace of the Urban Text from Blake to Dickens* (1998), *Deconstruction • Derrida* (1998), *The Rhetoric of Affirmative Resistance: Dissonant Identities from Carroll to Derrida* (1997) and *Being English: Narratives, Idioms, and Performances of National Identity from Coleridge to Trollope* (1994).

Kenneth Womack is Assistant Professor of English at the Pennsylvania State University's Altoona College. He has published widely on twentieth-century British and American literature, as well as on bibliography and textual criticism. In addition to serving as co-editor (with William Baker) of Oxford University Press's *The Year's Work in English Studies*, he is editor of *Interdisciplinary Literary Studies: A Journal of Criticism and Theory*. He is also co-editor, with Todd F. Davis, of *Mapping the Ethical Turn: Ethics and Literature in New Theoretical Contexts* (2001).

INDEX OF PROPER NAMES

Key Concepts
in Literary Theory

Edited by **Julian Wolfreys**, Associate Professor of
English with the Department of English at The University
of Florida, **Ruth Robbins**, Senior Lecturer in Literary
Studies at University College, Northampton *and*
Kenneth Womack, Assistant Professor of English at
Pennyslvania State University, Altoona

August 2001   0 7486 1519 9   224pp   £9.99

Key Concepts in Literary Theory provides the student of literature with clearly presented
and authoritative definitions of some of the most significant and often difficult to grasp
terms and concepts currently used in the study of literary theory. It brings together terms
from many areas of literary theory, including cultural studies, psychoanalysis,
poststructuralism, marxist and feminist literary studies, postcolonialism, and other areas of
identity politics with which literary studies concerns itself.

In addition, the volume provides accessible discussions of the main areas of literary, critical
and cultural study, supported by bibliographies and a chronology of major critics whose
work has informed critical studies of literature today, also accompanied by bibliographies.

Key Concepts in Literary Theory is an indispensable reference work for anyone interested
in the complexities of literary, critical and cultural theory.

Features

- Provides clear definitions of 300 terms in literary theory and criticism
- Provides readers with a range of essential literary concepts and period terms, including
  'irony', 'existentialism', 'symbolism' and 'modernism' and concentrates on literary criticism
  and theory, from 'aporia' and 'liminality' to 'phallocentrism' and 'simulacra'
- Reflects contemporary literary theory's rapidly changing terminology and looks to the
  future shape of literary theory in entries from 'technoscience' and 'cyberwar' to
  'mnemotechnic' and 'digitality'
- Includes terms such as 'gender parody', 'cyborg' and 'masquerade' to show that literary
  theory has made connections with gender studies and with media and popular culture
- Provides two accompanying reference sections:
  - Areas of Literary, Critical and Cultural study, which provides definitions of the
  significant movements and critical approaches within twentieth-century critical study,
  from Archetypal Criticism to Textual Criticism, each of which is accompanied by a
  bibliography of suggested reading
  - A Chronology of Critics, which covers thinkers from Karl Marx to Judith Butler, each
  entry being accompanied by a brief bibliography

Order from
Marston Book Services, PO Box 269, Abingdon, Oxon OX14 4YN
Tel 10235 465500 • Fax 01235 465555
Email: direct.order@marston.co.uk

Visit our website www.eup.ed.ac.uk

All details correct at time of printing but subject to change without notice

Literary Theories
A Reader and Guide

Edited by **Julian Wolfreys**, Associate Professor of English with the
Department of English at The University of Florida

June 1999   672pp
0 7486 1213 0   £52.50   •   0 7486 1214 9   £16.95

Literary Theories: A Reader and Guide is the first reader and
introductory guide in one volume. Bringing together theoretically
orientated readings by leading exponents of literary theory with lucid
introductions, the book offers the student reader a foundation
textbook in literary theory. Divided into 12 sections covering
structuralism, feminism, marxism, reader-response theory,
psychoanalysis, deconstruction, post-structuralism, postmodernism,
new historicism, postcolonialism, gay studies and queer theory, and
cultural studies, *Literary Theories* introduces the reader to the most
challenging and engaging aspects of critical studies in the humanities
today. Each section contains several influential texts that provide
discussion of theoretical positions and striking examples of close
readings of various works of literature from a number of perspectives. The introductions
introduce the theory in question, discuss its main currents, give cross-references to other
theories, and contextualise the readings that follow. An indispensable aid to
understanding theory, *Literary Theories* is a significant introduction to theoretical
approaches to literature.

- Unique combination of an anthology of core texts and a thorough introductory guide
  Each of the 12 sections contains:
  - Several key texts
  - An accessible 5000 word introduction
- Texts selected for their coverage of themes (ie questions of language, genre, the
  nature of reading, race and gender) and author (from Shakespeare to Virginia Woolf)
- Three bibliographies: an annotated bibliography introducing the reader to the
  arguments of influential texts in each field, a supplementary reading list and a list of
  works cited

"For those to whom this field of academic life is a vast
mystery or for those to whom its writings are a way of life,
this collection will be equally useful."

Contemporary Review

Order from
**Marston Book Services, PO Box 269, Abingdon, Oxon OX14 4YN
Tel 10235 465500   •   Fax 01235 465555
Email: direct.order@marston.co.uk**